HERBERT H. LEHMAN AND NEW YORK'S LITTLE NEW DEAL

HERBERT H. LEHMAN AND NEW YORK'S LITTLE NEW DEAL

ROBERT P. INGALLS

With a Foreword
BY GEORGE MEANY

New York · New York University Press · 1975

All Photographs
courtesy of
Herbert H. Lehman Papers

Copyright © 1975 by New York University
Library of Congress Catalog Card Number: 75-13744
ISBN: 0-8147-3750

Library of Congress Cataloging in Publication Data
Ingalls, Robert P   1941-
    Herbert H. Lehman and New York's Little New Deal.

    1. New York (State)—Politics and government—
1865-1950.   2. Lehman, Herbert Henry, 1878-1963.
3. United States—Politics and government—1933-1945.
4. United States—Economic policy—1933-1945.
I. Title.
F124.I53   974.7′04′0924   75-13744
ISBN 0-8147-3750-1

TO

George H. Mayer

SCHOLAR, MENTOR, AND FRIEND

FOREWORD

BY GEORGE MEANY

Herbert H. Lehman was the ideal public servant. No other man I ever met, or ever heard of, was more worthy of that title.

He had none of the average politician's guile, the average diplomat's evasiveness, the average banker's greed or the average statesman's aloofness.

He was a quiet man, completely honest, filled with compassion for others, truly dedicated to the democratic process and determined to make it work for the public good.

As Governor, Herbert Lehman was a trail-blazer. He sought and found new ways to serve the people of New York, and the record of social welfare legislation passed during his administration is unsurpassed. As a United States Senator, he was the conscience of the Congress. In both positions, he served with absolute integrity and rare distinction.

Throughout his public life, he put the problems of people—all people everywhere—above all else. He understood their needs, shared their aspirations, helped them achieve their goals.

To him, there were no national boundaries that, by right, denied some the freedom others enjoyed. He insisted that freedom and liberty, political and economic self-determination must never tolerate artificial barriers of race, creed, color, sex or geography.

To him, freedom was the God-given right of all people and he was, therefore, the unrelenting, implacable foe of dictators or would-be dictators.

It was a rare privilege for me to have known and worked with Herbert Lehman. It was a great and lasting honor to have been his friend.

To all who contemplate a life of public service, I recommend adopting Herbert H. Lehman as the model. There has never been—and I fear may never again be—his equal.

PREFACE

"A new deal" was pledged by Franklin D. Roosevelt during the 1932 presidential campaign, and the phrase stuck. But historians have debated whether the adjective "new" accurately describes the reforms of the 1930s. One school of thought argues that the New Deal had its roots in Progressivism and, therefore, "constituted only a stage in developments long under way." [1] However, other scholars question the degree of continuity between the two movements and picture the Depression as a turning point, a watershed in American history. [2]

One phase of the watershed controversy centers on the states. During the Great Depression, as in the Progressive Era, the reform impulse swept not only Washington but also a number of state capitals. Defenders of the discontinuity argument cite changes in states like Pennsylvania, Minnesota, and California as evidence that the 1930s marked a new departure in American politics. [3] Supporters of the opposite point of view contend that advances in the states simply extended the gains of Progressivism. Taking the continuity position a step further, some historians depreciate the importance of legislation adopted in both periods. In a study of state governments during the 1930s, James T. Patterson asserted that "few states enacted significant reforms." He concluded: "While state activity expanded in the 1930's, the change was far from dramatic." [4]

The present study examines the reforms adopted by New York State during the administration of Governor Herbert H. Lehman. After taking office in January 1933, Lehman served as chief executive until December 1942. During those ten years, state lawmakers approved a variety of reforms which quickly became known as the "Little New Deal," because the programs resembled in many ways those enacted in Washington. Under Lehman's guiding hand, Albany provided public assistance for the jobless, unemployment insurance, farm price supports, protective labor legislation, and other welfare measures. Organized topically, this study is an analysis of New York's Little New Deal rather than a biography of Lehman. However, Lehman played such an important role in the passage of the legislation that he merits equal billing in the title.

Although the rubric Little New Deal lacked precision, it clearly did not encompass every measure signed into law by Governor Lehman. Contemporary observers used the term loosely, but they never suggested that the Little New Deal covered minor matters such as the regulation of motor vehicles and nudist camps. Yet one might well debate whether some items should be included or excluded. Lehman himself is of limited help in this matter, since he rarely used the phrase, referring instead to "the achievements of Herbert H. Lehman" in campaign broadsides. Nevertheless, the topics discussed in this work made up the bulk of what Lehman considered his accomplishments as governor. The four other major issues—liquor control, reapportionment, anticrime legislation, and the reorganization of local governments—that occupied Albany officials are excluded here, either because they made little progress in the legislature or because they had no direct impact on the Welfare State which lay at the heart of Lehman's Little New Deal.

Since the focus of this study is Albany, little attempt is made to measure the impact of the national New Deal on New York. Washington enters into the discussion only at those points where state and federal programs intersected. Yet it should be kept in mind that the federal presence loomed especially large during the 1930s. In September 1933, one and a half million New Yorkers lined Fifth Avenue to watch another quarter of a million people march all day in support of the National Recovery Administration's Blue Eagle Campaign. By 1937, the Home Owners Loan Corporation had refinanced 80,000 mortgages in the state, thereby preventing foreclosure. Meanwhile, farmers debated and voted on federal marketing agreements for dairy products. Factory workers cast ballots in plant elections supervised by the National Labor Relations Board to decide whether or not to unionize. Another federal agency, the Public Works Administration, changed the face of the state. It built the Triborough Bridge linking the Bronx, Manhattan, and Queens; paid for the Lincoln Tunnel connecting New York and Jersey; helped finance Rochester's public library; provided new classrooms for over 100,000 children around the state and gave the 1500 citizens of Webster, New York, their first water-supply system. The Rural Electrification Administration brought utility lines to people in remote areas who could then enjoy everything from electric milkers to radios. In cities and towns around the state, the Federal Theatre Project staged productions like Sinclair Lewis' *It Can't Happen Here,* which attracted many New Yorkers who had never seen a play. Thousands of high school and college students—78,000 in New York City alone—were employed part-time by the National Youth Administration on projects which benefited both the young and their communities.[5]

While Washington implemented its far-reaching New Deal, another level of government—the state—also sought to improve the lives of New Yorkers. Since the country's most populous state faced nearly all the urban and rural problems created by industrialism and aggravated by the collapse of the economy, Albany's response provides a means of testing various hypotheses about the nature of reform in the 1930s. New York not only developed the best-known Little New Deal in the country, but it also had a strong progressive tradition which serves as a standard to measure the degree of change during Lehman's tenure in office. What was the character of New York's Little New Deal: did it continue Progressivism or mark a turning point? What were the accomplishments and shortcomings of the Little New Deal? Who benefited from it? What gave reform its momentum during the 1930s? What role did Herbert H. Lehman play in adoption of the Little New Deal? These are the questions this study seeks to answer through its focus on state legislation in the period 1933-42.

In the preparation of this work, I have benefited from the help and guidance of several people who deserve mention but naturally bear no responsibility for the judgments expressed herein. My greatest debt is to William E. Leuchtenburg, De Witt Clinton Professor of History at Columbia University, who first directed me to the Lehman Papers and subsequently gave unfailing advice and encouragement during the completion of this study. His careful readings at every stage not only strengthened the analysis but also improved the style. The Curator of the Lehman Papers, William B. Liebmann, immensely facilitated the research for this project through his knowledge of Herbert Lehman and his determination to make archives serve the student of history. His friendship and enthusiasm helped me in countless ways. Thomas McDaid, Assistant Curator of the Lehman Papers, generously offered suggestions which aided me at a number of points. My wife, Joèle, will probably never fully realize the importance of her contribution, but above all, she shared the burden, as well as the joy, involved in researching and writing this work. Finally, I would like to emphasize that the dedication to George H. Mayer is but a small expression of my gratitude to the man who first sparked my interest in history and then encouraged me to pursue that interest.

NOTES

1. Richard S. Kirkendall, "The New Deal as Watershed: The Recent Literature," *Journal of American History*, LIV (March 1968): 852.

2. For reviews of the New Deal literature, see ibid., and Richard S. Kirkendall, "The Great Depression: Another Watershed in American History?" in *Change and Continuity in Twentieth-Century America*, ed. by John Braeman et al. (Columbus, Ohio, 1964), pp. 145-90.

3. George H. Mayer, *The Political Career of Floyd B. Olson* (Minneapolis, 1951); Robert E. Burke, *Olson's New Deal for California* (Berkeley, Calif., 1953); Richard C. Keller, "Pennsylvania's Little New Deal" (unpublished Ph.D. dissertation, Columbia University, 1960).

4. James T. Patterson, *The New Deal and the States: Federalism in Transition* (Princeton, N.J., 1969), pp. 198, 202.

5. William E. Leuchtenburg, *Franklin D. Roosevelt and the New Deal, 1932-1940* (New York, 1963), pp. 66, 126-27, 129 et passim; Arthur M. Schlesinger, Jr., *The Coming of the New Deal* (Cambridge, Mass., 1958), p. 115 et passim; Public Works Administration, *America Builds: The Record of the PWA* (Washington, 1939), pp. 43, 136, 170-71, 226-30 et passim; "Final Report of the NYA for New York City and Long Island," p. 124, in National Youth Administration Records, Record Group 119, National Archives.

CONTENTS

ILLUSTRATIONS

PHOTOGRAPHS

FIGURES

TABLES

INTRODUCTION

During the generation before the Little New Deal, reform flourished in New York. Fathered at the state level by a Republican, Governor Charles Evans Hughes, Progressivism later thrived in the 1920s under the guiding hand of Alfred E. Smith, a Democrat. New York's next chief executive, Franklin D. Roosevelt, picked up where Smith left off and kept the ball rolling.[1] Despite differences in emphasis, these three governors sponsored similar remedies for the problems of an industrialized society. While serving in Albany, Hughes, Smith, and Roosevelt were "progressive"—in tune with the broad reform movement which dominated American politics after the turn of the century.[2]

In New York the forces of good government focused on administrative and political reforms to make the state more efficient and responsive. Determined to clean up the state bureaucracy, Charles Evans Hughes endorsed passage of the Moreland Act, which gave the governor authority to investigate any executive department. After winning approval of this measure as well as a corrupt practices law, Hughes devoted his second term to an unsuccessful fight for direct primaries.[3] Al Smith considered reorganization of the executive branch his greatest achievement. Compelled to rely on the lengthy procedure of amending the constitution, Smith worked throughout his four terms to reduce the state's 187 different agencies to eighteen departments, all but two of which were responsible to the governor. He also introduced business methods into New York's finances by pushing through a constitutional amendment establishing the executive budget. Finally, Smith showed his tie to pre-world war reform by advocating democratic political devices such as the referendum and the direct primary.[4]

Although progressives improved the machinery of government so that it could better regulate imbalances in society, they exercised caution in curbing business. Troubled by the abuses of monopolies, Governor Hughes won enactment of a law creating a state Public Service Commission (PSC) to oversee the operations of public utilities. After the PSC proved too weak to deal effectively with transportation and power interests,

Governor Roosevelt tried unsuccessfully twenty years later to gain legislative approval of bills strengthening the regulation of utilities. Both Hughes and Roosevelt also tightened the restrictions on banks, but FDR's proposals failed to prevent many questionable financial practices, because the governor too often accepted the advice of conservative bankers. Al Smith did little to constrain corporate interests, since he did not believe in interference with business.[5]

New York's working class benefited from the movement for social justice. Charles Evans Hughes largely confined his labor program to stricter enforcement of existing laws.[6] However, after the devastating fire in New York City's Triangle Shirtwaist Company which killed 145 workers in 1911, the legislature set up the Factory Investigating Commission, headed by lawmakers Robert F. Wagner and Alfred E. Smith, to study working conditions around the state. As a result of this panel's extensive recommendations, New York enacted dozens of factory safety laws governing standards of construction, fire prevention, and sanitary conditions. During the years 1912-14, the state also adopted a system of workmen's compensation and fixed a fifty-four-hour workweek for most women, with the notable exception of those employed in upstate canneries. In 1927, New York reduced the maximum to forty-eight hours for women, but exemptions continued to impair the law's effect. As a product of the progressive tradition, Al Smith's labor policy extended little protection to men. Governor Roosevelt formulated a broad labor program, but with few exceptions the Republican-dominated legislature blocked its enactment.[7]

Most studies of these three New York governors note their limited achievements. "Governor Hughes held up before the eyes of the people of New York a splendid vision of an improved state government, but the actual accomplishments were few," asserted an early history of the period.[8] Although one detailed examination of Smith's administration pictured it as "an embryonic welfare state," the author also declared that Smith's "progressive policies often reflected a concern with conservation rather than a desire for conscious innovation." [9] The Josephsons wrote: "Much of Smith's legacy to the people of New York State is confined to intangibles, such as the reorganization of the executive branch of government, or the shift in political power from the rural population to the city masses." [10] While generally building on the foundation laid by the Happy Warrior, Governor Roosevelt proceeded with caution, since he had his sights fixed on winning the presidential nomination.[11] As a result, one historian observed, "Roosevelt did not make the same crusading impact on New York's social, economic and political history that Smith made." [12]

In part, conservatives stood in the way of more sweeping change during the first generation of the twentieth century. Drawn from the ranks of big business and agriculture, most of New York's G.O.P. lawmakers opposed increases in government services which would benefit urban masses at the expense of more well-to-do taxpayers. In 1926, the Republican state platform pointed to "the Administration of President Coolidge as a model to restore economy, efficiency, and businesslike methods to Albany." [13] The Republican Old Guard often used its control of the state legislature to frustrate the plans of reform governors. Advances came about largely through a bipartisan coalition of liberal Republicans and Democrats, most of whom represented urban areas. However, throughout this period the Old Guard blocked enactment of the most radical proposals such as unemployment insurance and public development of the state's hydroelectric resources.[14]

Yet in spite of the fears of conservatives, Hughes, Smith, and Roosevelt favored a limited role for government in New York. All three rejected the idea of laissez-faire, but they exercised caution when enlarging public functions. Many of their proposals focused on negative state action such as restrictions on women's labor and prohibitions like those contained in the 1907 pure drug law. Positive government intervention was usually confined to improving traditional public services such as schools and hospitals. Al Smith devoted much of his time to creating a statewide network of parks. Although FDR had a more flexible and expansive view of government than his predecessor, he too emphasized the construction of public facilities, especially prisons to reduce overcrowding. Under the impact of the Depression, Roosevelt initiated state aid for unemployment relief, and he called for old age insurance. But his welfare program did not go much beyond this. With the possible exception of workmen's compensation, the Empire State generally failed to undertake activities which in any way guaranteed New Yorkers a minimum standard of living as a matter of right. Indeed, committed to the principle of balanced budgets, the state's liberal chief executives hesitated to increase current spending. Governor Smith cut taxes while supporting bond issues for needed public works. Not until 1932 did Roosevelt reluctantly give up the cherished policy of pay-as-you-go to borrow for unemployment relief.[15] In 1938, Roosevelt himself acknowledged that "during the twenties, I in common with most liberals did not at the start visualize the effects of the period, or the drastic changes which were even then necessary for a lasting economy." [16]

Most New Yorkers did not accept the need for "drastic changes" until the Depression hit bottom. By then FDR had moved to Washington, and his lieutenant governor, Herbert H. Lehman, had taken over the reins of government in Albany. His predecessors had generated a momentum for reform, but the question remained whether Lehman would follow the lines set down by Hughes, Smith, and Roosevelt or would venture in new directions.

NOTES

1. Hughes served as governor for four years (1907-10), Smith eight years (1919-20, 1923-28), and Roosevelt four years (1929-32). Most historians exclude Theodore Roosevelt, who held the office from 1899 to 1901, from the list of progressive governors. "During the progressive era, Roosevelt was the only New Yorker to gain greater renown [than Hughes] as a progressive; but Roosevelt owed his reputation to his activities in Washington rather than in New York." David M. Ellis et al., *A History of New York State* (Ithaca, N.Y., 1967), p. 385.

2. For discussions of Progressivism generally, see Richard Hofstadter, *The Age of Reform from Bryan to F.D.R.* (New York, 1955); Robert H. Wiebe, *The Search for Order, 1877-1920* (New York, 1967); George E. Mowry, *The Era of Theodore Roosevelt and the*

Birth of Modern America, 1900-1912 (New York, 1958); Arthur S. Link, *Woodrow Wilson and the Progressive Era, 1910-1917* (New York, 1954); Gabriel Kolko, *The Triumph of Conservatism* (New York, 1963); Arthur S. Link, "What Happened to the Progressive Movement in the 1920's?" *The American Historical Review,* LXIV (July 1959): 833-51.

3. Robert F. Wesser, *Charles Evans Hughes: Politics and Reform in New York, 1905-1910* (Ithaca, N.Y., 1967), pp. 124-45, 252-301; John Ellswerth Missall, *The Moreland Act: Executive Inquiry in the State of New York* (New York, 1946), pp. 9-23.

4. Oscar Handlin, *Al Smith and His America* (Boston, 1958), pp. 90-111; Matthew and Hannah Josephson, *Al Smith: Hero of the Cities* (Boston, 1969), pp. 237-40, 318; James T. Crown, "The Development of Democratic Government in the State of New York Through the Growth of the Power of the Executive Since 1920" (unpublished Ph.D. dissertation, New York University, 1956), passim; Paula Eldot, "Alfred Emanuel Smith, Reforming Governor" (unpublished Ph.D. dissertation, Yale University, 1961), pp. 35-129.

5. Wesser, *Hughes,* pp. 153-70; Bernard Bellush, *Franklin D. Roosevelt as Governor of New York* (New York, 1955), pp. 114-16, 243-68; Frank Freidel, *Franklin D. Roosevelt: The Triumph* (Boston, 1956), pp. 191-92; Josephsons, *Smith,* p. 288; Martin I. Feldman, "An Abstract of the Political Thought of Alfred E. Smith" (unpublished Ph.D. dissertation, New York University, 1963), p. 2 et passim; William E. Leuchtenburg, *The Perils of Prosperity, 1914-1932* (Chicago, 1958), pp. 231-33.

6. Irwin Yellowitz, *Labor and the Progressive Movement in New York State, 1897-1916* (Ithaca, N.Y., 1965), pp. 126-27, 154-55; Wesser, *Hughes,* pp. 309-10.

7. Leon Stein, *The Triangle Fire* (Philadelphia, 1962), passim; J. William Gillette, "Welfare State Trail Blazer: New York State Factory Investigating Commission, 1911-15" (unpublished M.A. essay, Columbia University, 1956), passim; Melvyn Dubofsky, *When Workers Organize: New York City in the Progressive Era* (Amherst, Mass., 1968), pp. 7-26; Jacob A. Lieberman, "Their Sisters' Keepers: The Women's Hours and Wages Movement in the United States, 1890-1925" (unpublished Ph.D. dissertation, Columbia University, 1971), pp. 139-257; Eldot, "Smith," pp. 312-78; Bellush, *Roosevelt,* pp. 191-207.

8. Alexander C. Flick, ed., *History of the State of New York* (10 vols.; New York, 1933-37), VII: 189.

9. Eldot, "Smith," pp. 131, 379.

10. Josephsons, *Smith,* p. 332. See also Handlin, *Smith,* p. 92.

11. Freidel, *Roosevelt,* p. 196; Rexford G. Tugwell, *The Democratic Roosevelt* (Garden City, N.Y., 1957), pp. 147-48.

12. Bellush, *Roosevelt,* p. ix.

13. Judith Stein, "The Birth of Liberal Republicanism in New York State, 1932-38" (unpublished Ph.D. dissertation, Yale University, 1968), pp. 8-32. Quotation on p. 14.

14. J. Joseph Huthmacher, "Urban Liberalism and the Age of Reform," *Mississippi Valley Historical Review,* XLIX (September 1962): 231-41; idem, "Charles Evans Hughes and Charles Francis Murphy: The Metamorphosis of Progressivism," *New York History,* XLVI (January 1965): 25-40; Herbert Hillel Rosenthal, "The Progressive Movement in New York State 1906-1914" (unpublished Ph.D. dissertation, Harvard University, 1955), passim; Eldot, "Smith," pp. 128-29.

15. Daniel R. Fusfeld, *The Economic Thought of Franklin D. Roosevelt and the Origins of the New Deal* (New York, 1956), pp. 99-100, 154, 181-82, et passim; Eldot, "Smith," pp. 130-252; Bellush, *Roosevelt,* pp. 66-75; Freidel, *Roosevelt,* pp. 218-27.

16. Quoted in Freidel, *Roosevelt,* p. 5.

HERBERT H. LEHMAN
AND NEW YORK'S
LITTLE NEW DEAL

FROM WALL STREET
TO STATE STREET

At about two o'clock in the morning of October 2, 1928, the call went through to Franklin D. Roosevelt in Warm Springs, Georgia. After numerous rebuffs, Democratic party leaders at the state convention in Rochester were trying once more to convince the unwilling Roosevelt to accept the nomination for governor. Alfred E. Smith, anxious to bolster his presidential bid with the strongest possible ticket in New York, begged FDR to run. When Roosevelt still demurred, in part because of his commitments to the Warm Springs Foundation, the Democratic national chairman, John J. Raskob, got on the line to say that he would take care of any financial obligations connected with the spa. Aware of Roosevelt's desire to continue receiving treatments for his paralysis caused by polio, Smith minimized the burden of the governor's job and suggested Herbert H. Lehman, a New York banker, as a possible lieutenant governor who could spell Roosevelt during his visits to Warm Springs. After Lehman himself took the phone and affirmed his readiness to run, Roosevelt finally relented and agreed to accept the nomination. Several hours later, joyful delegates formally endorsed the Roosevelt-Lehman ticket.[1]

The outcome of the state convention surprised Lehman as much as Roosevelt. Lehman had gone to Rochester devoted to the interests of Al Smith, whose national campaign he served as finance director. Although his name had been mentioned for the top spot on the state ticket after Republicans had nominated a Jew for governor, Lehman had discouraged any talk of his candidacy, because he did not like religion dictating the choice and he thought he had little chance in any case. Completely unaware that Rochester would mark a turning point in his life, Lehman had not even brought his closest confidant, his wife, Edith.[2]

With rising doubts about Al Smith's chances of winning the presidency, Herbert Lehman wanted the 1928 election to ensure at least a worthy successor for the Happy Warrior in Albany. Lehman later recalled: "I was so anxious to see the state remain under a liberal Democrat, which I knew Roosevelt to be, that I think I probably would have done almost anything that he asked me to do." When FDR finally agreed to serve if

Lehman joined him, the latter consented, thinking "it would be for two years, and at the end of two years I would return to my business." [3] Soon after the convention approved this team, Roosevelt attested to the importance of Lehman's candidacy in undermining his own reluctance to accept a draft. FDR wired his running mate: I DON'T NEED TO TELL YOU THAT YOUR NOMINATION MAKES ME VERY HAPPY AND IT IS FINE TO KNOW THAT I SHALL HAVE YOUR HELP IN THE DAYS TO COME. [4]

1

At the start of what became a new career, Herbert Henry Lehman contrasted sharply with the popular image of a New York politician. Short and almost completely bald except for a closely cut gray fringe of hair, he did not even look the part. Dark bushy eyebrows dominated a round face which made his trim figure appear stocky. Despite a solemn mien, Lehman could easily break into a friendly smile which would light up his entire face. He had, however, almost no sense of humor, perhaps because of a deep feeling of propriety which also underlay his abiding courtesy and kindness. Due to his basic reserve, Herbert Lehman came across as colorless—the word most often used to describe him. In many ways old-fashioned, he always wore a stiff collar and a tie held firmly in place by a pearl stickpin. When addressing any group, he read speeches mechanically with almost no inflection and few gestures. He never inserted a lively phrase, preferring instead dull prose laced with facts which appealed to reason rather than emotions. In an era of vibrant figures like the Happy Warrior and FDR, Herbert Lehman projected a particularly lackluster personality. [5]

Although Lehman was an anomaly in New York politics, his background prepared him for the life of public service he started at the unusually late age of fifty. Born on March 28, 1878, Herbert Lehman had grown up in the German-Jewish society centered in the rich surroundings of midtown Manhattan. His parents' wealth sprang from Lehman Brothers which Herbert's father, Mayer, and two uncles had founded after emigrating from Bavaria in the 1840s. Beginning as a small general store in Montgomery, Alabama, the family business had expanded into cotton trading and finally into investment banking after the firm relocated in New York City following the Civil War. The Lehmans prospered in the north and looked to the next generation for additional accomplishments. [6]

Herbert, the youngest of eight children, was closest to his brother Irving. Only two years older than Herbert, Irving seemed marked for greatness. A quiet, studious boy, he awed teachers at Dr. Sachs' School for Boys, the elite Manhattan institute where both Irving and Herbert received their early education. Herbert was less concerned with his studies and more excited by sports he could never quite master. He admired his brilliant brother who subsequently graduated from Columbia College and Law School. Their paths separated when Herbert went off to college in 1895, but they remained devoted to each other. Years later they worked in tandem after Herbert became New York's chief executive and Irving headed the state's highest tribunal, the Court of Appeals. [7]

Young Herbert chose a business career in spite of his parents' wishes. After the two

Herbert Lehman as a Williams College student, 1896.

eldest sons had gone into the family firm and Irving had settled on law, Mayer Lehman had expected Herbert to take up engineering at Columbia's School of Mines. However, the youth showed little appetite or aptitude for science, and a teacher at Sachs persuaded Mayer to send the boy to Williams College for a liberal education to prepare him for the business world. Herbert ultimately came to love Williams, but the first year at the small Massachusetts school tested the mettle of the nervous New Yorker who was forced to realize immediately that he and another boy from Sachs were the only Jews at Williams.[8] After a "desperately lonely" freshman year, Herbert finally overcame the suspicion and occasional hostility of classmates.[9] Determined to prove himself, he devoted his time to numerous extracurricular activities such as managing the track team, debating, acting in the drama society and writing for a campus literary magazine. By his senior year, Lehman's many contributions won him election into Gargoyle, the college's leading honor society. Finally, and least important in Herbert's mind, his classroom work usually earned him the proverbial gentleman's "C." [10]

After graduating from Williams in 1899, Herbert Lehman entered the world of business. With no previous training, he started working at $5.00 a week for the J. Spencer Turner Company, a New York City textile firm headed by a friend of his deceased father.[11] During his ten-year apprenticeship with this medium-sized company which sold canvas, the quiet and unassuming Herbert learned the ways of commerce and gradually moved into the ranks of management, ultimately rising to vice president and treasurer of the Turner Company. He enjoyed the work and stayed on until 1908, when he finally heeded his family's call to join Lehman Brothers as a full partner. There he participated in the firm's steady movement away from commodity trading and into investment banking and underwriting the first public issues of stock by large companies like F. W. Woolworth and Studebaker. His commercial experience helped Herbert solve management and distribution problems faced by client firms on whose boards of directors he often served.[12]

Soon after Herbert joined Lehman Brothers, he met Edith Altschul, a banker's daughter, who became his wife in 1910. Slender and slightly taller than Herbert, Edith Lehman displayed a graciousness and poise that her high-strung, awkward husband sometimes lacked. Yet even after Herbert went into politics, his cultivated wife remained a very private person who disliked speaking in public and who tried to shield their three adopted children from the limelight. Although she kept in the background, Edith Lehman followed politics closely and acted as a sounding board for her husband, who worried terribly when weighing decisions.[13] Toward the end of his life Herbert Lehman called his wife "a fine soldier [who] has not only never interfered in what I wished to do in public service, but has encouraged me in every possible way." [14]

Given his family background, Herbert Lehman's success in business was scarcely remarkable, but from the early days of his adult life he eagerly aided many less fortunate people. As a college student, he accompanied friends who visited Lillian Wald's settlement house on Henry Street in the heart of the slums on Manhattan's Lower East Side. After graduating from Williams, Lehman organized a boys' club at the settlement. Through his regular meetings with neighborhood youths and his exposure to the dynamic Miss Wald, he learned firsthand about the dismal living conditions in urban slums. Although he ran the boys' club for only a few years, Lehman remained close to the Henry Street Settlement as a board member and frequent contributor.[15] Expressing "very great affection and admiration for Miss Wald" at the time of her death in 1940, he declared that "with the exception of my wife and my parents no one has had as great an influence on my life as she." [16]

Herbert Lehman's generosity gradually led him into numerous philanthropic activities after he first secured his place in business. Closest to his heart was the Joint Distribution Committee (JDC), organized by American Jews during World War I to aid coreligionists, especially in eastern Europe. As one of the leaders of the JDC, Lehman helped raise over $43 million for relief during and immediately following the war. After 1920, the committee focused on the reconstruction of Jewish life in wartorn Europe. With the rehabilitation effort working through several subcommittees, Lehman directed the disbursement of economic aid which helped restore Jewish livelihoods in eastern Europe and the Soviet Union. During the 1920s, the JDC had surprising success, in part because of the tireless energy of Lehman, whose rise to vice chairman of the relief agency reflected the depth of his commitment.[17]

Lehman's work with the JDC strengthened his identification with Judaism. "If anything in my life has made me feel the value of . . . Jewish spirituality," he told an audience in 1928, "it is my connection with the cultural and religious activities of the joint distribution committee." [18] Significantly, this organization included Reform, Conservative, and Orthodox Jews who, in an unusual display of unity, collaborated without regard to long-standing doctrinal differences. Embracing Judaism as an entity, Lehman always kept ties with each of its three denominations. Like his father, Herbert attended Temple Emanu-El, a Reform synagogue, but he also worked closely with the Conservative Jewish Theological Seminary and ultimately served as chairman of its board of overseers. In addition, he contributed to a number of synagogues, including an Orthodox one built on the site where he was born.[19] Scarcely an intellectual who understood, let alone worried about, theological questions, Lehman declared late in his life that "denominations within the Jewish faith meant very little to me and . . . it made no difference to me whether a man went to a Reform, Orthodox or Conservative synagogue." [20]

Herbert Lehman never confined his philanthropy to Jewish groups. With unusual generosity, he gave to numerous Protestant and Catholic charities as well as to almost every imaginable civic cause from the Boy Scouts to the NAACP. By 1945, he was supporting almost three hundred different organizations, most of which received annual contributions on a systematic basis. Indeed, Lehman needed a full-time secretary just to keep track of his philanthropic activities. In 1962, he estimated that during his life he had donated well over $7 million to charity.[21]

2

Herbert Lehman got his first taste of government service in World War I. Although almost forty when America declared war in April 1917, he immediately applied for a direct commission. Before receiving appointment as a captain in the army, he did civilian

Herbert Lehman as an army officer in World War I.

work in the Navy Department where he first met Franklin D. Roosevelt, then assistant secretary of navy. Once commissioned, Lehman moved to the army's central purchasing division in Washington, which drew on his vast knowledge of textiles. Because of his expertise and administrative ability, he was soon shifted to the General Staff Corps and ultimately promoted to the rank of colonel, a title he proudly carried through the 1920s. Excited by his first government job, Lehman continued his military work more than seven months after the armistice.[22]

Following his two years in Washington, Lehman apparently did not relish returning to the business world. In 1920, he sought appointment as an undersecretary of war, because "I know that I should greatly enjoy the work and would approach it with much enthusiasm." If selected, he promised to relinquish his partnership in Lehman Brothers.[23] When the opening failed to materialize, Lehman naturally remained in the family business, but he devoted increasing amounts of time to outside interests during the 1920s. In addition to laboring tirelessly for the Joint Distribution Committee, the restless banker also turned his attention to politics.[24]

Herbert Lehman inherited his preference for the Democratic party from his parents. Living in Alabama, both had supported the Confederacy, and they brought their anti-Republican bias north with them. Although some of their children drifted into the party of Lincoln, Herbert unhesitatingly became a Democrat. Returning to Manhattan from Williams at the turn of the century, he joined his local Democratic club and was active enough to be selected as a delegate to the 1910 Democratic state convention. In 1912, Lehman contributed heavily to the campaign of William Sulzer, who won the election for governor but was impeached and removed from office after he broke with Tammany Hall. During the legislature's investigation of Sulzer, Lehman testified that he had given the future governor $5000 with no strings attached which, along with other contributions, Sulzer had failed to report as required by law.[25] After Lehman left the witness stand, a party leader plucked his sleeve and said in disbelief: "So you really gave $5,000 without any commitment as to its use." When Lehman answered affirmatively, the politician exclaimed: "Say, you're the kind of man the Democratic party needs!" [26] Unfortunately for the party, Sulzer's conviction temporarily soured Lehman's taste for politics. In addition, military service and Jewish relief work preoccupied him until the mid-1920s.[27]

Al Smith revived Lehman's interest in politics. After first hearing the Happy Warrior speak in 1922, Lehman learned more about Smith and met him socially through mutual friends like Joseph Proskauer and Belle Moskowitz, two of the governor's leading advisers. Gradually moving into the governor's inner circle, Lehman initially proved his value as a labor mediator. When a strike threatened the New York City garment industry in 1924, Smith appointed a mediation panel and asked Lehman to serve on it. Although he knew little about the clothing business, Lehman readily accepted. Several weeks of work produced an agreement between labor and management, but the commission continued its study for several years in hopes of bringing some order to the chaotic industry. Despite limited success, Lehman's efforts not only solidified his ties to Smith but also introduced him to leaders of the International Ladies Garment Workers Union who later became some of his strongest political supporters.[28]

Undoubtedly eyeing Lehman's wealth as well as his administrative ability, Al Smith selected him for numerous party jobs. In 1924, Lehman was treasurer of the governor's reelection drive, and he also became the largest individual contributor. Two years later, Lehman gave up his business duties for over a month to head Smith's campaign committee. In the wake of the 1926 victory, Smith wanted him to take charge of the Democratic state committee, but Lehman rejected the offer when Tammany chieftains expressed opposition to the appointment of a political newcomer not closely aligned with the New York City party machine. During 1927 and 1928, Lehman traveled widely throughout the western United States drumming up support for Smith's presidential bid. After the 1928 national convention, the Democratic nominee chose Lehman to head the campaign's finance committee. Although Lehman worked hard at raising funds, the bulk of the money came from a small group, including Lehman who personally gave over $500,000.[29]

The Happy Warrior rewarded Herbert Lehman's faithful service by backing him for lieutenant governor in 1928. Ironically, the selfless Lehman had sought no such quid pro quo, and he expressed genuine surprise at his selection as Franklin Roosevelt's running mate. Certain of victory, Lehman looked on his term in Albany as a brief two-year hiatus in his business career. Yet he had already shown a willingness to spend increasing amounts of time away from Lehman Brothers, and the excitement and personal satisfaction derived from government service kept him from ever returning to Wall Street.[30]

3

As promised, Herbert Lehman shared much of Franklin Roosevelt's burden in Albany. According to the constitution, the lieutenant governor's main task was to preside over the Senate, and Lehman won praise from Republicans as "the ablest and most impartial President of the Senate within any of our recollections." [31] In spite of his role in the upper house, the lieutenant governor's job had traditionally been a ceremonial post with little more than a title, but Roosevelt encouraged Lehman to make it a full-time position. The governor included Lehman in his inner circle, called the "Turkey Cabinet" because turkey was often served at the regular luncheon meetings of advisers and Democratic legislative leaders—a practice Lehman continued as chief executive. In addition to his work in the Senate, Lehman helped Roosevelt with a variety of administrative duties such as preparation of the annual budget and the inspection of state facilities, especially prisons and hospitals.[32]

Lehman often filled in for FDR, who frequently vacationed in Warm Springs and who also made trips in search of the presidential nomination. Lehman's days with the official title "acting governor" usually passed quietly, but crises inevitably arose. In December 1929, inmates at the state prison in Auburn killed a guard and held several others hostage along with the warden. Ignoring prisoners' demands for freedom and immunity from punishment, Lehman commanded a detachment of state troopers to rescue the hostages, which they did without further loss of life. On another occasion, the

City Trust Company of New York City collapsed during Roosevelt's absence from the state, and the acting governor immediately ordered an official investigation when he discovered that the recently retired head of the Banking Department was secretly preparing to leave the country. Concerned about the plight of the depositors, Lehman also personally took charge of reorganizing the defunct bank, and he gave one million dollars of his own money, none of which he ever recouped. Thanks to his diligence and sound judgment, Lehman proved so helpful to Roosevelt that the governor referred to him as "my good right arm." [33]

Lehman clearly benefited from this close association with FDR. More than anything else, Lehman's four-year apprenticeship provided the necessary experience to make him a successful governor in his own right. Having spent most of his life on Wall Street, he learned firsthand how things worked at the Capitol on State Street in Albany. The political novice found Roosevelt anxious to delegate responsibility in part, as Lehman later realized, because FDR "foresaw that someday I'd succeed him and [he] wanted to train me for the position." [34]

Lehman got his chance in 1932. After Roosevelt received the presidential nomination, New York Democrats gathered in Albany to choose a state ticket, but wounds suffered at the national convention had not yet healed. Still bitter about the failure to nominate Al Smith again, Democratic leaders from New York City and Albany expressed little enthusiasm for FDR's self-designated successor as governor. Smith, however, showed no personal animosity at the time, and he publicly threw his weight behind his old friend, Herbert Lehman, even though the lieutenant governor had supported Roosevelt at the national convention. Meanwhile, the anti-Roosevelt faction fixed on a ploy to deny Lehman the nomination. The bosses of the Brooklyn and Manhattan organizations proposed that Lehman take the spot of Senator Robert F. Wagner who was up for reelection and who might be persuaded to run for governor instead. Uncertain whether they could command a majority of the delegates, the pro-Lehman forces decided that their man should confront the tigers of Tammany in their lair.[35]

Mustering his courage, the determined lieutenant governor marched into the Albany hotel room of Tammany chieftain John Curry. Surrounded by other dissident county leaders, Curry declared that the slate would be Lehman for senator and Wagner for governor, but Lehman responded, as he remembered it years later:

Well, that won't suit me at all. I have stated that I expected to be nominated as governor, and I will not take the nomination to the United States Senate.

The local party bosses insisted that Lehman could hardly refuse if the convention selected him for the job in Washington. "Well," he answered, "I'll just get up and decline, but I can assure you that I will nonetheless have my name placed in nomination for the governorship." Lehman then walked out of the room, and shortly thereafter he received a phone call from Curry who said simply, "You win." [36] And so he did, going on to become New York's forty-ninth governor.

Governor and Mrs. Lehman at Atlantic City, 1933.

Franklin Roosevelt and Al Smith with Lehman at his inauguration as governor, January 2, 1933.

4

Once elected, Lehman had little trouble with the Tammany tiger, which lost most of its teeth during the 1930s. Although technically only the Democratic organization for New York County (Manhattan), Tammany Hall had long controlled the other county machines in the rest of New York City. However, after the death of the strong-willed Charles F. Murphy in 1924, Tammany's leadership passed through the hands of a series of mediocre politicians whose blunders included opposing the nominations of Roosevelt and Lehman in 1932. The following year, Fusionist candidate Fiorello La Guardia captured the mayor's office as a result of widespread exposures of corruption and division in Democratic ranks.[37]

Cut off from local patronage, the decaying Democratic machines of Manhattan and Brooklyn found little sympathy in Albany or Washington. Both Roosevelt and Lehman favored the astute and urbane leader of the Bronx, Edward J. Flynn, who had broken with other Democratic bosses in New York City and put his weight behind the president and the governor. After serving as FDR's secretary of state in Albany, Flynn held the same job under Lehman and became a trusted political adviser.[38]

Although no love was lost between Governor Lehman and local Democratic leaders around the state, he avoided an open break with them during his Albany years. Still in many ways a reserved businessman with an upper-class sense of propriety, Lehman, in the words of one observer, "never really felt either warm or close to any of.the practical politicians." [39] Nonetheless, whenever Democratic lawmakers blocked his plans for reapportionment or held up some New Deal measure, Lehman preferred to hammer away at them privately rather than risk splitting the party, which would have jeopardized his future and that of reform generally. Lehman reinforced his strong hand by remaining a loyal Democrat and casting a straight party vote at elections. Even when Tammany reached its low point in the 1930s, the governor continually supported its candidates for local office rather than any of the Fusionists, including Fiorello La Guardia.[40] Lehman also held local Democratic chieftains in line by consulting them on patronage, but he retained the last word on state appointments. Summing up his diplomatic handling of county bosses, Lehman later asserted:

> My relations with the political leaders, after the first couple of years, while never cordial or friendly, did not result in a public break with them, or any particular acrimony. . . . And I think that was due to one reason. From the very beginning of my administration, when these political leaders, like Curry and the O'Connells of upstate New York, came to me, I told them that I would not close the door to their recommendations; that as a Democrat I would be glad to appoint many Democrats; but that I felt that we had plenty of good Democrats who were qualified for appointment, so that it was not necessary to appoint poor ones for possible political advantage.[41]

Since Governor Lehman never thought of consulting party functionaries about any-thing but patronage questions, he relied heavily on a one-man brain trust, Charles Poletti, to advise him on state matters. Short and dark, this brilliant son of Italian immigrants worked his way through Harvard College while earning a Phi Beta Kappa key and then graduated from Harvard Law School. In 1933, at the age of thirty, Poletti came to Lehman's Albany staff highly recommended by Felix Frankfurter, who heralded the "disciplined and inventive mind" of his former student who also possessed "a strong desire to put his law to social use." [42] Finding the exuberant and affable Poletti of great assistance and a real comfort, Lehman soon elevated him to the official position of counsel to the governor, and he invited the young bachelor to move into the executive mansion, which also became the home of Poletti's wife after their marriage in 1934. As the governor's chief aid, the ubiquitous "Charlie" wrote speeches, drafted bills, advised on pending legislation, accompanied Lehman to meetings, and lobbied for the Little New Deal at the Capitol. Living in the same house, Lehman and Poletti often worked on state business after leaving the office and, as an ardent New Dealer, Poletti occasionally took advantage of late night talks to convince his more cautious boss of the need for some piece of reform legislation.[43] Midway through 1937, Poletti left Albany to serve as a judge on a lower state court, but the following year Lehman pushed for and won Poletti's nomination for lieutenant governor.[44]

5

Although Herbert Lehman ultimately held the governor's job for ten years, he tried to retire at the end of each term. In May 1934, Lehman disclosed to the president his reasons for not wanting to run again.

> No one knows better than you the sacrifice to oneself and to one's family which the holding of office of Governor during these trying days has entailed. . . . I can say, in all sincerity, that the enjoyment and satisfaction which have come to me from the knowledge of constructive work accomplished have more than compensated for the sacrifice which I have made. I cannot deny, however, that the strain has been great and that I feel in need of a rest.[45]

Several months later, however, Roosevelt convinced his old friend to accept renomination.[46] During 1936, Lehman's determination to relinquish the governorship was strengthened by setbacks in the legislature and the death of his brother, Arthur, a mainstay of the family business. In the spring of 1936, Lehman formally announced his decision to retire at the end of the year, but party leaders refused to take this as final. Anxious to buoy FDR's reelection campaign with a proven vote-getter in New York, Democrats staged a massive "draft Lehman" demonstration at their national convention in July.[47] The week following this overwhelming reception, Lehman yielded to entreaties from Democratic leaders and agreed to run because, he wrote a relative, "I realized that in loyalty to causes very dear to me I could not possibly refuse to at least offer myself for service to the people." [48]

From the beginning of his third term, Lehman again set his sights on leaving Albany.[49] When New York's Senator Royal S. Copeland suddenly died in June 1938, the governor quickly announced his candidacy for the vacant seat in Congress where, he revealed to his son, he hoped to "render good service to the people of the State and Nation . . . and yet have a great deal more time for my family and for my personal affairs, and be relieved to a great extent of the constant worry and responsibility which I am carrying." [50] Lehman went to the state convention in late September expecting to receive the Senate nomination, but after long discussions, Jim Farley and Ed Flynn convinced him that he was the only Democrat strong enough to defeat Thomas E. Dewey's bid for governor.[51] Although a recent constitutional amendment had extended the governor's term to four years, Lehman agreed to run again because he feared that Dewey would undo "much of the progress . . . made by Al Smith, FDR and [himself] over a period of twenty years." [52]

Lehman easily won his first three races for governor. In 1932, he faced William J. Donovan, renowned as "Wild Bill," the handsome World War I Medal of Honor winner who subsequently headed the OSS during World War II. In his only try for high elective office Donovan, a former Assistant Attorney General, was overwhelmed by the anti-Hoover tide.[53] Two years later, New York Republicans put the outspoken and bellicose Robert Moses up against Lehman. A Bull Moose Republican who had served in Al Smith's cabinet, Moses held the posts of New York City park commissioner and president of the state's Long Island Park Commission at the time of his nomination for governor. In a rough campaign Moses hit hard; with questionable accuracy he went so far as to call Lehman a liar during one heated exchange. Riding the wave of New Deal popularity, Lehman maintained his usual outward calm and ran up a plurality of over 800,000 votes, which was unprecedented in a nonpresidential election and which almost matched his record margin of victory in 1932.[54] As a result of the landslide, Democrats captured control of both houses of the state legislature for the first time since 1912. In 1936, according to one Albany correspondent, Republicans sought "a drab candidate who [could] trade monotony for monotony with Governor Lehman." [55] They found their man in a solemn-looking judge from Westchester County, William F. Bleakley, who rivaled Lehman for lack of color, but the invincible governor beat his anti-New Deal opponent by over 500,000 votes.[56]

Lehman faced his greatest challenge in the 1938 contest against "Mr. District Attorney," Thomas E. Dewey. The young lawyer from Michigan with his little black mustache and piercing dark eyes had won a national reputation as a rackets buster in New York City. At the age of only thirty-three in 1935, Dewey had received his big break when a Manhattan grand jury appealed to the governor for a special prosecutor to combat organized crime.[57] Following his usual practice, Lehman offered the position to several prominent Republican lawyers, since the appointee would need to investigate a Democrat, the New York County district attorney.[58] The governor's original choices begged off and unanimously recommended the selection of Thomas Dewey, who had

Governor Lehman and Mayor La Guardia at 1935 World Series.

President Roosevelt, Governor Lehman and Senator Wagner at 1938 campaign rally.

already held the post of chief assistant United States attorney for the New York City area. Lehman hesitated "because of [Dewey's] youth and his relative lack of experience," but pressed by time and circumstances, the governor finally acquiesced.[59]

Once installed as the state's prosecutor in Manhattan, Dewey soon launched a political career which brought him head-to-head with Lehman. After he had relentlessly pursued mobsters in a headline-making crusade, Dewey was elected Manhattan's district attorney in 1937. The following year, he received the G.O.P. nomination for governor, and national party leaders already talked about him as a potential presidential candidate.[60] Lehman finally agreed to oppose Dewey, in part because he resented the young challenger's ambition and his willingness to abandon local office so soon after accepting it. During the campaign, the governor attacked Dewey's unfamiliarity with the state's social and economic problems, but the tough country boy who had cleaned up the metropolis ran a strong race both upstate and in New York City. Lehman squeezed out a narrow victory by only 64,000 votes out of the almost five million cast.[61]

6

Herbert Lehman's popularity rested on his strikingly apolitical qualities. Humorless and colorless, he won respect for his single-minded devotion to the public interest rather than to party or person. Although this widely held opinion of Lehman sounded like the oldest of campaign clichés, it described him with surprising accuracy. As an upstate farm leader once pointed out, Lehman "lacked the radiant personal charm of Franklin Roosevelt, but he was virtually nonpartisan in his thinking and he seemed to be devoid of what we think of as the wiles of the politician and he conveyed a sense of worth and sincerity and a great desire to serve his state." [62] Even Lehman's poor speaking ability ultimately worked in his favor, since his flat and mechanical delivery carried conviction and encouraged trust.[63] "The Governor is not a good speaker," noted a Republican newspaper in Troy. "But, on the other hand, he gives an impression often lacking in presidential speeches, of sincerity and honesty of purpose." [64]

Frequently propelled by an aroused sense of the essential rightness of a cause, Lehman "was not prone to compromise." [65] Although his stubbornness sometimes annoyed more practical allies, it brought praise from ordinary New Yorkers, who liked their chief executive to rise above partisan considerations—or at least seem to.[66] A Utica newspaper once observed that "the Governor is regarded as an excellent businessman, with little of the politician about him." [67] An upstate woman wrote Lehman approvingly: "I know that you are not a Politician and therefore cannot play their game." [68]

Lehman also earned a well-deserved reputation as a conscientious governor. Unlike Al Smith who often commuted to Albany from New York City, Lehman moved his family to the state capital where he worked long days keeping in close touch with the variety of problems that arose not only during the brief legislative sessions but also in summer and fall when his predecessors usually escaped Albany. Seasoned Capitol reporters could not remember any governor laboring so hard and as efficiently since the days of Charles Evans Hughes.[69] "[Y]ou have an over-developed sense of duty" and "have given more of yourself to the state than it had any right to expect," Hickman Powell of the *Herald Tribune* wrote Lehman in 1936.[70] On those rare occasions when Lehman took a vacation to do some fishing, he invariably carried state business with him.[71] He once confided to his brother-in-law: "I unfortunately find it very difficult to cut myself off from work and have so many different worries and problems that it is pretty hard to relax." [72] Pointing to Lehman's "intensely serious mental attitude," James Farley observed that the governor "didn't have the faculty of easing the strain now and then with a hearty laugh or good outburst of anger." [73]

According to close friends, Lehman fretted over decisions.[74] "Once having made up his mind, that won't end it," Eleanor Roosevelt revealed. "He will think about it all night, and he will worry about it the next day, and will talk to everybody about it, and it will go on being a worry after there is no use worrying, because he's done it." [75] Most New Yorkers sensed the depth of Lehman's commitment to his job, and they trusted him, in the words of *Time* magazine, "as a decent, well-behaved, hard-working executive who is doing his level best for some 12,000,000 citizens." [76]

Herbert Lehman's streak of righteousness led to his celebrated split with Franklin Roosevelt in 1937. Although the two men saw each other infrequently after FDR became president, they remained good friends and cooperated on matters of mutual interest, especially at election time.[77] When Roosevelt presented his plan for liberalizing the Supreme Court by increasing the number of justices, Lehman privately took issue with the president early in 1937:

> I share your disappointment that many important measures have been declared unconstitutional by a narrow and unconvincing vote of the Supreme Court. Unfortunately, however, I feel that the end which you desire to attain does not justify the means which you recommend. . . . I feel, too, that nothing should be done which is merely an attempt to meet an immediate situation at the expense of orderly and deliberate processes of government.[78]

On this question, Lehman's innate caution was reinforced by his brother Irving, who also strongly opposed the Court reorganization plan. After months of stewing over the proposal, the governor finally came out against it publicly in a personally drafted letter to Senator Wagner. Repeating much of what he had previously told the president, Lehman charged that passage of enabling legislation would create a dangerous precedent which might permit less well-intentioned administrations to curtail constitutional rights in the future. By the time Lehman announced his stand on July 19, Roosevelt's plan already faced certain defeat in Congress, but the governor, probably unaware of recent developments in Washington, felt driven by his conscience to take sides on an issue he saw as fundamentally a matter of right and wrong.[79]

Lehman's letter predictably "burned the hell out of Roosevelt." [80] "If I were British," the president remarked privately, "I would say only one thing—'it isn't cricket.'" [81] Ironically, this comment summed up Lehman's own reason for opposing any change in the size of the Supreme Court.[82] As Lehman feared, his highly publicized declaration precipitated a breach in his relations with the president, which lasted until a reconciliation during Lehman's 1938 reelection campaign when FDR finally forgave, but he undoubtedly never forgot.[83]

7

Although Herbert Lehman's own performance contributed to his political success, the traditional voting behavior of New Yorkers best explains his string of election victories.[84] Since 1918, Democratic candidates for governor had won every contest but the one in 1920 when Harding's national landslide temporarily removed Al Smith from office. Although New Yorkers continued to give majorities to Republican candidates for president during the remainder of the decade, they regularly renewed the Democrats' two-year lease on the state's executive mansion. When the Depression transformed the country's political alignment and made Democrats the majority party, Lehman rode into the governor's office on a rising tide of Democratic popularity which also gave the state's electoral votes to Franklin Roosevelt (see Fig. 1).

In spite of Democratic victories in statewide elections during the 1920s and 1930s, Republicans dominated most of New York except for its largest city.[85] Since at least the turn of the century, the Empire State had divided politically between New York City and "upstate," a term used to describe everything lying outside the metropolis including suburban counties to the east on Long Island. According to a political axiom, New York City went Democratic, but the upstate region provided Republican majorities, with elections decided by the size of the turnout in each area. Although an oversimplification, this represented a fact of political life. Since 1900, Democratic candidates for governor had taken New York City while their opponents had carried the rest of the state except when Republicans split over Progressivism in 1912 and Prohibition in 1930 (see Fig. 2).[86]

Republican domination of upstate New York enabled their party to control the legislature. Recognizing the growing political split in the state, the G.O.P. pushed through a constitutional amendment in 1894 which stipulated that every county, except for two in the far north which were combined for this purpose, should have at least one representative in the Assembly, the lower house of the legislature. The state simultaneously fixed the number of assemblymen at 150. As a result of these provisions, Democrats won a majority of seats in both houses only once between 1918 and 1942, in spite of large pluralities in gubernatorial races.[87]

The upstate/New York City dichotomy both reflected and defied national political trends. After World War I, Democrats and Republicans outside the Solid South increasingly divided along urban/rural lines. While industrial workers and recent immigrants flocked to the party of Al Smith and Franklin Roosevelt, farmers and middle-class descendants of native-born Americans cast largely G.O.P. ballots.[88] Thus New York City, which pointed the way, had developed into a Democratic stronghold in the 1920s, and Republicans continually tightened their grasp on suburban and rural counties throughout the rest of the state.[89] However, contrary to their experience

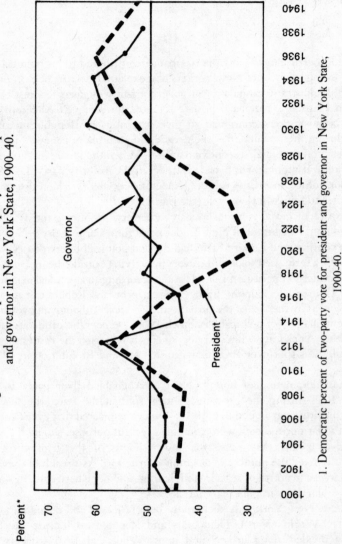

Fig. 1. Democratic percent of two-party vote for president and governor in New York State, 1900–40.

1. Democratic percent of two-party vote for president and governor in New York State, 1900-40.

* Includes minor party totals where candidates are the same as in the major parties.
Source: Percentages computed from vote totals reported in *New York Red Book* (Albany, 1900-1940).

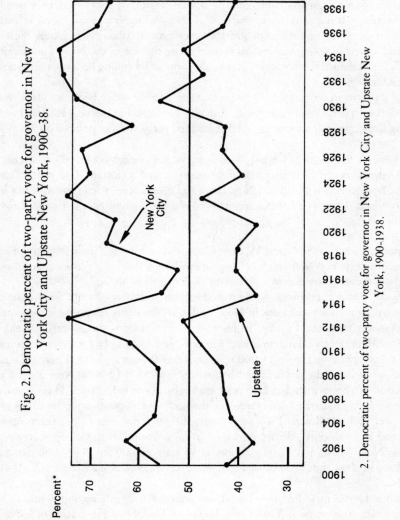

Fig. 2. Democratic percent of two-party vote for governor in New York City and Upstate New York, 1900–38.

2. Democratic percent of two-party vote for governor in New York City and Upstate New York, 1900-1938.

* Includes minor party totals where candidates are the same as in the major parties.
Source: Percentages computed from vote totals reported in *New York Red Book* (Albany, 1900-1940).

elsewhere, Democrats failed to capture control of the largest upstate cities, except for Utica and Albany which became Democratic bastions after World War I. Farther west, Syracuse, Rochester, and Buffalo remained in Republican hands. During the early 1930s, Democrats briefly held a majority of the local offices in Rochester and Buffalo, but weakened by factionalism and confronted by a well-organized opposition, they quickly reverted to their status as a minority party.[90] Although Democrats could not count on winning *local* elections in any major upstate cities except Albany and Utica, they did amass a sizable bloc of votes in industrial centers along the line of the New York Central Railroad, which enabled them to carry statewide contests by rolling up large pluralities in New York City.[91]

Political patterns in the Empire State proved remarkably stable because voters rarely questioned their party loyalty. Even during the Depression, Democrats had trouble converting Republican upstaters, as one discouraged party worker pointed out in 1936.

If everyone in this county [Lewis] votes as his or her pocket-book and conscience dictates, there should be a majority for Roosevelt and Lehman. The bitter fact remains, however, that Northern New York has been a Republican stronghold for so many years that it is a hard proposition to change enough people to make any impression.[92]

The Democratic chairman of rural Warren County stressed that "the voters are of such a character that it is very difficult to change them, and something extraordinary has to happen to get them to vote for any person other than a Republican." [93]

Traditional party allegiances worked in Herbert Lehman's favor. Swamping his opponents by as much as two to one in New York City, he easily overcame losses outside the metropolitan area (see Fig. 2). In his first two campaigns for governor, Lehman outpolled the Republican candidate in every one of New York City's sixty-two assembly districts (a unit containing from 15,000 to over 100,000 voters). Even Thomas Dewey could take only four of the city's assembly districts in 1938.[94] Outside New York City, Lehman often ran better than local Democrats, but he nevertheless trailed his opponents in most areas. Lehman carried only twelve of the fifty-seven upstate counties in his 1934 landslide over Robert Moses. Two years later, the governor lost all but three upstate counties, and in 1938 only Albany remained in his column. Of the state's thirty cities (excluding New York) with a population of at least 20,000 in 1930, Lehman took twenty-three in 1934, but his total dropped to eleven in 1936 and a mere five in his last race.[95]

Like other Democrats, Lehman found his political strength among workers and immigrants, especially in New York City. The New York State Federation of Labor, as well as politically active industrial unions, consistently endorsed Lehman in glowing terms.[96] The president of the International Longshoremen's Association declared in 1938: "Governor Lehman is the most sympathetic and understanding friend of organized labor that ever graced the Governor's chair in Albany or anywhere else." [97] Reflecting this opinion, first- and second-generation Americans who inhabited

Table 1
Lehman's Percentage of Total Vote in Predominantly
Jewish Assembly Districts, 1932–38

Assembly District	1932	1934	1936	1938
Manhattan's 4th (Lower East Side)	88	78	87	90
Manhattan's 9th (Central Park West)	71	71	67	73
Bronx's 2nd (Grand Concourse)	75	71	74	78
Brooklyn's 16th (Bensonhurst)	77	70	82	77

working-class assembly districts in Manhattan and Brooklyn regularly awarded Lehman from 60 to over 80 percent of their total vote.[98] Conversely, the governor ran poorest in his own home district, the "silk stocking" area east of Fifth Avenue, dominated by the city's wealthiest Protestants.[99]

Lehman received his greatest support from Jews who constituted 27 percent of New York City's population.[100] He rolled up his biggest pluralities in the Jewish slums of the Lower East Side where he consistently took almost 90 percent of all the ballots cast in the Fourth Assembly District. With his appeal to coreligionists cutting across class lines, Lehman ran almost as well in middle-class Jewish sections on the Upper West Side, along the Grand Concourse in the Bronx, and in Brooklyn's Bensonhurst (see Table 1). As the first Jew elected governor of the country's most populous state, Lehman brought prestige to this troubled minority during the period when anti-Semitism reached unheard-of heights.[101] In 1938, several Jewish leaders urging Lehman to remain in politics echoed the sentiment of many coreligionists: "Racially we feel that it would be important that you run at a time when so many people are engaged in creating race hatreds and in deprecating the contribution of the Jews to the welfare of this country." [102] During his four campaigns for governor, Lehman was openly attacked only once because of his religion. In the contest with Dewey, Lehman faced the first Protestant nominated for governor in almost a decade, and some upstate Republicans showed their enthusiasm by circulating anti-Semitic propaganda.[103]

Herbert Lehman's Wall Street background paid dividends throughout his public career. On the basis of his success as a banker, he entered government service near the top. Brought to Albany by Al Smith and FDR, Lehman owed no debts to local politicos. During his years in Albany, he frequently stressed the importance of applying business methods to state affairs.[104] Even after Lehman began giving New Yorkers a Little New Deal, many conservative voters trusted him, in part because of his reputation as a careful businessman. In 1934, Maurice C. Burritt, a Republican from a small upstate town who was a state public service commissioner, recorded his thoughts upon casting his ballot.

Stay home to vote today. Vote Republican ticket generally, to hold "new deal" in check and to prevent Tammany control in State but make exception to vote for Governor Lehman because of his honesty, sincerity [and] business [administration].[105]

While preserving the image of a cautious banker, Lehman helped push through the most comprehensive set of reforms ever enacted in New York.

NOTES

1. Ernest K. Lindley, *Frankin D. Roosevelt: A Career in Progressive Democracy* (Indianapolis, 1931), pp. 11-21; Elliott Roosevelt, ed., *F.D.R.: His Personal Letters, 1905-1938* (New York, 1948), pp. 644-46; James A. Farley, *Jim Farley's Story: The Roosevelt Years* (New York, 1948), pp. 59-60; Eleanor Roosevelt, *This I Remember* (New York, 1949), pp. 44-47, Herbert H. Lehman Memoir, Columbia Oral History Collection, pp. 244-47. (Hereinafter referred to as COHC.)
2. HHL Memoir, pp. 242-43, 247.
3. Ibid., p. 248. See also Edward J. Flynn Memoir, COHC, p. 16.
4. Roosevelt to HHL, October 2, 1928, Special File, Herbert H. Lehman Papers, Columbia University. (Hereinafter referred to as HHLP.)
5. Hickman Powell, "Profile: The Governor—I," *The New Yorker,* May 2, 1936, p. 21; Interview of Edward Weinfeld by Allan Nevins, Decmeber 9, 1961, Interview of Henry Epstein by Nevins, December 10, 1961, Nevins Research File, HHLP; Warren Moscow, *Politics in the Empire State* (New York, 1948), pp. 21-23.
6. *A Centennial: Lehman Brothers, 1850-1950* (New York, 1950), pp. 1-25; HHL to James L. Loeb, April 15, 1947, "HHL—Biographical Data," Special File, HHLP.
7. The best single source of information about Herbert Lehman's early life is Allan Nevins, *Herbert Lehman and His Era* (New York, 1963). Irving Lehman won election to the Court of Appeals as an Associate Judge in 1924, and he became its Chief Judge in 1940. Bernard L. Shientag, "Chief Judge Irving Lehman, Citizen and Jurist: An Appreciation," *The Menorah Journal,* XXXV (Spring 1947): 155-75; William M. Wiecek, "The Place of Chief Judge Irving Lehman in American Constitutional Development," *American Jewish Historical Quarterly,* LX (March 1971): 280-303.
8. HHL to Clifford W. Hall, August 7, 1947, "HHL—Biographical Data," Special File, HHLP; HHL Memoir, pp. 38-45.
9. HHL to Allan Nevins, March 16, 1961, Special File, HHLP.
10. Williams College Scrapbook, HHLP; HHL Memoir, pp. 46-50.
11. Upon his death in 1897, Mayer Lehman left an estate of over $5 million, of which Herbert's share was $400,000. Nevins, *Lehman,* p. 422. n. 5. For a discussion of the difficulty of estimating the Lehman family wealth from public records, see Phillip Lappin, "Herbert H. Lehman: His Background and Public Career" (unpublished M.A. essay, Columbia University, 1958), pp. 50-51.
12. HHL to Carolin Flexner, January 27, 1949, "HHL—Biographical Data," Special File, HHLP; HHL Memoir, pp. 56-66; *A Centennial,* pp. 16, 26-38.

13. *New York World-Telegram*, November 1, 1934; S. J. Woolf, " 'Ten Commandments' of Democracy," *New York Times Magazine*, November 5, 1939. Both articles in "Lehman, Edith A.," Special File, HHLP. See also Jared Van Wagenen, Jr., *Days of My Years: The Autobiography of a York State Farmer* (Cooperstown, N.Y., 1962), p. 197; Charles Poletti Memoir, COHC, p. 8.

14. HHL to David Dubinsky, March 12, 1958, Special File, HHLP.

15. Lillian Wald to HHL, December 20, 26, 1916, HHL to Wald, December 23, 1916, January 11, 1917, Special File, HHLP; Wald to HHL, May 13, 1935; January 15, 1936, Lillian Wald Papers, New York Public Library; HHL Memoir, pp. 34, 148-50, 187-90; William B. Liebmann, "A Friendship: Pro Bono Publico," *Columbia Library Columns,* XVIII (November 1968): 10-15.

16. HHL to Katherine Faville, March 18, 1940, "Henry Street Visiting Nurse Service," General Correspondence, 1933-40, HHLP. (Hereinafter referred to as Gen. Corr.)

17. Zosa Szajkowski, "Disunity in the Distribution of American Jewish Overseas Relief, 1919-1939," *American Jewish Historical Quarterly,* LVIII (March 1969): 376-407; idem, "Budgeting American Jewish Overseas Relief, 1919-1939," ibid., LIX (September 1969): 83-113; idem, " 'Reconstruction' vs. 'Palliative Relief' in American Jewish Overseas Work, 1919-1939," *Jewish Social Studies,* XXXII (January 1970): 14-42; Nevins, *Lehman,* pp. 68-76.

18. *New York Times,* December 10, 1928.

19. Marc Tanenbaum Memoir, COHC, pp. 5-6, 32-36; HHL Memoir, pp. 10, 153.

20. HHL to Allan Nevins, March 16, 1961, Special File, HHLP.

21. "List of Organizations to which HHL Contributes," October 30, 1945, "HHL—Biographical Data," Special File; Carolin Flexner to Basil O'Connor, January 20, 1956, Special File; [Proposed] "Appendix III: Resources and Philanthropies," enclosed in Allan Nevins to HHL, December 13, 1962, Special File, HHLP; Carolin Flexner Memoir, COHC, passim.

22. World War I Scrapbook, HHLP; HHL Memoir, pp. 99-115; Nevins, *Lehman,* pp. 55-62.

23. HHL to Benedict Crowell, January 19, 1920, "War Department," Gen. Corr., 1913-26, HHLP.

24. Flexner Memoir, p. 12; Nevins, *Lehman,* pp. 66-67.

25. HHL Memoir, pp. 13-14, 55-56, 95-96; Henry Morgenthau, Sr., to HHL, June 23, 1913, Special File, HHLP.

26. Related by Henry Epstein in interview by Nevins.

27. HHL Memoir, pp. 145-46.

28. HHL to George Gordon Battle, December 29, 1925, Morris Hillquit to HHL, June 10, 1926, Special File, HHLP; HHL Memoir, pp. 193-98; Dwight Edwards Robinson, *Collective Bargaining and Market Control in the New York Coat and Suit Industry* (New York, 1949), pp. 43-57; Jesse Thomas Carpenter, *Competition and Collective Bargaining in the Needle Trades* (Ithaca, N.Y., 1972), pp. 131-38, 444-47, 582-84 et passim.

29. *New York Times,* October 1, December 24, 1926, March 19, 24, 1927, July 12, 1928; HHL Memoir, pp. 210-19, 227-41; Nevins, [Proposed] "Appendix III."

30. HHL to Mary W. Dewson, June 21, 1954, Special File, HHLP. After his 1928 election victory, Lehman relinquished his position as a full partner in Lehman Brothers. Although he held the title of "special partner" while lieutenant governor, he paid little attention to business affairs. Once elected governor in 1932, Lehman severed all ties with Lehman Brothers as well as with other firms. He retained his considerable stock holdings, but he

disposed of all stock in companies that had any dealings with the state. Lehman's foresight prevented opponents from making any political capital out of his former Wall Street connections. HHL to Harold M. Lehman, December 6, 1932, "Lehman Brothers," Special File, HHLP; HHL to John E. Mack, April 15, 1935, "JOHNST," Gen. Corr., 1933-40, HHLP; HHL to Carolin Flexner, September 25, 1936, "Flexner, C.A.," ibid.; Norman Thomas to HHL, October 30, 1940, Special File, HHLP.

31. Henry D. Williams to HHL, April 1, 1929, Partial Personal Correspondence, 1929-31, HHLP.

32. FDR to HHL, November 17, 1930, Special File, HHLP; Albany *Knickerbocker Press,* January 21, 1936; Henry Morgenthau, Jr., Memoir, COHC, pp. 6-7; Samuel I. Rosenman Memoir, COHC, p. 1; Samuel I. Rosenman, *Working with Roosevelt* (New York, 1952), pp. 53-54. Frances Perkins, who then headed New York's Department of Labor, later recalled that Lehman provided "an enormous load of detailed assistance to Franklin Roosevelt when he was Governor." Perkins to HHL, October 5, 1949, Special File, HHLP.

33. HHL Memorandum Regarding Auburn Riot, n.d., "Prisons" folder, Campaign File # 1, HHLP; HHL Address, November 3, 1932, Speech File, 1928-32, p. 1007, HHLP; HHL Memoir, pp. 372-78; Bernard Bellush, *Franklin D. Roosevelt as Governor of New York* (New York, 1955), pp. 58-68, 103-17; Frank Freidel, *Franklin D. Roosevelt: The Triumph* (Boston, 1956), pp. 68-69, 124-25, 187-89; Jewel Bellush, "Roosevelt's Good Right Arm: Lieutenant Governor Herbert H. Lehman," *New York History,* XLI (October 1960): 423-43.

34. HHL Memoir, pp. 265-66. According to James Farley, Roosevelt decided in 1930 that Lehman should replace him two years later. Farley, *Jim Farley's Story,* pp. 135-36.

35. James A. Farley, *Behind the Ballots* (New York, 1938), pp. 172-77; James A. Farley Memoir, COHC, p. 8; Edward J. Flynn, *You're the Boss: The Practice of American Politics* (New York, 1947), pp. 105-10; J. Joseph Huthmacher, *Senator Robert F. Wagner and the Rise of Urban Liberalism* (New York, 1968), pp. 102-4.

36. HHL Memoir, pp. 299-303.

37. Flynn, *You're the Boss,* pp. 7-11, 46-63; Charles Garrett, *The La Guardia Years, Machine and Reform Politics in New York City* (New Brunswick, N.J., 1961), pp. 3-113; Nancy J. Weiss, *Charles Francis Murphy, 1858-1924: Respectability and Responsibility in Tammany Politics* (Northampton, Mass., 1968), pp. 92-96 et passim; Alfred Connable and Edward Silberfarb, *Tigers of Tammany: Nine Men Who Ran New York* (New York, 1967), pp. 269-90; Warren Moscow, *The Last of the Big-Time Bosses: The Life and Times of Carmine De Sapio and the Rise and Fall of Tammany Hall* (New York, 1971), pp. 23-30; Eugene J. Keogh Memoir, COHC, pp. 15-16.

38. HHL Memoir, pp. 221, 225-27, 272-73, 306-7; Flynn Memoir, pp. 9-10.

39. Rosenman Memoir, p. 3. Lehman's cool relationship with party leaders included James Farley who officially headed both the New York State Democratic party and the National Democratic Committee during this period. Farley devoted little attention to New York affairs except at election time, in part because he and Lehman never got along particularly well despite mutual respect for each other's obvious abilities. Farley to HHL, December 9, 1942, HHL to Frank Altschul, August 27, 1960, Special File, HHLP; HHL Memoir, pp. 262-63; Farley Memoir, pp. 5-7.

40. HHL Memoir, pp. 365-66, 603-4, 613-14; HHL to Allan Nevins, January 4, 1962, Special File, HHLP. More independent liberals roundly condemned Lehman for backing regular

Democrats against La Guardia. A. A. Berle, Jr., to FDR, October 25, 1934, PPF 1306, Franklin D. Roosevelt Library. (Hereinafter referred to as FDRL.) See also Kate M. Weinberger, "The Life and Political Philosophy of Herbert H. Lehman," (unpublished M.A. essay, Columbia University, 1940), pp. 104-6.

41. HHL Memoir, pp. 332-33.

42. Frankfurter to HHL, December 7, 1932, Charles Poletti Papers, in HHLP, Columbia University. See also HHL to Frankfurter, December 5, 1932, Frankfurter to Poletti, January 4, 1933, ibid.; *Current Biography, 1943,* pp. 599-602.

43. HHL to Frankfurter, April 3, 1933, Special File, HHLP; Charles Poletti Memoir, COHC, passim.

44. James Farley to Poletti, October 3, 1938, Poletti Papers. Lehman did not get along very well with William Bray, his lieutenant governor for the first three terms. As the Democratic boss of Utica and an Irish Catholic with ties to Tammany leaders, Bray was nominated in 1932 to balance the ticket. Lehman went along with this, but he never relied on the lethargic lieutenant governor, who preferred to tend to his law practice in Utica and spend as little time as possible in Albany. HHL Memoir, pp. 265-68; Farley Memoir, pp. 24-25; Flexner Memoir, p. 57; Poletti Memoir, pp. 12-22.

45. HHL to FDR, May 12, 1934, Special File, HHLP.

46. HHL to FDR, August 7, 1934, FDR to HHL, August 8, 1934, ibid.

47. HHL to FDR, March 17, May 20, 1936, HHL to Eleanor Roosevelt, May 27, 1936, ibid.; FDR to Henry Morgenthau, Jr., March 19, 1936, Elliott Roosevelt, ed., *F.D.R.: His Personal Letters, 1928-1945* (New York, 1950), I: 572; *New York Times,* August 9, 1936; HHL Memoir, pp. 592-97; Farley Memoir, p. 14; Keogh Memoir, p. 19; Poletti Memoir, pp. 10-11.

48. HHL to Arthur L. Goodhart, July 22, 1936, Special File, HHLP. See also FDR to HHL, June 29, 1936, ibid.; James Farley to HHL, June 30, 1936, Clipping Books, vol. 43, HHLP (hereinafter referred to as CB); Charles Poletti to Robert F. Wagner, June 30, 1936, "Politics, 1933-40," Robert F. Wagner Papers, Georgetown University.

49. HHL to Edgar Stern, January 22, 1937, HHL to Felix Rose, December 10, 1937, HHL to Hilda Jane Lehman, January 11, 1938, Gen. Corr., 1933-40, HHLP.

50. HHL to Mr. and Mrs. Peter G. Lehman, July 1, 1938, Special File, HHLP.

51. Vincent Dailey to Edith A. Lehman, November 23, 1938, ibid.; Stephen Early to Raymond Clapper, October 1, 1938, PPF 93, FDRL; Henry Morgenthau, Jr., Diaries, Book 144, pp. 18-23, FDRL; Farley, *Jim Farley's Story,* p. 147; HHL Memoir, pp. 651-54, 670-73; David Dressler Memoir, COHC, pp. 83-84.

52. HHL to Arthur Corscadden, June 30, 1947, "Farley, James A.," Special File, HHLP.

53. HHL to William Clark, November 7, 1932, Gen. Corr., 1932, HHLP; HHL Memoir, pp. 310-12; Corey Ford, *Donovan of OSS* (Boston, 1970), pp. 11-76.

54. *New York Times,* October 24, 1934; Cleveland Rodgers, *Robert Moses, Builder for Democracy* (New York, 1952), pp. 220-25 et passim. After the election, Moses apologized for his invective. Refusing to engage in any vendetta, the governor soon thereafter reappointed Moses to another term as chairman of the State Council of Parks, and the two men retained a mutual respect for each other. HHL Memoir, pp. 564-67; Robert Moses, *Public Works: A Dangerous Trade* (New York, 1970), pp. 878, 883.

55. Powell, "Profile," p. 21.

56. *New York Times,* September 30, 1936; S. J. Woolf, "Lehman or Bleakley?" *New York Times Magazine,* October 11, 1936; HHL Memoir, p. 598.

57. Rupert Hughes, *Attorney for the People: The Story of Thomas E. Dewey* (Boston, 1940), passim; Stanley Walker, *Dewey: An American of this Century* (New York, 1944), pp. 1-106.

58. The Republicans asked to serve were Charles Evans Hughes, Jr., George Z. Medalie, Thomas D. Thacher, and Charles H. Tuttle.

59. HHL Memoir, p. 640. See also Poletti Memoir, pp. 15-17.

60. George H. Mayer, *The Republican Party, 1854-1966* (New York, 1967), pp. 453-54.

61. HHL Address, September 30, 1938, *Public Papers of Herbert H. Lehman, Forty-ninth Governor of the State of New York* (10 vols.; Albany, 1934-47), *1938,* p. 555 (hereinafter referred to as *Public Papers); HHL Memoir, pp. 650-54; Warren Moscow Memoir, COHC, pp. 18-19. Dewey actually outpolled Lehman's Democratic vote, and the governor received his margin of victory from 420,000 votes cast for him on the line of the American Labor Party. New York's ALP had been organized in 1936 at the instigation of FDR to give him an extra line on the ballot to attract the support of pro-New Deal and anti-Tammany voters of the political left. Robert F. Carter, "Pressure from the Left: The American Labor Party, 1936-1954" (unpublished Ph.D. dissertation, Syracuse University, 1965), pp. 2-25.

62. Van Wagenen, *Days of My Years,* pp. 196-97.

63. Mary Yorke Allen to HHL, January 7, 1933, Arthur Corscadden to HHL, March 27, 1938, Special File, HHLP; *Brooklyn Daily Eagle,* November 4, 1934, clipping, Box A-56, Citizens Union Papers, Columbia University; Rosenman Memoir, pp. 1-2; Tanenbaum Memoir, p. 22.

64. Troy *Times-Record,* January 2, 1937, CB, 46, 848.

65. Poletti Memoir, p. 7.

66. Farley Memoir, p. 26; Rosenman Memoir, p. 3; Anna Rosenberg Memoir, COHC, p. 5.

67. *Utica Press,* February 3, 1937, CB, 46: 875.

68. Flo Garon to HHL, June 4, 1936, CB, 41. See also Lee T. Smith to HHL, May 25, 1936, CB, 40; William D. Bosler to HHL, June 25, 1936; David M. Ellis et al., *A History of New York State* (Ithaca, N.Y., 1967), pp. 421-22.

69. Russell Owen, "The Man Behind the 'Little New Deal,' " *New York Times Magazine,* March 15, 1936; S. J. Woolf, "Lehman Outlines His Social Philosophy," ibid., August 9, 1936; George S. Van Schaick Memoir, COHC, pp. 42-54, 92.

70. Powell to HHL, June 3, 1936, "HER," Gen. Corr., 1933-40, HHLP.

71. Thomas V. Brunkard to Carolin Flexner, September 8, 1937, Gen. Corr., 1933-40, HHLP; HHL to Peter G. Lehman, May 8, 1938, Special File, HHLP.

72. HHL to Frank Altschul, November 12, 1935, Special File, HHLP.

73. Farley, *Behind the Ballots,* p. 175.

74. Julius C. C., Edelstein Memoir, COHC, p. 27; Rosenman Memoir, pp. 4-5.

75. Eleanor Roosevelt Memoir, COHC, p. 5.

76. *Time,* December 31, 1934, p. 9.

77. HHL Memoir, pp. 546-47; Eleanor Roosevelt Memoir, p. 10. See also the HHL- FDR correspondence, Special File, HHLP.

78. HHL to FDR, February 26, 1937, Special File, HHLP. See also Edith A. Lehman to Robert F. Wagner, February 25, 1937, ibid.

79. HHL to Robert F. Wagner, July 19, 1937, Irving Lehman to HHL, July 24, 1937, ibid.; Interview of Weinfeld by Nevins; Joseph Alsop and Turner Catledge, *The 168 Days* (Garden City, N.Y., 1938), pp. 219-94; William E. Leuchtenburg, "Franklin D.

Roosevelt's Supreme Court 'Packing' Plan," in *Essays on the New Deal,* ed. by Harold M. Hollingsworth and William F. Holmes (Austin, Texas, 1969), pp. 100-7.

80. Farley Memoir, p. 1.

81. FDR to Felix Frankfurter, July 22, 1937, Max Freedman, ed., *Roosevelt and Frankfurter: Their Correspondence, 1928-1945* (Boston, 1967), pp. 403-4.

82. Poletti Memoir, p. 12.

83. HHL to FDR, August 30, September 9, 1938, FDR to HHL, September 7, 1938, Special File, HHLP; FDR to HHL, October 10, 1938, Elliott Roosevelt, *F.D.R.: His Personal Letters,* IV: 815; New York *Herald Tribune,* January 6, 1939, CB, 75: 6868; HHL Memoir, pp. 606-7, 687-89; Eleanor Roosevelt Memoir, pp. 7-8; Rosenman Memoir, pp. 9-10.

84. For explanations of voting behavior and the long-term impact of party identification, see: Angus Campbell et al., *The American Voter: An Abridgement* (New York, 1964); Lawrence H. Fuchs, ed., *American Ethnic Politics* (New York, 1968); William H. Flanigan, *Political Behavior of the American Electorate* (Boston, 1968); Walter Dean Burnham, *Critical Elections and the Mainsprings of American Politics* (New York, 1970).

85. As a result of their prowess in state contests, Democrats held both of New York's U.S. Senate seats from 1926 to 1946.

86. Flynn, *You're the Boss,* pp. 78-82; Moscow, *Politics in the Empire State,* pp. 36-53, 70-101, 125-47; Frank J. Munger and Ralph A. Straetz, *New York Politics* (New York, 1960), pp. 39, 52-53; Lorraine Colville, "A Comparison and Evaluation of the Organization and Techniques of the Major Political Parties in New York City and the Reaction of the Electorate to the Organizations, 1929-1949" (unpublished Ph.D. dissertation, New York University, 1954), passim; Marvin G. Weinbaum, "New York County Republican Politics, 1897-1922: The Quarter Century after Municipal Consolidation," *The New-York Historical Quarterly,* L (January 1966): 63-94.

87. N. Y. Const., art. Ill, secs. 2,5; Lynton K. Caldwell, *The Government and Administration of New York* (New York, 1954), pp. 60-63.

88. Samuel Lubell, *The Future of American Politics* (3rd ed., rev.; New York, 1965), passim; David Burner, *The Politics of Provincialism: The Democratic Party in Transition, 1918-1932* (New York, 1968), passim.

89. For a graphic depiction of the Democrats' decline upstate from 1860 to 1954, see the color-coded maps in *Richards Atlas of New York State,* ed. by Robert J. Rayback (rev. ed.; New York, 1965), pp. 37-44.

90. *Buffalo Evening News, Rochester Times-Union,* November 8, 1933; Robert H. Jackson to James A. Farley, September 14, 1936, Charles Stanton to Farley, October 15, 1936, Box 83, OF 300, FDRL; Blake McKelvey, "Rochester's Political Trends: An Historical Review," *Rochester History,* XIV (April 1952): 1-24; idem, *Rochester: An Emerging Metropolis, 1925-1961* (Rochester, 1961), pp. 21-32, 63-67, 75-93; John T. Horton, Edward T. Williams, and Harry S. Douglass, *History of Northwestern New York: Erie, Niagara, Wyoming, Genesee and Orleans Counties* (3 vols: New York, 1947), I: 232-35, 311, 389, 428; Munger and Straetz, *New York Politics,* pp. 40-57.

91. Moscow, *Politics in the Empire State,* pp. 41-42. In 1938 the proportion of the total vote for governor cast by each part of the state divided as follows: New York City (47.9 percent); New York City suburbs (10.1 percent); upstate urban (28.3 percent); upstate rural (13.7 percent). Munger and Straetz, *New York Politics,* P. 65.

92. Bill Easton to James Farley, September 9, 1936, Box 83, OF 300, FDRL.

93. J. Edward Collings to James Farley, October 25, 1938, Box 91, ibid.

94. In 1936, Lehman lost Manhattan's "silk stocking" area, the 15th AD, and two suburban ADs in Queens (nos. 4 and 6). Two years later, Dewey picked up these three ADs plus a similar one, the 20th, in Brooklyn. Vote totals can be found in *Manual for the Use of the Legislature of the State of New York,* published annually.

95. Lehman's vote in all counties, as well as in many cities, is conveniently summarized in *Record of Vote Cast for Herbert H. Lehman, 1928-1938* (n.p., n.d.), in HHLP.

96. Luigi Antonini and Alex Rose to HHL, August 27, 1936, "ALP," Gen. Corr., 1933-40, HHLP; John M. O'Hanlon to HHL, August 31, 1936, "New York State Federation of Labor," ibid.; Sidney Hillman to HHL, November 3, 1936, Sidney Hillman Papers, Amalgamated Clothing Workers of America Library; *New York State Federation of Labor Bulletin,* October 15, 1932, October 10, 1934, October 5, 1936, October 14, 1938.

97. New York *Herald Tribune,* July 7, 1938, CB, 69: 6468.

98. The best discussion of voting behavior in New York City in this period can be found in Arthur Mann, *La Guardia Comes to Power, 1933* (Chicago, 1965), pp. 125-52. In addition to socioeconomic data on the city's population, the book includes an appendix with maps showing the location of Assembly Districts. See also Burner, *Politics of Provincialism,* which contains an analysis of the city's presidential vote from 1916 to 1932. Of limited use for the 1930s are two works which cover local elections in the forties: John Albert Morsell, "The Political Behavior of Negroes in New York City" (unpublished Ph.D. dissertation, Columbia University, 1950); William Spinrad, "New Yorkers Cast Their Ballots" (unpublished Ph.D. dissertation, Columbia University, 1955).

99. Lehman's proportion of the total vote cast in Manhattan's 15th AD ranged from a high of 52 percent in 1934 to a low of 41 percent in 1936. In the latter year that represented his worst showing in any New York City Assembly District.

100. Walter Laidlaw, ed., *Population of the City of New York, 1890-1930* (New York, 1932) p. 275.

101. Lehman was "perhaps the most prominent Jew ever elected to public office in the United States." Lawrence H. Fuchs, *The Political Behavior of American Jews* (Glencoe, Ill., 1956), p. 163. For evidence of Jewish voters' identification with him on a religious basis, see the letters in CB, 40, 41, 43.

102. Victor F. Ridder et al., to HHL, September 16, 1938, Special File, HHLP.

103. Matthew J. Murphy to James Farley, December 12, 1938, Jesse Jacobs to Farley, December 12, 1938, Arthur J. Leonard to Farley, December 29, 1938, Harry Nugent to Farley, October 26, 1938, Box 91, OF 300, FDRL; Moscow Memoir, p. 19; Moscow, *Politics in the Empire State,* p. 22.

104. See, for example, Herbert H. Lehman, "A Business Man Looks at Politics," *Atlantic Monthly,* CXLVIII (November 1931): 555-64.

105. Burritt Diary, November 6, 1934, Maurice C. Burritt Papers, Collection of Regional History, Cornell University.

II

EMERGENCY UNEMPLOYMENT RELIEF

Herbert H. Lehman took over as governor in the midst of the worst crisis that ever hit the Empire State. By January 1933, after three years of the Depression, more than 1,500,000 New Yorkers, one-quarter of the labor force, were unemployed, and 23 percent of the state's male wage earners worked only part-time. Over 250,000 families and single persons, almost 10 percent of the state's population, depended on public relief which often proved inadequate.[1]

Behind the mounting data indicating the severity of the Depression stood New Yorkers who suffered as they never had before. The report of one social worker described the typical case of an unemployed longshoreman living with two sons on Manhattan's Lower East Side.

> He was in a terrible financial position. With no one working, he had only 3¢ to his name. He was in fear of being dispossessed, and the gas bill was unpaid. . . . The only food in the house consisted of a few tomatoes.[2]

Forced to leave their homes when they fell too far behind in rent, many families throughout the state doubled up with friends or relatives, but they needed more than a roof over their heads during the particularly harsh winter of 1932-33.[3] "The cold felt on the streets," concluded an observer, "can scarcely be less than in homes heated by furnaces for which there is no coal and stoves for which there is no wood, lighted by candles and furnished with beds for which there are few if any blankets." [4] After months, even years, of idleness, the unemployed lost more than wages. In December 1932, many applicants for relief in New York City showed symptoms of nervous and emotional disorders due to the "lack of vacation with pay, need of new clothes, sleeplessness from worry, constant moving from one lodging to another, the pawning or selling of cherished possessions, as well as the complete loss of stability resulting from unemployment." [5]

In an era of unparalleled destitution, government gradually expanded public assistance for the needy. After the demand for aid had outrun municipal and county resources, New York State had broken with tradition by opening its coffers for local unemployment relief beginning in the fall of 1931. Under the supervision of the Temporary Emergency Relief Administration (TERA), the state paid 40 percent of community welfare bills by 1933, but even this proved insufficient. Appeals soon went out to Washington and, early in 1933, the federal government started supplementing state and local aid for the jobless. The unprecedented infusion of funds from Albany and Washington marked a turning point in the public welfare system, but New Yorkers initially considered this a temporary measure. As late as 1934, state officials generally believed that cities and counties would resume exclusive responsibility for unemployment relief once the crisis abated. During Lehman's first term as governor, Albany lawmakers annually prolonged the life of the TERA, but they continued to stress the emergency nature of state aid for the jobless.

1

At the time of Lehman's inauguration, New York's relief machinery faced an imminent financial breakdown. In New York City the head of the Emergency Work and Relief Administration had recently declared that this bureau had almost depleted existing funds.[6] At the other end of the state, the mayor of Buffalo warned that the "problem of caring for our citizens who are without means to procure the necessities of life is the most serious and at the same time the most complicated that has ever confronted the city." Although Buffalo had spent more for public assistance in the month of December 1932 than in the entire fiscal year of 1925, it could not help all those in need.[7] Relief recipients in the state's second largest city complained that their welfare allotments included dirty, used clothing which was beyond repair.[8] When Rochester launched a clothing drive for the unemployed late in 1932, it met with limited success, because, as some citizens pointed out, "if we had any old clothes we'd be wearing them." [9] With most communities suffering from a similar lack of funds, the State Conference of Mayors appealed to Lehman for increased assistance from the Temporary Emergency Relief Administration. However, Harry Hopkins, head of TERA, simultaneously reported that under existing policies the agency would exhaust by mid-1933 the $30 million designed originally to subsidize local relief for the entire year.[10]

Lehman looked to Washington for financial help to alleviate the distress caused by limited funds. In his inaugural address he declared: "We need as never before the wholehearted cooperation and the unselfish pooling of the resources of federal, state and municipal governments, and of private communal agencies." [11] Although New York could have borrowed federal funds from the Reconstruction Finance Corporation (RFC) since July 1932, Governor Roosevelt's administration had refused to take this step, because the RFC required a governor applying for aid to certify that local and state resources were inadequate. Since this amounted to a declaration of bankruptcy or "pauper's oath," both Roosevelt and Hopkins had opposed it. Upon assuming office, Lehman appealed for a modification, or at least a broader interpretation, of the federal Emergency Relief and Construction Act of 1932 to enable New York to receive its benefits.[12]

New Yorkers divided over the issue of federal assistance for unemployment relief. The Republican leader of the state Senate declared that New York should claim its fair share of U.S. funds; hard-pressed local officials and private welfare agencies overwhelmingly agreed.[13] "Those of us who know this situation best . . . rejoiced when we saw your statement indicating the need of getting money from the Reconstruction Finance Corporation," a director of the Association for Improving the Condition of the Poor wrote Lehman.[14] However, many newspaper editors spoke out against the principle of federal aid, which they labeled "regrettable" and "dangerous." [15] Decrying New York's appearance as "a mendicant at the door of the national Treasury," the *Herald Tribune* hoped the state could avoid "this fundamentally unsound procedure" which would set a bad precedent for poorer states.[16]

When RFC officials intimated that a loan to New York would raise no problems, Lehman decided to circumvent remaining obstacles. With the full backing of G.O.P. leaders, the legislature authorized the governor to apply for federal funds with the understanding that they would not represent a public loan prohibited by the state's constitution.[17] Meanwhile, Lehman filed for an immediate RFC allocation of $34,600,000 to supplement local and state relief for the following six months. With a verbal sleight of hand, he disposed of the "pauper's oath" by simply revising the usual declaration of necessity to make it more palatable.[18]

The directors of the RFC accepted New York's broad interpretation of the application procedure but rejected Lehman's attempt to introduce a degree of long-range planning into relief financing. Although the governor had sought assurances for the next six months, the RFC persisted in making decisions on a monthly basis. This hand-to-mouth arrangement ultimately brought New York $26,400,000 for the months of February through May and helped to carry the unemployed into the spring and a new era of federal aid.[19]

After moving into the White House in March, Franklin Roosevelt took immediate steps to aid the jobless. On May 12, the president signed the Federal Emergency Relief Act which authorized $500 million in outright grants to the states for unemployment relief. Enabling legislation divided the appropriation with one-half going to states on a matching basis and the other half forming a discretionary fund to be spent according to the relative needs of each state.[20] Congress created the Federal Emergency Relief Administration (FERA), modeled after New York's TERA, to oversee distribution of the federal grants-in-aid.[21]

The president chose Harry Hopkins to head the FERA. Although Lehman strongly protested the loss of his own relief coordinator, Hopkins' departure gave New York a friend in court who was personally acquainted with the state's welfare officials and their problems.[22] The same week Hopkins took up his duties in Washington, Lehman and

TERA leaders met with him to determine what the Empire State would receive from FERA. On the basis of past expenditures by the state and its communities, Hopkins promised to give New York about $25 million in grants over the next five months, by which time he expected to deplete the initial Congressional appropriation of $250 million in matching funds. As a result of this commitment, TERA hoped to disburse a total of $12 million per month throughout the state during this period with the federal government paying 42 percent, the state 13 percent, and local communities the remaining 45 percent. These proportions show the importance of the sudden influx of federal and state funds into cities which only two years before had paid the entire cost of unemployment relief.[23]

2

During the early years of the Depression, the Empire State relied largely on loans to finance its share of relief. This spared hard-pressed taxpayers from bearing immediately the full cost of public assistance, but constitutional restrictions made borrowing a lengthy and cumbersome process for raising money. First, lawmakers had to approve any bond issue, and then the state's voters had to add their consent at a general election. Since the legislature convened in January and a referendum went before the electorate in November, TERA needed to plan relief financing almost a year in advance.

In April 1933, TERA predicted that the state would require a bond issue of $60 million to cover its portion of relief expenses during the upcoming winter. Since this would amount to double the previous bond issue, TERA feared that the governor would not approve the full sum. Lehman, however, accepted the judgment of welfare experts, as did the vast majority of the state legislators who voted to place the question on the November ballot.[24] Although the state had earmarked money for the unemployed in the 1933 budget, Lehman chose to rely exclusively on loans for the next year in order to lighten the immediate burden on taxpayers.[25] During the summer of 1933, the governor took action to ensure passage of the bond issue by New York voters. Since TERA wanted to avoid becoming involved in politics, he accepted the offer of Homer Folks to arrange the necessary publicity. Lehman could not have found a better coordinator.[26]

Since 1893, the energetic Folks had served as head of the State Charities Aid Association and built the private agency into one of the most powerful pressure groups in New York. The gentle social worker inspired confidence, but he could fight doggedly for causes he considered just. During the first three decades of the twentieth century, he had spearheaded successful campaigns for improved public health and welfare services. Rising to the top of his profession, Folks was twice elected president of the National Conference of Social Work. By 1933, this "statesman of the public good" had already passed his sixty-fifth birthday, but with no thought of retirement Folks turned his attention to the new problems created by the Depression. He and Lehman had known each other for years, and the governor called on his friend for advice in fields such as relief, child welfare, and mental health.[27]

Having led the drive for the 1932 relief bond issue, Folks organized another low-key, bipartisan campaign in 1933. Through a citizens' committee and extensive publicity, he rallied support throughout the state. In order to keep the question free of party politics, Folks got endorsements from both Republican and Democrat state chairmen and from mayoral candidates in forty-two cities. Several days before the election, Mrs. Lehman delivered an unusual statewide radio appeal on behalf of her ailing husband, who had suffered complications from a recent appendectomy. The citizenry responded with an overwhelming five to one vote in favor of the bond issue.[28]

3

Within the Empire State, New York City had the most severe unemployment crisis. The metropolis contained about half the state's factory workers and, by 1933, two out of five had lost their jobs.[29] As they exhausted their personal resources and faced eviction and starvation, the unemployed sought help wherever they could find it. Traditionally, private charities had carried most of the local welfare burden, but after several years of heroic efforts, they depleted their funds.[30] Although the city increased its spending for public assistance, it could scarcely succor all those in need without state or federal help, since throughout this period New York City had more people on its welfare rolls than the rest of the state combined. As Lorena A. Hickok, FERA's chief investigator, graphically pointed out in 1933, New York City struggled "with the biggest community relief job on earth—the biggest job of its kind ever undertaken by any city since the world began."

Two years ago, in 1931, the entire load carried by official and semi-official agencies consisted of less than half a million persons, aided at a cost of a little more than $30,000,000. During the first six months of this year those agencies cared for—or attempted to care for—1,417,675 human beings, at a cost of $50,524,309. And the amount they spent was many millions of dollars below what it should have been!

The magnitude of the relief job in New York City and its complexities are breath-taking. One city block will contain almost 200 families on the relief rolls. Those 1,250,000 human beings represent a complete cross-section of the population, the best and the worst—the most intelligent, the most highly educated and the most helpless and most ignorant. Among them are represented more than 30 nationalities. Thousands of them cannot speak a word of English. And among them are business and professional men whose incomes five years ago ran into many thousands of dollars.

There they are, all thrown together into a vast pit of human misery, from which a city, dazed, still only half awake to the situation, is trying to extricate them.[31]

Initially, New York City financed unemployment relief by borrowing money. During 1932 and early 1933, municipal officials negotiated a series of short-term loans, but in the spring of 1933, local bankers refused to extend any more credit as the city's financial condition steadily deteriorated as a result of the Depression.[32] Since New York, like most cities, depended on real estate levies to support public services, its revenues dropped sharply as harried property owners withheld tax payments. At the depth of the economic crisis in 1932-33, the tax delinquency rate hit 26 percent. Moreover, the city suffered from the effects of an era of free spending and padded payrolls which helped drive the municipal budget to a record high in 1932, when the Staten Island borough president earned more than the state's lieutenant governor.[33] A popular verse accurately summarized Mayor Jimmy Walker's carefree attitude.

> "Mayor, may we economize?"
> "Boys, I won't begrudge it—
> Hit the depression between the eyes
> But don't go near the budget." [34]

When bankers declined to lend the city any more money, Tammany leaders expected the state to bail them out. In May 1933, they appealed to TERA for a cash advance of $5 million to pay the full cost of unemployment relief for the month of June.[35] At a conference with state welfare officials, Governor Lehman called for "a hard-boiled attitude," because he feared that otherwise local communities would shift the entire relief burden to the state and federal governments.

> If we go ahead and start to carry the load of New York City, we will never get out of it. The bankers will be pleased and the City will be pleased, but where will we be[?] If this thing will bring it to a head, let it be brought to a head. Public opinion I think will be in favor of continuing relief work by the City. I certainly won't take any other position.[36]

Agreeing with the governor, TERA turned down the city's request. Nevertheless, when New York City ultimately managed to raise but half its share of relief for June, TERA was forced to grant an extra $2 million to prevent the complete collapse of public assistance. The following month, state and federal authorities again balked at paying all the city's welfare expenses.[37]

Unable to win a complete state takeover of relief, Mayor John P. O'Brien's administration turned to Albany lawmakers. In July, municipal leaders called for a special session of the legislature to enact some new state tax to be handed over to localities for unemployment relief. Although the governor agreed to convene the legislature, he refused to sanction any additional state imposts. Instead, he recommended that the state empower New York City to levy specific emergency taxes, limited in duration and earmarked for home and work relief. This method, according to Lehman, would maintain a degree of local responsibility for public assistance and also encourage economies in other municipal expenditures. City officials briefly held to their demand for state funds, but they soon relented. With Lehman's approval, the legislature gave New York City blanket authority to impose taxes for unemployment relief during the next six months. The city used its emergency power to pass several business taxes, but the revenues failed to cover its share of relief costs.[38]

Stepping into the breach, Lehman facilitated the resumption of private loans. At the invitation of New York bankers in September 1933, the governor held a series of conferences in his apartment along Manhattan's Park Avenue.[39] Sitting in the Lehmans' magnificently wood-paneled living room decorated with Dutch old masters, municipal and banking officials drafted a four-year plan which rescued the city financially and assured adequate relief for the indigent. According to the so-called Bankers' Agreement, New York City pledged to segregate all tax payments for the next four years, budget specific sums to cover tax delinquencies, and limit imposts on real estate. In return for these guarantees, representatives of the city's leading banks promised to refinance short-term municipal loans, purchase bonds for relief, and create a revolving tax fund from which the city could borrow with future tax revenues as security.[40]

Bankers immediately fulfilled their part of the bargain. In November, they bought municipal bonds which furnished New York City with $31 million to pay its share of unemployment relief for the succeeding ten months. State and federal grants of $2.00 for every $1.00 put up locally guaranteed at least $9 million monthly for home and work relief in the metropolitan area. This sum approached the $10 million which the private Welfare Council considered the absolute minimum necessary for the care of the city's destitute.[41]

4

The winter of 1933-34 held the harsh prospect of intensified suffering for millions of people in the Empire State. Autumn welfare rolls were double those of the previous year because thousands of families had finally exhausted their personal resources and sought public assistance for the first time.[42] Other less fortunate New Yorkers braced for their third winter as public charges, and a community social worker described their steady deterioration.

> The first winter they were fairly well clothed, in pretty good physical condition, and hopeful. They felt themselves that they needed only temporary help—until they could get back to work.
>
> Last winter their clothes were patched, they were beginning to show signs of undernourishment, and they were worried.
>
> Now their clothing is in rags. They are sick, mentally and physically. They have given up even trying to look for work. The majority have become so apathetic that they accept without questioning us whatever we give them, no matter how pitifully inadequate it is or how badly administered. A few, whose spirit is not entirely broken, say to us bitterly: "What hope have you to offer?" [43]

To alleviate the worsening conditions, both Albany and Washington expanded their aid. Beginning in November 1933, TERA raised its rate of reimbursement for local home and work relief from 40 to 66⅔ percent. This meant that each level of government paid one-third of the total relief in every community, but state and federal authorities limited their commitment to three months owing to the usual shortage of money.[44]

During November, the president also announced the formation of the Civil Works Administration (CWA). Under this program the federal government temporarily suspended FERA grants and took direct responsibility for all work relief in the nation. Through an infusion of U.S. funds, Washington looked for a rapid expansion of local projects to give jobs to over four million Americans. Conceived as a means of "priming the pump" as well as assisting the needy, CWA promised work until mid-February for 396,000 unemployed New Yorkers regardless of whether or not they qualified for relief.[45] Since the Empire State already had a thriving system of work relief, it filled almost half its quota by merely transferring people on existing projects to CWA, which paid higher wages. The other half came from the lists of state and federal employment bureaus. However, when thousands of new applicants, many of whom had waited all night in the streets, swamped government employment offices, the demand for CWA jobs quickly threatened to outrun the state's allotment.[46]

Although at least two people applied for every position available during the first month, CWA never filled its original quota in New York State. Various delays occurred largely because of the magnitude of the program which had as its goal the employment of almost 400,000 New Yorkers, 10 percent of the national total. Simply devising projects for that many people consumed valuable time, and once communities found appropriate civil works, they deluged the state with applications which TERA had to process before actual labor could begin. Consequently, enrollment in CWA did not reach its peak in New York until February 1934, and by then Washington had started to dismantle the program.[47]

CWA tried to place the jobless according to their particular training. Since 75 percent of the New Yorkers put on civil works were unskilled, they spent most of their time repairing public facilities and shoveling snow. Yet some workers got the opportunity to do more satisfying labor. Sixty-five unemployed lawyers in Buffalo compiled, recodified, and indexed county and town statutes. In Rochester, a group of painters organized an art gallery, and over a hundred jobless musicians gave free concerts. Throughout the state, former teachers set up nursery schools which served as child-care centers for CWA employees.[48]

Lehman became an ardent supporter of CWA even though he had originally feared that the sudden federal takeover of all work relief would disrupt existing public assistance programs.[49] Once CWA showed its usefulness in supplying jobs, the governor fought to delay its scheduled termination. On January 17, 1934, he warned the president that the end of civil works would "bring grave economic and social consequences." Since the state could not afford to continue all the projects, reductions in U.S. expenditures would result in layoffs. Lehman feared that if CWA employees were "deprived of their jobs, unrest might . . . assume serious proportions." [50] The president responded that CWA was designed as a temporary aid for the winter and that other public projects and private employment would take up the slack caused by its demise.[51]

The predictions of the New York State Department of Labor were less sanguine. While CWA gave work to about 340,000 New Yorkers, 600,000 others had filed with employment services in hopes of getting on the government payroll. The Public Works

Administration (PWA), a federal program of aid for heavy construction, had furnished only 20,000 jobs in the state and held little promise of adding soon to that total.[52] Surveys indicated a mere 30,000 factory openings by the end of March, and even a doubling of this estimate to 60,000 left 90 percent of those registered for work with little chance of placement in private industry.[53] Reflecting the growing sense of desperation, one woman pleaded with a social worker in Manhattan:

> You've got to do something for me. There's four men sitting in my kitchen all day—my husband and the three boys. They go out early every day looking for jobs and then come home and just sit. I know its better than the corner but I think I'm going crazy if *one* of them doesn't [get] a job.[54]

For people like this, the termination of CWA would close off the only immediate avenue of escape from forced idleness.

Lehman's protests, along with thousands of others from across the country, finally brought a pledge of federal assistance to replace CWA in the spring of 1934. At a White House conference on March 16, FDR, Hopkins, Lehman, TERA officials, and Albany legislative leaders agreed on a plan to assure unemployment relief for the rest of 1934. The president promised over $100 million in FERA grants, which amounted to about 50 percent of New York's estimated relief bill. The state had enough from the 1933 bond issue to cover 25 percent of the expenses, and it would require each community to furnish the remaining 25 percent.[55]

5

Although Washington had eased the local burden by paying the cost of all work relief during the winter of 1933-34, New York City still had trouble raising money for home relief. As a result, Governor Lehman had again found himself deep in the morass of municipal finances early in 1934. When the newly elected mayor, Fiorello La Guardia, took office in January, he inherited a budget of $551 million that was unbalanced by about $30 million. Short of funds for unemployment relief and saddled with a low credit rating which barred the city from receiving additional federal aid from the PWA, La Guardia requested the governor's support for emergency legislation permitting the mayor to cut local expenses. The economy bill proposed by La Guardia sought a balanced budget through the reorganization or abolition of city agencies, the reduction of certain municipal and county salaries, and the imposition of one-month furloughs without pay for most city employees. The measure exempted teachers, firemen, and policemen from the wage provision, but the furloughs applied to all except court personnel. The suggested legislation placed all the powers enumerated in the hands of one man—the mayor of New York City—for a period of two years.[56]

Writing to La Guardia, Lehman expressed shock at the "essentially un-American" and "completely dictorial [sic] authority which you ask the Legislature to grant." He agreed with the urgent need for retrenchment in municipal expenses but argued that the city government already possessed sufficient power to achieve the goals desired by the mayor. Although Lehman opposed giving the mayor unilateral authority, he assured La Guardia of his willingness to cooperate "in any legitimate attempt by orderly processes to reduce the cost of government in the city." [57]

The state divided sharply on the economy bill, but most spokesmen echoed Lehman's reservations. Upstate newspapers used words like "radical" and "un-American" to describe the measure, and they generally concluded that the city could roll back expenditures without resorting to a one-man dictatorship.[58] Although New York City editors sympathized more with La Guardia's problems, about half the major dailies opposed his economy plan.[59] Others, including the *Times* and the *Herald Tribune,* rallied behind the Republican mayor.[60] Two influential groups, the Citizens Union and the Merchants' Association of New York, also endorsed the economy bill.[61]

La Guardia responded to the heavy criticism in a cool but conciliatory letter to Lehman which included "only two or three little drops of acid." [62] Obviously disturbed by accusations of dictatorship, the mayor insisted that he desired only sound city management but found himself hamstrung by Tammany Hall, which still controlled one branch of the municipal legislature. In short, political realities necessitated an extraordinary grant of additional authority. While repeating his opposition to one-man rule, the governor invited La Guardia to confer on possible alternatives.[63]

After their initial sparring, the two executives quickly settled on a compromise which vested emergency powers in the Board of Estimate until October 1, 1934. Enactment of any of the measures described in the original bill required at least ten of the board's sixteen votes, three of which the mayor himself cast, but the city legislature retained the authority to repeal or amend any such actions in accordance with its normal procedures. Lehman expressed satisfaction with these revisions, which preserved democratic processes but made possible the implementation of economies through the Board of Estimate which was controlled by La Guardia's Fusion party.[64] The compromise won the immediate and overwhelming approval of newspapers throughout the state.[65]

Democratic state legislators proved less receptive. Despite Tammany's defeat in the 1933 city election, Democrats still held most of the county offices, which faced cuts under the terms of the economy bill. This strong personal interest generated opposition not only from Tammany representatives but also from staunch allies of Lehman such as Secretary of State Edward J. Flynn who ran the Bronx's Democratic organization. Furthermore, groups of teachers and civil service employees from New York City flocked to Albany to fight the economy bill with its mandatory furloughs and prospective salary cuts for city personnel. Since the legislation constituted a home-rule measure that required a two-thirds majority in each house, Democratic votes would ultimately be crucial.[66]

Ignoring pressure from the governor and national party leaders, Democratic lawmakers blocked passage of the economy bill. When Lehman insisted on action at the end of January, all but four of the sixty-five Democratic assemblymen responded with a no vote. Since this left the proposal nineteen votes short of the necessary two-thirds, the governor then took the unusual step of meeting with all assemblymen from his party and personally asking them to approve the economy bill, but only seven Democrats heeded his advice on the next ballot in the lower house. Belated endorsements by James Farley and the president also failed to budge legislative chieftains and city Democrats, who defeated La Guardia's plan a total of four times in the Assembly.[67]

The recalcitrant Democrats finally forced the mayor to compromise again. Early in April, he agreed to a series of amendments which severely limited the impact of the economy bill. While the number of votes required in the Board of Estimate was increased from ten to twelve, other revisions prohibited the board from lowering the salary of any employee making less than $3000 annually and excluded county departments from any reorganization. Although the legislature quickly adopted this version of the economy bill, twenty-three of the fifty Democratic assemblymen from New York City held out against any retrenchment in the municipal budget.[68] Using its new powers to impose furloughs and reorganize departments, the Board of Estimate saved about $14 million, which eliminated half the estimated deficit in the 1934 budget. This step, combined with the Bankers' Agreement of the previous fall, helped revive investor confidence in New York City, which enabled the city to float additional loans for aid to the jobless.[69]

Despite recurrent crises, New York City gradually raised the quality of unemployment relief. While some improvement occurred in 1933, welfare remained inadequate because of the shortage of funds, which left little money to pay the rent and utilities of destitute New Yorkers. Moreover, when the city periodically ran out of funds at the end of a month, it often removed thousands of families from the relief rolls for a few days or even a week. In the interim, the stranded people observed what they called "foodless holidays." During 1934, welfare standards made significant advances as a result of changes in administrative and financial procedures. Within two months after La Guardia took office, for example, the average relief allotment for a family jumped from $36.00 to $43.00 a month.[70] In 1934, the La Guardia administration, with Lehman's support, also won a revision of state enabling legislation to permit relief in cash so that the poor could decide for themselves how to spend money received from the city.[71]

During Lehman's first term, the Empire State as a whole led the nation in the drive to relieve distress caused by the Depression. In September 1933, FERA's perceptive investigator, Lorena Hickok, reported that relief activities in upstate New York were two or three years in advance of the rest of the country. She wrote: "I found relief administration and adequacy so far ahead of what I had seen in other states that there just isn't any basis for comparison at all." [72]

Throughout this period, Lehman himself played an important role in rescuing victims of the Depression. Although his experience as a banker led him to see relief as essentially a problem of dollars and cents, the governor had a genuine interest in the plight of the unemployed. He usually accepted TERA estimates of the need for funds, and he fought for joint financial participation by local, state, and federal governments. Once a fund was established for a specific period, Lehman tried to make it last by allotting a limited percentage for each month. In the spring of 1934, TERA's executive director privately called the governor "cagey" and "pretty hardboiled" because of his unwillingness to spend relief monies at a faster rate, but this tightfistedness guaranteed that the state would not exhaust the funds before it arranged for additional appropriations.[73] Lehman also assured bipartisan support for public assistance by appointing many Republicans to TERA and consulting G.O.P. legislative leaders before embarking on any new relief policy.[74]

New Yorkers on relief fared better than other needy Americans primarily because of the infusion of both state and federal aid. The Empire State began supplementing local relief in 1931, but hard-pressed communities soon found they needed more than a 40 percent contribution from Albany. Thanks to the addition of federal funds in 1933, TERA managed to pay two-thirds of all local relief costs by the end of the year and, the following spring, it started footing three-quarters of the total bill.

In spite of the unprecedented extension of state and federal funds, New Dealers in Albany and Washington conceived of this step as a temporary expedient to meet an emergency situation. Overwhelmed by the immediacy of the unemployment crisis, officials continued through 1934 to devise relief programs on virtually a month-to-month basis, since they scarcely had time to think about the future, let alone plan for it. The reliance on loans to finance unemployment relief indicated the stopgap nature of assistance. During Lehman's first term as governor, many New Yorkers still expected a business revival, which would end the need for state and federal subsidies. Yet despite the temporary character of aid for the jobless, Albany and Washington had accepted responsibility for the welfare of indigent citizens for the first time in history. The next few years would determine whether New York would return to the primitive "poor relief" system of pre-Depression days.

NOTES

1. "Statement for the TERA re: Necessity for Federal Funds," January 10, 1933, folder "Hopkins, Harry," Microfilm Reel 45, Governorship Papers (hereinafter referred to as GP), HHLP; David M. Ellis et al., *A History of New York State* (Ithaca, N.Y., 1967), p. 416.
2. Quoted in Harry Manuel Shulman, *Slums of New York* (New York, 1938), pp. 120-21.
3. *Buffalo Courier-Express,* April 7, 1933.
4. Emergency Unemployment Relief Committee statement, *New York Times,* December 19, 1932.
5. Report of the Women's Director of the Emergency Work Relief Bureau, *New York Evening Post,* December 19, 1932.
6. *New York Times,* December 2, 1932.
7. *Buffalo Evening News,* January 3, 1933.
8. *Buffalo Courier-Express,* December 7, 1932.
9. Rochester *Democrat and Chronicle,* December 30, 1932.
10. William P. Capes to HHL, December 29, 1932, "Conference of Mayors, 1932-33," Reel 20, GP, HHLP; Hopkins to HHL, December 21, 1932, Special File, HHLP; U.S., Congress, Senate, Committee on Manufactures, Hearings before a Subcommittee of the

Committee on Manufactures, U.S. Senate, on S. 5125, 72d Cong., 2d sess., 1933, pt. I, pp. 102, 106.

11. HHL Address, January 2, 1933, *Public Papers of Herbert H. Lehman, Forty-ninth Governor of the State of New York, 1933* (Albany, 1934), pp. 12-13. (Hereinafter referred to as *Public Papers.*)

12. U.S., Congress, Senate, Hearings before a Subcommittee of the Committee on Manufactures, *op.cit.,* p. 85; "Suggested Reference in Message to Obtaining [sic.] Relief Funds from Reconstruction Finance Corporation," n.d., "RFC–General, 1933," Reel 81, GP, HHLP; Harry Hopkins to HHL, December 15, 1932, "Hopkins, Harry," Reel 45, GP, HHLP; HHL Message to the Legislature, January 4, 1933, *Public Papers, 1933,* p. 31.

13. State Charities Aid Association Press Release, January 20, 1933, "SCAA," Reel 90, GP, HHLP; Albany *Knickerbocker Press,* January 5, 1933; *New York Times,* January 3, 17, 1933.

14. William H. Matthews to HHL, January 17, 1933, Gen. Corr., 1933-40, HHLP.

15. *Buffalo Evening News,* January 3, 1933; *New York Evening Post,* January 3, 1933; *New York Sun,* January 3, 1933; Rochester *Democrat and Chronicle,* January 5, 1933.

16. New York *Herald Tribune,* Jaunuary 3, 5, 1933.

17. The constitution barred the state from contracting any debt unless authorized by law and approved in a general election by a majority of the voters. N.Y. Const., art. VII, sec. 4 (1920). *New York Times,* January 3, 6, 19, 1933; HHL Statement, January 19, 1933, *Public Papers, 1933,* pp. 455-57; *Laws of New York, 1933,* chap. 8.

18. HHL to the RFC, January 19, 1933, *Public Papers, 1933,* pp. 457-58; HHL to the RFC, January 28, 1933, "RFC–General, 1933," Reel 81, GP, HHLP. Lehman also tried to pry loose money from the RFC for self-liquidating public works. Local applications had been pending for months, but even a high-level commiteee, headed by Robert Moses and appointed by Lehman, failed to expedite the release of RFC funds for public construction in the state. HHL Statements, January 27, February 1, 1933, *Public Papers, 1933,* pp. 458-60; Moses to HHL, June 1, 1933, "Emergency Public Works Commission," Reel 29, GP, HHLP.

19. *New York Times,* January 20, 1933; Fred C. Croxton to HHL, January 31, February 28, March 25, April 28, 1933, "RFC–Fred C. Croxton," Reel 82, GP, HHLP. The first RFC allotment for February allowed New York to increase by 16 percent the number of families receiving relief. Despite its late start, New York finally ranked third among the states, after Illinois and Pennsylvania, in total relief funds granted by the RFC. *New York Times,* March 27, May 10, 1933.

20. The matching fund provided $1.00 of federal money for every $3.00 of public monies from all sources spent in the state during the preceding three months. Josephine C. Brown, *Public Relief, 1929-39* (New York, 1940), p. 146.

21. Ibid., pp. 140-51. In addition to FERA, which depended on states for the administration of relief funds, Congress established the Civilian Conservation Corps (CCC) which excluded any significant role for state or local governments. In its nine-year history the CCC provided jobs in the country's forests for over 200,000 young New Yorkers who returned more than $41 million in wages to their indigent families. John A. Salmond, *The Civilian Conservation Corps, 1933-1942: A New Deal Case Study* (Durham, N. C., 1967), pp. 26-47; "Final Report of the Director of the Civilian Conservation Corps," Washington, 1942, pp. 108, 109, 115, Civilian Conservation Corps Records, Record Group 35, National Archives.

22. FDR to HHL, May 19, 1933, HHL to FDR, May 19, 1933, OF 444, FDRL; Hopkins to HHL, May 19, 1933, HHL to Hopkins, May 19, June 1, 1933, "TERA Correspondence,

1931-33," Harry Hopkins Papers, FDRL. To replace Hopkins, Lehman selected Alfred H. Schoellkopf, a member of TERA, an upstate Republican, and vice president of the Niagara-Hudson Power Company. Frederick I. Daniels, a former commissioner of public welfare in Syracuse, served as executive director of TERA after March, 1933, and became chairman upon Schoellkopf's resignation in October 1935.

23. Transcript, "Meeting of TERA on Federal Aid and New York City," May 27, 1933, "TERA, 1933," Reel 95, GP, HHLP.

24. Harry Hopkins to Charles Poletti, April 3, 1933, "Hopkins, Harry," Reel 45, GP, HHLP; *Laws of New York, 1933,* chap. 260.

25. HHL Messages to the Legislature, January 4, April 8, 1933, *Public Papers, 1933,* pp. 31-32, 118-19.

26. Folks to HHL, July 12, 1933, HHL to Folks, July 14, 1933, Alfred H. Schoellkopf to HHL, July 17, 1933, "Unemployment Relief Bond Issue," Reel 98, GP, HHLP.

27. Walter I. Trattner, *Homer Folks: Pioneer in Social Welfare* (New York, 1968), pp. 251-63 et passim; HHL to Folks, February 4, 1933, Folks to HHL, February 6, 1933, Homer Folks Papers, Columbia University; HHL Address, July 9, 1936, *Public Papers, 1936,* pp. 895-96; Homer Folks Memoir, COHC, pp. 91-92.

28. *New York Times,* October 25, 28, 1933; Edith A. Lehman Address, November 3, 1933, *Public Papers, 1933,* pp. 784-85; *The New York Red Book* (Albany, 1934), p. 405.

29. New York State Department of Labor, *Trend of Employment in New York State Factories from 1914 to 1939* (Albany, 1940), pp. 67-70.

30. For a discussion of the collapse of private relief, see Lilian Brandt, "Relief of the Unemployed in New York City, 1929-1937," (preliminary draft, 1939), pp. 1-169, 442-47.

31. Lorena Hickok Report, October 2-12, 1933, "Hickok Reports," Hopkins Papers.

32. It should be noted that the New York banking community had its own problems. By March 1, 1933, a virtual cessation of deposits, combined with steady withdrawals, had brought banks around the country to their knees. With state after state declaring bank holidays, New York bankers called on Lehman to take a similar step. Unable to wait for Roosevelt's inauguration and a national bank holiday, Lehman closed the state's banks for two days beginning March 4, and they remained closed for an additional four days when FDR declared a national bank holiday from March 6 through 9. Henry Bruere to HHL, October 15, 1935, Joseph A. Broderick to HHL, December 14, 1935, "Bank Holiday," Special Subject File, HHLP.

33. William Whyte, *Financing New York City,* American Academy of Political and Social Science, Pamphlet Series, No. 2 (New York, 1935), passim; New York State Constitutional Convention Committee, *Problems Relating to Taxation and Finance* (New York, 1938), p. 303; Cushman McGee, *The Finances of the City of New York* (New York, 1940), p. 124.

34. Whyte, *Financing New York City,* p. 35.

35. Samuel Untermyer to Marvin McIntyre, May 20, 1933, OF 88, FDRL; Frank J. Taylor to Frederick I. Daniels, May 23, 1933, "O'Brien, John P.," Reel 72, GP, HHLP.

36. Transcript, "Meeting of TERA," May 27, 1933.

37. Frederick I. Daniels to John P. O'Brien, May 31, 1933, Alfred H. Schoellkopf to O'Brien, July 12, 1933, "O'Brien, John P.," Reel 72, GP, HHLP; Harry Hopkins to FDR, July 7, 1933, OF 444, FDRL.

38. Joseph F. Higgins to HHL, July 13, 1933, Report of New York City Comptroller on Financial Condition of City, July 11, 1933, HHL to the Board of Estimate and

Apportionment, July 16, 1933, *Public Papers, 1933,* pp. 612-27; Samuel Untermyer to HHL, August 16, 1933, HHL to Untermyer, August 17, 1933, "Special Session, October 18, 1933," Reel 89, GP, HHLP; *Laws of New York, 1933,* chap. 815; *New York Times,* August 24, September 8, October 15, 1933.

39. Lehman was unusually qualified to help the city, since he not only had been a banker himself but also had headed a committee appointed by Mayor Walker to study municipal finances in 1926. HHL to Lindsay Rogers, October 1, 1926, Lindsay Rogers Papers, Columbia University; Herbert H. Lehman et al., *The Finances and Financial Administration of New York City: Recommendations and Report of the Subcommittee on Budget, Finance, and Revenue, of the City Committee on Plan and Survey* (New York, 1928).

40. Clearing House Banks to John P. O'Brien, September 13, 1933, Frank L. Polk and Samuel Untermyer to HHL, September 18, 1933, HHL to Polk and Untermyer, September 18, 1933, "New York City Finances," Reel 69, GP, HHLP; HHL to Polk and Untermyer, October 9, 1933, "Special Session, October 18, 1933," Reel 89, ibid. In a brief special session the state legislature granted New York City the powers needed to implement the Bankers' Agreement. *Laws of New York, 1933,* chaps. 831-33; *New York Times,* October 19, November 1, 1933.

41. Alfred H. Schoellkopf to Frank J. Taylor, October 21, 1933, Charles Poletti Memorandum, "TERA and New York City Relief," October 29, 1933, "TERA, 1933," Reel 95, GP, HHLP; Solomon Lowenstein to Board of Estimate and Apportionment of the City of New York, September 23, 1933, "Welfare Council of New York City," Reel 103, ibid.; *New York Times,* November 21, 1933.

42. *New York Times,* November 15, 1933.

43. Quoted in Hickok Report, October 2-12, 1933.

44. Harry Hopkins to Frederick I. Daniels, October 10, 1933, New York, 400, Federal Emergency Relief Administration Records, Record Group 69, National Archives. Through use of discretionary funds, the state and federal governments actually had been paying over 50 percent of New York State's total relief bill since February 1933. TERA to Mayors et al., October 16, 1933, "United States Federal Emergency Relief Administration," Reel 99, GP, HHLP. (Hereinafter referred to as "USFERA.")

45. One member of TERA who attended a CWA orientation meeting in Washington reported: "The major purpose of the government is ... 'priming the pump.'" William Hodson to Members of the Board of Directors [of the Welfare Council], November 16, 1933, "Welfare Council of New York City," Reel 103, GP, HHLP.

46. Harry Hopkins to Alfred H. Schoellkopf, November 10, 1933, Administrative Correspondence, New York, State Series, Civil Works Administration Records, Record Group 69, National Archives; Schoellkopf to Hopkins, November 20, 1933, "USFERA," Reel 99, GP, HHLP; *New York Times,* November 25, 28, 1933.

47. *New York Times,* December 18, 20, 1934; Alexander Leopold Radomski, *Work Relief in New York State, 1931-1935* (New York, 1947), pp. 163-65. The final report of the CWA in New York presents contradictory evidence on the maximum number employed by the CWA and the exact date when that was reached. The total, however, was approximately 340,000, or some 50,000 less than the original goal. TERA, "Review of C.W.A. Activities in New York State," 1934, pp. 18, 56, WPA Research Library, Record Group 69, National Archives.

48. TERA, "Review of C.W.A.," pp. 12-13; *Buffalo Courier-Express,* January 21, 1934; *Rochester Times-Union,* January 8, 16, 1934; "The Civil Works Administration and

Nursery Schools in New York," *Schools and Society,* XXXIX (January 20, 1934): 79-80.

49. HHL to Harry Hopkins, November 13, 1933, "USFERA," Reel 99, GP, HHLP.

50. HHL to Harry Hopkins, January 17, 1934, HHL to FDR, January 17, 1934, ibid.

51. FDR to HHL, February 10, 1934, ibid.

52. The PWA, created in June, 1933, was another New Deal agency which had little impact on the state government, since most of its loans and grants-in-aid for public construction went to local communities. In the Empire State, which received more money from the PWA than any other state, 95 percent of the grants went to local public bodies and only 5 percent to the state government itself. Estimated percentages computed from the following sources: U.S., Congress, House, Committee on Appropriations, Hearings before a Subcommittee of the Commiteee of Appropriations, U.S. House of Representatives, on the Emergency Relief Appropriation Act of 1938 and Public Works Administration Appropriation Act of 1938, 75th Cong., 3d sess., 1938, pp. 441-42; "Status of Completed Non-Federal Allotted Projects," January 3, 1940, p. 29, Public Works Administration Records, Record Group 135, National Archives.

53. Elmer F. Andrews, "Memorandum to Governor Lehman Regarding the Unemployment Situation," n.d., enclosed in Paul Sifton to J. J. Canavan, January 29, 1934, "Labor, Department of, 1933-38," Reel 54, GP, HHLP.

54. Quoted in Helen Hall, *Unfinished Business in Neighborhood and Nation* (New York, 1971), p. 14.

55. Harry Hopkins to HHL, February 27, 1934, HHL to Hopkins, February 28, 1934, "USFERA," Reel 99, GP, HHLP; HHL to FDR, March 12, 14, 1934, Marvin McIntyre to HHL, March 14, 1934, OF 444-Misc., FDRL; HHL Statement, March 16, 1934, HHL Message to the Legislature, April 4, 1934, *Public Papers, 1934,* pp. 93-94, 634; *New York Times,* March 17, 1934; Searle F. Charles, *Minister of Relief: Harry Hopkins and the Depression* (Syracuse, N.Y., 1963), p. 61.

56. La Guardia to HHL, December 20, 1933, Box 2565, Fiorello La Guardia Papers, New York City Municipal Archives; La Guardia to HHL, January 4, 1934, *Public Papers, 1934,* p. 608; Charles Garrett, *The La Guardia Years: Machine and Reform Politics in New York City* (New Brunswick, N.J., 1961), pp. 142-43. For the complete text of the original economy bill, see *New York Times,* January 3, 1934.

57. HHL to La Guardia, January 5, 1934, *Public Papers, 1934,* pp. 612-17.

58. *Auburn Advertiser,* January 6, 1934, Albany *Times Union,* January 9, 1934, *Elmira Star Gazette,* January 10, 1934, *Niagara Falls Gazette,* January 8, 1934, *Salamanica Press,* January 6, 1933, *Syracuse Herald,* January 8, 1934, Syracuse *Post Standard,* January 7, 1934, *Troy Observer,* January 7, 1934, *Troy Times,* January 6, 1934, CB, XV: 126-32, HHLP.

59. *New York American,* January 8, 1934, *New York Journal,* January 8, 1934, *New York Post,* January 9, 1934, *New York Sun,* January 6, 1934, CB, VI: 125-32, HHLP.

60. *New York Times,* January 3, 1934; New York *Herald Tribune,* January 8, 1934; New York *Daily News,* January 6, 9, 1934; *New York World-Telegram,* January 2, 6, 1934; *New York Daily Mirror,* January 8, 1934, CB, XV: 131, HHLP.

61. *New York Times,* January 9, 1934; S. C. Mead to HHL, January 12, 1934, "New York City—Economy Bill," Reel 69, GP, HHLP.

62. *New York Times,* January 8, 1934.

63. La Guardia to HHL, January 7, 1934, HHL to La Guardia, January 8, 1934, *Public Papers, 1934,* pp. 617-21.

64. La Guardia to HHL, January 12, 1934, Box 2565, La Guardia Papers; HHL to Jerome D.

Barnum, January 10, 1934, "NYC—Economy Bill," Reel 69, GP, HHLP; HHL to Lillian Wald, January 11, 1934, Special File, HHLP; HHL Statement, January 10, 1934, *Public Papers, 1934*, pp. 621-22. For the text of the compromise bill, see ibid., pp. 608-12.

65. For a broad sampling of editorial opinion, see CB, XV: 136-43, HHLP. Of the eighteen editorials preserved here, not one opposed the compromise bill.

66. *New York Times*, January 17, February 17, March 19, 1934.

67. HHL Message to the Legislature, January 30, 1934, *Public Papers, 1934*, pp. 75-76; *New York Times*, January 18, 31, February 7, 15, 18, 19, March 7, 17, 29, 1934.

68. *New York Times*, April 4, 6, 10, 1934; *Laws of New York, 1934*, chap. 178. For a detailed account of the economy-bill fight in Albany, see Jewel Bellush, "Selected Case Studies of the Legislative Leadership of Governor Herbert H. Lehman" (unpublished Ph.D. dissertation, Columbia University, 1959), pp. 239-302.

69. Whyte, *Financing New York City*, p. 41; Garrett, *The La Guardia Years*, pp. 144-45.

70. *New York World-Telegram*, October 3, 1933; Hickok Report, October 2-12, 1933; Lorena A. Hickok to Harry Hopkins, December 29, 1933, Arch Mandel to Hopkins, June 20, October 15, December 17, 1934, Mandel to Aubrey Williams, August 2, 1934, New York, 406, FERA Records; Martha Luginbuhl to Corrington Gill, May 1, 1934, New York, 400, FERA Records; "The Welfare Council of New York City, Summary of Activities in 1934," February 20, 1935, "Welfare Council of New York City," Reel 103, GP, HHLP.

71. La Guardia to HHL, February 6, 1934, Box 2565, La Guardia Papers; Lillian Wald to HHL, February 6, 1934, Lillian Wald Papers, New York Public Library; Paul Kellogg to HHL, March 9, 1934, Gen. Corr., 1933-40, HHLP; HHL Message to the Legislature, March 7, 1934, *Public Papers, 1934*, p. 399; *Laws of New York, 1934*, chap. 65. Only one other city followed New York's lead and provided cash relief. TERA, *Five Million People, One Billion Dollars* (Albany, 1937), pp. 35-36.

72. Hickok Report, September 12-19, 1933, "Hickok Reports," Hopkins Papers.

73. Transcripts of Harry Hopkins and Frederick I. Daniels Conversations, March 28, April 4, 1934, "Telephone Conversations with State Relief Directors, *et al.*, New York," Hopkins Papers.

74. HHL Address, October 19, 1934, *Public Papers, 1934*, p. 783.

III

FROM EMERGENCY RELIEF TO THE WELFARE STATE

During the mid-1930s, New Yorkers reconsidered the emergency and temporary character of the state's relief activities. With no end of the Depression in sight, the state launched a sweeping inquiry into government's responsibility for poverty-stricken people unable to find jobs. A commission of experts appointed by the governor concluded that the state should permanently cooperate with local communities in financing and supervising unemployment relief. With an amazing display of unanimity, Albany lawmakers accepted this recommendation, thereby guaranteeing New Yorkers a minimum standard of living even if they never returned to work.

1

The nation suffered through the fifth year of the Depression during 1934. Relief rolls continued to grow as more and more people reached the end of their resources after years of forced idleness. The city manager of Rochester declared that "the problem of public welfare continues to be the most perplexing problem facing this and other cities." [1] In New York City, applications for public assistance poured in at the rate of over 1200 per day during the summer months when warm weather had previously brought a decline in the demand for relief.[2] Furthermore, increasing numbers of middle-class workers went on relief, but they did so with the greatest reluctance, according to Lorena Hickok of the Federal Emergency Relief Administration (FERA).

If you are the kind of person the government really should be interested in helping, you go there only as the last resort. You have used up all your resources and have strained the generosity of your relatives and your friends to the breaking point. Your credit is gone. You couldn't charge a nickle's [sic] worth at the grocery store. You owe several months' rent. The landlord had lost his patience and is threatening to throw you out. Maybe you've already gone through an eviction or two. I quote

48

one of the case supervisors: "It does something to a family to go through a couple of evictions." The chances are you've been hungry for some time. And now there's no food in the house. You've simply got to do something.[3]

On Morningside Heights in Manhattan, another representative of Harry Hopkins noted that former Columbia University professors and students often passed the welfare bureau six or seven times before getting up the courage to walk in and ask for help.[4] "Mentally," he concluded, "the havoc wrecked [sic] among skilled and white collar people cannot be estimated, but it is serious. Many skilled men will never be useful again because of this interlude of worry." [5]

Yet the same observer found a different attitude among most New Yorkers at this time, the end of 1934.

No private jobs are in sight. . . . Relief workers report a complete lack of faith in the vast majority of clients that private jobs are coming back. . . .

Secondly, the psychology of relief has gone through the whole population within the past year. Relief is regarded as permanent by both clients and relief workers. Clients are assuming that the government has a responsibility to provide [it]. The stigma of relief has almost disappeared except among white collar groups.

In short, "the word 'emergency' disappeared out of the relief picture." With little hope of business reviving sufficiently to absorb all the able-bodied unemployed, New York City welfare officials expected public funds to assure a minimum standard of living for people unable to earn it themselves.

There is a surprisingly uniform belief . . . among supervisors and case workers that they feel the government has a definite responsibility and obligation to provide a minimum subsistence level for every person, regardless of jobs. If private jobs bring in income below this level, then the government should supplement. This feeling has also gained amazing tenacity among clients, who are definitely more dependent on the government.[6]

As New York moved steadily toward the Welfare State, David C. Adie became an early champion of "the new philosophy of collective responsibility." [7] Born and educated in Scotland, Adie had emigrated to the United States at the age of twenty-five in 1913. After working for various private welfare agencies in Minneapolis, New York City, and Buffalo, he was appointed to the New York State Board of Social Welfare by Governor Roosevelt in 1929. This group set down policy for the State Department of Social Welfare whose chief executive officer—a commissioner—the board selected. In 1932, Adie was elevated to the post of state commissioner of social welfare where he won a reputation as a far-sighted liberal. Governor Lehman came to rely heavily on the shrewd social worker for advice throughout the 1930s.[8]

During 1934, David Adie began to spell out the implications of the Welfare State.

Although he believed that the nation's economy would continue to improve, he thought many of the jobless would never again find productive work. "It is my opinion," the commissioner declared, "that we will find ourselves with a permanent unemployment of 6,000,000 as compared with the norm of about 1,500,000 in pre-depression times and about 13,000,000 at the depression peak." [9] Since the country faced a long-term problem, Adie suggested necessary changes in public assistance.

> The general public must fully comprehend that Queen Elizabeth is dead, that the instruments which were good enough in her day and the social philosophy which may or may not have been justified have no longer validity in a highly industrialized state. The concept of needy persons as paupers carrying with it all the stigma and loss of status which characterized a less complicated social order is simply farcical today, let alone unjust. We can no longer view persons in receipt of public assistance as characterized by less capacity, dependence, or moral instability. Our attitude, however, must not only change in relation to social status but we must change also in regard to relief as an instrument. Call it what you will, the different forms of relief administered today are entirely different in their nature from the relief of yesterday. . . .
>
> We have experienced . . . the completion of the relief circle. Beginning with an uncomplicated social economy which found relatively adequate social care motivated by pity, fear, and false philanthropy, we have arrived at a complicated social order in which we view social security as necessitating the operation of a variety of social services.[10]

In tying relief to social security, Adie saw the unemployed as a category of dependent citizens needing public assistance as much as the aged or the handicapped: "The new group which has probably assumed permanence is the result of a labor surplus existing in a world which will conceivably have less and less need for the totality of . . . human power as a result of the growing and increasing substitution of mechanical." Economic developments, according to the commissioner of social welfare, required security for the unemployed through cash allowances and public jobs, and this step necessitated "federal, state, and local governments working out a co-ordinated national welfare program." As early as 1934, David Adie called for a government-guaranteed minimum income for those in society excluded from gainful employment, and New York gradually moved in this direction.[11]

2

With welfare rolls steadily growing and many social workers talking of permanent government aid, New York took steps to terminate emergency financing of relief during 1934. In April, Governor Lehman told Albany lawmakers that the state could not rely indefinitely on bond issues and that "within a reasonable time" the entire cost of relief should come from current revenues. Toward this end, he called for a reduction in the amount obtained from bond issues and a gradual assumption of annual welfare expenses by taxpayers. The governor and legislative leaders settled on a $40 million relief bond issue which went on the November ballot. Although this sum would cover only a portion of the state's share of unemployment relief for 1935, it would tide New York over until the 1935 legislature could study the situation and appropriate additional funds out of the regular budget.[12] Homer Folks again led a successful bipartisan campaign for the bond issue, which voters overwhelmingly approved.[13]

During the summer of 1934, Mayor La Guardia also sought a permanent method of financing municipal relief. Since the demand for public assistance remained unexpectedly high, the city faced exhaustion of the loans negotiated in 1933. La Guardia warned that New York could no longer treat unemployment as a temporary problem, because, he argued, even a complete revival of business would bring the technological displacement of workers. Faced with a long-term commitment to relief, the mayor branded additional borrowing as "costly, wasteful and unscientific." Therefore, he called for a shift from loans to taxation as the primary means of raising the city's share of relief, which then totaled about $5 million per month.[14] With the backing of a special committee of municipal lawmakers, La Guardia appealed to the governor for expansion of the city's taxing powers to put relief on a pay-as-you-go basis. Lehman forwarded this request to the state legislature, which was already meeting in an extraordinary session. Senators and assemblymen quickly adopted a law authorizing New York City to levy emergency taxes through 1935 but only for relief purposes.[15]

Local officials had the usual trouble agreeing on what form the taxation should take. While the city debated the merits of various imposts during the fall of 1934, it received interim bank loans which kept money flowing to the needy. With the depletion of relief coffers imminent, municipal legislators levied taxes on business revenues and personal incomes, but these did not cover the entire relief bill. Finally, in late November, New York City assured enough funds for the coming year by enacting a local sales tax, a levy on public utilities, and an inheritance tax.[16] Although the state had limited the duration of these imposts to one year, it subsequently granted New York City periodic extensions of its emergency taxing powers which allowed the city to subsidize public assistance without relying any longer on loans.[17]

New York City's experience showed the effect of placing a large share of the relief burden on local governments. Like most municipalities, New York had traditionally drawn most of its revenues from property taxes, which could not be readily increased, particularly during a depression. When forced to look elsewhere for funds, the La Guardia administration confronted stiff opposition from groups affected by proposed levies on businesses and personal incomes. As a last resort, the city passed the sales tax, which brought in sufficient revenues but fell heaviest on low-income families who could least afford it. Thus economic and political considerations produced a regressive impost as the primary source of local relief funds in the country's largest city. Despite the disadvantages of the sales tax, it at least provided enough money so that New York finally could give public assistance without interruption.[18]

3

During the summer of 1934, the Temporary Emergency Relief Administration concluded that New York approached "the cross-roads of emergency planning and long-range planning." Therefore, the agency suggested that an independent study should determine the type of machinery which could deal most efficiently and economically with the prolonged suffering of the jobless.[19] In response to this proposal, Governor Lehman created the Commission on Unemployment Relief, an unofficial body of thirty-four members, which he directed to investigate the existing welfare system and recommend necessary changes. The governor's appointments to the commission included social workers, business and labor leaders, and Albany lawmakers from both parties.[20] Lehman selected Allen Wardwell of New York City as chairman of the group. Although a lawyer, Wardell was much like the governor—deliberate and cautious, yet capable of making tough decisions. With the aid of federal and private funds, the Wardwell Commission engaged over twenty technical experts and mounted an extensive inquiry. During the following two years, the group issued a series of reports on various phases of the relief problem.[21]

Commission members divided on the immediate question of the future of TERA. While some favored setting a date for abolishing the emergency relief agency, others led by Allen Wardwell argued that such a decision was premature because of uncertainties about prospective relief loads and federal policies. Therefore, the panel recommended early in 1935 that the legislature extend the life of TERA for another year, until February 15, 1936, by which time the state could better evaluate the agency's ultimate role in public assistance. Meanwhile, in order to provide for improved coordination of temporary and permanent welfare programs, the Wardwell Commission advised that TERA expand its executive committee by including someone from the State Board of Social Welfare and also adding the commissioner of social welfare, David Adie, as a nonvoting member. In accepting these suggestions, Lehman agreed that the frequency of changes in relief policies precluded for the moment any possibility of making a final decision about the fate of TERA.[22]

G.O.P. legislators resisted the idea of postponing consideration of TERA's future. Complaining that previous cooperation with the governor on a bipartisan relief program had benefited him politically at their expense, Republicans threatened to pursue an independent course during the 1935 session. "We are firmly of the opinion," declared G.O.P. leaders in January, "that unemployment should be dealt with in a scientific manner and that a definite permanent policy must be evolved by the state. . . . Anything else is unfair to those who through no fault of their own are unable to provide for themselves and their families." [23] Specifically, Republicans wanted a gradual takeover of TERA's activities by the Department of Social Welfare so that New York could achieve a full integration of all public assistance programs by June 1936. However, since Republicans lacked a majority in either house of the legislature, Lehman persuaded them to drop their proposal and thereby keep unemployment relief a nonpartisan issue. After a series of meetings with the governor, G.O.P. lawmakers voted for his bill to extend TERA for another year and enlarge its membership.[24]

The Depression continued to reap its toll during 1935, when 25 percent of New York's industrial workers were still unemployed. Thousands of people who had survived on their own since 1929 exhausted their money and sought public aid as a last resort. In January 1935, 48,700 families in the state received their first relief allowances, and one out of six New Yorkers, over two million people, depended on government assistance. The average weekly grant for a family of five in New York City was $12.00, which barely kept people alive, as shown by the fact that 18 percent of the city school children suffered from malnutrition.[25]

With the welfare rolls expanding during 1935, New York State confronted the annual problem of raising sufficient funds to care for the destitute. It proved more difficult than usual to estimate the state's share of relief costs, because federal plans were again in flux. On January 4, President Roosevelt asked Congress to replace the so-called "dole" of FERA with a national works program which would provide jobs for employable relief recipients. Stressing his desire to cooperate with Washington, Lehman tried unsuccessfully to find out more about the proposal from Harry Hopkins.[26] In the absence of detailed information, the governor suggested that the state furnish as much money for relief as the previous year by appropriating $10 million to supplement the $40 million already available from the most recent bond issue. The total would permit the state to contribute over $4 million monthly to victims of the Depression during 1935.[27] Looking ahead to 1936, Lehman recommended a $55 million bond issue with $35 million for direct grants to communities and the remainder for state construction "to give employment to our people and to stimulate industry." The legislature approved this request, as did the state's electorate.[28]

The year 1935 marked a turning point in federal/state cooperation on unemployment relief. In April, Congress adopted the Emergency Relief Appropriation Act which signaled the end of the two-year-old system of grants-in-aid for the poor. As a replacement for the FERA "dole," the law established the Works Progress Administration (WPA) to give federally created jobs to able-bodied people on relief. State and local governments were left in charge of caring for the needy incapable of working.

The separation of federal and state obligations deeply disturbed Albany leaders. TERA officials feared this arrangement "would endanger the general well being [sic] and financial condition of the State and its local subdivisions." [29] Lehman initially liked the new setup. After talking with Roosevelt in May, the governor favored divorcing the federal works program from TERA, because he understood the former would encompass large public works like those handled by the PWA. However, upon learning more about the nature of the WPA, Lehman found it "so definitely a work relief program that his previous position could no longer hold." He agreed with the entire TERA that federal, state and local relief activities should remain fully integrated for both financial and administrative reasons.[30]

In June 1935, Lehman and members of TERA pleaded their case before Harry

Hopkins who was to head the WPA. The Albany officials asked for incorporation of the new federal projects into New York's existing relief structure, but Hopkins refused because the president had already decided on "relieving the federal government of any relief activity or responsibility, and of establishing a works program of a non-relief character." Since the thinking of local welfare bureaus "must inevitably be colored with their psychology of relief," they could not implement the WPA, which would provide jobs without any stigma of government handouts. In short, Hopkins wanted the WPA to be a distinct organization staffed entirely by federal employees.[31]

The inauguration of the WPA required changes in New York's relief system. The federal takeover of most work relief led TERA to abandon this field completely, because home relief was a less costly means of caring for people excluded from the WPA. The impending cutoff of federal grants also forced TERA to modify its reimbursement policy. Late in the summer of 1935, the state agency notified communities that the proportion of relief costs paid locally would have to be increased as Washington eliminated FERA grants and the WPA absorbed a large portion of people on welfare. Although the local share had been 25 percent for at least a year, Lehman directed TERA to return to the original 1931 plan under which cities and counties paid 60 percent and the state covered the remaining 40 percent. Despite the jump in the local rate, it was assumed that community welfare bills would stay about the same, since most relief recipients would transfer to the federal works program.[32]

The WPA failed to take care of as many indigent New Yorkers as originally planned. Both FDR and Harry Hopkins had promised WPA jobs for 70 percent of the relief clients, and pending achievement of this goal, Washington was to subsidize the cost of any part of the quota still on home relief. But in September 1935, New York faced the imminent cessation of federal grants, although the WPA had fallen behind in absorbing its share of welfare cases. Troubled by Washington's apparent unwillingness to uphold its end of a bargain, Lehman demanded that the private understanding be spelled out publicly.[33] Under pressure from the governor, Roosevelt called a meeting at his Hyde Park estate, attended by Lehman, TERA officials, Hopkins, and Mayor La Guardia. In recognition of their previous commitment, Roosevelt and Hopkins pledged to provide jobs for 396,000 needy New Yorkers and to pay home relief for that portion of the quota not employed on federal projects. Fulfillment of this agreement brought the state over $7 million in supplementary funds from Washington for local relief in November. Meanwhile, the president moved to expedite development of the WPA in New York.[34]

In the wake of the Hyde Park conference, Harry Hopkins privately attacked Lehman's approach to relief questions. "The Governor wants to deal with me . . . in a very formal fashion," Hopkins remarked in a conversation with Mayor La Guardia. Whenever the federal relief administrator mentioned a particular objective to Lehman, ". . . the next thing I know," Hopkins exclaimed, "he is pinning me down to write another letter. Confidentially, I don't like to do business that way." Yet Hopkins felt compelled to add, in describing the governor, "I like him and God knows he has cooperated."[35] Although Lehman sometimes irritated other officials by fighting against any relaxation of federal or local commitments, his tactics often got more money from both levels of government than would have otherwise been forthcoming.

Conflicting interpretations of the Hyde Park agreement added to the growing tension between Albany and Washington. In November, the Roosevelt administration informed Lehman that the offer of jobs for almost 400,000 New Yorkers would include employment not only by the WPA but also by all other federal agencies such as the Civilian Conservation Corps and the PWA. Since most of the people working under programs other than the WPA had never been local relief recipients, Lehman complained that their inclusion in the goal of 400,000 would undermine the plan to reduce the state's public welfare burden. Therefore, he urged the president to continue supplying funds for the part of the quota which had not come directly from relief rolls. FDR refused on the grounds that limited congressional appropriations did not permit such action and that under the circumstances "the federal government is discharging its obligations in New York State in the fullest possible manner." In line with this position, Washington made its last grant for local home relief in December 1935.[36]

Relations between Albany and Washington deteriorated during 1935, as officials became more and more frustrated in trying to deal with problems created by the Great Depression. Since many of the unemployed had lost all hope of ever returning to work, the federal government had established the WPA with an initial appropriation of $1.5 billion to give the poor something meaningful to do. Yet even this astronomical sum proved too little to supply jobs for all employables on relief. As a result, TERA asserted, Washington put "a terrific burden on state and local funds for [a] larger relief load than was anticipated . . . due to [the] failure of WPA to reach its objectives and the Federal Government to live up to its earlier pledge." [37]

4

On New Year's Day, 1936, Governor Lehman solemnly declared that care of the unemployed still constituted the country's greatest single problem. While the WPA provided work relief for about 360,000 of the jobless in New York State, over 300,000 others remained on home relief jointly paid for by the state and its communities. The total of 660,000 represented an increase of about 10 percent over the maximum relief load carried the previous winter. The government supported 25 percent of Buffalo's population and 20 percent of the people in New York City. Emphasizing that "we still have a very long way to go before we reach normal conditions of employment," the governor called for agreement on a long-range program to deal with destitution. As a first step, he suggested that the state dissolve TERA and transfer its duties to the Department of Social Welfare.[38]

On January 3, 1936, Lehman forwarded to the legislature a report by his Commission on Unemployment Relief. After almost two years of study, the Wardwell Commission concluded that the jobless would require public assistance for the foreseeable future. While favoring retention of a locally administered relief system, the panel decided that efficient and adequate care of the indigent necessitated both state supervision and financial support. Since emergency methods wasted time and money, a regular state agency should take permanent charge of unemployment relief. Toward this end, the commission advocated reorganization of the State Department of Social Welfare and its supervisory parent, the State Board of Social Welfare, so that they could assume the burden of directing relief operations by January 1, 1937, when TERA would pass out of existence. The investigators called for the expansion of the duties of the Board of Social Welfare, reduction of its size from twelve to eight members and transfer to the governor of its power to appoint the head of the Department of Social Welfare.[39]

The Depression and four years' experience with TERA prepared New Yorkers to accept permanent government aid for the poor. According to a history of public welfare written during the late 1930s, many people "no longer looked upon [economic dependency] as primarily the result of a lack of moral fiber and character on the part of the needy themselves." Forced unemployment had struck masses of hard-working members of the middle class, which taught New Yorkers "to regard destitution and its consequences not as a question of individual weakness and breakdown, but fundamentally as a problem that must be attacked by society as a whole." [40]

Evidence of this new attitude came from a variety of sources. After a year of study, a local committee of prominent citizens appointed by Mayor La Guardia declared in 1935:

> [I]t is now clear that private industry will increase its production substantially without re-employing a large number of the men and women who are unemployed. . . .
>
> This community must . . . therefore decide whether the millions of unemployed families who are not re-employed in private industry or on public works shall be given just enough to continue their existence, or shall be guaranteed a minimum standard of living which will maintain standards of health and decency for themselves and the communities of which they form an important part. In our opinion the latter choice must be made.[41]

At the other end of the state, a Republican newspaper in Buffalo noted the growing acceptance of relief by 1936:

> Before the depression, the phrase "on the welfare" was anathema to the average worker. The bulk of those cared for by public funds was made up by alcoholics, chronic loafers, the physically incapacitated and a few other derelicts. . . .
>
> During the years 1932-34, the public became acutely aware of the predicament in which thousands of neighboring families had been placed for lack of employment. Relief shifted from the character of a stigmatized public service to an essential public service. . . .
>
> After . . . 1933, it became apparent that this army of unemployed could not be classified on a par with the normal indigent family. These people had been self-respecting, self-supporting, independent family units throughout their lives.

They had built up reserves on normal expectancy. Through no fault of their own their incomes were cut off and their reserves were exhausted. The national, state and local governments realized that they deserved different treatment and different classification than the so-called pauper relief families.[42]

Since "we are teaching . . . workers to expect a standard income from one source or another as long as they live," an official in the Buffalo welfare bureau concluded, "the social revolution which has been discussed in America for 25 years has actually taken place during the depression."[43]

The radical change in attitude toward relief paved the way for adoption of the Wardell Commission recommendations in 1936. Endorsements came from Homer Folks and other leaders of voluntary agencies, including the Welfare Council of New York City, who fully backed long-term state participation in local unemployment relief. Speaking through the State Conference of Mayors, municipal governments not only applauded the guarantee of continued state aid, but they also asked that Albany share equally the cost of home relief.[44]

Although the state welfare officials supported most of the Wardell report, they disagreed with some of the proposed revisions in the state bureaucracy. The Board of Social Welfare favored an increase rather than a decrease in its membership and opposed surrendering its right to choose the head of the Department of Social Welfare. The present commissioner, David Adie, also objected to changing the method of appointment, because he feared that this might bring partisan politics into the department and divide the loyalty of the person most responsible for executing policies laid down by the Board of Social Welfare.[45]

Republicans initially took advantage of the discussion over relief to attack the New Deal in Washington and the Little New Deal in Albany. Although G.O.P. legislators approved of transferring TERA's duties to the Department of Social Welfare, they charged that enactment of all the commission's proposals would give the governor "czarlike powers." One lawmaker, well aware that an election year had dawned, equated the appointment by the governor of the welfare commissioner with "the usurpation by the New Deal of the functions of Congress."[46] Members of the opposition in Albany introduced a bill creating a legislative inquiry into the handling of relief, but they had little hope of putting the proposal into law, since Democrats controlled the Assembly.[47]

Disregarding Republican rhetoric, Lehman kept his usual outward calm. With all concerned groups, including Republicans, agreeing that the state should accept permanent responsibility for helping the unemployed, the governor tried to iron out minor differences over the administrative setup. During February and March, he held a series of meetings with legislative leaders and representatives of the Wardell Commission, TERA, and the Department of Social Welfare.[48] These conferences produced unanimous agreement on a compromise which closely resembled the Board of Social Welfare's revisions of the Wardell recommendations. The enabling bill, later passed by the legislature, provided for expiration of TERA on June 30, 1937, by which time the Department of Social Welfare would take over its functions. The law also established the regulatory and advisory role of an enlarged Board of Social Welfare which retained its right to name the commissioner of social welfare. In order to complete the changeover to a regular system of public assistance for the jobless, the 1936 legislation directed local emergency relief bureaus to transfer their duties to existing community welfare departments which would receive state reimbursements for 40 percent of their expenditures for unemployment relief.[49] Lehman hailed the enactment of this bill "which recognizes and provides relief for our unemployed as a permanent policy of the State government." As a result of lessons learned during the Depression, the governor proclaimed in the 1936 campaign, "we have decreed that in the humane and progressive Empire State we will never again countenance private bread lines and we will never again force men and women out of work to go begging from door to door for food and clothes." [50]

5

Soon after the State Department of Social Welfare took over directing relief activities, a new wave of unemployment swept across the country. In the middle of 1937, a recession reversed four years of slow but steady improvement in the economy. Lasting about a year in New York, the recession cut the state's industrial work force by 13 percent, which lowered factory employment to the level of January 1935. Welfare bureaus soon felt the impact of the economic setback. Within six months, the home relief population more than doubled in the hard-hit upstate area although New York City, with its more diverse economy, showed an increase of only 15 percent. By the spring of 1938, 345,000 families and individuals, over one million New Yorkers, were receiving home relief. As in previous expansions of the welfare rolls, thousands of families—81,000 in the winter of 1937-38—which had weathered years of the Depression without any government aid sought public assistance for the first time.[51]

The swelling demand for unemployment relief brought renewed pressure for increased state and federal spending. By the time the recession struck, New York had completed the transition from loans to taxes as the primary means of financing relief. The 1936 bond issue for $30 million was the state's last for this purpose. In his 1937 budget message, Governor Lehman called for new taxation to put relief on a pay-as-you-go basis. For the coming fiscal year, he advocated a 2 percent tax on the gross receipts of utility companies other than railroads. To expand local tax revenues, the governor also urged that the state give municipalities the power to impose a similar levy of 1 percent exclusively for unemployment relief. Albany lawmakers adopted both measures without any question.[52] After 1937, New York stopped earmarking specific taxes for relief and simply financed it like any other item in the normal state budget. This step, in the words of the Board of Social Welfare, indicated "widespread acceptance of public assistance as a basic element of government service in a democracy." [53]

Although Albany had committed itself to pay 40 percent of local relief expenses, community leaders regularly lobbied for more state aid. In 1938, Mayor La Guardia temporarily cut welfare allotments 10 percent as a means of putting pressure on the state to contribute more funds to the city, but Governor Lehman stood firmly against any increase in the rate of reimbursement. When, as a result, New York City was forced to enact additional local imposts, La Guardia branded them "State negligency taxes." [54] During 1939, several organizations of local officials, stressing the limits of municipal resources based almost entirely on real estate taxes, petitioned Lehman for new state levies to be turned over to cities and counties for unemployment relief. The governor, however, declared that the state also had financial problems and, therefore, could not undertake additional responsibilities.[55] Lehman was so strongly committed to keeping the state contribution at 40 percent that he worked behind the scenes to eliminate exceptions to the maximum rate of reimbursement.[56]

Defending his tightfistedness, Lehman argued that he had to balance the needs of the unemployed against those of the hard-pressed taxpayer. In 1938, he asserted that the administration of public welfare should have "for its objective the care of human beings and the conservation of the interests of the general taxpayer." [57] Yet the governor often overlooked the fact that the incidence of taxation varied according to which level of government imposed it. While the state could easily levy progressive taxes on businesses and personal incomes, cities depended on regressive measures, notably the sales tax. Thus protection of "the interests of the general taxpayer" dictated greater participation by the state in the financing of aid for the jobless.[58]

Another consideration forced heavy reliance on local resources. Both the governor and the state welfare commissioner feared that if communities paid little or nothing toward the cost of public assistance, they would lose all incentive to keep expenditures at a minimum through devices such as adequate investigation of applicants. However, acceptance of this principle did not require arbitrary insistence on a maximum state reimbursement of 40 percent, regardless of differing conditions in New York's many cities. Although Lehman would not approve increased contributions for public assistance, he could take pride in the fact that New York already paid a larger portion of local relief bills than any other state in the Union.

While mayors appealed to Albany for additional funds during the late 1930s, Lehman tried to get more money from Washington for unemployment relief. In 1937, he requested the president not to curtail the WPA until its workers could find jobs in private industry, because otherwise they would fall back on home relief rolls. When Roosevelt refused to make any such commitment, Lehman asked several governors if they thought "some of the larger industrial states acting together could do [anything] to bring the situation forcefully to the attention of the President and the Congress." The chief executives of Pennsylvania and Connecticut expressed little interest, but the governors of Wisconsin, Rhode Island, Minnesota, Illinois, and Massachusets accepted Lehman's invitation to gather at his Manhattan apartment so they could coordinate a joint appeal to Washington.[59] After their meeting on February 28, 1937, the conferees immediately sent a telegram to the president calling for fulfillment of the initial goal of the WPA—federal jobs for all employable relief recipients. In addition, the governors endorsed Lehman's suggestion that the WPA drop only those workers absorbed by private business and replace them with other able-bodied people still on relief. This group of chief executives, or their representatives, subsequently met twice with Roosevelt, but they failed to gain assurances from the president that he would not further cut back the WPA during 1937.[60] Although the governors then abandoned their common drive to reverse the decline in federal spending, their actions produced an unexpected side effect. Lehman's role in organizing the unsuccessful campaign contributed to the impending personal split between him and Roosevelt. They finally broke in July over the issue of the Supreme Court, but the president first criticized Lehman, according to Arthur Krock of the *Times,* for his failure to cooperate in cutting relief costs and balancing the national budget.[61]

Nevertheless, Lehman continued to call for more federal aid. In his annual message to the legislature for 1938, he repeated his hope that Washington would "assume its share of the cost of caring for the needy unemployed." [62] Since the president returned to a policy of spending in the wake of the 1937 recession, Lehman found little cause for complaint during 1938.[63] The following year, when slashes in WPA appropriations seemed imminent, the governor renewed his fight against such moves. Directing his appeals to Congress, he cited evidence that unemployment relief remained the most serious municipal problem in New York State and stressed that cutbacks in federal expenditures had previously necessitated increases in local relief. However, Washington disregarded this plea and again began reducing the federal works program.[64]

6

Despite gradual improvements in the economy after 1938, unemployment remained a heavy burden in the early 1940s. The 1940 census reported that New York's labor force had the country's highest rate of unemployment—13.7 percent. Although defense and war production helped reduce the ranks of the jobless, over 150,000 families and single persons were on local relief rolls as late as June 1942. This represented one-third the peak caseload of March 1935.[65]

As New York slowly recovered from the worst years of the Great Depression, the composition of the relief population changed dramatically. By 1940, the state classified the majority of welfare recipients as "unemployable." A survey of a typical upstate city in 1941 found that half the families on home relief contained no one capable of working, because they were too young or too old, physically handicapped or needed to take care of dependent children. Although the Board of Social Welfare expected the definition of unemployable to vary according to the demands of the labor market, it declared that many on relief "certainly cannot find a place in the competitive world of commerce and industry. They will constitute a charge upon society in good times as well as bad, for they are not affected to any important degree by the ebb and flow of prosperity." [66]

The waning of the Depression noticeably transformed the group of relief recipients described as "employable." Gradual improvements in the economy enabled most middle-class professionals, such as doctors, teachers, and engineers, to regain their jobs. However, many members of the lower class were forced to remain on relief, because they either lacked skills or faced discrimination in hiring. By 1941, 15 percent of the state's employable public charges were aliens, excluded from the WPA and most defense work.[67] At the same time, New York City contained almost three-quarters of the state's relief load, and the majority of the city's cases consisted of aliens and blacks. Although both groups included many unskilled workers, even many men with a trade found that a variety of discriminatory practices kept them unemployed.[68] As early as 1937, blacks, who constituted only 5 percent of the city's total population, made up 22 percent of the welfare rolls. In a remarkable statement, the executive director of New York's Urban League pointed out the implication of these figures: "Unless there is a change in the attitude of those responsible for this condition, which more and more tends to force Negroes on relief and bar them from participation on regular jobs, the Negro population of our urban centers will inevitably become wards of the State." [69]

Beginning in 1939, the La Guardia administration spearheaded a campaign against able-bodied people still on the dole. With federal appropriations for the WPA dropping, New York City looked to the state to take up the slack through a revival of the 40 percent reimbursement for local work relief. Pointing to the large number of aliens on home relief, Mayor La Guardia asserted privately that "the City and State [are] entitled to something in return for assistance." [70] Furthermore, the WPA's ban on the use of noncitizens, "instead of penalizing the aliens, . . . gives them a most favored status," La Guardia complained in 1941. "While others on home relief are assigned to do some work on WPA, the aliens for the past two years have sat comfortably and idly and uselessly enjoying home relief without any risk or requirement to do any work." [71] A return to work relief would also give welfare bureaus a means of checking up on clients who sometimes earned extra money on the side. "If we had a case of which we were suspicious," La Guardia asserted, "we could send a person to a job where he would be assigned at odd times which would prevent him from having another job." [72]

Support for La Guardia's proposal came from upstate Republicans. An assemblyman from Gloversville, who sponsored legislation to restore local work relief, declared that naturalized citizens on the WPA felt "worse off than aliens, who may be fed and clothed by the community but can't be put to work." In addition, he argued that it was not "fair to ask the taxpayers to shell out relief without getting something back." Rejecting the principles of the Welfare State, the assemblyman concluded:

> There is no point, as I see it, in feeding, clothing, and housing able-bodied men who contribute nothing to their own maintenance, let alone their self-respect. . . .
>
> Now neither the man is satisfied, nor the community and its taxpayers who support him. If able-bodied, he is nothing more than a glorified pauper—glorified by the New Deal or some other outlandish mode of thinking whose theme is:
>
> "I will not work unless I get paid what I think I am worth; and I will not beg. Take care of me. . . ."
>
> I believe that able-bodied men should work for their bread, if that is un-American, if that is inhuman, if that is contrary to the conception of the New Day and the New Deal, so long to human character, and so long to Mr. Tax Payer.[73]

In the late 1930s, a number of states resorted to local work relief not only to supplement the WPA but also to enforce a kind of "work test" for people on home relief. The staff of the WPA considered this step "a veneered return to Queen Elizabeth's theory of pauper relief." Often it turned welfare clients into a source of cheap labor which displaced regular municipal employees.[74] In New York, significant opposition to the dole did not surface until middle-class professionals had gone off relief and welfare rolls included a noticeably large proportion of immigrants and blacks. At that point, many New Yorkers suddenly wanted relief recipients to prove their worthiness by working for welfare payments. "Frankly," La Guardia admitted to Lehman, "I do not expect to get much work out of them but the check and control, I believe, will mean a great deal to us." [75]

The New York State Department of Social Welfare objected to the plan, which became known as "work for relief." The department feared it would lead to the exploitation of welfare clients and further curtailment of the WPA. In addition, it would necessitate restoration of a state works division to supervise the projects.[76] During the 1939 legislative session, Democratic lawmakers also opposed the idea of state aid for work relief, but Republican majorities in both houses passed several bills designed to implement such a program. G.O.P. legislators expected many relief recipients to refuse public assistance if they had to work for it. The governor, however, recognizing that Republicans had a distorted view of the welfare population, vetoed the legislation for strictly financial reasons. Since most public charges relied on government aid through no fault of their own, Lehman declared that a return to more expensive work relief would inflate the cost of public assistance by millions of dollars.[77]

Sentiment in favor of municipal work relief mounted in New York State year by year. "Man has been decreed by an Authority wiser than the State Board of Social Welfare to 'earn his bread by the sweat of his brow,'" asserted one of La Guardia's advisers on welfare matters.[78] In the 1940 legislature, work relief bills picked up the support of most Democrats as well as Republicans, and there was speculation that the governor would add his approval. Nevertheless, Lehman again followed the advice of the Department of Social Welfare and blocked enactment of the measure.[79]

After taking a similar position in 1941 the governor finally acquiesced in 1942. During the latter year, the State Board of Social Welfare withdrew its opposition because the outbreak of war changed the situation. On the one hand, minority groups and noncitizens confronted obvious discrimination in securing employment in war industries, and, on the other hand, some cities had difficulty completing minor maintenance owing to the growing labor shortage. As a temporary means of coping with both problems, the Board of Social Welfare endorsed the restricted work relief measure adopted for one year by the legislature in 1942. This act, signed by the governor, provided for a 40 percent state reimbursement for work relief wages on approved local projects. The law also contained safeguards against the misuse of either the program or its workers.[80]

New York City quickly established numerous projects, which furnished 14,000 jobs, particularly for needy aliens and blacks. The city also cut off aid for several hundred indigent persons who refused to work for relief. Describing this as a "work-or-starve" program, social welfare journals considered it a backward step.[81] Above all, it showed that continued acceptance of the Welfare State might depend on who received government benefits. Even before the Depression ended, some New Yorkers questioned whether unemployed blacks and immigrants deserved home relief as a matter of right.

In defense of this apparently permanent welfare class, the State Board of Social Welfare tried to get help from Washington. During the early 1940s, the board called for the resumption of federal grants-in-aid to supplement state and local expenditures for home relief. Since the enactment of the Social Security Act in 1935, the federal government had subsidized the cost of public assistance for three categories of needy people—the aged, dependent children, and the blind. In addition to contributing to social security recipients, the state and local communities paid entirely for all other impoverished through home relief, or "general assistance" as it became known. Throughout this period, more money went for home relief in New York State than the other three categories combined, since those in need of general assistance outnumbered the people receiving social security (see Fig. 3). The extension of national grants for home relief would not have decreased the total cost of public assistance, but it would have given access to the greater tax resources of the federal government.[82]

Since New York could afford the expense of unemployment relief, it stressed that the issue involved more than fiscal considerations. According to the Board of Social Welfare, the movement of indigent families from one state to another made public assistance a national problem. Federal aid, based on minimum guidelines, would improve welfare standards throughout the country and help remove any stigma still attached to idleness forced on able-bodied people who were excluded from the Social Security Act. When added to the three types of categorical relief already covered by social security, federal grants for general assistance "would complete the circle of Federal responsibility for the needy." [83]

Washington's failure to aid all the indigent showed in part the political weakness of those needing general assistance. Unskilled blacks and aliens, who composed much of New York's welfare population by 1940, were unorganized and received little attention in the halls of Congress. Relief recipients without citizenship lacked even the most basic tool of political leverage—the vote. Thus a large number of people dependent on the government gained none of the federal benefits extended to better-organized groups like the aged and the handicapped.[84]

Albany made up for some of the shortcomings of federal welfare services. Until 1931, the state had supplied absolutely nothing for local poor relief, but during the succeeding six years, it borrowed $215 million for unemployment relief and appropriated $60 million from tax revenues (see Table 2, columns 2 and 3). During Lehman's last term in Albany, over 10 percent of the state budget annually went for general assistance (see Table 2, column 4).

Under the impact of the Depression, New York State assumed a new role in unemployment relief. Beginning in 1931, Albany added its funds, and two years later

Fig. 3. Obligations incurred for public assistance*
in New York State, 1932–40.

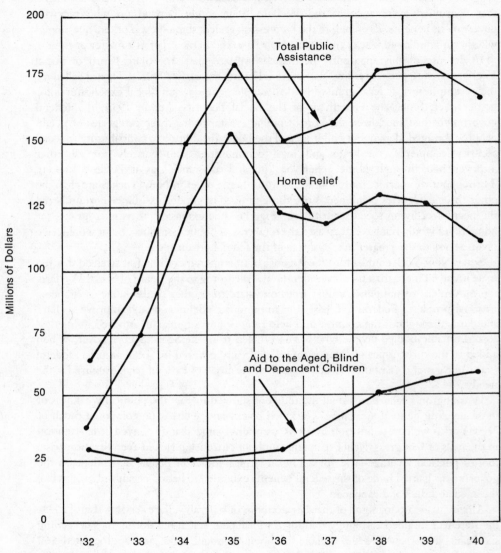

3. Obligations incurred for public assistance in New York State, 1932-40.*

* Exclusive of work relief.

Source: New York State Department of Social Welfare, *Democracy Cares*, p. 77.

Table 2
New York State Expenditures for
Unemployment Relief, 1931–42

Fiscal Year	Relief Outlay from Bond Issues	Current Revenues	
		Relief Outlay[a]	Percentage of Total Budget
(1)	(2)	(3)	(4)
1931	....	....	..
1932	$15,000,000	$25,000,000	
1933	27,000,000	....	8
1934	58,000,000	....	..
1935	30,000,000	10,000,000	..
1936	70,000,000	10,000,000	3
1937	15,000,000	15,006,670	3
1938	....	44,000,000	5
1939	....	48,500,000	11
1940	....	59,917,400	12
1941	....	53,537,596	15
1942	....	50,000,000	14
			12

[a]Exclusive of debt service for the retirement of relief bonds.

Sources: HHL, *Public Papers, 1933-42;* New York, *Annual Report of the Department of Audit and Control* (Albany, 1932-42).

those of Washington, to local relief efforts. During almost six years of temporary, emergency service, TERA supervised the distribution of over one billion dollars to five million New Yorkers, about 40 percent of the state's population.[85]

In 1936, New York State accepted permanent responsibility for supplementing community welfare expenses. This step marked a significant advance in the gradual transition from poor relief to a system of general assistance which recognized the causes of economic dependence as social rather than personal and provided public aid to the unemployed as a matter of right rather than charity. Following the example of TERA, Albany furnished grants-in-aid at the rate of 40 percent and set guidelines to assure a minimum level of quality. Although local welfare bureaus continued to distribute relief funds, they did so on the basis of the Welfare State, which guaranteed a minimum standard of living for all New Yorkers unable to earn it themselves. After surveying municipal services in 1938, a group of delegates to the state's constitutional convention exclaimed: "The most revolutionary change . . . has taken place in the sphere of welfare activities." [86]

NOTES

1. *Rochester Times Union,* October 15, 1934.
2. *New York Times,* September 23, 1934.
3. Hickok Report, October 2-12, 1933, "Hickok Reports," Harry Hopkins Papers, FDRL.
4. Wayne W. Parrish to Harry Hopkins, November 17, 1934, "Narrative Field Reports," ibid.
5. Wayne W. Parrish to Harry Hopkins, November 11, 1934, ibid.
6. Ibid.
7. David C. Adie, "A State Handles Its Public Welfare Problems," *Social Service Review,* VII (September 1933): 420.
8. *The New York Red Book, 1933* (Albany, 1933), p. 316; "In Memoriam: David C. Adie, 1888-1943," *Social Service Review,* XVII (June 1943): 227-28; Interview of HHL by Allan Nevins, February 2, 1959, Nevins Research File, HHLP.
9. *Buffalo Evening News,* April 5, 1934. See also Adie Address, May 22, 1934, "Social Welfare—General, 1933-36," Reel 88, GP, HHLP.
10. David C. Adie, "The Organization of a National Welfare Program," *Social Service Review,* VIII (September 1934): 424-25.
11. Ibid., pp. 426-28.
12. HHL Message to the Legislature, April 18, 1934, *Public Papers, 1934,* pp. 122-25; *Laws of New York, 1934,* Chap. 718.
13. Alfred H. Schoellkopf to HHL, July 13, 1934, HHL to Schoellkopf, July 20, 1934, Gen. Corr., 1933-40, HHLP; Folks to HHL, September 28, October 30, 1934, HHL to Folks, October 1, 1934, "$40,000,000 Bond Issue," Reel 34, GP, HHLP. The results of the balloting were 1,422,177 votes in favor and 368,589 opposed. New York State, *Legislative Manual, 1935* (Albany, 1935), p. 980.
14. *New York Times,* May 31, June, 5, 24, 1934.
15. HHL Message to the Legislature, July 24, 1934, *Public Papers, 1934,* pp. 146-47; *Laws of New York, 1934,* chap. 873; A. A. Berle, Jr., to Franklin D. Roosevelt, July 25, 1934, PPF 1306, FDRL.
16. *New York Times,* August 30, September 15, 26, 30, October 2, November 11, 21, 1934.
17. *Laws of New York, 1935,* chap. 601; *Laws of New York, 1936,* chap. 414; *Laws of New York, 1937,* chap. 327; *Laws of New York, 1938,* chap. 444; *Laws of New York, 1939,* chap. 659; *Laws of New York, 1940,* chap. 245; *Laws of New York, 1941,* chap. 200.
18. In 1942, the state gave all its communities additional taxing authority on a permanent basis, which made unemployment relief a regular item in municipal budgets. *Laws of New York, 1942,* chap. 755; *New York Times,* April 1, 1942.
19. Preliminary draft, Alfred H. Schoellkopf to HHL, June 4, 1934, Frederick I. Daniels to HHL, June 8, 1934, "Unemployment Relief Commission, 1933-35," Reel 98, GP, HHLP. (Hereinafter referred to as "URC.")
20. Commission members included Winthrop W. Aldrich (chairman of the board of the Chase National Bank), William P. Capes (secretary of the State Conference of Mayors,), Homer Folks, Fred J. Freestone (head of the State Grange), Mary L. Gibbons (director of the New York City Emergency Relief Bureau), Porter R. Lee (a former president of the National Conference of Social Workers), Thomas J. Lyons (a vice president of the State Federation

of Labor), and G. William Magly (an official of the Association of Real Estate Boards). For a complete list of the thirty-four members, see *Public Papers, 1934,* pp. 426-27.

21. Press Release, August 3, 1934, Wardwell to HHL, April 6, 1935, "URC," Reel 98, GP, HHLP; Interview of Hugh Jackson by Allan Nevins, December 12, 1961, Nevins Research File, HHLP. For the commission studies, see New York State Commission on Unemployment Relief, *The Public Employment Services in the State of New York* (Albany, 1935), *The Administration of Home Relief in New York City* (Albany, 1935), *Work Relief Projects of the Public Works Type in the State of New York* (Albany, 1935), *State and Local Welfare Organization in the State of New York* (Albany, 1936), *Public Relief for Transient and Non-Settled Persons in the State of New York* (Albany, 1936), *Work Relief in the State of New York* (Albany, 1936).

22. "Preliminary Report of the Commission on Unemployment Relief," January 19, 1935, *Public Papers, 1935,* pp. 78, 82-83; Allen Wardwell to HHL, February 1, 1935, HHL to Wardwell, January 26, 1935, "URC," Reel 98, GP, HHLP.

23. *Buffalo Evening News,* January 14, 1935.

24. *New York Times,* January 10, 11, 14, February 5, 1935; *Laws of New York, 1935,* chap. 25.

25. HHL Address, November 1, 1935, *Public Papers, 1935,* p. 938; TERA, *Administration of Public Unemployment Relief in New York State: Its Scope, Accomplishments and Cost, April 1, 1934-March 31, 1935* (Albany, 1935), p. 5; *New York Times,* March 18, 31, 1935.

26. HHL to Hopkins, January 17, 1935, "TERA," 1935, Reel 95, GP, HHLP; Hopkins to HHL, January 23, 1935, "Hopkins, Harry," Reel 45, ibid.

27. HHL Message to the Legislature, January 28, 1935, *Public Papers, 1935,* pp. 95-96.

28. HHL Message to the Legislature, March 28, 1935, *Public Papers, 1935,* pp. 140-42; *Laws of New York, 1935,* chap. 505.

29. "Minutes of Meeting of the TERA," May 28, 1935, New York, 400, Federal Emergency Relief Administration Records, Record Group 69, National Archives. (Hereinafter referred to as FERA Records.)

30. Transcript of Harry Hopkins and Alfred H. Schoellkopf Conversation, May 13, 1935, "Telephone Conversations with State Relief Directors, *et al.,* New York," Hopkins Papers; "Minutes of Meeting of the TERA," June 14, 1935, NY, 400, FERA Records.

31. "Minutes of a Special Meeting of the TERA, Held in Washington," June 15, 1935, NY, 400, FERA Records. The WPA divided New York State into two administrative regions with New York City forming one unit and the rest of the state another. The fiercely bellicose Hugh Johnson, formerly chief of the National Recovery Administration, served as first head of the WPA in New York City. His selection undoubtedly impressed upon New Yorkers the high degree of independence the president expected from the WPA. Harry Hopkins to Lester W. Herzog, June 25, 1935, New York, 610, State Series, Works Progress Administration Records, Record Group 69, National Archives; *New York Times,* June 26, 1935.

32. Transcript of Harry Hopkins and Hugh Johnson Conversation, July 2, 1935, "Telephone Conversation, New York," Hopkins Papers; "Minutes of Meeting of the TERA," July 31, September 5, 26, 1935, NY, 400, FERA Records.

33. HHL to FDR, September 11, 1935, HHL to Harry Hopkins, September 11, 1935, Memorandum for the President [unsigned], September 11, 1935, OF 91, FDRL.

34. Hopkins to HHL, September 19, 1935, "USFERA," Reel 99, GP, HHLP; James Farley to FDR, October 11, 1935, FDR to Comptroller General McCarl, October 14, 1935,

Hopkins to Corrington Gill, October 15, 1935, OF 444-C, FDRL; Hopkins to Lester Herzog, October 27, 1935, Aubrey Williams to Frederick I. Daniels, November 1, 1935, NY, 610, WPA Records.

35. Transcript of Hopkins and Fiorello La Guardia Conversation, November 7, 1935, FERA Box 65, Hopkins Papers.

36. Corrington to Gill to FDR, November 11, 1935, OF 444-C FDRL; Aubrey Williams to FDR, November 11, 1935, OF 91, FDRL; HHL to FDR, November 13, 1935, FDR to HHL, November 27, 1935, "TERA, 1935," Reel 95, GP, HHLP; *New York Times,* December 3, 1935.

37. Draft of a telegram to Harry Hopkins, enclosed in Frederick Daniels to HHL, December 4, 1935, "TERA, 1935," Reel 95, GP, HHLP.

38. HHL Message to the Legislature, January 1, 1936, *Public Papers, 1936,* pp. 9-11; *Buffalo Evening News,* May 5, 1936; *New York Times,* November 14, 1938.

39. HHL Message to the Legislature, January 3, 1936, *Public Papers, 1936,* pp. 44-45; New York State Governor's Commission on Unemployment Relief, *State and Local Welfare Organizations in the State of New York,* in *Public Papers, 1936,* pp. 46-49.

40. David M. Schneider and Albert Deutsch, *The History of Public Welfare in New York State, 1867-1940* (Chicago, 1941), pp. 376-77.

41. *Report of Mayor La Guardia's Committee on Unemployment Relief* (New York, 1935), pp. 57-58.

42. *Buffalo Evening News,* May 6, 1936.

43. *Buffalo Evening News,* May 13, 1936.

44. Homer Folks to HHL, January 29, 1936, "URC, 1936," Reel 98, GP, HHLP; Robert P. Lane to HHL, February 24, 1936, "Welfare Council of New York City," Reel 103, ibid.; Barklie M. Henry to HHL, February 27, 1936, "Association for Improving the Condition of the Poor," Reel 6, ibid; *New York Times,* January 4, 9, 1936.

45. Adie, "Memorandum Relative to the Wardwell Commission Recommendations," n.d., Adie to HHL, December 26, 1935, "URC, 1936," Reel 98, GP, HHLP.

46. *New York Times,* January 4, 1936.

47. Ibid., January 16, 19, February 23, 26, 1936.

48. HHL to Irving Ives, Irwin Steingut, George R. Fearon, John J. Dunnigan, Allen Wardwell, Frederick I. Daniels and Victor Ridder, January 29, 1936, "Unemployment Relief Conference, February 6, 1936," Reel 98, GP, HHLP; HHL Statement, February 6, 1936, *Public Papers, 1936,* p. 770; HHL to William H. Matthews, February 27, 1936, "Social Welfare, Board of—Reorganization," Reel 88, GP, HHLP.

49. *New York Times,* March 21, 27, 1936; *Laws of New York, 1936,* chap. 873.

50. HHL Memorandum, June 5, 1936, HHL Address, October 30, 1936, *Public Papers, 1936,* pp. 511, 1011. A constitutional amendment adopted in 1938, specifically empowered the state to provide aid for the needy. N.Y. Const., art. VII, sec. 8 (1938).

51. New York State Department of Labor, *Trend of Employment in New York State Factories from 1914 to 1939* (Albany, 1940), pp. 17, 108; New York State Board of Social Welfare, *Annual Report for the Year 1938,* p. 18, in New York State, *Legislative Documents* (Albany, 1939), No. 68 (hereinafter referred to as Leg. Doc.); *New York Times,* April 4, 29, 1938.

52. *New York Times,* April 8, 1937; HHL Message to the Legislature, April 12, 1937, *Public Papers, 1937,* pp. 243-45; *Laws of New York, 1937,* chap. 321. Forty-seven cities quickly enacted the 1 percent utility tax. William P. Capes to HHL, September 28, 1937, "Conference of Mayors, 1936-1942," Reel 20, GP, HHLP.

53. New York State Board of Social Welfare, *Annual Report for the Year 1940,* Leg. Doc. No.

68 (1941), p. 24. See also New York State, *Report of the Joint Legislative Committee on State Fiscal Policies,* Leg. Doc. 41 (1938), pp. 124-39.

54. La Guardia to HHL, February 7, March 5, 8, 17, 1938, La Guardia and the Board of Estimate to Isidore Dollinger, March 14, 1938, Alex Rose to HHL, March 8, 1938, HHL to La Guardia, February 8, March 3, 10, 24, 1938, "New York City—Relief Tax," Reel 70, GP, HHLP; HHL Message to the Legislature, March 18, 1938, *Public Papers, 1938,* p. 517; *New York Times,* March 23, April 6, 12, 1938.

55. *New York Times,* December 29, 1938; Leon H. Abbott to HHL, March 3, 1939, "New York State Association of Public Welfare Officials, " Reel 70, GP, HHLP; Alice Wood Wynd to HHL, December 11, 1938, HHL to Wynd, December 29, 1938, "Social Welfare—General, 1937-38," Reel 88, ibid.

56. HHL to Frederick I. Daniels, May 15, December 22, 1936, "TERA, 1936," Reel 95, ibid.; HHL to Daniels, July 29, 1937, HHL to Victor F. Ridder, February 28, 1938, "Social Welfare—General, 1937-38," Reel 88, ibid.

57. HHL Address, June 23, 1938, *Public Papers, 1938,* p. 517.

58. For a discussion of state taxation during this period, see *infra,* chap. X.

59. HHL to FDR, December 21, 1936, January 18, 1937, FDR to HHL, January 14, 1937, OF 444-C, FDRL; HHL to Philip LaFollette, Charles F. Hurley, Wilbur L. Cross, George H. Earle, Henry Horner, M. Clifford Townsend, Martin Davey, Elmer Benson, February 3, 1937, Earle to HHL, February 9, 1937, Cross to HHL, February 26, 1937, LaFollette to HHL, February 8, 1937, Robert E. Quinn to HHL, February 8, 1937, Benson to HHL, February 11, 1937, "Unemployment Relief—Governor's Conference, April 9, 1937," Reel 98, GP, HHLP; *New York Times,* February 27, 1937. Frank Murphy of Michigan sympathized with the objectives of the conference but was unable to attend. Murphy to HHL, February 28, 1937, "Governor's Conference, 1937," Reel 98, GP, HHLP.

60. Benson, Hurley, Horner, LaFollette, Lehman, and Quinn to FDR, February 28, 1937, *Public Papers, 1937,* pp. 607-8; *New York Times,* March 7, April 10, 12, 1937.

61. *New York Times,* July 20, 1937.

62. HHL Message to the Legislature, January 5, 1938, *Public Papers, 1938,* pp. 39-40.

63. For a discussion of the shift in federal policy, see William E. Leuchtenburg, *Franklin D. Roosevelt and the New Deal, 1932-1940* (New York, 1963), pp. 244-51, 256-57.

64. HHL to Robert F. Wagner, James Mead, and Thomas H. Cullen, January 13, 1939, HHL to the Chairman and Members of the Appropriations Committee of the U.S. Senate, January 18, 1939, "Works Projects Administration—General, 1939-1940," Reel 105, GP, HHLP; HHL to Edward T. Taylor, May 24, 1939, "WPA—Questionnaire," ibid. From 1936 to 1941, WPA appropriations dropped 72 percent while New York's home relief expenditures fell only 49 percent. During the period 1937 to 1940, at least 50 percent of the workers discharged from the WPA returned to municipal welfare rolls shortly after dismissal. New York State Board of Social Welfare to the Congressional Representatives of New York State, April 10, 1940, "WPA—General," ibid.; New York State Department of Social Welfare, *Democracy Cares; The Story Behind Public Assistance in New York State* (Albany, 1941), p. 73.

65. U.S., Department of Commerce, Bureau of the Census, *Sixteenth Census of the United States, 1940: Population,* vol. II, pt. I, p. 90; New York State Board of Social Welfare, *Annual Report for the Year 1941,* Leg. Doc. No. 28 (1942), p. 26.

66. New York State Board of Social Welfare, *Annual Report, 1940,* p. 25; idem, *Annual Report, 1941,* pp. 19-20.

67. In 1939, Washington barred noncitizens from holding WPA jobs. Salvatore J. LaGumina,

"The New Deal, the Immigrants and Congressman Vito Marcantonio," *The International Migration Review,* IV (Spring 1970): 72-73.

68. New York State Board of Social Welfare, *Annual Report, 1941,* p. 21; New York State, *Annual Report of the Department of Social Welfare, July 1, 1941-June 30, 1942,* Leg. Doc. No. 11 (1943), p. 8.

69. *New York Times,* February 18, 1937.

70. La Guardia to HHL, April 13, 1940, Box 2565, Fiorello La Guardia Papers, New York City Municipal Archives.

71. La Guardia to HHL, April 21, 1941, Box 2566, ibid.

72. Draft of letter, La Guardia to HHL, May 1939 ["not used"], Box 2565, ibid.

73. Albany *Knickerbocker News,* February 3, 1939.

74. Howard O. Hunter to Lester Herzog, November 17, 1939, NY, 610, WPA Records; Corrington Gill, "Local Work Relief," *Survey Midmonthly,* LXXVI (May 1940): 157-59.

75. La Guardia to HHL, April 21, 1942, chap. 926 (1942), New York State Bill Jacket Collection, New York Public Library. (Hereinafter referred to as Bill Jackets.) For a discussion of the punitive aspects of the work test for welfare recipients, see Frances Fox Piven and Richard A. Cloward, *Regulating the Poor* (New York, 1971).

76. Memorandum, "Re: Lake Work Relief Bill," February 28, 1939, "WPA—Questionnaire," Reel 105, GP, HHLP.

77. *New York Times,* March 21, 1939; HHL Veto Message, May 13, 1939, and Veto Memorandum, June 15, 1939, *Public Papers, 1939,* pp. 261-62, 333.

78. Edmond Borgia Butler to La Guardia, April 12, 1940, Box 2565, La Guardia Papers.

79. Lester Herzog to F. C. Harrington, November 14, 1939, April 12, 1940, NY, 610, WPA Records; Elsie M. Bond to HHL, April 28, 1942, George Hallett to HHL, May 11, 1942, Bill Jackets, chap. 926 (1942); *New York Times,* March 30, 1940; "Memorandum Re Work Relief," February 2, 1940, "Social Welfare—General, 1940-42," Reel 88, GP, HHLP; HHL Veto Memorandum, April 27, 1940, *Public Papers, 1940,* pp. 293-94.

80. New York State Board of Social Welfare, *Annual Report for the Year 1942,* Leg. Doc. No. 38 (1943), pp. 11-12; *Laws of New York, 1942,* chap. 926; David C. Adie to HHL, March 20, 1942, Bill Jackets, chap. 926 (1942).

81. "Notes and Comments," *Social Service Review,* XVI (September 1942): 529; "The Social Front," *Survey Midmonthly,* LXXVIII (September 1942): 247.

82. New York State Board of Social Welfare, *Annual Report for the Year 1939,* Leg. Doc. No. 67 (1940), p. 18; idem, *Annual Report, 1941,* pp. 34-35; New York State Department of Social Welfare, *Democracy Cares,* p. 52.

83. New York State Board of Social Welfare to the Congressional Representatives of New York State, June 18, 1941, "Social Welfare—General, 1940-42," Reel 88, GP, HHLP. See also William Haber, "Relief: A Permanent Program," *Survey Graphic,* XXVII (December 1938): 591-94.

84. For a discussion of the role of pressure groups in the shaping of federal welfare policies, see Gilbert Y. Steiner, *Social Insecurity: The Politics of Welfare* (Chicago, 1966).

85. TERA, *Five Million People, One Billion Dollars* (Albany, 1937), p. 10.

86. New York State Constitutional Convention Committee, *New York City Government Functions and Problems* (Albany, 1938), p. 74.

IV

THE SEARCH FOR SECURITY

The Depression exposed the insecurity of life in modern America. As people watched the scourge of unemployment strike indiscriminately at every segment of society, they suddenly felt vulnerable and helpless. Remembering those days, a former white-collar employee of a publishing house recalled:

> Everyone was emotionally affected. We developed a fear of the future which was very difficult to overcome. Even though I eventually went into some fairly good jobs, there was still this constant dread: everything would be cut out from under you and you wouldn't know what to do. It would be even harder, because you were older.[1]

Facing an uncertain future, Americans finally recognized that not only unemployment but also old age, sickness, and fatherless families produced widespread poverty. In search of security against want, the country sought ways to cushion individuals against hazards beyond their control.

Advocates of government-sponsored social security won a series of victories during the 1930s. Although a small band of reformers had long campaigned for protection against the various causes of economic dependency, they had little success until the Depression brought massive destitution.[2] After the collapse of the economy focused public attention on the need for enhanced security, New York adopted a number of measures designed to guarantee a minimum standard of living for specific groups such as the unemployed and the aged. Often acting in concert with Washington, the Empire State extended both public assistance to relieve want and social insurance to keep people from becoming public charges. The enactment of this legislation marked another step in New York's acceptance of the Welfare State.

1

The drive for social security initially concentrated on insuring workers against unemployment, the most pervasive cause of destitution during the Depression. As the horrors of unemployment became apparent, reformers moved quickly to win adoption of mandatory compensation for the jobless, but they failed to agree on the best means of protecting laborers in the future. By 1933, proponents of job insurance divided into two major camps with their respective headquarters in Wisconsin and Ohio.

Wisconsin, the first state to pass an unemployment compensation law, followed the so-called American plan which was intended primarily to prevent unemployment. This uniquely American proposal required contributions from employers to be placed in separate company reserves. If the amount of money in a firm's exclusive compensation fund dropped below a certain minimum for each wage earner, the company had to replenish its account. Since the liability of each employer was limited to his own workers, this scheme assumed that businessmen would curb unemployment rather than pay the cost of compensation. The American plan excluded the spreading of risk through a single fund used in ordinary insurance and European social security programs, but supporters of this system hoped to avoid organized opposition from employers and private insurance companies by segregating contributions and limiting the role of government.[3]

The chief architect of the American plan, John B. Andrews, intentionally distinguished his proposal from European social insurance. As secretary of the American Association for Labor Legislation (AALL), a reform group which sought better government protection of workers, Andrews had first questioned the relevance of foreign experience in the wake of World War I, when Americans rejected compulsory health insurance modeled after the system established by Bismarck in the late nineteenth century. Throughout the United States opponents of state health insurance raised the cry of "Made in Germany," which helped to defeat the legislation. When the AALL then turned its attention to unemployment compensation, Andrews decided to avoid any connection with Europe.

> I think it is a mistake for us in this country to spend an undue amount of time discussing the British or any other system of European unemployment insurance. I think we can much more wisely build out of our own American experiences with accident insurance a practical unemployment compensation system with much better prospects of enactment here.[4]

Using the analogy of workmen's compensation, Andrews and his colleagues ultimately developed the scheme which they significantly called "An American Plan for Unemployment Reserve Funds."[5]

Soon after Wisconsin adopted a version of the American plan in 1932, the Ohio Commission on Unemployment drafted a competing proposal which drew heavily on European principles of job insurance. The Ohio plan, as it became known, stressed the goal of economic security for wage earners rather than the prevention of unemployment.

Since, it was reasoned, fluctuations in work forces lay largely beyond the control of individual firms, the Ohio measure sought adequate protection for the jobless through both employer and employee donations to a single statewide fund. This pooling of assessments spread the cost of job insurance among all businesses, which guaranteed that workers in industries plagued with unemployment would still receive ample benefits.[6]

While Wisconsin and Ohio prepared differing measures, the campaign for unemployment compensation gained momentum in the Empire State. Socialists had introduced a job insurance bill in the New York legislature as early as 1921, but the movement for mandatory benefits languished until the Depression. In 1931, John B. Andrews formed the New York Conference for Unemployment Insurance Legislation to promote this reform in the Empire State. Acting as an umbrella organization, the conference brought together leaders of a number of sympathetic groups including the League of Women Voters, the Consumers' League, and the Women's Trade Union League. Although headed in name by Howard S. Cullman, a millionaire businessman who helped with the election campaigns of Roosevelt and Lehman, the statewide job insurance lobby was largely the tool of Andrews, who tried to use it to further his American plan.[7]

With interest in unemployment insurance growing, Governor Roosevelt sponsored the creation of two commissions which studied the question and reported during 1932. One, an interstate panel made up of representatives from New York and six other industrial states, strongly recommended the establishment of compulsory unemployment reserves paid for by employers.[8] Although a New York legislative committee also advocated the eventual adoption of job insurance, its members suggested another year of hearings before the state committed itself to a particular system. The Republican-dominated legislature authorized continuation of the inquiry, but lawmakers rejected appeals from Roosevelt for the immediate passage of a compensation bill.[9]

As 1933 approached, the prospects for enactment of unemployment insurance in New York suddenly improved. The American Federation of Labor (AFL), which had traditionally resisted government intervention in labor-management relations, dramatically reversed its opposition to state-controlled compensation for the jobless. After the AFL endorsed the principle of compulsory job insurance at its national convention in December 1932, the New York State Federation of Labor put this item at the top of its agenda for legislative action.[10] Meanwhile, New York Republicans had revealed that they were now prepared to disregard the objections of businessmen. Despite appeals for further delay from employer organizations, the Republican chairman of the Joint Legislative Committee on Unemployment indicated repeatedly that his group would soon present a bill for speedy adoption of job insurance. In late 1932, he predicted state creation of a compensation system, "possibly within a year." [11]

The state's incoming chief executive proved more cautious. While campaigning for governor, Herbert Lehman had dedicated himself to a "program looking toward unemployment insurance," but he had expressed concern that a new compensation system might retard recovery if implemented during the depths of the Depression. Therefore, Lehman had urged the enactment of "moderate and conservative unemployment reserve legislation," which would not go into effect until business activity had revived sufficiently.[12] In his first message to the legislature, the new governor repeated his lukewarm call for a law "looking toward a system of unemployment insurance." [13]

Ignoring Lehman's go-slow attitude, leading pressure groups submitted compensation bills to Albany lawmakers. On behalf of the New York Conference for Unemployment Insurance Legislation, Senator Seabury C. Mastick, an upstate Republican, offered the latest version of the AALL plan, which established individual company reserves but permitted limited pooling of funds by industry or locality if this was found desirable by the state administration. The State Federation of Labor sponsored a similar piece of legislation, which largely copied the Mastick bill except for the provision of greater compensation. As introduced by Senator William T. Byrne, an Albany Democrat, the union proposal raised the maximum weekly payment from $12.50 to $15.00, extended the maximum benefit period from thirteen to sixteen weeks, and increased the rate of employer contributions from 2 to 3 percent. Both measures covered only workers making less than $2000 annually, and they set a three-week waiting period before payments could begin.[14]

During February 1933, the campaign for unemployment reserves suffered an unexpected setback. In the long-awaited report of the Joint Legislative Committee on Unemployment, the majority again endorsed the principle of compulsory compensation but recommended further postponement of its enactment.[15] All but one of the Republican members joined representatives of business and labor in accepting the arguments of employers, who contended that if forced to establish unemployment reserves before an upturn in the economy, they would fire part-time workers rather than build accounts for them. Since such action might ultimately expand welfare rolls, the committee's majority suggested that the state defer creation of job insurance.[16] This conclusion overlooked the fact that the Mastick bill, first introduced in 1931, specifically excluded part-time wage earners. Furthermore, as dissenting committee members pointed out, the state could overcome the objections of businessmen by passing enabling legislation which stipulated that compulsory compensation go into effect when evidence indicated an improvement in economic conditions.[17]

Organized labor's endorsement of the majority report revealed the weakness of its recent conversion to job insurance. The union representative who participated in the legislative inquiry voted for postponement because officials of the State Federation of Labor still feared that implementation of this reform might undermine organizing campaigns among workers. Several powerful union chiefs in New York continued to oppose unemployment insurance publicly, while others appeared at best indifferent to the outcome of the pending legislative battle. Thus delay apparently suited cautious labor leaders as much as businessmen who worried about the economic impact of compulsory compensation.[18]

Governor Lehman also hesitated to endorse any of the job insurance bills. In a private interview on February 14, John Andrews found that Lehman favored the idea in principle but was concerned about the proper time for putting it into effect. The governor feared that October 1, 1933, as stipulated by both the Mastick and Byrne bills, would be too soon with unemployment running so high. When Andrews suggested the possibility of waiting for a 10 percent rise in manufacturing employment instead of setting a specific date for implementation, Lehman countered that New York could also delay until other states or the Congress passed such legislation. Rejecting these alternatives as impractical, the head of the American Association for Labor Legislation left Albany with serious doubts about the depth of Lehman's liberalism. "In this state," Andrews concluded, "we have become accustomed to liberal Governors and I fear we are in for some disappointment during this administration." [19] However, soon after his meeting with Andrews, Lehman agreed to accept a job insurance law with "a broadly flexible formula" for fixing the time to inaugurate the system.[20]

Advocates of unemployment reserves decided to press for quick passage of a statute with a mechanism to postpone the date of implementation. Such delay represented a small concession, since most reformers conceived of state compensation as a means of dealing with future periods of unemployment. Although they assumed that the existing crisis would subside before industry could build up sufficient reserves, proponents of insurance sought an immediate legislative commitment to the principle because the Depression had generated widespread support for measures to enhance social security.[21] Experience showed, according to John B. Andrews, that "industrial leaders and legislators forget about unemployment as soon as business revives." [22] In hopes of overcoming resistance from the governor and businessmen, both the Conference for Unemployment Insurance and the State Federation of Labor amended their bills to defer the start of employer contributions until New York's employment index rose 20 percent above the level of February 1933.[23]

Disregarding this compromise, spokesmen for employers persisted in attacking unemployment insurance. The Chamber of Commerce charged that mandatory benefits for the jobless would tend to "lessen the interest of the worker in keeping his job or in getting other work." The group found job insurance "objectionable for social, political, and economic reasons." [24] In April, twenty-two leaders of business organizations called for a moratorium on legislation that would increase the financial burdens on New York firms and place them at a competitive disadvantage nationally.[25]

When Lehman failed to endorse either of the amended insurance bills, over seven hundred prominent New Yorkers appealed to him for action. Stressing that public concern with the problems of unemployment would dissipate with the return of prosperity, the petitioners asked that the state take immediate steps to set up a system of compensation for the jobless. Lehman responded to this plea by issuing a special message which called for the prompt approval of compulsory unemployment reserves. Since he expected compensation under the American plan to help stabilize factory employment, the governor defended job insurance as part of a "conservative program for the well-being of the industries of this State." Lehman did not endorse any particular bill before the legislature, but he suggested that the one adopted not take effect until the index of state employment rose twenty points and remained there for at least six months.[26]

Lehman's endorsement put new life in the drive for unemployment insurance. Three days after lawmakers received his message, the Senate approved labor's Byrne bill with the delaying amendment dictated by the governor. Although Democrats controlled the upper house by a bare majority, the desertion of an upstate senator made success dependent upon aid from members of the opposition. Two Republicans, one from Rochester and the other from Brooklyn, defied their party leaders and joined twenty-five Democrats to provide one more than the minimum number of votes needed for passage. However, with adjournment approaching, Republicans who dominated the Assembly killed the Byrne measure in committee.[27]

Soon after the end of the 1933 legislative session, a new force joined the crusade for unemployment insurance. The American Association for Old Age Security, organized in 1927 to fight for old age pensions, expanded its activity to encompass unemployment and health insurance. Led by the fiery Abraham Epstein, the group changed its name to the American Association for Social Security (AASS) and turned its attention to compensation for the jobless. As champions of social insurance modeled after European examples, Epstein and his collaborators sought an alternative to the American plan of the AALL. After a series of conferences in New York during the summer and fall of 1933, the AASS completed drafting a job insurance bill which resembled the Ohio plan. The AASS proposal called for contributions from employers, employees, and the state to go into a single pooled fund from which unemployed laborers would draw insurance benefits.[28]

The emergence of the American Association for Social Security rekindled an old feud between Abraham Epstein and John B. Andrews. After winning broad agreement on his American plan in the Empire State, Andrews naturally resented the appearance of a competing proposal which might divide the coalition he had brought together.[29] Moreover, Epstein's leadership of the rival faction made a bitter confrontation almost inevitable because he and Andrews had quarreled before and, by 1933, they scarcely spoke. In spite of their common interest in social reform, the two men differed in everything from principles to temperament. Andrews, a native-born American with his roots in Wisconsin, had long tried to divorce the social security movement from European experience which held little attraction for many Americans. His cautiousness carried over into political battles where, as secretary of the American Association for Labor Legislation, he readily compromised in order to win even the smallest legislative advance. Epstein, a Russian immigrant, admired European social insurance systems and sought to transplant them to his adopted country. In 1927, the impatient young Epstein organized the American Association for Old Age Security as an alternative to Andrews' more conservative American Association for Labor Legislation. Although this move produced much ill will, Epstein had never hesitated to fight anyone, including fellow reformers, who failed to stand for the fullest measure of economic security for the helpless and indigent.[30]

The controversy surrounding alternative systems of unemployment compensation focused on the type of fund to be established. At one extreme stood John Andrews and supporters of the American plan who favored segregated company reserves as a means of stimulating the prevention of unemployment. At the other extreme, Abraham Epstein and defenders of the single state fund contended that adequate protection of laborers required statewide pooling which would spread the risk among all employers in a manner approaching ordinary insurance. New York became the battleground for these competing principles, since both Andrews and Epstein recognized that any law enacted by the nation's most populous state could well serve as a model for the rest of the country.[31]

Another Andrews—Elmer F. Andrews, New York's industrial commissioner—tried to bring the two sides together. As a civil engineer who had become an expert in workmen's compensation, Elmer Andrews had won the respect of Frances Perkins while he had held the post of assistant industrial commissioner in New York. When Perkins had taken over as FDR's Secretary of Labor in 1933, she had recommended Andrews to succeed her as head of the state's Department of Labor. In accepting the advice, Governor Lehman had promoted a man who turned out to be an ardent champion of the Little New Deal.[32] However, Elmer Andrews failed in his initial attempt to win agreement on a single job insurance bill late in 1933. He held a series of meetings with representatives of labor, the AALL, the AASS, and the Conference for Unemployment Insurance, but the only possible compromise—some form of partial pooling—generated little enthusiasm. In December, the talks collapsed, with both John Andrews and Abraham Epstein sticking to their own schemes while other participants, including Commissioner Andrews, could not decide which course to follow.[33]

A thirty-nine-year-old labor leader, George Meany, ultimately determined the shape of job insurance in New York. Heavy set and bald, with a broad, stubby nose, this Irishman from the Bronx looked like a bulldog and often acted like one. Born in New York City, Meany had followed in his father's footsteps and become a plumber. In 1922, young George had won election as business agent of the Manhattan-Bronx plumbers' local which his father had once headed. Hard working and completely honest in a position often riddled with graft, Meany had risen to vice president of the State Federation of Labor in 1932 and, soon thereafter, he had taken over leadership of the federation's committee on unemployment insurance. His mastery of this complex issue and successful defense of union interests catapulted Meany into the office of president of the New York State Federation of Labor, which he held from August 1934 until his election as secretary-treasurer of the AFL in 1939.[34]

During the winter of 1933-34, George Meany decided what stand organized labor should take on the job insurance fund. Although the state federation had initially backed John Andrews' American plan, union officials had remained aloof from the dispute that subsequently developed between Andrews and Epstein. In the discussions held by the industrial commissioner, Meany said only that as labor's representative he wanted the best possible protection for workers. When these conferences failed to produce an agreement, Andrews and Epstein each set out to win over organized labor.

While John Andrews carried on a rearguard holding action, Epstein destroyed union support for the American plan.[35] The head of the AASS exposed the weakness of segregated reserves to George Meany. Epstein pointed out that an "individual company reserve plan is not much better than any other company welfare plan," because segregated accounts would cripple trade unionism by tying workers to employers who had built up ample compensation funds. Moreover, firms plagued by seasonal unemployment beyond their control, such as those in the construction industry, could never accumulate sufficient reserves to protect their own employees. Epstein stressed that adequate security for all wage earners demanded real insurance through the statewide pooling of compensation funds, which would spread the risk among all employers.[36] These arguments converted George Meany to the single pool.[37] Shortly after the legislature convened in January 1934, Meany repudiated previous union backing of segregated accounts, because labor leaders saw a strong threat of company unions in any system of plant reserves. "Let's be plain," Meany concluded, "the State Federation has decided on the state pool and won't support anything else." [38] Organized labor's adoption of "the left wing single pool system," as John Andrews scornfully called it, marked a significant move in the direction of real insurance.[39]

The governor refused to commit himself to labor's new position. Although he personally preferred the more conservative American plan offered in 1933, Lehman knew too little about the concept of the single pool either to endorse or to reject it.[40] Having already called for the "immediate enactment" of unemployment insurance in his annual message for 1934, the governor chose to remain neutral in the controversy of reserves versus pooling, since reformers themselves could not agree on the best method. Lehman implied that he would sign into law any compensation measure that cleared the legislature.[41]

The absence of an official administration bill weakened the campaign for job insurance in 1934. The New York Conference for Unemployment Insurance, though deeply divided over the issue of pooling, decided to reaffirm its long-standing support for John Andrews' American plan of company reserves. However, as a small concession to advocates of pooling, the new Mastick-Steingut bill provided that one-tenth of each employer's donations should go into a contingency fund to supplement any individual reserves that ran out.[42] Senator Byrne again sponsored the State Federation of Labor measure, which copied the Mastick-Steingut draft except for the addition of a pooled fund. This reliance on the AALL proposal troubled Abraham Epstein, who found the union bill badly drawn and full of contradictions.[43] However, the American Association for Social Security decided against introducing its model bill, because that would further divide advocates of insurance. "Personally I feel that no matter how bad the Federation bill, . . . it is wiser for us to stick with them," Epstein concluded.[44]

In April 1934, a legislative hearing revealed a growing consensus on job insurance. Divorcing himself from John Andrews' hard-line position, Howard Cullman of the Conference for Unemployment Insurance pleaded for quick action on either of the leading compensation measures before people forgot the evils of the Depression and the horrors of unemployment. Backing for this point of view unexpectedly came from four of New York City's Republican county committees. Despite some support for both the Mastick and the Byrne bills, most proponents of insurance appealed for a common state fund because, as one lawyer put it, "Unemployment insurance is not a scheme to avoid unemployment, but to relieve it." [45]

Businessmen generally opposed compulsory compensation of any kind. Only Eastman Kodak and General Electric, two of the state's largest corporations, endorsed the principle of company reserves, though they rejected any pooling of funds. Since both firms usually had low rates of unemployment and had already established their own systems of compensation, they could expect the state's creation of segregated accounts to cost them little.[46] Smaller businessmen, represented by the Chamber of Commerce, Associated Industries, and the Merchants' Association, stood firmly against the imposition of any additional financial burdens which would place New York firms at a competitive disadvantage in interstate business.[47]

In spite of increased support for unemployment compensation in 1934, legislation advanced no further than the previous year. The Democratic-controlled Senate again passed the Byrne bill by the slimmest of margins. When an insurgent Democrat refused to go along with the other twenty-five members of his party, a Brooklyn Republican cast the deciding vote, as he had in 1933. However, upstate Republican assemblymen blocked consideration of the measure by the lower house. With Mayor La Guardia's backing, eight Republicans from New York City and another from Westchester joined a virtually solid bloc of Democrats in favor of job insurance, but the coalition fell eight votes short of the majority required to dislodge the legislation from committee.[48]

Abraham Epstein considered the 1934 legislative session a great success: "I never for one moment believed that New York was ready for the enactment of an unemployment insurance law this year, and everything we accomplished was more than we could possibly have hoped for." [49] His campaign for a single state fund had won over the Federation of Labor, which brought many other converts into the fold. Since most reform groups had lined up behind the union bill, Epstein concluded that "the entire issue of reserves vs. a state pooled fund in New York state is now settled." [50] The dimensions of Epstein's achievement soon became fully apparent. In June 1934, the members of the New York Conference for Unemployment Insurance Legislation voted unanimously to endorse in the future a proposal that provided for greater pooling than the Mastick bill they had previously sponsored.[51]

Although most New Yorkers had deserted company reserves by the summer of 1934, John Andrews remained committed to his American plan. He warned state union officials of "the apparent conspiracy to bring about forced contributions by workers" through the introduction of a common fund.[52] The leader of the AALL linked this conspiracy to "the 'adroit propaganda' carried on by some of the Socialist and Communist advocates of the British or Ohio system of so-called unemployment 'insurance.' " [53]   Addressing himself to businessmen, Andrews asked if they wanted assessments for the jobless "thrown into one promiscuous pool as is done under some foreign schemes." [54] Despite his sniping at Epstein and the single-fund idea, Andrews failed to reverse the direction of the social insurance movement in the Empire State.

In preparation for the 1935 legislative session, advocates of job insurance finally

formed a united front. At a conference called by Industrial Commissioner Elmer
Andrews, all representatives of reform groups, with the exception of John Andrews,
agreed to back labor's demand for a pooled fund. Those previously committed to
employer reserves, including the industrial commissioner, had reached the conclusion
that a statewide fund provided greater security for workers. In explaining his conversion
to pooling, Elmer Andrews pointed out that an individual store or factory owner could
not prevent unemployment, and he added that the government could more easily
administer a single pool than segregated accounts.[55]

Having accepted the principle of a state fund, the conferees endorsed a new bill which
incorporated features of both the Wisconsin and the Ohio plans. While creating the
pooled fund proposed in Ohio, the measure copied Wisconsin by drawing exclusively on
contributions from employers. The other provisions of the New York legislation
generally followed the old Byrne and Mastick bills, which made New York's coverage
broader than that of Wisconsin, the only state that had already enacted unemployment
compensation. The federal Department of Labor considered New York's 1935 bill,
sponsored by Senator Byrne and Assemblyman John F. Killgrew, better than any yet
introduced in the country.[56]

When the Byrne-Killgrew measure went into the legislative hopper in January 1935,
all signs indicated its prompt passage. During his 1934 campaign for reelection, Lehman
had put job insurance at the top of his twelve-point labor program, and he had
condemned Old Guard Republicans who had blocked adoption of this reform in 1933
and 1934. With Democrats in control of the legislature, proponents of compensation
anticipated quick action in the upcoming session. But unexpected delays soon
developed.[57]

On January 17, 1935, President Roosevelt asked Congress for national social security
legislation, a proposal which raised the thorny issue of federal/state coordination. The
federal plan, sponsored by New York's Senator Wagner, encouraged the creation of
state unemployment insurance schemes through a tax-offset plan. Congress would levy a
federal payroll tax of a fixed percentage, but would permit employers to credit any
contributions they paid under a state job insurance law. Thus, if states passed statutes
requiring a payroll tax at least as large as that set by Congress, local businessmen remitted
nothing to Washington. If states failed to act, they lost the money that otherwise could
have formed a fund to compensate their jobless. The prospect of other states soon
establishing unemployment insurance undermined the position of New York opponents
who had argued that action by a single state would put its businessmen at a competitive
disadvantage. However, the Congressional bill set a minimum rate of employer
contributions which fell below that proposed in New York. While the Byrne-Killgrew
measure directed a flat 3 percent tax on payrolls, the federal rate would vary from 1 to 3
percent depending on the index of industrial production. This sliding scale meant that
the minimum national levy would initially be less than that proposed in the Empire
State.[58]

New York leaders tried to eliminate this potential differential so that foes of job
insurance could not use it as a weapon to defeat state legislation. Since a lower rate of

contributions would force a reduction in benefits, a committee of New Yorkers lobbied in Washington for an increase in the standards specified by the Wagner bill. When this effort failed, the state revised the Byrne-Killgrew proposal to provide for a sliding scale of from 1 to 3 percent during the first two years of operation. Thereafter, the payroll tax would remain a flat 3 percent.[59] Senator Wagner deplored this backward step, because his measure was designed to raise the minimum standards of poorer states, not to pull the wealthiest states down to that level. Lehman, however, took the position of businessmen and contended that New York should make its legislation coincide with that enacted by Congress. The governor wrote Wagner: "I believe that it would be detrimental to the interests of employers, employees and the general public of the State of New York if our State were to adopt a bill that went beyond the Federal measure, as it would obviously place us at a competitive disadvantage." [60]

In March 1935, the New York legislature held a public hearing on the amended Byrne-Killgrew bill. Spokesmen for interested groups revealed little change in their respective positions. Urging further delay, most business representatives argued that New York should await the enactment of federal legislation before committing itself to a specific program. Although a few large corporations favored compulsory compensation, they uniformly opposed the pooling of funds because that offered no incentive for management to stabilize employment. On the other hand, Elmer Andrews defended a statewide fund as the best means of guaranteeing minimum security for workers, particularly those in industries with high rates of unemployment. Furthermore, the industrial commissioner asserted that New York's approval of the Byrne-Killgrew measure would give a tremendous impetus to the movement for federal legislation. In a surprise move, John B. Andrews endorsed the administration proposal with its pooled fund, but his last-minute gesture went largely unnoticed.[61]

The week after the hearing, opponents of job insurance presented their case to the governor. In a private meeting with Lehman, business leaders argued against any state action before Washington instituted its system of tax incentives. They also appealed for revision of New York's plan in order to permit company reserves and employee contributions, but the governor stood firmly against any further tampering with the Byrne-Killgrew bill.[62]

Soon thereafter, Lehman notified Democratic leaders of the legislature that he wanted prompt passage of the Byrne-Killgrew measure without any more changes. On the following day, March 20, the Assembly approved the bill. Republicans first tried to add an amendment which would have permitted implementation of job insurance only when and if Congress adopted the federal social security program. After rejecting this proposal by a strict party vote, the lower house approved the Byrne-Killgrew measure by a tally of 103 to 41. On the final vote, twenty-six Republicans cast their ballots in accord with the entire bloc of Democrats.[63]

The bill then moved to the Senate where Democrats suddenly staged a revolt. Signs of mutiny first surfaced at a party caucus when a test of sentiment showed a large majority of members opposed to passage of the insurance legislation in its present form.[64] The issue again focused on the question of delay. While some Democrats favored the amendment already defeated in the Assembly, others preferred changing the date of implementation from January 1 to March 1, 1936, which would have given the next legislature an opportunity to revise the system before it went into effect.[65]

The resistance of Senate Democrats raised doubts about the sincerity of their previous commitment to unemployment insurance. Although Democrats in the upper house had passed such legislation during the last two sessions, they had voted with the assurance that the Republican-controlled Assembly would reject compulsory compensation for the jobless. In 1935, after affirmative action by the lower house, Senators faced the reality that another Yes vote would mean the actual adoption of job insurance by the state. Reportedly under pressure from business groups—"powerful but hidden forces," as George Meany called them—many Democrats had second thoughts and suddenly echoed employers' fears about competitive handicaps if New York proceeded ahead of other states.[66] In addition, lawmakers chafed at being constantly whipped into line by Lehman during 1935, when the governor took advantage of Democratic majorities to push for a number of his proposals, which included a reapportionment plan opposed by Tammany Democrats because it would reduce Manhattan's representation in the legislature. Therefore, partly as a gesture of independence, some Democrats insisted on amendments to the insurance bill after it reached the upper house at the end of the session. When Lehman refused to give in, the rebels declared that they preferred to see the Byrne-Killgrew measure go down to defeat rather than approve it without revisions. In defiance of the governor, the majority of Senate Democrats demanded that New York's insurance system take effect only when and if Congress adopted its plan of tax incentives to encourage similar action by other states.[67]

After their show of strength, the Democratic senators finally compromised with Lehman. While they dropped their demand that implementation await federal action, the governor agreed to postpone the first collection of payroll taxes from January 1 to March 1, 1936. Since this change did not alter the substance of the legislation, its acceptance by the insurgents represented a victory for the governor. The Republican minority leader of the state Senate chided his Democratic colleagues for cringing under "the whip of a Simon Legree" and sacrificing their convictions, but the amended Byrne-Killgrew bill passed the upper house with the approval of all Democrats and two Republicans.[68]

As the second state to enact unemployment compensation, New York won immediate recognition for adopting a more liberal system than Wisconsin's. Early defeats of the Wisconsin plan in the Empire State had given proponents of social insurance the opportunity to gain support for a statewide pooled fund. Lehman had initially favored the more conservative company reserves, but after reformers switched their allegiance to pooling, the governor followed their lead.[69] The resulting legislation provided New Yorkers with one of the basic guarantees of the Welfare State. If they lost their jobs, insured workers received compensation as a matter of right without any test of need. This represented an unprecedented commitment by the state to furnish a degree of security against the perils of unemployment. With justification Lehman called job insurance "one of the most progressive enactments in the history of this State." Secretary of Labor Frances Perkins hailed the principal features of the New York statute and suggested that it might well serve as a model for other states.[70]

Although unemployment compensation created a new responsibility for government, it supplied only limited protection for New Yorkers. The 1935 law covered "manual labor" paid less than $2500 annually in a business with at least four wage earners. The legislation specifically excluded farm workers and anyone employed by the government or a nonprofit organization. Starting in 1938, insured laborers who lost their jobs were to receive 50 percent of their previous wages but not more than $15.00 weekly. After a waiting period of three weeks, benefits lasted a maximum of sixteen weeks. Considering these restrictions, New York's industrial commissioner accurately observed that the Byrne-Killgrew Act represented "merely a modest and cautious beginning in providing some security to the wage earners of the State." [71]

Soon after New York adopted unemployment insurance, opponents of compulsory compensation appealed to the courts in hopes of overturning the law. Two upstate firms, aided by New York's most powerful organization of businessmen, instituted test cases which proceeded quickly through the state and federal courts during 1936. Since the parties involved in these suits did not dispute any facts, they sought a ruling simply on the constitutionality of the job insurance statute.[72]

The first case originated in Syracuse where two small employers joined in a legal challenge to the Byrne-Killgrew Act. Associated Industries, which had long led the opposition to job insurance, participated in the Syracuse litigation as a friend of the court. The plaintiffs argued that New York's statute violated fundamental guarantees of both state and federal constitutions. Since the insurance system excluded certain businesses, it allegedly denied equal protection of the laws to companies forced to contribute. The Syracuse firms also contended that the collection of payroll taxes would deprive employers of their property without due process of law. Furthermore, the legislation reputedly misused the taxing power by raising revenues for essentially private purposes. The employers' suit concluded that the arbitrary and discriminatory provisions of the law could not be justified by a resort to the police power of the state. In response, the New York Department of Labor asserted that insuring workers against "the economic and social evils of unemployment" came within the public welfare and taxing powers of the state and in no way abridged any constitutional rights.[73]

The judge in the Syracuse case rejected the employers' claims and upheld the state law.[74] Supreme Court Justice William F. Dowling observed that "the act is novel, revolutionary, and unusual . . . ; but this does not mean it is unconstitutional." Writing in the midst of the Depression, Dowling did not question the legislative finding that "economic insecurity due to unemployment is a serious menace to the welfare of the people of the state." Since the scope of unemployment made government assistance both reasonable and necessary, the judge concluded that New York's system of job insurance promoted the general welfare without infringing on constitutional rights.[75]

Soon thereafter, another lower court issued a contrary decision. Ruling on a suit brought by Associated Industries in Albany County Supreme Court, Justice Pierce H. Russell declared the entire job insurance law unconstitutional. In his decision, the judge seemed most disturbed by the concept of a pooled fund through which the state forced employers to pay the cost of compensation for workers of other companies in addition to their own. Russell asserted that this "is without validity under our system of government, and constitutes an unwarranted, unreasonable, and arbitrary transfer of the property of one to another in violation of the due process clause of the [United States] Constitution." [76]

Since New York's highest tribunal had already accepted the Syracuse case on appeal, it quickly agreed to review the two lower court decisions together. In arguments for the Court of Appeals, both sides reiterated points previously made. Lawyers for the state stressed the breadth of government's police and public welfare powers.[77] The New York Department of Labor's economic brief amassed evidence to show that unemployment represented a growing burden which weighed heavily on all classes and localities. According to the state agency, the "economic interdependence of all industries, geographic areas and social groups" necessitated dealing with unemployment as a public problem.[78] Although attorneys and economists for the employers tried to raise doubts about the validity of statistics mustered by the state, they placed their main emphasis on the contention that job insurance violated state and federal constitutional rights of due process and equal protection of the laws.[79]

The Court of Appeals moved with unusual haste to resolve the constitutional issues that had already divided two lower court judges. On April 15, 1936, New York's highest tribunal upheld the entire insurance law by a five to two margin. Speaking for the court's majority, which included Irving Lehman, Chief Judge Frederick E. Crane focused on the question of the state's power to relieve distress wrought by the loss of jobs. Well aware that massive unemployment had recently brought the country to its knees, Crane declared:

> When such a matter becomes general and affects the whole body politic, a situation has arisen which requires the exercise of the reserve power of the State. . . .
> Power in the State must exist to meet such situations.

The court's majority concluded that the legislature had the authority to create a system of unemployment insurance.

> Whether or not the legislature should pass such a law or whether it will afford the remedy or the relief predicted for it, is a matter for fair argument but not for argument in a court of law. Here we are dealing simply with the power of the Legislature to meet a growing danger and peril to a large number of our fellow citizens, and we can find nothing in the act itself which is so arbitrary or unreasonable as to show that it deprives any employer of his property without due process of law or denies to him the equal protection of the laws.[80]

This sweeping decision overjoyed advocates of social insurance. Upon hearing the ruling, Elmer Andrews declared: "This is a red-letter day in the new order which is based upon the ideal and the rapid achievement of social security for the wage-earners of the State and the nation." [81] "Friends of social insurance," Abraham Epstein asserted, "owe the deepest debt of gratitude to the five judges of the New York Court of Appeals for the greatest contribution made toward genuine social insurance in America." Epstein thought the court had delivered "the death blow . . . to all opponents of governmental action for social security." [82]

Despite the rejoicing in New York, the insurance statute still had to clear perhaps the greatest obstacle—the United States Supreme Court. The nation's highest tribunal had proved unreceptive to many state and federal welfare measures, and the fate of New York's job insurance law attracted national attention. Since the case represented the first court test of social security legislation, the validity of similar programs in other states hinged on the outcome of the New York litigation. The ultimate decision on the constitutionality of the New York statute would also affect the form of pending insurance legislation throughout the country, because the Empire State had adopted the most progressive type of compensation with a pooled fund. With so much at stake, the federal Social Security Board helped New York State attorneys polish their legal and economic briefs for submission to the Supreme Court. [83]

After hearing both sides in the dispute repeat their respective arguments, the Supreme Court issued an unusual decision in November 1936. With one justice absent and not voting, the tribunal divided evenly, four to four, on the constitutionality of New York's insurance law. [84] This left the statute on the books, because in the event of tie votes the Court simply reaffirmed the decision being appealed. Moreover, since the missing justice was a liberal, New Dealers considered the Court's action a good omen for any future test of social security legislation. New York's successful defense of its insurance system prompted numerous other states to adopt similar programs. In the month following validation of the New York statute, eighteen states enacted compensation laws. [85] After years of legislative and legal battles, job insurance had finally become a permanent feature of America's growing Welfare State.

2

Unemployment insurance provided some protection against distress resulting from the loss of jobs, but the causes of economic insecurity in an industrial society went far beyond periodic unemployment. Old age and sickness also frequently led to widespread poverty and destitution. Although disease and unemployment struck every segment of the population, they combined in the case of the elderly to produce one of the nation's largest groups of dependent people. During the 1920s, the United States Census reported that 54 percent of the paupers in almshouses were at least sixty-five years old, and evidence indicated a steady expansion of this proportion. [86]

In modern America, the elderly suffered from the impact of several impersonal trends. As progress in medical care reduced infant mortality, the life expectancy of the average American jumped ten years between 1900 and 1930, and the proportion of the population over sixty-five rose from 4 to almost 6 percent. Even more important, industrialization had turned most people into employees who had little control over their economic lives. When automation displaced workers, the older ones faced the greatest difficulty finding another job. Forced to retire with much of their lives still before them, many of the aged exhausted their personal resources and spent their last years in misery. In pre-industrial societies, relatives usually shielded the elderly against the perils of growing old, but the modern economy encouraged mobility, which loosened home ties and family solidarity. Thus a combination of demographic, economic, and familial factors made old-age dependency a serious problem in twentieth-century America.[87]

Under the leadership of Governor Franklin Roosevelt, New York finally took steps to relieve destitution among elderly people. After the defeat of a pension bill for the third consecutive year in 1929, Roosevelt prodded the legislature to create a temporary commission to investigate the condition of the aged and recommend "the most practical and efficient method of providing security against old age want." [88] In a lengthy report the following year, the Commission on Old Age Security estimated that the Empire State contained more than 600,000 persons over sixty-five. While only half of this group could count on friends and relatives for support, less than 4 percent received public and private charity that had changed little since the institution of poor relief by Queen Elizabeth in the sixteenth century. About 6000 of the elderly New Yorkers lived in the state's sixty-three almshouses, dehumanizing places where able-bodied, healthy inmates lived in the same dormitories with the chronically ill. "Worthy people," observed the state commission, "are thrown together with moral derelicts, with dope addicts, with prostitutes, bums, drunks—with whatever dregs of society happen to need the institution's shelter at the moment." [89]

The aged poor struggled heroically to avoid the poorhouse. Some went hungry rather than part with their homes, and many worked well past their seventieth birthdays. When one man reached seventy-two and could no longer shine shoes,'he turned to peddling pretzels in a futile attempt to provide for himself and his wife. A New York City welfare agency told of finding a job for a seventy-five-year-old man in a toy factory where he labored for six years. A private charity in Syracuse reported the case of another couple:

> Mr. S. is 72 years of age. His wife is 69. They live in a three-room flat in a large apartment house. . . . There is a toilet but no bath. They have been married 44 years, [and] have no children. Both are handicapped with marked disabilities. Mr. S. is almost totally deaf. Mrs. S. has arthritis and walks on crutches. She can sew, however, and obtains work through the Employment Bureau. She earns $1.50 a week from the first of November to the first of May. Mr. S. is janitor of the building for which services he receives his rent ($25). Aside from this he does odd jobs about the place and averages from $3 to $5 a week.

The specter of the poorhouse apparently helped the elderly bear such hardships. When faced with the prospect of entering an almshouse, a former engineer of seventy recoiled and said, "An institution is a place where people live with no plan except to die." [90]

Yet after exposing the misery experienced by many of the elderly, New York's

Commission on Old Age Security recommended only limited improvements in public aid. With surprising optimism the investigators depreciated the need for government-sponsored pensions. They suggested instead that the state share equally with local communities the cost of direct assistance to the needy over seventy years of age. Although this expansion of the outdoor relief system would keep the able-bodied poor out of the despised almshouses, the plan promised little security. The commission estimated that 51,000 New Yorkers over seventy would qualify for old age assistance, but it gave no reason for excluding another 25,000 indigent persons between the ages of sixty-five and seventy. The state study also recommended that assistance go only to citizens who had resided in New York for the preceding ten years. After receiving this report, the Republican-dominated legislature adopted the proposals for an improved relief system to aid the elderly.[91] Within three years, 54,000 New Yorkers were receiving an average of $24.00 per month under the 1930 law, but the beneficiaries represented only 8 percent of the state's population over sixty-five.[92]

In 1933, the aged poor felt the pinch of government belt-tightening in New York. Although Lehman had long backed state aid to the elderly, he showed more concern with the needs of the budget during his first year as governor.[93] To help keep down a burgeoning public debt, Lehman proposed a cut of $1,100,000 in the state's share of old age assistance. The legislature slashed an additional $500,000, which brought the total reduction to more than 20 percent of the appropriation for the previous year. This economizing inevitably forced local welfare bureaus to trim the number of old age relief recipients and the size of their individual allowances. After labor and social welfare organizations, led by Abraham Epstein, spoke out against these harsh measures, Lehman restored a portion of the severed funds in his budget for 1934-35.[94]

Confronting an economy-minded governor and legislature, reformers tried in vain to expand the coverage of old age assistance. During Lehman's first term, the New York branch of Epstein's American Association for Old Age Security sponsored bills to eliminate the citizenship requirement and reduce the minimum age from seventy to sixty-five. Epstein also wanted a state study of contributory pension systems, but his proposals received little attention in Albany where neither Republican lawmakers nor Lehman would consider any amendments that would increase state costs. Aware that a lowering of the age limit to sixty-five would raise expenditures by one-third, the governor stated privately that he would back this reform only if the federal government contributed the additional funds.[95] By the mid-1930s, improved security for elderly New Yorkers depended on the extension of aid from Washington.

3

On August 15, 1935, the president signed the Social Security Act which pledged federal assistance to a variety of groups including the elderly. The omnibus law created three distinct programs to aid different categories of needy Americans. First, the measure established a national system of compulsory old age insurance financed by most wage earners and their employers. Washington also promised to share equally with the states the cost of public assistance for the aged poor excluded from the government pension system. The second major provision of the Social Security Act set up federal incentives for the development of state unemployment insurance.[96] Finally, the law extended grants-in-aid for public health services and for state care of dependent children, the crippled, and the blind. Since most programs in the Social Security Act relied on federal/state cooperation, each state had to adopt enabling legislation before its citizens could benefit from the 1935 law.[97]

New York seemed certain to fall in line for the federal monies. Even before Congress had acted, the Empire State had adopted its unemployment insurance scheme which met national guidelines.[98] Although Albany lawmakers needed to approve the receipt of all other social security benefits, this step promised to be a mere formality, since either the state or its communities already extended various kinds of public assistance to all the groups covered by the federal law. Participation in the new system of federal grants-in-aid necessitated only slight revisions in state practices and standards of eligibility.[99]

When the legislature convened in January 1936, Lehman recommended several measures so that the state could qualify for federal funds under the Social Security Act. First, he called for a lowering of the minimum age for old age assistance from seventy to sixty-five. Since most social security programs depended on matching grants, the governor also suggested that the state begin contributing to existing local aid for dependent children, the blind, and the crippled. In addition, New York needed to expand its system of public health and its services for maternal and child welfare. On March 2, Lehman submitted an eight-point social security bill to implement these proposals. Although this legislation increased state expenditures for public welfare, it promised to cut local costs by permitting an influx of money from Washington. The governor estimated that during the first year New York would obtain $15 million to $20 million in U.S. funds if the state invested an additional $4 million in aid to the needy. He suggested that the necessary revenue be raised through a 20 percent hike in liquor taxes.[100]

Many Republican legislators unexpectedly balked at allowing New Yorkers to receive social security benefits. Looking ahead to the November elections, they decided to stake their political lives on an anti-New Deal campaign. Several barometers of public opinion prompted reliance on this strategy. Republicans who had just regained leadership of the Assembly interpreted their election victory as a defeat for the New Deal policies of Lehman and Roosevelt.[101] One exuberant lawmaker declared: "We came back to control because the people wanted to end the subservience of the great State of New York to the brain trusters in Washington." [102] In their enthusiasm Republicans overlooked their failure to win a majority of the Senate, and they refused to acknowledge the unrepresentative character of the Assembly, which Democrats rarely controlled. Other evidence probably prevented Republicans from appreciating these facts. During January 1936, *The Literary Digest* reported the results of a poll which indicated that 69 percent of New York voters opposed the New Deal. With this in mind many Republican legislators expected social security to prove unpopular, since it increased spending and dictated certain standards to the states.[103]

Accepting the challenge of the anti-New Dealers, Lehman decided to fight for social security. His chances of success seemed good, since Democrats had a majority in the Senate and were outnumbered by only seven Republicans in the Assembly. Although Republicans complained about rising taxes and subservience to Washington, the governor could not believe they would vote against public assistance for groups like the elderly, widowed mothers, and dependent children. In any case, Lehman wanted the electorate to know exactly where each party stood on the issue of social security, because he was confident that the state's voters would overwhelmingly endorse the New Deal if asked to do so in November.[104]

At a legislative hearing on March 17, the governor's omnibus security bill won virtually unanimous approval. Both social welfare and business organizations backed the measure. The latter recognized that enactment of the plan would bring a net decrease in the burden of New York taxpayers through a sizable reduction in local welfare costs. Business spokesmen insisted, however, that additional state funds for matching grants should come from economies in other areas of the budget rather than from new taxes.[105]

When no resistance to social security surfaced in New York, G.O.P. lawmakers began to hedge their bets. In March, the Assembly passed unanimously a Republican measure making persons over sixty-five eligible for state and federal old age assistance. Although this proposal required no immediate increase in state expenditures, its acceptance by Republicans raised doubts about the sincerity of their professed opposition to social security. They had condemned Lehman's eight-point program which called for the same change in age limit, but Republicans finally acquiesced in this one tie to the federal Social Security Act.[106]

G.O.P. lawmakers agreed to go along with improved old age benefits, because they feared the growing power of this bloc of voters. Throughout the upstate area many elderly New Yorkers had endorsed Dr. Francis Townsend's call for a national pension scheme which would have provided every citizen over sixty with $200 a month on the condition the money was spent within thirty days. After the California doctor visited Buffalo in January 1935, dozens of Townsend Clubs had sprung up in that part of the state, and organizers talked of running their own candidates for office in the 1936 election. Since most of the Townsendites were normally Republican, G.O.P. legislators proved sympathetic to pleas for increased assistance for the elderly.[107] One newspaperman called the Republican bill to lower the minimum age for benefits "a sop to the Townsendites." [108]

After Republican assemblymen yielded to part of Lehman's social security package, their colleagues in the upper house capitulated completely. At the end of March, the entire bloc of G.O.P. senators joined the Democratic majority to pass the governor's omnibus bill unanimously. When the Assembly failed to follow suit by April 1, New York began losing $654,000 a month in federal grants. The split between Republicans in the upper and lower houses resulted from conflicting readings of public opinion. George R. Fearon, the minority leader of the Senate who wanted to run for governor, thought his party's best chance for victory lay in quick adoption of social security legislation, thereby eliminating it as an election issue. During Senate debates, he declared that New York should do everything necessary to share in federal benefits.[109]

When the Assembly adamantly refused to pass the bill, Lehman took his case to the people. In a statewide radio address on April 19, the governor sketched the outlines of the proposed security program which would improve welfare services for thousands of New Yorkers. He emphasized that unless the state acted immediately it would lose millions of dollars in federal aid. Pointing to the intransigence of the Assembly, Lehman called on New Yorkers to let their voices be heard so that their state might join over seventeen others that had already been receiving U.S. funds under the Social Security Act.[110]

Ten days after Lehman's appeal, the Assembly again blocked a vote on his security bill. Although three Republicans from the cities of Buffalo and New York joined a solid bloc of Democrats, the motion to discharge the measure from committee lost, 71 to 73. When the governor rebuked the lower house for its inaction, the rhetoric of the opposition reached new heights. "Reckless spending," declared one assemblyman, "is at an end so far as Republicans are concerned and we want the taxpayers to know it." [111] Another lawmaker attacked the growth of federal power:

> The whole question turns on whether New York, with the most humane laws of any state, is going to be governed from Albany or Wahington. It's a question of whether we're to be permitted to take care of our own, in our own way, or have a superimposed government at Washington tell us what to do.[112]

Fighting as he never had before, Lehman refused to accept defeat. On May 4, only five days after the last rejection of social security, the governor sent another appeal to the legislature in an attempt to pick up the few Republican votes he needed for victory in the lower house. Lehman emphasized the nonpartisan support given his bill by Mayor La Guardia, the Conference of Mayors, and the State Board of Social Welfare.[113] When only one assemblyman reversed his position, Lehman went on the radio again in hopes that the pressure of public opinion could pry loose three more votes. Addressing the people on May 7, the usually reserved governor pounded on his desk as he hammered home his points. He argued that the social security measure created nothing experimental but, rather, expanded existing services. Cooperation with Washington in this endeavor involved no more dictation than other programs such as flood control, which Albany legislators had readily accepted.[114]

In spite of his numerous appeals, Lehman failed to arouse any significant response from the electorate. Although the governor reported receiving hundreds of letters supporting his position, he lacked the organized effort needed to channel the reservoir of pro-social-security sentiment into a force capable of converting Republican assemblymen.[115] Pressure groups like the American Association for Social Security which usually marshaled public opinion behind New Deal measures neglected to do so in this case because they expected the enabling bills to sail through the legislature. "Frankly," Abraham Epstein of the AASS told the governor in May, "we never conceived that the Republican leadership would be as short-sighted and as stupid as they seem to be. Their adamant stand has taken us all by surprise." [116] Caught off guard, the reformers had no time to mount a well-orchestrated campaign for improved assistance to dependent children, the blind, and the crippled.

The debate over social security exposed a widening split in G.O.P. ranks. In a rejoinder to the governor, James J. Wadsworth, chairman of the Assembly's Public Relief and Welfare Committee and son of the former U.S. senator, said over a statewide radio hookup that social security in the modern world was impossible, and he dismissed the federal program as "just another New Deal boondoggle." [117] Rejecting this "reactionary and tory" attitude, the one-time G.O.P. state chairman, W. Kingland Macy, called it an example of a "selfish and contemptuous philosophy." Even Congressman Hamilton Fish, Jr., a staunch anti-New Dealer, publicly warned fellow Republicans that they would never regain control of New York "if we continue in the same reactionary course of trying to sweep back the waves of progress and changing conditions in a great industrial State." [118] Much of the upstate Republican press also questioned the strategy of die-hard G.O.P. assemblymen. Declared the *Ithaca Journal News:* "The Republican party is a minority party in New York, because for 20 years it has fought the social programs of a line of Democratic governors. Must the Assembly give this Democratic governor another popular issue?" [119]

Soon after his second address to the people of New York, Lehman made his last attempt to push through the security package. In an unusual personal appearance before a joint session of the legislature on May 11, the governor raised his normally low voice and virtually shouted his disappointment over the stalemate on social security. He noted the inconsistency of lawmakers who condemned the new welfare program but nevertheless approved that part which permitted federal aid to the aged. Yet despite the last-minute support of several Republican county leaders from New York City and Buffalo, Lehman's security measure again fell three votes short of the majority needed to discharge it from committee in the lower house.[120] During the final debate, a Republican from Jamestown reflected the sentiment of the opposition when he exclaimed: "I am willing to stay here all summer if I can prevent this monstrosity, commonly called the New Deal, from gaining any further foothold in New York State." [121]

As the longest legislative session in twenty-five years drew to a close, the Assembly's majority leader, Oswald D. Heck, praised the action of party stalwarts.

> You Republicans have taken a stand against so-called Social Security which will bring to you the plaudits of the taxpayers. You have demonstrated that once and for all New York State is not going to be hitched to the chariot of the New Deal; that you are not going to be bought by federal contributions.[122]

While extolling the Republican commitment to principle, Heck chose to overlook his party's approval of state legislation to allow elderly New Yorkers to benefit from social security. The enactment of this Republican bill by both houses brought the Empire State federal grants for old age assistance, but meanwhile, New York would receive no funds for other groups covered by the Social Security Act.[123]

The final showdown on social security came in the 1936 election. The Republican state platform denounced the federal Social Security Act as "unsound financially and unworkable in practice." [124] During the campaign, the Republican candidate for governor, William Bleakley, condemned Lehman for permitting "the State to become the baggage coach hitched to the New Deal locomotive [which] . . . hurtled through the nation ripping up the roadbeds of [state] sovereignty." [125] Although Bleakley attacked increased spending and the growth of government, he tried to minimize differences over social security.

> No one is against social security. Opposition to social security comes, however, in the manner of its administration, in the method of enabling taxation and, in many instances, in duplication of effort. . . .
>
> There is no issue of social security as far as I am concerned. I am absolutely and unqualifiedly in favor of social security. . . . I do differ with the Governor of this State, however, as to the method of administration of social security.[126]

Lehman refused to accept his opponent's protestations. The governor called on Bleakley to denounce the "small group of reactionary and heartless Republican Assembly leaders," who had dismissed social security as unattainable. Reminding voters of the 1936 legislative battle, Lehman promised to continue his fight for expanded aid to the needy. "If I am returned to Albany . . . ," he declared, "I pledge you unremitting effort to secure the speedy adoption of this social security program." [127]

The rout of Republicans on election day gave Lehman the mandate he had sought. As one Albany correspondent observed, "The people . . . not only spoke but shouted their acclaim of the Roosevelt program in the nation and the Lehman program in the State. This has had its sobering effect on the Republicans." [128] Although Republicans retained control of the malapportioned state Assembly, their majority was cut from seven to two, and resistance to social security disappeared. Lehman's omnibus bill, which became the first order of business in the 1937 session, passed quickly with little debate and only twenty dissenting votes in the entire legislature of two hundred members.[129]

The adoption of enabling legislation for social security marked another step in New York's expansion of the Welfare State. Although public assistance to groups like dependent children and the blind had existed before the 1920s, it was locally financed and went to only a fraction of needy New Yorkers. By 1940, the state's welfare department noted that a radical change had occurred in government policy after the Depression had exposed the depth of economic dependency in America.

> Once the blinders were removed, we saw the realities that confronted us. We knew then that our economic system could, and did, produce dependency on a mass basis. . . .
>
> We have seen and recognized the major economic hazards of our time— unemployment, destitute old age, fatherless families, sickness and accidents. . . . And we saw that public assistance programs were created to meet the needs of each group . . . , and how, finally, a whole national public aid system had to be set up to meet the unprecedented onslaughts of our most malignant depression. . . .
>
> Today New York State . . . guarantees at least a minimum of security for those who need it.[130]

The New Deal significantly increased government expenditures for social security programs. Although aid to dependent children (or mothers' allowances) and assistance to the blind dated in New York from 1915 and 1922, respectively, they remained grossly inadequate county relief measures until the state and federal governments added their funds and supervision in 1937 (see Table 3, columns 3 and 4). New York began to share the cost of local old age assistance in 1931 but, after 1936, federal grants permitted the state to double such aid within three years (see Table 3, column 2). The total amount spent for these three categories varied little until Albany and Washington inaugurated their social security plans (see Table 3, column 5).

While helping a variety of dependent groups, New Dealers failed to enact protection against one of the greatest causes of insecurity—sickness. Health insurance had long been a feature of European Welfare States; yet the American movement for similar coverage met insuperable obstacles.[131] In 1919, the AALL and the State Federation of Labor pushed a compulsory health insurance bill through the New York Senate, but the Assembly killed the measure. Medical societies and insurance companies led a coalition of opponents that included druggists, fraternal organizations, and employers.[132] Following this defeat, the campaign for health insurance languished until the 1930s. The New Deal revived interest in government-insured medical care, but advocates of this reform despaired of overcoming the concerted resistance of powerful pressure groups. Although bills were introduced in the New York legislature from 1935 through 1941, they received little attention and died in committees without the benefit of public hearings.[133] None of these proposals got any support from Lehman, who took the

Table 3
Total Expenditures for Selected Public Assistance
Programs in New York State, 1932–40

Year	Old Age Assistance	Aid to Dependent Children	Aid to the Blind	Total
(1)	(2)	(3)	(4)	(5)
1932	$15,457,968	$12,678,473	$350,000	$28,486,441
1933	13,592,592	11,725,797	363,213	25,681,602
1934	12,651,600	12,015,964	374,093	25,041,657
1935	13,934,452	12,207,926	393,065	26,535,443
1936	16,053,337	12,387,783	416,178	28,857,298
1937	26,317,288 *	13,219,117	515,861	40,052,266
1938	31,341,834	18,329,248 *	709,853*	50,380,935
1939	33,301,124	21,003,834	800,539	55,105,497
1940	36,661,968	19,784,271	877,432	57,323,671

* First full year of state and federal grants under the Social Security Act.
Source: New York State Department of Social Welfare, *Democracy Cares,* p. 89.

position that health insurance should be a national program integrated into the federal social security system.[134]

During the 1930s, the enactment of various welfare programs guaranteed that New Yorkers would receive government protection against the perils of unemployment, old age, and some disabilities. The state's commitment to provide insurance and public assistance grew out of the Depression, which reformers, lawmakers, and judges repeatedly cited as proof that neither individuals nor private agencies could deal adequately with economic dependency in an industrial society. Although local communities had furnished some aid to the indigent before the 1930s, relief had been given sparingly as a matter of charity. Under the New Deal, Albany and Washington not only greatly improved existing public assistance programs, but also instituted novel social insurance schemes. During 1936, Lehman noted the new role of government:

> There have been important changes in the public view of the standards of care due to dependent groups, and at the same time an appreciation that the State's responsibility for the welfare of human beings does not end with the institutional care of unfortunates.
>
> The purpose of government is not only to protect the lives and property of its people . . . , but also to bring increased happiness, contentment and *security* into the homes of its people.[135]

In pursuit of security, New Yorkers embraced the primary goal of the Welfare State—a government-guaranteed minimum standard of living as a matter of right.

NOTES

1. Ward James quoted in Studs Terkel, *Hard Times: An Oral History of the Great Depression* (New York, 1970), p. 423.
2. According to Roy Lubove, "Workmen's compensation was the earliest social insurance program in the United States and the only one in operation before the 1930's." In 1913, New York State had established its system of workmen's compensation which required mandatory benefits for job-related injuries or accidents. Under the Little New Deal, the state extended the law to cover occupational diseases. Roy Lubove, *The Struggle for Social Security, 1900-1935* (Cambridge, Mass., 1968), p. 45; *Laws of New York, 1935*, chap. 254; *Laws of New York, 1936*, chap. 887.
3. Lubove, *The Struggle for Social Security*, pp. 144-70; Harry Malisoff, "The Emergence of Unemployment Compensation: I," *Political Science Quarterly*, LIV (June 1939): 242-44.
4. Andrews to Jeffrey R. Brackett, December 6, 1921, quoted in Lubove, *The Struggle for Social Security*, pp. 113-14.
5. *American Labor Legislation Review*, XX (December 1930): 349. The terms unemployment compensation, unemployment insurance, and unemployment reserves are hereinafter used interchangeably as they usually were during the 1930s despite Andrews' attempts to distinguish reserves from insurance.

6. Lubove, *The Struggle for Social Security*, pp. 171-73; Daniel Nelson, *Unemployment Insurance: The American Experience, 1915-1935* (Madison, Wis., 1969), pp. 179-85.

7. For Cullman's background see his obituary in the *New York Times*, June 30, 1972.

8. Connecticut, Massachusetts, New Jersey, New York, Ohio, and Rhode Island participated in the interstate study.

9. Bernard Bellush, *Franklin D. Roosevelt as Governor of New York* (New York, 1955), pp. 184-89; William Haber and Merrill G. Murray, *Unemployment Insurance in the American Economy* (Homewood, Ill., 1966), p. 65; Nelson, *Unemployment Insurance*, pp. 162-69.

10. *New York Times*, November 21, 29, December 1, 1932; *New York State Federation of Labor Bulletin*, December 9, 1932, pp. 5-6.

11. *New York Times*, November 11, December 2, 3, 25, 1932, January 8, 1933.

12. HHL Address, October 31, 1932, Speech File, 1928-32, p. 966, HHLP.

13. HHL Message to the Legislature, January 4, 1933, *Public Papers, 1933*, p. 29.

14. John B. Andrews to Mrs. Walston Chubb, December 24, 1932, Andrews to Seabury C. Mastick, January 26, 1933, Andrews to Olga S. Halsey, February 2, 1933, American Association for Labor Legislation (John B. Andrews) Papers, New York School of Industrial and Labor Relations, Cornell University. (Hereinafter referred to as Andrews Papers.) The New York Conference for Unemployment Insurance Legislation tried to win labor's support for the Mastick bill by liberalizing its coverage to meet most of labor's demands, but the conference refused to back a provision of the Byrne bill which permitted strikers to receive unemployment compensation. Statement of the New York Conference for Unemployment Insurance Legislation, February 10, 1933, Andrews to Francis B. Tyson, March 7, 1933, ibid.

15. The week before publication of the report, proponents of job insurance expected the legislative committee "to make a unanimous report and put in a bill." John B. Andrews to Mary Dreier, February 16, 1933, ibid.

16. *Report of the Joint Legislative Committee on Unemployment*, February 20, 1933, Leg. Doc. No. 66 (1933), pp. 11-13.

17. Ibid., pp. 17-18; John B. Andrews to Paul A. Raushenbush, February 21, 1933, Andrews to Dorothy W. Douglas, February 25, 1933, Andrews Papers.

18. John B. Andrews Memorandum, Telephone Conversation with Ward B. Arbury, January 30, 1933, Andrews to Dorothy W. Douglas, February 25, 1933, Andrews Papers.

19. John B. Andrews to Mary K. Simkhovitch, February 21, 1933, Andrews Memorandum, Conference with Governor Lehman, February 14, 1933, Andrews Papers. For additional evidence of Lehman's cautiousness on this issue, see Charles Poletti to Felix Frankfurter, February 27, 1933, "Minimum Wage—Laws and Hearings," Reel 63, GP, HHLP.

20. HHL to Mary K. Simkhovitch, February 16, 1933, "Unemployment Relief Commission, 1933-35," Reel 98, GP, HHLP.

21. Howard Cullman to HHL, January 23, 1933, "Cullman, Howard," Reel 24, GP, HHLP; Mary K. Simkhovitch to HHL, February 8, 1933, "Unemployment Relief Commission, 1933-35," Reel 98, GP, HHLP.

22. Andrews to Stewart Browne, February 21, 1933, Andrews Papers.

23. John B. Andrews to Seabury C. Mastick, February 25, 1933, Andrews to HHL, February 28, 1933, Andrews Papers; New York State Federation of Labor, *Official Proceedings, 70th Annual Convention* (1933), pp. 70-72.

24. Chamber of Commerce of the State of New York, *Monthy Bulletin*, XXIV (April 1933): 551, 554.

25. *New York Times,* April 2, 4, 1933.
26. Ibid., March 29, 1933; HHL Message to the Legislature, April 5, 1933, *Public Papers, 1933,* pp. 115-17. See also HHL to Albert G. Milbank, April 17, 1933, Gen. Corr., 1933-40, HHLP.
27. *New York Times,* April 9, 11, 1933; John B. Andrews Report, April 14, 1933, Abbot Low Moffat to Andrews, April 25, 1933, Andrews Papers.
28. Epstein to Francis D. Tyson, June 8, 1933, Epstein to William Haber, June 9, 1933, Box 4, Abraham Epstein Papers, Columbia University [hereinafter referred to as Epstein Papers (Columbia)]; "Suggestions Received from Paul H. Douglas," June 9, 1933, Epstein to Douglas, July 10, 1933, Box 11, ibid. Isaac M. Rubinow, chief architect of the Ohio plan, was a close associate of Epstein and helped draft the AASS job insurance bill. Rubinow to Epstein, January 22, 1934, Box 51, ibid.; AASS, *Social Security,* VII (September 1933): 1, 6. In 1933, New York State Senator Albert Wald had introduced a bill modeled after the Ohio plan, but the measure had generated little support. John B. Andrews to Paul A. Raushenbush, March 25, 1933, Andrews Papers.
29. Andrews to John A. Ryan, July 31, 1933, Andrews Papers.
30. Lubove, *The Struggle for Social Security,* pp. 42-43, 113-14, 138-39, 141-43 et passim; *John B. Andrews Memorial Symposium on Labor Legislation and Social Security* (Madison, Wis., 1949), passim.
31. Isaac M. Rubinow to Epstein, January 29, 1934, Box 51, Epstein Papers (Columbia).
32. Perkins to Lillian Wald, March 15, 1933, Lillian Wald Papers, New York Public Library; *New York Red Book, 1934* (Albany, 1934), pp. 263-64. In 1938, FDR chose Andrews to head the new federal division to enforce the Fair Labor Standards Act. *New York Times,* July 16, 1938.
33. Elmer F. Andrews to John B. Andrews, September 29, 1933, John B. Andrews to Paul A. Raushenbush, October 27, December 20, 1933, John B. Andrews to Josephine Goldmark, November 10, 18, 1933, Joseph P. Chamberlain to Elmer F. Andrews, November 21, 1933, John B. Andrews to Elmer F. Andrews, December 1, 1933, John B. Andrews Memorandum, Conference with Commissioner Andrews et al., December 1, 1933, Andrews Papers; Walter Gellhorn to Joseph P. Chamberlain, December 1, 1933, Box 49, Walter Gellhorn Papers, Columbia University.
34. Joseph C. Goulden, *Meany* (New York, 1972), pp. 3-47; George Meany Memoir, COHC, pp. 1-3.
35. John B. Andrews to John M. O'Hanlon, November 1, December 5, 1933, January 22, 1934, Andrews Papers.
36. Abraham Epstein to George Meany, December 2, 1933, Box 28, American Association for Social Security (Abraham Epstein) Papers, Cornell University. [Hereinafter referred to as Epstein Papers (Cornell).] See also S. J. O'Brien to Meany, December 18, 1933, January 17, 1934, ibid.
37. George Meany to Fred Gaa, January 8, 1934, Abraham Epstein to Alvin H. Hansen, January 18, 1934, ibid.
38. Quoted in Walter Gellhorn to Joseph P. Chamberlain, January 27, 1934, Gellhorn Papers.
39. Andrews to J. Sidney Stone, May 1, 1934, Andrews Papers.
40. HHL to Frances Perkins, December 18, 1933, "U.S. Department of Labor," Reel 99, GP, HHLP.
41. HHL Message to the Legislature, January 3, 1934, *Public Papers, 1934,* p. 49; Abraham Epstein to Isaac M. Rubinow, January 25, 1934, Box 51, Epstein Papers (Columbia); New

York State Federation of Labor, *Official Proceedings, 71st Annual Convention* (1934), p. 116.

42. New York Conference for Unemployment Insurance Legislation, Minutes of Meeting, January 26, 1934, John B. Andrews to HHL, January 29, 1934, Andrews to Paul A. Raushenbush, January 31, 1934, Andrews Papers.

43. *New York Times,* February 10, 1934; Epstein to Henry L. O'Brien, February 23, 1934, Box 28, Epstein Papers (Cornell); Epstein to Isaac M. Rubinow, March 2, 1934, Epstein Papers (Columbia), Box 51.

44. Abraham Epstein to Isaac M. Rubinow, February 2, 1934, Box 51, Epstein Papers (Columbia).

45. *New York Times,* April 5, 1934. Socialists refused to back the Byrne bill unless it was amended to provide greater benefits. Norman Thomas to Louis Waldman, March 28, 30, 1934, Norman Thomas Papers, New York Public Library.

46. The Mastick-Steingut bill permitted employers who had already set up company reserves to continue administering their own compensation funds. John B. Andrews to Irwin Steingut, May 2, 1934, Andrews Papers

47. *New York Times,* April 5, 1934. See also Mark Daly to HHL, January 16, 1934, "Daly, Mark," Reel 24, GP, HHLP; Brooklyn Chamber of Commerce, "Special Bulletin RE: N.Y. State Unemployment Insurance," April 11, 1934, Box 25, Epstein Papers (Cornell); *New York Times,* April 17, 22, 1934.

48. Howard S. Cullman to HHL, April 24, 1934, "Cullman, Howard S.," Reel 24, GP, HHLP; *New York State Federation of Labor Bulletin,* May 5, 1934; New York Conference for Unemployment Insurance Legislation, Minutes of Special Meeting, May 15, 1934, Andrews Papers.

49. Epstein to Isaac M. Rubinow, May 3, 1934, Box 51, Epstein Papers (Columbia).

50. Abraham Epstein to Isaac M. Rubinow, April 27, 1934, ibid.

51. New York Conference for Unemployment Insurance Legislation, "Resume of Membership Meeting," June 6, 1934, Andrews Papers.

52. Andrews to John M. O'Hanlon, June 5, 1934, ibid.

53. John B. Andrews to John M. O'Hanlon, May 24, 1934, ibid.

54. John B. Andrews, "Unemployment Reserves," *The Management Review,* XXIII (December 1934): 357.

55. John B. Andrews to Paul A. Raushenbush, November 28, 1934, Elmer F. Andrews to John B. Andrews, December 18, 1934, Andrews Papers.

56. *New York Times,* November 27, December 5, 1934, January 6, 1935; V. A. Zimmer to James Corcoran, January 7, 1935, Classified General Files, Unemployment—New York, Division of Labor Standards Records, Record Group 100, National Archives.

57. HHL Addresses, October 25, 31, 1934, *Public Papers, 1934,* pp. 801, 819; William T. Byrne to Abraham Epstein, December 19, 1934, Box 38, Epstein Papers (Columbia).

58. Arthur J. Altmeyer, *The Formative Years of Social Security* (Madison, Wis., 1966), pp. 117-25; *New York Times,* January 19, 1935; Walter Gellhorn to Joseph P. Chamberlain, January 21, 1935, Box 50, Gellhorn Papers.

59. James Corcoran et al., Memorandum to Elmer F. Andrews, January 22, 1935, "United States Legislation—Unemployment Insurance Law," Reel 100, GP, HHLP; *New York Times,* February 6, 8, 17, 22, March 2, 1935. Several minor amendments were also made in the Byrne-Killgrew bill to eliminate conflicts between it and the federal measure.

60. HHL to Robert F. Wagner, January 25, 1935, "United States Legislation—Unemployment Insurance Law," Reel 100, GP, HHLP; Wagner to Stanley M. Isaacs, February 21, 1935,

"Assorted Important Subjects, 1933-38," Robert F. Wagner Papers, Georgetown University Library; Abraham Epstein to Joseph Schlossberg, March 1, 1935, Box 28, Epstein Papers (Cornell).

61. *Buffalo Evening News,* March 6, 7, 1935; *New York Times,* March 7, 1935; John Andrews to HHL, March 7, 1935, Andrews Papers.
62. *New York Times,* March 14, 1935.
63. New York *Herald Tribune,* March 21, 1935; *New York Yimes,* March 20, 1935; New York, *Assembly Journal, 1935* (Albany, 1935), p. 2175.
64. Since Democratic senators expressed their opposition in party conferences closed to the press, there was no indication which lawmakers led the resistance. Reports of the exact number involved also varied, but it was a majority of the Democrats and included their leader, John J. Dunnigan of New York City.
65. *New York Times,* March 21, 22, 1935.
66. *New York Times,* March 23, 1935.
67. Albany *Knickerbocker Press,* March 22, 1935, April 3, 1935; New York *Hearld Tribune,* March 22, 29, 1935; *New York Times,* March 29, April 1, 3, 1935.
68. New York *Herald Tribune,* April 10, 1935; *New York Times,* April 10, 1935; *Laws of New York, 1935,* chap. 468.
69. George Meany Memoir, COHC, pp. 12-13.
70. HHL to John F. Killgrew, May 24, 1935, Gen. Corr., 1933-40, HHLP; *New York Times,* September 3, 1935.
71. *New York Times,* April 28, 1935.
72. Ibid., January 14, 1936.
73. *W. H. H. Chamberlin, Inc., and E. C. Stearns v. Elmer F. Andrews, et al.,* 286 N.Y.S. 252-53 (1936).
74. In New York the State Supreme Courts are inferior courts. The state's highest tribunal is the Court of Appeals.
75. 286 N.Y.S. 260-79. Justice Dowling ruled unconstitutional one section of the 1935 law which provided payments to workers on strike.
76. *Associated Industries of New York State v. Department of Labor, et al.,* 286 N.Y.S. 465 (1936).
77. *Respondents-Appellants Brief on the Law,* p. 11, in *Records and Brief of the New York State Court of Appeals* (1936), No. 200.
78. *Economic Brief for Respondents,* pp. v. vi et passim, ibid.
79. *Reply Brief for Plaintiff-Respondent in Answer to Economic Brief for Defendants-Appellants,* passim, *Brief for the Respondents,* passim, ibid.
80. *W. H. H. Chamberlin, Inc. v. Elmer F. Andrews et al.,* 271 N.Y. 9, 14, 15 (1936).
81. *New York Times,* April 16, 1936.
82. AASS, *Social Security,* X (May 1936): 2.
83. Wilbur J. Cohen to Edwin E. Witte, March 3, 1936. Chairman's Files, 095, Social Security Administration Records (hereinafter referred to as SSA Records), Record Group 47, National Archives; Alanson W. Willcox to Henry Epstein, August 19, October 10, 1936, "New York Law Department," Central Files, State File—New York (hereinafter referred to as CF, SF—NY), 092, SSA Records; Merrill G. Murray to Louis Resnick, September 1, 1936, CF, SF—NY, 510, SSA Records; Willcox to Epstein, October 28, 1936, Thomas H. Eliot to Epstein, November 3, 1936, CF, SF—NY, 513, SSA Records.

THE SEARCH FOR SECURITY

84. *W. H. H. Chamberlin, Inc. v. Elmer F. Andrews, et al.*, 299 U.S. 515. Justice Harlan F. Stone was sick at the time of the decision.
85. Wilbur J. Cohen to Meredith B. Givens, December 5, 1936, CF, SF–NY, 510, SSA Records; Alanson W. Wilcox to Henry Epstein, December 9, 1936, 092, ibid.; Malisoff, "The Emergence of Unemployment Compensation," pp. 255-56.
86. Abraham Epstein, *The Challenge of the Aged* (New York, 1928), p. 33.
87. Ibid., pp. 4-11; Ernest W. Burgess, "Aging in Western Culture," Philip M.·Hauser and Raul Vargas, "Population Structure and Trends," in *Aging in Western Societies*, ed. by Ernest W. Burgess (Chicago, 1960), pp. 5-20, 29-44.
88. *Laws of New York, 1929,* chap. 664.
89. *Report of the New York Commission on Old Age Security,* Leg. Doc. No. 67 (1930), pp. 39, 398, 399, 437. Quotation from p. 398.
90. Ibid., pp. 605, 635, 644, 661, 662. Quotations from pp. 605 and 661.
91. Ibid., pp. 11-24; Bellush, *Roosevelt,* pp. 177-81; *Laws of New York, 1930,* chap. 387.
92. Abraham Epstein, *Insecurity: A Challenge to America* (New York, 1933), pp. 534-36.
93. For expression of Lehman's early commitment to old age assistance, see HHL to William H. Matthews, February 23, 1929, April 3, 1930, "Matthews, William H.," Reel 29, LGP, HHLP.
94. Epstein to HHL, February 18, 1933, "American Association for Social Security," Reel 4, GP, HHLP; Epstein to HHL, August 17, 1933, Box 38, Epstein Papers (Columbia); *New York Times,* August 24, 1933. For a list of annual appropriations for old age assistance, see Table 3, *infra*, p. 93.
95. Minutes of the Executive Committee Meeting of the New York Permanent Conference on Old Age Security, January 17, December 19, 1933, Box 40, Epstein Papers (Columbia); Abraham Epstein to Samuel Mandelbaum, January 17, 1933, January 2, 1934, Mandelbaum to Epstein, February 16, 1933, Box 42, ibid.; HHL to Kent E. Keller, December 31, 1934, "KEL," Reel 51, GP, HHLP.
96. See *supra,* p. 80.
97. Altmeyer, *Formative Years of Social Security,* pp. 3-42; Leuchtenburg, *Franklin D. Roosevelt and the New Deal,* pp. 130-33. Old age insurance was the only part of the Social Security Act that operated independently of the states.
98. Only minor changes in wording were necessary to make the New York law conform to the federal Social Security Act. Herman A. Gray to HHL, December 21, 1935, "Unemployment Insurance Law," Reel 98, GP, HHLP.
99. *New York Times,* September 14, 1935.
100. HHL Messages to the Legislature, January 1, March 2, 1936, *Public Papers, 1936,* pp. 36-43, 226-29.
101. New York *Herald Tribune,* January 5, 1936; *New York Times,* January 2, 3, 5, 1936.
102. Albany *Knickerbocker Press,* January 23, 1936.
103. *Literary Digest,* January 18, 1936, p. 11; New York *Herald Tribune,* April 19, 1936; *New York Times,* March 8, 1936.
104. HHL to Carolin E. Flexner, January 4, 1936, Gen. Corr., 1933-40, HHLP; HHL Memoir, COHC, p. 473.
105. New York *Herald Tribune,* March 18, 1936; *New York Times,* March 18, 1936. See also Louis K. Comstock to HHL, April 22, 1936, "Social Security Act–Federal," Reel 88, GP, HHLP.

106. Albany *Knickerbocker Press*, March 19, 1936; New York *Herald Tribune*, March 19, 1936; *New York Times*, March 8, 1936.
107. *Buffalo Evening News*, January 12, 1935, January 3, 7, 11, 1936; William O. Dapping to James A. Farley, September 8, 1936, F. J. Sisson to Farley, September 12, 1936, Mark E. Monaghan to Farley, September 14, 1936, Box 83, OF 300, FDRL.
108. *New York Times*, March 27, 1936.
109. New York *Herald Tribune*, May 10, 1936; *New York Times*, March 27, April 19, May 11, 1936.
110. HHL Address, April 19, 1936, *Public Papers, 1936*, pp. 871-75.
111. New York *Herald Tribune*, May 1, 1936.
112. Albany *Knickerbocker Press*, May 1, 1936.
113. HHL Message to the Legislature, May 4, 1936, *Public Papers, 1936*, pp. 298-300. See also Fiorello La Guardia to HHL, April 14, 1936, William P. Capes to New York Mayors, April 17, 1936, "Social Security—Federal," Reel 88, GP, HHLP.
114. Albany *Knickerbocker Press*, May 7, 1936; New York *Herald Tribune*, May 8, 1936; *New York Times*, May 7, 1936; HHL Address, May 7, 1936, *Public Papers, 1936*, pp. 880-82. To show its support for Lehman, the Senate took the unusual step of unanimously passing his security bill for the second time. New York *Herald Tribune*, May 5, 1936.
115. *Buffalo Evening News*, May 8, 11, 1936.
116. Epstein to HHL, May 5, 1936, "Appreciation Letters," Special File, HHLP.
117. *New York Times*, May 9, 1936.
118. Ibid., May 11, 1936.
119. *Ithaca Journal News*, May 11, 1936, CB, 35: 727, HHLP. See also other clippings in ibid.
120. HHL Message to the Legislature, May 11, 1936, *Public Papers, 1936*, pp. 300-10; Albany *Knickerbocker Press*, May 13, 14, 1936; *Buffalo Evening News*, May 12, 1936; New York *Herald Tribune*, May 12, 14, 1936; *New York Times*, May 12, 1936; HHL to Thomas Parran, May 12, 1936, Special File, HHLP; W. Kingsland Macy to HHL, May 16, 1936, Gen. Corr., 1933-40, HHLP.
121. *Buffalo Evening News*, May 13, 1936.
122. *New York Times*, May 14, 1936.
123. *Laws of New York, 1936*, chap. 693; Frank Bane to HHL, June 19, 1936, SSA Records, CF, SF—NY, 621; Abbot Low Moffat to Lillian Wald, June 3, 1936, Special File, HHLP.
124. *New York Times*, September 30, 1936.
125. Ibid., October 20, 1936.
126. Ibid., October 15, 1936.
127. HHL Addresses, October 30, 31, 1936, *Public Papers, 1936*, pp. 1009, 1015.
128. W. A. Warn in *New York Times*, January 10, 1937.
129. Ibid., January 14, February 11, 1937; *Laws of New York, 1937*, chap. 15. New York became the twenty-eighth state to accept federal social security grants for dependent children and the twenty-seventh state to extend similar aid to the blind. Social Security Board, Bureau of Research and Statistics, *Public Assistance: Monthly Statistics for the United States*, vol. II, no. 2 (February 1937), pp. 3-4.
130. New York State Department of Social Welfare, *Democracy Cares: The Story of Public Assistance in New York State* (Albany, 1941), pp. 14, 20.
131. Lubove, *The Struggle for Social Security*, pp. 66-90; Forrest A. Walker, "Compulsory Health Insurance: 'The Next Great Step in Social Legislation,' " *The Journal of American History*, LVI (September 1969): 290-304.

132. Lubove, *The Struggle for Social Security,* pp. 84-89.
133. John B. Andrews to Esther M. Hilton, November 11, 1935, Andrews Papers; Abraham Epstein to William T. Byrne, January 24, 1935, Epstein to Irving D. Neustein, February 18, 1937, Epstein to Rose Weiss, February 8, 1938, Box 26, Epstein Papers (Cornell); *New York Times,* January 28, 1936, March 30, 1939, February 29, 1940, January 23, 1941; Albany *Knickerbocker Press,* February 1, 1935.
134. HHL Message to the Legislature, January 3, 1940, *Public Papers, 1940,* pp. 18-20; HHL Message to the Legislature, January 8, 1941, *Public Papers, 1941,* p. 36.
135. HHL Address, April 25, 1936, *Public Papers, 1936,* p. 876. (Italics added.)

V

DEFENDING THE
DEFENSELESS

Many laborers who managed to keep their jobs during the Depression suffered as much as people on relief. The onslaught of massive unemployment gave businessmen the opportunity to exploit helpless workers by sharply reducing wages and lengthening the workday. Although the cost of living also fell after 1929, the wages of many New Yorkers dropped faster, and working conditions deteriorated as fly-by-night sweatshops reappeared in numerous industries. The collapse of labor standards hit women and child employees hardest because they held the lowest-paying jobs and remained largely unorganized. Under the impact of the Depression, one clothing manufacturer in New York instituted a system of piecework which cut the weekly paychecks of skilled women employees from $11.00 in 1931 to $3.00 in 1933. During this period, a girl in another factory found her wages slashed from $20.00 a week to 20 cents a day for the same job. To compensate for these cuts, some women in the garment industry started taking work home at night, and they labored until two or three o'clock in the morning to earn $2.00 a day. Many less fortunate families turned their homes into factories where they produced a variety of articles under the age-old system of industrial homework.[1]

Long-time defenders of women and child wage earners expressed dismay at seeing the return of conditions which undermined many achievements of the previous generation. An official of the Women's Trade Union League lamented in 1933: "We have discovered during this depression that American workers stand for a great deal more than we ever supposed they would." [2] Mary W. Dewson, a leader of the Consumers' League, observed: "Industrial standards built up inch by inch after years of struggle are going down like card houses before the demand of the unemployed for work at any price." [3] Often unprotected by state labor laws or even by trade unions in many cases, women and child workers were at the mercy of employers who followed the dictates of the competitive system.

102

However, reformers who had long battled for expanded government regulation of industry seized the opportunity presented by the Depression to win a number of victories. "Faced with the utter breakdown of wage standards and working conditions," one veteran of previous crusades declared in 1933, "organizations interested in improving social conditions must co-operate this year more closely than ever before in the campaign for labor legislation." [4] Within four years this newly aroused conscience brought enactment of the most complete array of labor reforms ever adopted by New York. Under Governor Lehman's guidance and with the prodding of numerous organized lobbies, the legislature passed statutes designed especially to protect women and children in industry. These laws established minimum wages, reduced maximum hours, further restricted child labor, and permitted the abolition of industrial homework.

1

The wages of women and children initially generated the most attention because they plunged to alarming depths as a result of the Depression. By 1933, the earnings of children in New York factories had fallen about 50 percent in three years. While relief officials in New York City estimated that a single woman had to earn at least $10.00 a week to subsist, a survey of experienced women in New York industries revealed that they received an average weekly wage of $10.34.[5] A group of clerical workers averaged only $11.39 for the same period, and an expert typist who translated German into English for a law office took home $8.00 a week. "I eat only two meals a day," she explained, "just enough food to give me strength to keep going. My shoes are paper thin. I suffer with a toothache—but a filling costs half a week's salary." Less skilled laborers had even greater difficulty making ends meet. One woman in the garment industry who supported her two children and jobless husband averaged between $5.50 and $6.50 for a sixty-hour week. Among a group of factory women whose incomes were sharply reduced in 1932, a report showed 49 percent had to go without some essential piece of clothing, such as a winter coat; 41 percent lacked nourishing food; 58 percent moved to cheaper housing; and 61 percent postponed much-needed medical care. Such revelations stirred New Yorkers to demand a state minimum wage for women and children.[6]

The Consumers' League led the campaign for this reform. Organized in New York City just before the turn of the century, the National Consumers' League (NCL) had local affiliates in a number of states, but the New York branch had remained the closest ally of the national association, since the two groups shared offices in New York City. The League's battles had produced several seasoned leaders, notably Josephine Goldmark and Mary W. Dewson, whose careers extended from Progressivism through the New Deal. As a recent graduate of Bryn Mawr College, the slight and modest Goldmark had joined the staff of the NCL soon after its founding, and she quickly became the principal lieutenant of Florence Kelley, the association's guiding light. In 1907, Josephine Goldmark persuaded her brother-in-law, Louis D. Brandeis, to cooperate in the League's defense of Oregon's maximum-hour law for women. While the Boston lawyer concentrated on the legal arguments for presentation to the Supreme Court, Goldmark amassed economic facts and figures to demonstrate the need for protective legislation. The "Brandeis brief," as the resulting document became known, made legal history and helped catapult Brandeis into a seat on the Supreme Court.[7]

In 1919, Mary W. Dewson succeeded Josephine Goldmark as research director of the NCL. Dewson, a graduate of Wellesley College with a degree in economics, first won the League's attention in 1911, when she served as executive secretary of the Massachusetts commission which investigated women's wages and engineered adoption of the country's first minimum wage law. After joining the NCL's staff in New York, the energetic Dewson collaborated with Felix Frankfurter, the Harvard law professor, in preparation of a brief for the defense of a minimum wage law for women in the District of Columbia. The Frankfurter-Dewson team produced a lengthy brief of 1138 pages, over 1000 pages of which were devoted to marshaling facts to prove the economic need of minimum wages. After unfavorable court decisions in the early 1920s, Mary Dewson resigned as research director of the NCL and took over as secretary of the Consumers' League of New York.[8] Still a persistent fighter for social reform, she became closely associated with Governor Franklin D. Roosevelt during his years in Albany and, after he moved to the White House, Dewson served as head of the women's division of the Democratic National Committee. Always a pragmatist, she later recalled: "When the Supreme Court checkmated us for the moment, I was glad to work for FDR's election. It was the same field." [9]

In 1923, the Supreme Court had overthrown a minimum wage law and halted the initial movement for this reform. During the preceding decade, a crusade by the NCL had brought passage of minimum wage laws in fourteen states and the District of Columbia.[10] These statutes applied either to women exclusively or to women and minors, but none included men because trade unions opposed such regulations, and courts had proved unreceptive to legislation limiting conditions of employment for adult male workers. The 1923 decision by the Supreme Court struck down the federal measure which prohibited the payment to women in Washington, D.C., of wages "insufficient to maintain them in good health and morals." [11]

Despite a vigorous defense led by Mary Dewson and Felix Frankfurter, the nation's highest tribunal ruled by a vote of five to three that the federal law unconstitutionally abridged the freedom of women workers and their employers to make a contract regarding the price paid for certain labor. While rejecting the District of Columbia measure, the Court seemed to accept the legality of minimum wages if defined in different terms. Speaking for the majority in the *Adkins* case, Justice George Sutherland declared:

> A statute requiring an employer to pay in money, to pay at prescribed and regular intervals, to pay *the value of services rendered,* even to pay with fair relation to the extent of the benefit obtained from the service, would be understandable.[12]

Since existing laws did not fit this apparent loophole based on "the value of services rendered," they languished in the wake of the *Adkins* decision. Only Massachusetts continued to apply its weak system of advisory minimum rates for women, which relied not on legal penalties but on publication of the names of offending employers.[13]

When the Depression revived interest in minimum wages for women and children, the *Adkins* ruling plagued Consumers' League officials. While drafting a new bill early in 1933, Josephine Goldmark and Mary Dewson looked to Felix Frankfurter for expert advice. The Harvard law professor warned that reformers should not expect the Supreme Court to reverse the 1923 decision, and he suggested that the group try to get a minimum wage law sustained by distinguishing it from the federal measure already rejected by the Court.[14] Frankfurter took his lead from Justice Sutherland's emphasis on "the value of services rendered" as an appropriate measure of legal minimum wages, although this standard would severely limit the effect of any state law. In its model bill, drafted largely by Frankfurter, the NCL did not attempt to set uniform wage rates for all workers. Instead, it proposed that whenever a substantial number of women and children in a single occupation received less than subsistence wages, the state could conduct an investigation to determine whether the earnings were "fairly commensurate with the value of services rendered." If convincing proof showed that incomes fell below this level, a representative minimum wage board could, after hearings, recommend that the state institute minimum wage standards for that particular occupation. During the first nine months, the state could enforce such orders by publicity alone, as in Massachusetts. After this trial period and more hearings, the minimum rate could be made mandatory and backed up by legal penalties if violations persisted.[15]

While a committee framed this proposal in January 1933, the Consumers' League garnered support for it in the Empire State.[16] At a conference held in New York City on January 9, the League brought together representatives of over fifty civic, labor, and religious organizations. Speakers emphasized that the Depression had made minimum wage legislation an economic as well as a social necessity, since reduced earnings cut the purchasing power of workers, thereby undermining efforts to stimulate recovery. "The real case in favor of the minimum wage at the present time should be put much less in terms of the welfare of the workers than in terms of the need to safeguard the stability of society—economic society itself," declared Professor Eveline Burns, a Columbia economist. Attesting to the effect of the Depression on the thinking of businessmen in industries plagued by sweatshops, a spokesman for a group of laundry owners commented:

We find that the wages of the workers in laundries have been cut to such an extent that it is jeopardizing not only the welfare of the workers but the entire structure of the industry. The better employers in the industry have to meet the competition at the wage levels of their competitors, which are really destructive to the industry as well as unfair to the workers. The group I represent would support a minimum wage bill today, although it would not have been willing to do so a few years ago.[17]

After hearing evidence of the deplorable working conditions in local businesses, the conferees organized themselves into the New York State Labor Standards Committee, and they issued a call for a mandatory minimum wage and an improved maximum-hour law.[18] Mary Dewson became chairman of this group which coordinated the statewide campaign for legislative action.[19] Additional support soon came from an official conference of eastern states which recommended minimum wages for women and children to protect not only workers but also "fair-minded employers" who suffered as a result of cutthroat competition.[20]

Herbert Lehman proved a reluctant ally of the minimum wage movement in New York. Although he had endorsed the principle of advisory minimum wages in both his 1932 campaign and his first message to Albany lawmakers, the new governor worried about the competitive handicap which mandatory legislation might impose on local businesses if New York acted before other states. Felix Frankfurter and Mary Dewson, with the strong backing of both Frances Perkins and Charles Poletti, quickly overcame the governor's fears by pointing out that interstate competition had little effect on leading exploiters of women's labor such as laundries, hotels, and restaurants.[21] At a meeting in early February 1933, according to Frankfurter, Mary Dewson finally won over Lehman by "reading him the riot act." [22]

Once convinced that minimum wages would not undermine business, Lehman put the full weight of his office behind the drive for this reform. On February 27, the governor recommended that the legislature enact a minimum wage for women and children which, he argued, would serve "not as a burden but as a protection to industry." Stressing the economic consequences of low earnings, Lehman declared:

> [U]nfair trade practices are inimical to recovery. They prevent stabilization of industry; they are a source of unfair competition to firms who seek to maintain decent standards; they depress prices, whereby goods become cheaper and cheaper while the great masses are less and less able to buy; eventually, they add to unemployment.[23]

Lehman left the details of enabling legislation in the hands of state lawmakers. Democrats immediately introduced two measures modeled after the proposal drafted by the NCL. One, the Wald-Eberhard bill, copied the League's plan for mandatory wage scales, but the other, sponsored by party leaders John Dunnigan and Irwin Steingut, omitted the penalty provisions scheduled to take effect nine months after the establishment of minimum wage standards. As a purely advisory system under which the state could only publicize the names of violators, the weaker Dunnigan-Steingut measure was designed to reduce the possibility of unfavorable court decisions by following the example of Massachusetts.[24] However, the ineffectiveness of the Massachusetts experiment with permissive wage scales led the New York Labor Standards Committee and other reform groups to back the stronger Wald-Eberhard bill, which made noncompliance with minimum wage rates a misdemeanor after the trial period of nine months.[25]

In 1933, economic conditions largely eliminated opposition to minimum wages for women and children. The Consumers' League cleared the way for passage by effectively exposing the prevalence of starvation wages which no one dared defend. Since drastic wage cutting had undermined price structures in many industries, some businessmen endorsed the reformers' call for state intervention.[26] An official of the Laundry Board of Trade noted in 1934: "The better element in the laundry industry in this State has realized for a long time that if competition was to be levelled out, and disastrous price wars . . . were to be minimized, *it would be necessary not only to tell the industry as a whole how long it could work its employees, but what minimum wages it could pay its employees.*"[27] At a legislative hearing on March 2, 1933, none of the state's leading business organizations even bothered to attend.[28] With most employers either neutral or actually in favor of minimum wages for women and children, the only significant resistance came from some women's organizations, such as the National Women's Party and the Federation of Business and Professional Women's Clubs, which argued that labor legislation should apply to all workers, regardless of sex, to prevent unemployed men from replacing women. In response to this criticism, Assemblyman Herbert Brownell, a Republican from Manhattan just beginning a public career which would ultimately take him into President Eisenhower's cabinet as attorney general, sponsored a minimum wage bill in cooperation with another Republican, Senator Thomas Desmond. The Desmond-Brownell measure covered all workers regardless of age or sex.[29]

Minimum wage legislation took precedence over other labor proposals in 1933. On March 23, the Democratic Senate adopted the Wald bill, which reportedly had the backing of Governor Lehman. Opponents first tried to limit the effect of the proposed minimum wage system to an emergency period. After Democrats defeated this crippling amendment by a strict party vote, eleven Republicans (the majority of them from urban districts) joined a solid bloc of Democrats in approving the original measure.[30] In the Republican-controlled Assembly the Wald bill passed by the wide margin of 100 to 43, as Republicans split generally along urban/rural lines.[31] The legislature also adopted overwhelmingly the Desmond-Brownell wage bill which covered men as well as women and minors. Lawmakers, including Democratic party leaders, who voted for both the Wald and Brownell measures apparently felt that the final decision on whether or not to extend protection to men should be left up to the governor.[32]

After the legislature passed the two proposals, Lehman weighed carefully their respective merits for almost a month while interested groups bombarded him with advice. The Consumers' League and its allies argued that only the Wald bill could withstand a test of constitutionality, since the Surpeme Court had generally refused to accept legislation which interfered with the so-called freedom of contract of male workers. The State Federation of Labor stressed that it had never endorsed government regulation of wages for men in private industry. Furthermore, proponents of the Wald measure pointed out that it provided legal penalties for violators of minimum wage scales. When Lehman announced his intention of signing the Wald bill but indicated he might also approve the Brownell proposal, reformers countered that this would only create confusion, since the two measures had different provisions regarding definitions, enforcement procedures, and the period of application. The governor finally held a hearing where various groups aired their views, but only women's rights organizations spoke in favor of the Desmond-Brownell bill.[33] On April 29, Lehman signed the tougher Wald measure, because he concluded that it stood a better chance of meeting constitutional standards. The governor also noted that "progressive associations and organizations interested in labor legislation in this State have urgently recommended to me the approval of the [Wald] bill." [34]

Adoption of a minimum wage law for women and children marked the first great victory of Lehman's Little New Deal. After the legislature's favorable action, President Roosevelt called on other states to follow New York's lead and pass similar laws.[35] Credit for the successful campaign in the Empire State belonged to the Consumers' League which, as Charles Poletti correctly observed, was "largely responsible for the enactment of the legislation." [36] Veterans of previous battles for minimum wages, including Josephine Goldmark and Mary Dewson, had dramatically exposed the prevalence of miserable wages which undermined the lives of workers and the stability of businesses. While mobilizing public opinion, these NCL officials had drafted a new model bill, brought together a coalition of allies, and persuaded Lehman to assume leadership of the movement. At the depth of the Depression, with its harrowing impact on women and child workers, the stalled drive for minimum wages regained its momentum in New York, and seven other states enacted similar laws during 1933.[37]

2

Implementation of New York's minimum wage act revealed its weakness. The statute did not set a state minimum wage for women and children but, rather, provided for the creation of a state-appointed wage board for any industry suspected of paying laborers less than the value of services rendered. This panel, composed of representatives of employers, employees, and the public, could suggest minimum rates only after determining the value of services rendered by workers. If the board's recommendation was accepted by the state's industrial commissioner, it became the minimum for that particular industry after interested groups presented their views at public hearings. During the first nine months of the order, the so-called "directory period," violation of wage standards brought only the publication of an offender's name. Upon expiration of this trial period, the state could establish a mandatory order and institute legal action for noncompliance which could bring fines and imprisonment. The legislature initially hampered administration of this complicated law by failing to appropriate funds for the first year of its operation.[38] When employers, troubled by cutthroat competition, flooded the Department of Labor with requests that their particular industry immediately receive the benefit of minimum wage standards, Elmer Andrews, the state's new industrial commissioner, appointed an advisory committee of civic, labor, and business leaders to decide which industry his limited staff should investigate first.[39]

On May 15, 1933, the advisory panel recommended that the state initially set minimum wages for commercial laundries. As one of New York's largest employers of women, with 22,000 on its payrolls, this industry cried out for government intervention, since it was infested with fly-by-night sweatshops. Its "slaves" were black women, and Italian and Puerto Rican immigrants, who labored long hours for earnings as low as $3.00 a week. After looking into such conditions throughout the state, the Laundry Wage Board, appointed by Commissioner Andrews, proposed minimum rates of 31 cents an hour ($12.40 for a forty-hour week) for the New York City area and 27½ cents an hour ($11.00 for a forty-hour week) for the rest of the state. When no serious objections developed at public hearings, this order went into effect on October 2, 1933. Within a month, the median weekly earnings of women and minors in the state's laundries rose from $10.41 to $12.12. Even greater gains occurred in hourly wages, since the former figure was based on an average forty-five-hour week and the latter on a forty-hour week.[40]

Despite the ardent support of many laundry owners, enforcement of these wage scales proved difficult. The Department of Labor's small group of inspectors had to cover more than two thousand plants spread around the state, and they had to deal with unscrupulous operators who tried every conceivable means to avoid paying workers as much as 31 cents an hour. One laundry reported that it had seventeen partners and only nine employees, and it argued that laborers listed as partners should not have to receive minimum wages. According to a more common practice, some owners paid workers the correct amount but illegally forced them to kick back part of their earnings with threats of firings. Several months after the wage scales went into effect, reports from laundries themselves showed that 27 percent paid some of their workers less than the required minimum. When violations continued, the Department of Labor invoked the full penalty of the law, but during the directory period, publicity constituted the only weapon with which to fight notorious owners who scorned public opinion. In the spring of 1934, the state released a list of eighty-nine chronic offenders in New York City who paid as little as 10 cents an hour. The weakness of this enforcement procedure could be seen in June, when the state reported that 158 laundries in New York continued to pay less than the minimum. After the directory period of nine months, the Department of Labor made the wage order mandatory, which enabled the state to prosecute violators. The attempt to punish offenders quickly precipitated a legal challenge of the law's validity.[41]

The constitutional test of minimum wages originated in Brooklyn where the most flagrant violations had occurred. Soon after the mandatory order took effect in August 1934, a state inspector making the rounds of Brooklyn laundries discovered that the Spotlight Laundry had paid its women employees only $10.00 for a forty-seven-hour week instead of the required $14.88. The manager, Joseph Tipaldo, passed this off as "a misunderstanding" and asked the bookkeeper to give $4.88 to each girl. When the inspector learned subsequently that the women had not received the money, he ordered that each be paid $4.88 in his presence. However, all were forced to return the money as soon as the state official left. The following week, the Spotlight's payroll showed that each girl had earned exactly the minimum wage for the number of hours worked, but interviews revealed that the employees had to endorse their checks without seeing the face. Each worker had then received $10.00 in cash. The checks, subpoenaed from the bank by the attorney general of New York, were made out for $13.64. On the basis of this and other evidence, the state got indictments from a grand jury which charged the Spotlight's owner, his agent, his bookkeeper, and Tipaldo with third-degree forgery and failure to pay the minimum wage.[42]

Through a series of adroit maneuvers, Tipaldo's lawyers prevented the case from ever reaching a jury. Although the Spotlight's manager was out of jail on bail, his attorneys returned him to prison and then sought a writ of habeas corpus to free their client. In State Supreme Court for Kings County, they argued that the minimum wage act was unconstitutional on the basis of the 1923 *Adkins* decision. However, the Brooklyn judge rejected the plea by distinguishing the New York statute from the one invalidated in Washington, D.C. The former, he declared, reflected "a humane legislative intent to ameliorate human distress by affording a measure of security to women who, by reasons of the unprecedented adverse conditions . . . were unable to adequately protect themselves." [43]

When Tipaldo appealed this decision, he found an unexpected ally. Organized laundry owners refused to defend him, because they thought an end to minimum wages "would result in the resumption of the evil methods of exploitation of workers and destruction of decent standards in the trade." [44] However, the New York State Hotel Association came to Tipaldo's rescue and financed his legal costs, which ultimately totaled $70,000. Aware that the Department of Labor planned to issue a wage order covering hotels and restaurants, these industries hoped to forestall this action by winning invalidation of the 1933 wage law.[45] While hotel and restaurant owners helped fill his war chest, Tipaldo prepared for a bright future. The Spotlight Laundry rechristened itself "Bright Light," installed $8000 worth of new equipment and doubled its work force. Showing a surprising lack of concern over this investment, Tipaldo boasted publicly: "I expect to get it back eventually on what I save in wages."[46]

When Tipaldo's case reached the New York Court of Appeals, it focused on the *Adkins* decision of 1923. The state submitted both legal and economic briefs to defend its statute. The so-called factual brief, which the State Department of Labor prepared with the aid of the Consumers' League, mustered 127 pages of statistics to prove that women, both single and married, constituted a growing segment of the work force who labored not for "pin money" but to support themselves and their dependents. Furthermore, data showed that women often earned wages so low that they did not receive the value of services rendered. Since they remained largely unorganized, only the state could protect them through minimum wage legislation. New York's legal brief stressed that the 1933 wage law was a valid exercise of the state's police power because, as contrasted with the invalidated District of Columbia statute, it provided a definite standard for minimum wages.[47] Tipaldo's attorneys, led by Nathan L. Miller who had served both as governor of New York and as a judge on the Court of Appeals, did not challenge the state's economic arguments but, rather, dismissed them as "old straw thoroughly threshed in the *Adkins* case." Governor Miller contended that this 1923 decision applied to the New York law, because "any [wage] standard set by others than the parties to the contract must necessarily be an arbitrary compromise of individual opinion. Free men and women cannot be ruled in that way under our system." [48] Although the New York State Hotel Association filed a brief in support of this position, several groups of laundry operators submitted a counter document which defended the state's minimum wage law.[49]

On March 3, 1936, New York's highest tribunal issued an unexpected decision. By a four to three vote, the Court of Appeals ruled the minimum wage act unconstitutional.[50] Resting the majority's short decision on *Adkins,* Chief Judge Frederick E. Crane declared that he saw "a difference in phraseology and not in principle" between the federal law overthrown in 1923 and the New York statute enacted in 1933.[51] Judge Irving Lehman, the governor's older brother, rejected this view in a dissenting opinion. After noting the plight of women workers, Lehman stressed the vital differences between the two laws and concluded that the state had the power to adopt a minimum wage based on the value of services rendered.[52]

New York State appealed this decision to the United States Supreme Court, which accepted the case. *Adkins* again became the focal point of the legal arguments, with New York contending that its statute was "vitally dissimilar" and Tipaldo's attorneys taking the opposite stand.[53] A number of interested parties also filed briefs as friends of the court. The Consumers' League secured Dean Acheson as a special counsel on behalf of six states which had minimum wage laws similar to that of New York. Ohio filed a separate supporting brief as did New York City which expected the outcome of the litigation to affect the size of local relief rolls. Backing for Tipaldo came from both the New York State Hotel Association and the National Women's Party in concert with some women's professional organizations.[54]

On June 1, 1936, the Supreme Court handed down its decision. By a five to four vote, the tribunal refused to review the validity of the *Adkins* precedent, because New York's appeal had allegedly not challenged that ruling. Speaking for the Court's majority, Justice Pierce Butler declared that New York's Court of Appeals "rightly held that the *Adkins* case controls this one and requires that [Tipaldo] be discharged." [55] This conclusion elicited two dissenting opinions. Chief Justice Charles Evans Hughes argued: "In view of the difference between the statutes involved, I cannot agree that the case should be regarded as controlled by *Adkins.*" [56] Justice Harlan F. Stone went even further and declared that his colleagues should have reconsidered the 1923 decision on the basis of the country's subsequent experience and the Court's intervening rulings. In conclusion Stone eloquently brought into focus the plight of women laborers.

> There is grim irony in speaking of the freedom of contract of those who, because of their economic necessities, give their services for less than is needful to keep body and soul together. But if this is freedom of contract no one has ever denied that it is freedom which may be restrained . . . by a statute passed in the public interest.[57]

Revulsion at the Court's decision quickly swept the country. Newspapers, including those generally hostile to the New Deal, overwhelmingly disagreed with the *Tipaldo* ruling. Even Herbert Hoover spoke out against it. Expressing shock, New York's Republican Congressman Hamilton Fish told the House of Representatives that just as his party had freed three million slaves, both parties needed to emancipate three million women and child workers. A disappointed Governor Lehman deplored the Court's action, which knocked down the law he considered one of the most important enacted by his administration.[58]

Defenders of New York's minimum wage statute immediately sought reconsideration of the Court's ruling. Noting that the majority opinion had specifically avoided any reexamination of the *Adkins* precedent, the National Consumers' League implored Lehman to seek a rehearing before the Supreme Court. With the governor's fervent support, New York's attorney general, John J. Bennett, Jr., formally requested a rehearing on June 23.[59] The state pointed out that its original petition for a review of the *Tipaldo* decision had asked for "a reconsideration of the *Adkins* case in the light of the New York act and conditions aimed to be remedied thereby." [60] In October 1936, the Supreme Court turned down the request for a rehearing, and the *Tipaldo* case finally came to an end.[61] However, the apparent victor in the contest soon suffered defeat. A few months after the Court ruled the minimum wage law unconstitutional, Joseph Tipaldo lost his job as manager of the Bright Light Laundry. Explaining his fate, Tipaldo subsequently told newspapermen:

> I was swamped daily with mail condemning my actions in the case, and my customers wouldn't give the drivers the wash. I didn't have enough available cash to operate the laundry, so I ultimately wound up behind "the eight ball," a victim of bad circumstances.[62]

3

In spite of the *Tipaldo* decision, New Yorkers did not relax their efforts to assist women and child workers. After the overthrow of the 1933 statute, supporters of minimum wages considered various means of either meeting constitutional objections or circumventing the Court entirely. While a group of New York lawyers remained convinced that the state could design a law that the Supreme Court would accept, some reformers thought that amending the Constitution might prove the only alternative.[63] In October 1936, Industrial Commissioner Andrews brought together a group of labor and civic leaders to recommend a course of action for New York. After a month of deliberations, this committee decided on a two-pronged approach. First, it called for a new minimum wage law fully distinguishable from both statutes already rejected by the Supreme Court. Second, this group of citizens suggested that New York join with other states in pushing for a constitutional amendment specifically authorizing such legislation.[64] Meanwhile, mounting evidence indicated the need for reinstituting minimum wage standards. In late 1936, an employee of a Brooklyn laundry complained to the Department of Labor about deteriorating wage levels.

My employer pays the girls from eight to ten dollars a week [for] which we have to work forty-five hours a week and during the working hours which [sic] we are waiting for work some time he will take that time out and won't pay us for it which by the time the week is over we only get seven to nine dollars.[65]

When the legislature convened in January 1937, prompt passage of a new minimum wage law seemed a certainty. In his first address of the year, Lehman called for the immediate enactment of a measure to protect women and children. If it proved necessary, he also favored a constitutional amendment "so that government may not find itself impotent in its desire to give our working women a decent wage to preserve an American standard of living." [66] The week after delivering his annual message, Lehman again urged quick state action on minimum wages. In achieving this goal, he could expect support from Republicans, because during the recently concluded election campaign both their party platform and their gubernatorial candidate had pledged to back minimum wage legislation designed to meet constitutional objections.[67]

Despite widespread agreement on the need for a minimum wage law, differences arose over the best way of gaining the Supreme Court's approval. New Yorkers still sought a means of distinguishing a statute from the acts ruled unconstitutional in the *Adkins* and *Tipaldo* decisions. The study group that Commissioner Andrews had appointed the previous fall drafted a bill which closely resembled New York's 1933 measure except for the description of a minimum wage. Whereas the act rejected by the Court had defined "an oppressive and unreasonable wage" as "*both* less than the fair and reasonable value of the services rendered *and* less than sufficient to meet the minimum cost of living necessary for health," the new bill based "a fair wage" only on the "value of services rendered." Introduced by New York City Democrats Irwin Steingut and Leon A. Fischel, the administration's measure won endorsements from the Consumers' League, the Women's Trade Union League, and the League of Women Voters. These organizations hoped that elimination of the vaguest part of the previous definition of a fair wage would make the legislation constitutional in the eyes of the Supreme Court. Republican lawmakers Thomas Desmond and Herbert Brownell, still opposed to confining minimum wages to women and children, revived their proposal for including men which Lehman had vetoed in 1933. Another Republican, Assemblyman Abbott Low Moffat, sponsored a third measure which he drafted in consultation with Henry Epstein, Lehman's solicitor general, who had represented the state in the *Tipaldo* case. The Moffat proposal attempted to meet the Court's objections by making no distinction between men and women and by using a complicated formula to determine labor costs as the basis of minimum wages.[68]

At a public hearing on February 4, 1937, lawmakers took testimony on the three bills. Although no one opposed the principle of minimum wages, participants sharply debated the merits of the various proposals for six hours. A majority of the speakers, led by the Consumers' League, favored the Fischel-Steingut bill to protect women and children exclusively.[69] However, women's rights groups objected to legislation confined to women because they claimed it encouraged employers to replace women with men.[70] In a surprise move, Solicitor General Henry Epstein attacked the administration's proposal which, he argued, flaunted rulings of the Supreme Court. George Meany, president of the State Federation of Labor and a supporter of the Fischel-Steingut measure, doubted that the Court would accept any of the bills, but he hoped that "the Court has had its eyes and its ears opened to the desire for this legislation, as expressed in the ballot box last fall."[71]

Soon thereafter, Meany's wish came true. On March 30, banner headlines told the story.

MINIMUM WAGE LAW CONSTITUTIONAL
Washington Law Akin to Voided New York Act
Is Sustained—Adkins Ruling Reversed.[72]

Nine months after the Court divided five to four in the *Tipaldo* case, the switch of Justice Owen J. Roberts tipped the balance to the liberals' side, and the nation's highest tribunal upheld the Washington State law which established a minimum wage for women and children. This statute broadly defined a minimum wage as one sufficient to supply the "necessary cost of living and to maintain the workers in health." [73] New Yorkers were jubilant. "Now that the United States Supreme Court has changed its mind, or at least one-ninth of its mind . . . , New York can enact a law which will go directly to the point," declared Elmer Andrews.[74]

Four days after the decision, the industrial commissioner called a meeting of the committee that had drafted the Fischel-Steingut bill. With the governor present, the group discussed what form legislation should now take. Debate focused on the question of whether or not to include men, since President Roosevelt had just come out in favor of extending such protection to all workers. Senator Fischel suggested a compromise that would have empowered the state to apply minimum wages to men in any cases where they replaced women covered by wage orders. Mary Dewson and Consumers' League officials approved this amendment, but George Meany emphatically rejected it because, he claimed, men did not want state intervention in matters that collective bargaining could resolve. Backing up organized labor's position, Lehman declared that he also opposed the inclusion of men, because it might invite a negative court ruling. With both the State Federation of Labor and the governor lined up against minimum wages for men, the committee decided to limit the bill's coverage to women and children. Other provisions of the measure closely followed the 1933 act except for some improvements including reduction of the trial period for wage orders from nine to three months.[75]

On April 5, Lehman recommended immediate action on the revised Fischel-Steingut bill. In a special message to the legislature, the governor explained carefully the constitutional and economic reasons for excluding men, and he cited George Meany's opposition as proof that such coverage was neither required nor desired. Nevertheless, Senate Republicans tried to amend the bill to include all workers. After the Democratic majority defeated this proposal, the original Fischel-Steingut measure passed with merely one dissenting vote. When the Republican-dominated Assembly followed suit, only three Republicans cast negative ballots. On April 27, Lehman signed the bill into law.[76]

The following year, Congress passed legislation which supplemented state minimum wage laws. In 1938, the Fair Labor Standards Act set a minimum wage of 40 cents an hour and a maximum forty-hour week for all laborers engaged in interstate commerce.[77] Although the federal law contained numerous exceptions, it permitted New York to focus on protecting workers employed in intrastate business, particularly service industries such as laundries, hotels, and restaurants. By 1940, New York's Department of Labor had applied the state law to six different industries thereby bringing wage increases averaging 16 percent to 153,000 women and children. However, the use of wage boards for each occupation, rather than a statutory minimum for all businesses, meant that extension of the minimum wage absorbed tremendous time and money and also produced a mass of separate regulations that were difficult to enforce.[78] These weaknesses in New York's minimum wage act resulted from unfavorable court decisions which the state had tried to circumvent by a cautious approach based on the conditions peculiar to each industry. Thus, although judges ultimately failed to prevent the application of minimum wages, their rulings hampered efforts to protect women and minors.

4

Children long remained the most defenseless and pitiful victims of the industrial revolution. As America entered the twentieth century, New York State employed an estimated 400,000 children between the ages of five and eighteen. In spite of some restrictive legislation, they labored long hours for low wages in every type of business establishment from heavy industry to department stores. Many plied city streets hawking newspapers or delivering packages while others worked in dirty, overcrowded tenements helping their mothers make clothes or small items such as toys. A typical report told of Angeline Perati who

according to her employment certificate . . . was 15 years old, but her actual age was 12. She worked in an artificial flower factory from 7:30 in the morning until 6 in the evening. In the evening she helped her mother and younger sister make artificial flowers at home. She was in a pitiful physical condition, being subject to epileptic fits and being troubled with a weak heart. In all her life she has attended school just one month.[79]

The case of Angeline pinpointed some of the problems confronted by reformers who forced the state to adopt protective child labor laws. While employers and parents violated the statutes extensively, New York had only a few factory inspectors to cover the state's more than 40,000 manufacturing establishments.

Despite enormous obstacles, New York gradually expanded the restrictions on child labor during the first three decades of the twentieth century. Led by the New York Child Labor Committee (NYCLC), organized in 1902, reformers won a broad prohibition on the employment of youths under fourteen, but the patchwork legislation exempted fields such as farm labor and street trades which were still widely thought to benefit children. Although fourteen- and fifteen-year-old youths had to secure employment certificates in order to work, the state granted about 50,000 of these annually during the 1920s. New York also limited the work of children under sixteen to an eight-hour day and forty-four-hour week. The major weakness in all these laws remained enforcement, which continued to be inadequate owing to a shortage of funds and often a lack of determination on the part of public officials.[80]

Demands for improved minimum standards and enforcement met stiff opposition from many businessmen and their allies in government. They argued that additional restrictions would inhibit the ability of children to supplement family incomes. Moreover, opponents of protective legislation invoked America's traditional commitment to the work ethic and other middle-class values to defend child labor, which allegedly kept youths busy and out of trouble. "Surely," declared one employer spokesman in 1933, "the boy who learns business fundamentals, who meets human nature, who learns the value of business policies of dependability, honesty, courtesy and promptness is better equipped to make his way in the world than is the youngster who secures his education wholly within the four walls of a schoolroom." [81]

Unfortunately, young entrepreneurs such as newsboys also gained other knowledge from their contacts on the streets. A study make in 1916 showed that street traders accounted for over 70 percent of Manhattan's juvenile delinquents. As one historian has vividly pointed out: "A life characterized by shaking down customers by pretending to be out of change, making small pay-offs to the patrolman, and learning the 'ropes' about prostitution, drinking, and gambling was hardly the kind of training Horatio Alger would have approved for future captains of industry." [82]

Often stymied at the state level, reformers looked to federal legislation as a means of controlling child labor. During President Wilson's administration, progressives won enactment of two laws which effectively prohibited the interstate transportation of goods manufactured by children, but the Supreme Court ruled both measures unconstitutional.[83] Temporarily frustrated by court decisions, proponents of federal action decided to press for a constitutional amendment specifically empowering Congress to regulate child labor. After the Senate and House passed such an amendment in 1924, the campaign shifted to the states, thirty-six of which had to approve the proposal in order for it to become a part of the Constitution.[84]

A powerful coalition of diverse interest groups blocked New York's ratification of the child labor amendment. Although businessmen had long grumbled about alleged competitive disadvantages suffered as a result of New York's restrictive child labor laws, they rejected the proposal for national standards because they feared it might prove the opening wedge for extensive federal labor legislation. Less obvious opponents of national action emerged during the 1920s. The agricultural community, one of the state's largest and least regulated employers of child labor, overwhelmingly opposed the amendment.

In a poll taken by the Farm Bureau Federation, New York farmers voted ten to one against the proposal. The hierarchy of the Catholic Church also fought the measure because it worried about the effect of federal intervention on parochial education. According to the state's diocesan newspapers, the amendment might open the door to federal aid to public education and infringe upon parental control over family life. In addition, if Congress used this grant of authority to raise the school-leaving age higher than New York's minimum of fourteen, parishes might have to expand Catholic educational facilities. A vast reservoir of public opinion supported the opposition among businessmen, farmers, and Catholics. While some New Yorkers raised the specter of nationalization of the country's youth, others pointed to the failure of the recently enacted prohibition amendment to achieve its goal.[85]

The great array of forces opposing the child labor amendment overwhelmed the civic, labor, and welfare groups that favored it. In 1925, New York's legislature failed to take any action on the proposal. By the following session, the measure appeared dead nationally, since only six states had ratified it. Bills endorsing the amendment were introduced annually in New York, but they never even emerged from committee until 1935.[86]

The Depression and the New Deal revived interest in the abolition of child labor. Although the number of youths employed in factories actually declined as a result of massive unemployment, wages and working conditions grew worse. Some children earned only 35 cents for a day's work. As a new spirit of reform swept the country, fourteen states—the first to act since 1925—ratified the child labor amendment during 1933.[87]

In New York the same forces that had long blocked passage of the amendment frustrated attempts to adopt it during the New Deal. While business and farm organizations voted resolutions condemning the proposal, local officials of the Catholic Church carried the brunt of the attack against the measure.[88] Religious leaders still worried about the impact of federal controls on parochial education, but in public they generally raised legal and constitutional objections to the amendment. The superintendent of Brooklyn's Catholic schools declared that the "Prohibition debacle has taught us the folly of placing in our organic law propositions which the common people will not respect in practice." [89] A Long Island branch of a Catholic laymen's society went to the heart of the controversy when it expressed fear that raising the minimum age for child labor would mean increased educational costs for new schools, additional equipment, and extra teachers.[90]

During the 1930s, significant support for the anti-amendment crusade came from newspapers throughout New York which employed children to sell papers. After the National Recovery Administration (NRA) attempted to deal with the child labor problem in its code for newspapers, editorials against the child labor amendment suddenly multiplied. The vast majority of upstate journals opposed the measure, and the New York Publishers' Association went on record against it. Despite endorsements from the *New York Post,* the *New York World-Telegram* and the *Daily News,* the *New York Times* did not back the proposal until 1937.[91] Many editors claimed that freedom of the press, not child labor, was the real issue, but the *Daily News* disagreed: "When our fellow-publishers talk of freedom of the press they mean freedom to hire children to deliver newspapers before light on winter mornings, because children are cheaper." [92]

Several prominent New Yorkers emerged as spokesmen for opponents of the child labor amendment. From the editorial pages of the magazine *New Outlook,* Alfred E. Smith hammered away at the proposal. "The pending child labor amendment," he declared, "gives the Federal government complete control over the lives and daily habits of every person in this country below the age of eighteen. . . . Over a period of years, everyone would have a large part of his life regulated under it." [93] Nicholas Murray Butler, Columbia University's politically active president, became New York's foremost opponent of the amendment. Butler emphasized what he considered the measure's "revolutionary implications." As proof of this charge, he pointed out in 1937: "Every Communist gathering which has recently met has endorsed it with unanimous enthusiasm." [94] In a nationwide radio address, Columbia's president concluded that "the effect of this proposal [is] not upon child labor, for that would be quite negligible, but upon our American form of government, upon the home, the family, the school and the church." [95] The New York Child Labor Committee found that the criticism leveled by men like Smith and Butler "divided thinking people in an amazing fashion." [96]

Proponents of the child labor amendment in New York failed to overcome the formidable collection of forces allied against them. Both the National and the New York Child Labor Committees gathered endorsements from an impressive array of groups and individuals including the president, the governor, the League of Women Voters, the YMCA, the State Federation of Labor, the American Legion, the Federal Council of Churches, and clergymen such as Rabbi Stephen S. Wise and Dr. Harry Emerson Fosdick. In vain attempts to explode some of the myths surrounding the amendment, reformers pointed out that Prohibition incorporated an outright ban into the Constitution, but the child labor proposal simply enabled Congress to legislate on the problem. However, these arguments remained unconvincing in light of the amendment's broad grant of authority which many people interpreted as an actual ban on all labor by youths under eighteen.[97]

Until the mid-1930s, New York's legislature kept the child labor amendment bottled up in committee. Owing to the deep divisions caused by the issue, most lawmakers hoped to avoid a recorded vote on the measure. Even many Democrats overlooked their party's commitment to the proposal as voiced by Roosevelt, Lehman, and Farley.[98] George A. Hall, long-time secretary of the New York Child Labor Committee, observed that some legislators "are Catholics first and democrats second." [99] Hall remarked privately in 1935: "Unless the 'church' calls off its opposition, I am sure that we will fail in getting enough votes to pass the bill." [100]

This prediction proved true. Despite Democratic majorities in both houses that year, the ratification measure never came to a vote in the Senate and went down to defeat in the Assembly. The lower house brought the proposal out of committee for the first time after Lehman persuaded Speaker Irwin Steingut to toe the party line, but out of 150 Assemblymen, only thirty-two Democrats and three Republicans cast ballots for the amendment.[101] Among the Democrats, six identifiable Catholics voted for the child labor measure while at least nineteen followed the advice of their religious leaders.[102] After this stunning defeat, the NYCLC considered the child labor amendment a dead issue in the state, although routine endorsements still poured from reform groups and leaders of the Democratic party.[103]

To everyone's suprise, the ratification bill passed one house of the legislature in 1937. As a result of Democratic support, the enabling measure sailed through the state Senate before the opposition had a chance to rally its forces that year. In addition, Democrats were reportedly told at a party conference prior to the vote that the Catholic Church had withdrawn its objections.[104] However, the Catholic hierarchy soon reaffirmed its traditional position. In an unusual appearance at an Assembly hearing on the bill, the bishop of Albany, Most Reverend Edmund F. Gibbons, spoke on behalf of all the bishops of New York and their flock of 3,500,000 parishioners who constituted one-fourth of the state's population.[105] The Albany prelate quoted Patrick Cardinal Hayes, archbishop of New York, who argued that federal regulation of child labor "would contravene the principles of our form of government and seriously endanger the rights of parents." Responding to criticisms of the church's attitude, Bishop Gibbons concluded that "menaces of alarming proportions to religion and morality, the family, the home, the child, the workingman, the capitalist, the businessman, and the lawfully constituted government itself, demand that we clergy be conservative." [106] In the wake of this stinging denoucement of the amendment, the Assembly rejected it by a vote of 102 to 42, with only thirty-three Democrats in favor of the measure. The majority of the forty-one Democrats who opposed the amendment were Catholics.[107] The powerful influence of the church, coupled with the conservative attitude of upstate Republicans, again doomed the child labor amendment.[108]

The pressure for a constitutional amendment soon disappeared. Encouraged by more liberal Supreme Court decisions, Congress passed the Fair Labor Standards Act of 1938, which banned the employment of minors under sixteen in businesses engaged in interstate commerce. The effectiveness of the law was severely limited by exemptions for children working for their parents or in agriculture when not required to attend school. But contemporaries overlooked the shortcomings of the statute and assumed that America had finally licked the problem of child labor in interstate commerce.[109] Meanwhile, New York had already adopted the sixteen-year-old standard.

5

The minimum school-leaving age had long served as a weapon to combat child labor. Simply by raising the age at which youths could stop their formal education, the state could effectively curb the exploitation of children in factories. In 1889, New York set the minimum age for factory employment at fourteen where it remained until the 1930s. During the Progressive Era and several times in the 1920s, the New York Child Labor Committee called for lifting the school-leaving age from fourteen to sixteen, but this proposal met with opposition from local education officials who claimed that the new standard would create both enforcement problems and overcrowding in the schools.[110]

The Depression renewed interest in this reform. With fewer children working and with so many men unemployed, the NYCLC sponsored a fifteen-year-age bill during the years 1930-32. The committee hoped that a reduction in their traditional demand for a sixteen-year cutoff would eliminate some opposition.[111] Although the new proposal picked up the support of many public school superintendents, it continued to meet resistance from the State Council of Catholic School Superintendents whose spokesmen lobbied against any change which might require increased expenditures for parochial education. Lieutenant Governor Lehman, a long-time member of the NYCLC who had first contributed to the cause in 1909, delivered speeches on behalf of the fifteen-year-old measure, but the bill made no headway in the legislature.[112]

Beginning in 1933, the New Deal gave momentum to the campaign for abolition of child labor. Many federal codes adopted by the NRA set a minimum age of sixteen for employment in affected industries. When enforcement of this standard precipitated no serious economic or educational crisis, the NYCLC intensified its crusade for a sixteen-year-old minimum school-leaving age for New York. In addition to taking advantage of the NRA's experience, the committee hoped to exploit the arguments often used by opponents of the federal child labor amendment who claimed to prefer the local regulation of minors. However, resistance to raising the minimum age of school attendance continued during 1933 and 1934, despite Lehman's firm support of the reform. The strongest opposition came from Catholic educational officials and rural school authorities who still feared the financial impact of the proposal.[113]

In 1935, the Democratic-controlled legislature finally strengthened the restriction on child labor. At an Albany hearing, Associated Industries stood alone in its opposition to raising the school-leaving age to sixteen. On March 5, enabling legislation sailed through the Senate with merely eight dissenting votes from the Republican minority. Several weeks later the measure went down to defeat in the Assembly by a vote of sixty-five to sixty-seven, in which twenty-one Democrats joined the opposition. After a frantic lobbying effort by the Lehman administration and the NYCLC, the lower house adopted the sixteen-year minimum on April 12, but it first added a minor amendment which permitted mentally deficient children to leave school at fifteen.[114] The NYCLC hailed the school-age bill as "one of the most progressive child labor measures of the last thirty years." [115] Within a year after it went into effect, this law practically eliminated the factory employment of youths under sixteen. Yet children still toiled on farms and in retail and street trades after school hours. In New York, as elsewhere, reformers had no answer for the continued use of child labor, because they largely overlooked the problem.[116]

6

Much of the exploitation of women and child workers took place in their own homes. Families engaged in so-called homework industries produced handmade commodities ranging from all types of clothing to toys, artificial flowers, and lamp shades. After picking up material at employers' offices, homeworkers lugged it to their cramped houses and apartments where they toiled long hours for pay based usually on the number of articles turned out. This form of manufacturing encouraged the use of all members of the family, including young children and grandparents, who could perform many of the simple but tiring tasks. Despite workweeks as long as sixty and seventy hours, homeworkers received notoriously low wages, which even in the prosperous year of 1928 averaged only $6.19 for a typical week in all New York industries. Most of the state's home manufacturing was centered in the slums of New York City where immigrants and their children labored in dark, unventilated tenements. Of course, they also cooked, ate, and slept in the same crowded rooms.[117]

Although homework created more suffering than many factories, it proved difficult to regulate. Beginning in the 1890s, New York State passed laws restricting home manufacturing largely for health reasons in order to protect consumers, but the effect of the regulations was minimal owing to numerous exemptions and enforcement problems. By the end of the Progressive Era, exposures of unsanitary conditions led the state to outlaw the production in tenements of food, dolls, and children's clothing. The legislature also forbade the employment in homework of children under fourteen, and it required licenses for tenement houses that had any home manufacturing. All these statutes excluded from their coverage one- and two-family dwellings, which permitted businessmen to shift their operations to small houses in suburbs and upstate cities. Employers and poor families interested in making money also easily evaded the laws, which were difficult to enforce in more than 20,000 licensed tenements throughout the state. When an inspector appeared in a neighborhood, word spread quickly, and parents simply concealed forbidden articles while underaged children turned briefly from work to play. The complete abolition of homework became the only practical remedy for its shortcomings but, during the 1920s, the legislature refused even to extend the list of prohibited goods because of the strong opposition of employers.[118]

After the collapse of the economy in 1929, already outrageous conditions in home manufacturing grew rapidly worse. By 1934, reports circulated of women receiving as little as fifty cents for a fourteen-hour day spent making ties in their apartments. The State Department of Labor revealed numerous cases of experienced homeworkers who earned anywhere from 25 to 75 cents a day for long hours. One manufacturer admitted paying 2 cents an hour to a skilled embroidery worker. Hidden from public view, homework employed an unknown number of people, estimated in New York from 30,000 to 50,000. A large proportion of them, perhaps a majority, labored in one- and two-family houses over which the state exercised no control. Impoverished by the Depression and isolated from fellow laborers, homeworkers remained at the mercy of unscrupulous businessmen who had little contact with their own employees. Low wages forced many full-time homeworkers to rely on supplements from public and private relief agencies in order to provide even the bare necessities of life.[119]

The Depression and the New Deal made the abolition of homework desirable economically, as well as socially. Beginning in 1933, Washington attempted through NRA codes to prohibit home manufacturing in businesses engaged in interstate commerce. Although the federal ban proved difficult to enforce, it stimulated some employers to back similar controls on local intrastate businesses which could still farm out homework at low wages. After the Depression diminished markets, companies which operated factories felt the pinch from home manufacturers who had little overhead and could afford to cut prices drastically. In 1934, the New York Department of Labor sponsored a sweeping legislative attack on homework to protect not only exploited laborers but also hard-pressed employers who suffered as a result of the competition. The state proposed to issue certificates to all homeworkers, to license all places where homework was done, and to license all home manufacturers for fees to cover the cost of enforcement. This legislation won the support of Governor Lehman, organized labor, reform groups, and some employers, particularly in industries which had already eliminated homework. Albany lawmakers unanimously adopted the bill, but only after they exempted workers in one- and two-family houses in cities with a population under 200,000.[120]

The following year, Democrats used their control of the legislature to strengthen restrictions on home manufacturing. First, they abolished the exemption for communities of less than 200,000 people and, second, they added a provision which gave the state's industrial commissioner the power to ban homework entirely in a particular industry.[121] The Women's Trade Union League hailed this legislation which it hoped would free "thousands of overworked and underpaid women from ruthless exploitation."[122] Within three years, the state invoked its new authority to prohibit home manufacturing in men's outer clothing and neckwear and in the artificial flower and feather industry. Although New York continued to permit some exceptions in each industry, it gradually extended the list of forbidden goods. As a result, the number of state certificates issued to homeworkers dropped from 52,026 in 1937 to 5616 in 1955. Washington backed up this effort through the Fair Labor Standards Act of 1938, which applied minimum wages to both factories and homes, thereby making the latter less attractive as places of employment. After years of limited and ineffective restrictions on home sweatshops, New Dealers successfully began the eradication of homework and confined manufacturing to factories where employees received government protection against low wages, long hours and deplorable working conditions.[123]

During the 1930s, New Yorkers went to the rescue of women and child laborers who, it was assumed, could not defend themselves. Largely unorganized for their own protection, many of these workers held the lowest-paying and least-skilled jobs which others like them could easily fill should they fight for their rights. Often scarcely earning subsistence wages and laboring under deplorable conditions, women and children "lucky" enough to have jobs found the Depression a harrowing experience. Social welfare groups such as the Consumers' League and the New York Child Labor Committee took advantage of the economic crisis and exposed the plight of these workers. In the midst of the Depression, reformers finally won significant advances in labor legislation after many years of frustration.

Lehman's administration proved sympathetic to the suffering of women and children. In demanding legislative relief, Lehman found crucial support not only among the state's voters but also in the ranks of Republican lawmakers. Beginning in 1933, New York adopted a series of reforms designed specifically to aid women and child workers. Despite a temporary setback as a result of the *Tipaldo* decision, the state successfully offered the first guarantee of minimum wages for New Yorkers. It also initiated the gradual abolition of industrial homework, which had long produced some of the country's worst sweatshops. Although New York failed to ratify the federal child labor amendment, the state improved its own restrictions on child labor by raising the minimum school-leaving age from fourteen to sixteen. All these reforms expanded the Welfare State by guaranteeing minimum standards for the protection of particular groups in the industrial labor force.

NOTES

1. Elinore M. Herrick, "Brief in Support of Minimum Wage Legislation," [1933], pp. 7-9, copy in "Wages and Hours—Standard Wage Act, New York" folder (hereinafter referred to as "Wages and Hours—SWA, NY"), National Consumers' League Papers (hereinafter referred to as NCL Papers), Library of Congress; Frances Perkins, "The Cost of a Five-Dollar Dress," *Survey Graphic*, XXII (February 1933): 75-78; Rita S. Halle, " 'Lucky' to Have a Job," *Scribner's Magazine*, LXLIII (April 1933): 235-38; John T. Flynn, "Starvation Wages: The Plight of the Employed," *The Forum*, LXXXIX (June 1933): 327-31.
2. "Minutes of Conference on Breakdown of Labor Standards," January 9, 1933, pp. 2-3, "Consumers' League of New York," Reel 21, GP, HHLP.
3. "Minutes of Meeting, "What Concerned Action Can Do About It," December 1932, folder 17, Mary W. Dewson Papers, Schlesinger Library, Radcliffe College.
4. Mabel Leslie to Lucy Mason, February 3, 1933, "Wages and Hours—SWA, NY," NCL Papers.
5. New York *Herald Tribune*, March 3, 1933, "Factual Brief for Appellant," p. 32, *Morehead v. New York ex rel. Tipaldo*, in *U.S. Briefs, 1935* (396).
6. Herrick, "Brief in Support of Minimum Wage Legislation," pp. 5-8; Josephine Goldmark, "The New Menace in Industry," *Scribner's Magazine*, LXLIII (March 1933): 141-43.
7. *New York Times*, December 16, 1950; Josephine Goldmark, *Impatient Crusader: Florence Kelley's Life Story* (Urbana, Ill., 1953), pp. 82-83, 143-49; Robert H. Bremner, *From the Depths: The Discovery of Poverty in the United States* (New York, 1956), pp. 232-33; Clement E. Vose, "The National Consumers' League and the Brandeis Brief," *Midwest Journal of Political Science*, I (November 1957): 267-90; *Muller v. Oregon*, 208 U.S. 412 (1908).
8. Mary W. Dewson to Isador Lubin, April 16, 1957, folder 17.1, Dewson Papers (Radcliffe).
9. Quoted in James T. Patterson, "Mary Dewson and the American Minimum Wage Movement," *Labor History*, V (Spring 1964): 150.
10. Despite a thorough survey of the problem, New York failed to enact a minimum wage law during this period. Thomas J. Kerr, IV, "The New York Factory Investigating Commission and the Minimum Wage Movement," ibid., XI (Summer 1971): 373-386.
11. Alice S. Cheyney, "The Course of Minimum Wage Legislation in the United States," *International Labor Review*, XXXVIII (July 1938): 26-27; *Adkins v. Children's Hospital*, 261 U.S. 525 (1923).

12. 261 U.S. 559. (Italics added.)
13. Cheyney, "The Course of Minimum Wage Legislation in the United States," p. 28.
14. Frankfurter to Goldmark, January 10, 1933, Dewson to Elizabeth Brandeis, January 19, 1933, Dewson to Arthur Holcombe, January 19, 25, 1933, "Wages and Hours—SWA (1933 Drafts)," NCL Papers.
15. Felix Frankfurter, "Why We Believe the Standard Minimum Wage Bill May Be Declared Constitutional," [February 1933], ibid.
16. Mary W. Dewson, "An Aid to the End," I, 92, Mary W. Dewson Papers, Franklin D. Roosevelt Library.
17. "Minutes of Conference on Breakdown of Labor Stardards," pp.3-5.
18. For strategic reasons, the Labor Standards Committee soon dropped the demand for a maximum forty-four-hour week because the state already had a forty-eight-hour law (with numerous exemptions), and the group thought it more important to concentrate its efforts on minimum wage legislation. Lucy R. Mason to Labor Standards Committees, March 11, 1933, "Minimum Wage—General," Consumers' League of New York Papers, New York School of Industrial and Labor Relations, Cornell University. (Hereinafter referred to as CLNY Papers.) In 1935, the state eliminated most exceptions to the forty-eight-hour week for women. Laws of New York, 1935, chap. 106.
19. Dewson to Mary Anderson, January 12, 1933, "New York Labor Standards Committee," CLNY Papers.
20. "Recommendations of Second Interstate Eastern States Conference on Uniform Labor Laws," January 27-28, 1933, p. 4, "Minimum Wage—Laws and Hearings," Reel 63, GP, HHLP. (Hereinafter referred to as "MW—L & H.")
21. Frankfurter to Dewson, January 28, February 9, 1933, Frankfurter to Perkins, February 9, 1933, "Wages and Hours—SWA, NY," NCL Papers; Frankfurter to Poletti, February 28, 1933, "MW—L & H," Reel 63, GP, HHLP; Poletti Memoir, COHC, pp. 4-6.
22. Frankfurter to FDR, April 14, 1933, Max Freedman, ed., Roosevelt and Frankfurter: Their Correspondence, 1928-1945 (Boston, 1967), p. 126. See also Dewson, "An Aid to the End," I, 103; HHL to Elinore M. Herrick, April 27, 1936, Special File, HHLP.
23. HHL Message to the Legislature, February 27, 1933, Public Papers, 1933, p. 96.
24. Charles Poletti to Felix Frankfurter, February 27, 1933, "MW—L & H," Reel 63, GP, HHLP; "History of Minimum Wage in Albany at the Present Session," [1933], "Wages and Hours—SWA (1933 Drafts)," NCL Papers.
25. Mabel Leslie to HHL, February 28, 1933, Mary E. Dreier to HHL, March 1, 1933, David Dubinsky to HHL, February 28, 1933, "MW—L & H," Reel 63, GP, HHLP; New York State Federation of Labor Bulletin, March 21, 1933; League of Women Voters, Weekly News, March 24, 1933, clipping, in "Wages and Hours—SWA (1933 Drafts)," NCL Papers.
26. Mary Dewson to FDR, [February 1933], folder 20, Dewson Papers (Radcliffe); New York Times and New York World-Telegram, March 1, 1933.
27. H. K. Wilder to Lucy R. Mason, August 31, 1934, "Wages and Hours—NY Minimum Wage Case," NCL Papers. (Italics in original.)
28. The only businessman to speak in opposition to the legislation was a representative of the hotel association. New York Herald Tribune, March 3, 1933.
29. Ibid., March 20, 1933; New York Times, February 1, March 1, 3, 19, 21, 1933; Buffalo Evening News, March 3, 1933.

30. New York *Herald Tribune, New York Times,* March 24, 1933.
31. Thirty-two Republicans voted with the Democratic minority.
32. Only fourteen legislators, all Republicans, cast ballots against both minimum wage bills. New York, *Assembly Journal, 1933* (Albany, 1933), pp. 2300, 2306; New York, *Senate Journal, 1933* (Albany, 1933), p. 1426. For information on legislators and their districts, see *New York Red Book, 1933* (Albany, 1933).
33. Josephine Goldmark to HHL, April 10, 1933, John M. O'Hanlon to HHL, April 10, 13, 1933, Dorothy Kenyon to HHL, April 11, 1933, Chapter 584, New York State Bill Jacket Collection, New York Public Library; Elinore M. Herrick to Mary W. Dewson, April 12, 1933, Box 20, Dewson Papers (FDRL); Elinore M. Herrick, "Analysis of Terms of Desmond Minimum Wage Bill Contradicting and Conflicting with Terms of Wald Minimum Wage Bill," n.d., Albert Wald to HHL, April 13, 1933, "MW—L & H," Reel 63, GP, HHLP; Albany *Knickerbocker Press,* April 14, 28, 1933; New York *Herald Tribune,* April 28, 1933; *New York Times,* April 14, 22, 28, 1933.
34. HHL Memorandum, April 29, 1933, *Public Papers, 1933,* p. 302; *Laws of New York, 1933,* chap. 584.
35. FDR to HHL, FDR to Governor of New Jersey et al., April 11, 1933, OF 91, FDRL.
36. Poletti to John J. Bennett, Jr., July 11, 1933, "MW—L & H," Reel 63, GP, HHLP.
37. Cheyney, "The Course of Minimum Wage Legislation in the United States," pp. 30-31.
38. The Department of Labor partially overcame this obstacle by diverting funds and staff from other duties.
39. Elmer F. Andrews to Joseph J. Canavan, June 22, 1933, "MW—L & H," Reel 63, GP, HHLP; New York State Department of Labor, *Report of the Industrial Commissioner, 1933,* Leg. Doc. No. 21 (1934), pp. 34-35.
40. Albert Parry, "A Minimum Wage Comes to New York," *American Mercury,* XXXIV (February 1935): 236; New York State Department of Labor, *Minimum Wage and the Laundry Industry* (Special Bulletin No. 201, 1938), pp. 17-18; New York State, Department of Labor, "Report to the Industrial Commissioner: The Effect of Directory Order No. 1," July 2, 1934, pp. 7-9, copy in Box 14, Dewson Papers (FDRL).
41. New York State Department of Labor, *Minimum Wage and the Laundry Industry,* pp. 18-19; H. K. Wilder to Elmer F. Andrews, July 19, 1934, "Wages and Hours—NY Minimum Wage Case," NCL Papers; New York State Department of Labor, *Report of the Industrial Commissioner, 1934,* Leg. Doc. No. 21 (1935), pp. 24-25.
42. Beulah Amidon, "Due Process," *Survey Graphic,* XXV (July 1936): 413-14. Here and throughout this discussion of the *Tipaldo* case, I have relied heavily on John W. Chambers, "The Big Switch: Justice Roberts and the Minimum-Wage Cases," *Labor History,* X (Winter 1969): 44-73.
43. *People ex. rel. Tipaldo v. Morehead,* 282 N.Y.S. 581.
44. Herman Brickman to Lucy Mason, January 23, 1936, "Wages and Hours—NY Minimum Wage Case," NCL Papers.
45. New York State Department of Labor, *Report of the Industrial Commissioner, 1935,* Leg. Doc. No. 21 (1936), p. 34; idem, *Minimum Wage and the Laundry Industry,* p. 22.
46. *New York World-Telegram,* April 9, 1936, clipping, "Minimum Wage—Central," CLNY Papers.
47. *Factual Brief for Respondent, Respondent's Brief on the Law,* passim, New York State Court of Appeals, *Records and Briefs, 1936,* No. 80. Many people, especially leaders of the NCL,

cooperated in the preparation of the state's briefs. See Josephine Goldmark to Frieda Miller, August 21, September 3, 1935, Miller to Goldmark, September 13, 1935, NCL Papers, "Wages and Hours—New York Minimum Wage Case."

48. *Appellant's Reply Brief,* pp. 2, 20, New York State Court of Appeals, *Records and Briefs, 1936,* No. 80.

49. *Brief of New York State Hotel Association, Brief of Interborough Coat and Apron Supply Association, Inc., et al.,* ibid.

50. The NCL had originally focused its campaign for minimum wages in New York partly because of the expectation that the Court of Appeals would render a favorable decision in any test of constitutionality. Felix Frankfurter to Benjamin V. Cohen, February 1933, "Wages and Hours—SWA (1933 drafts)," NCL Papers.

51. *People ex rel. Tipaldo v. Morehead,* 270 N.Y. 238.

52. Ibid., 252-53.

53. *Appellant's Brief on the Law,* p. 32, *Brief for the Respondent,* passim, *U.S. Briefs, 1935* (396).

54. Nicholas Kelley to Dean Acheson, April 11, 1936, "Wages and Hours—NY Minimum Wage Case," NCL Papers. United States Department of Labor, Women's Bureau, *A Brief History of the New York Minimum Wage Case* (Washington, 1936), p. 4.

55. *Morehead v. New York ex rel. Tipaldo,* 298 U.S. 609.

56. Ibid., 618-19.

57. Ibid., 632.

58. *New York Times,* June 2, 3, 1936; HHL to Dorothy Kenyon, June 10, 1936, "MW—L & H," Reel 63, GP, HHLP; Chambers, "The Big Switch," pp. 54-55.

59. Dorothy Kenyon to HHL, June 15, 25, 1936, Rose Schneiderman and Mary E. Dreier to HHL, June 18, 1936, HHL to Bennett, June 15, 18, 1936, Bennett to HHL, June 18, 1936, Henry Epstein to HHL, June 18, 1936, Charles Poletti to Elinore Herrick, June 18, 1936, "MW—L & H," Reel 63, GP, HHLP.

60. *Petition for Rehearing,* pp. 2-3, *U.S. Briefs, 1936.* (334).

61. *New York Times,* October 13, 1936.

62. Quoted in New York State Department of Labor, *Minimum Wage and Laundry Industry,* p. 22.

63. Lucy R. Mason to Mary Anderson, June 1, 1936, "Minimum Wage, New York," 5-3 (34), Division of Labor Standards Records (hereinafter referred to as DLS Records), Record Group 100, National Archives; Mason to Benjamin V. Cohen, October 5, 1936, "New York Minimum Wage—Legislative Proposals," CLNY Papers.

64. *New York Times,* October 13, 14, November 7, 28, 1936.

65. New York State Department of Labor, *Minimum Wage and Laundry Industry,* p. 24.

66. HHL Message to the Legislature, January 6, 1937, *Public Papers, 1937,* p. 22. The governor made his endorsement of a constitutional amendment conditional, because he, like other reformers, awaited the outcome of the Supreme Court's review of Washington State's minimum wage statute, which state courts had upheld. A final decision in this case was expected early in 1937. Chambers, "The Big Switch," pp. 58-60.

67. HHL Message to the Legislature, January 12, 1937, *Public Papers, 1937,* pp. 40-41; *New York Times,* October 14, 1936, January 7, 10, 1937.

68. Elinore M. Herrick, "Analysis of 1937 Minimum Fair Wage Legislation," n.d., Felice J. Louria, "An Analysis of Minimum Wage Bills to Be Considered at Albany on February 4th," n.d., "New York Minimum Wage—Legislative Proposals," CLNY Papers; HHL to

Elmer F. Andrews, February 9, 1937, "ANDES," Gen. Corr., 1933-40, HHLP; Andrews to HHL, December 30, 1936, *Public Papers, 1937,* pp. 41-58; Albany *Knickerbocker Press,* January 14, 19, 1937; *New York Times,* January 14, 17, 18, 1937.

69. New York *Herald Tribune,* February 5, 1937.

70. Surveys of the laundry industry after the imposition of minimum wages for women showed that "there was virtually no change in the percentage of women working in the plants, thus indicating that the wage order did not cause a reduction in their numbers." New York State Department of Labor, "Maintaining Labor Standards in 1939," p. 7, "Labor Department—State Insurance Fund, 1939-40," Reel 54, GP, HHLP.

71. Albany *Knickerbocker Press,* February 5, 1937.

72. *New York Times,* March 31, 1937.

73. *West Coast Hotel Co. v. Parrish,* 300 U.S. 387. For an excellent discussion of this decision, see Chambers, "The Big Switch."

74. *New York Times,* March 30, 1937.

75. M. L. Mel to Verne Zimmer, April 7, 1937, "Minimum Wage, New York," 5-3 (34), DLS Records.

76. HHL Message to the Legislature, April 5, 1937, *Public Papers, 1937,* pp. 236-39; New York *Herald Tribune,* April 16, 1937; *New York Times,* April 16, 22, 1936; *Laws of New York, 1937,* chap 276. In 1944, New York extended minimum wage standards to include men. *Laws of New York, 1944,* chap. 792.

77. William E. Leuchtenburg, *Franklin D. Roosevelt and the New Deal, 1932-1940* (New York, 1963), pp. 261-63.

78. Isador Lubin and Charles A. Pearce, "New York's Minimum Wage Law: The First Twenty Years," *Industrial and Labor Relations Review,* XI (January 1958): 205, 210, 218; New York State Department of Labor, *Report of the Industrial Commissioner, 1940,* Leg. Doc. No. 21 (1941), p. 55.

79. New York Child Labor Committee Report, 1903, quoted in Jeremy P. Felt, *Hostages of Fortune: Child Labor Reform in New York State* (Syracuse, 1965), p. 49. Here and throughout this discussion of child labor reforms, I have relied heavily on Felt's excellent study.

80. Mary Stevenson Callcott, *Child Labor Legislation in New York* (New York, 1931), pp. 255-58; Felt, *Hostages of Fortune,* passim.

81. H. S. Stodghill, Remarks before the NRA Newspaper Code Hearing, September 22, 1933, quoted in Felt, *Hostages of Fortune,* p. 153.

82. Ibid., pp. 160-61.

83. *Hammer v. Dagenhart,* 274 U.S. 251 (1918); *Bailey v. Drexel Furniture Co.,* 259 U.S. 20 (1922).

84. Clarke A. Chambers, *Seedtime of Reform: American Social Service and Social Action, 1918-1933* (Ann Arbor, 1963), pp. 29-37; Goldmark, *Impatient Crusader,* pp. 114-17.

85. Felt, *Hostages of Fortune,* pp. 198-205; Vincent A. McQuade, *The American Catholic Attitude on Child Labor Since 1891* (Washington, 1938), pp. 84-91. The wording of the child labor amendment stimulated many misgivings, because it gave Congress "power to limit, regulate, and prohibit the labor of persons under 18 years of age." In the 1920s, this seemed to many people an extremely broad grant of power, and the public often confused the authority to legislate with actual legislation.

86. Felt, *Hostages of Fortune,* pp. 208-10.

87. Elizabeth Brandeis, "Organized Labor and Protective Labor Legislation," in *Labor and the New Deal*, ed. by Milton Derber and Edwin Young (Madison, Wis., 1957), p. 199; Felt, *Hostages of Fortune*, p. 94.

88. Chamber of Commerce of the State of New York, *Monthly Bulletin*, XXVI (February 1935): 371-74; New York State Farm Bureau Federation Resolution, November 10, 1933, "New York State Farm Bureau Federation," Reel 71, GP, HHLP; Lillian Wald to HHL, December 17, 1934, Lillian Wald Papers, New York Public Library.

89. Joseph V. X. McClancy to HHL, January 17, 1935, "Child Labor, 1935-36, "Reel 16, GP, HHLP. See also McClancy to the Editor, *New York Times*, September 21, 1933.

90. St. Pancras Holy Name Society of Glendale, Long Island, to HHL, March 8, 1934, "Federal Child Labor Amendment," Reel 31, GP, HHLP. Of all the Catholic newspapers and periodicals in New York, *The Catholic Worker* was the only one to endorse the amendment. McQuade, *The American Catholic Attitude*, pp. 130-31.

91. George A. Hall to Heywood Broun, January 18, 1934, Hall to John H. Finley, April 6, 1934, Box 19, Group I, New York Child Labor Committee Papers (hereinafter referred to as NYCLC Papers), New York State Library; Albany *Knickerbocker Press*, February 6, 1935; New York *Daily News*, January 6, 1935; *New York Post*, January 4, 7, 1935; *New York Times*, January 14, 1934, February 22, 1937; *New York World-Telegram*, January 18, 1935.

92. Quoted in Dorothy Dunbar Bromley, "The Newspapers and Child Labor," *Nation*, January 30, 1935, p. 131.

93. Alfred E. Smith, "Child Labor," *New Outlook*, CLXIII (March 1934): 12.

94. Butler to HHL, February 4, 1937, "Child Labor, 1937," Reel 16, GP, HHLP.

95. *New York Times*, February 3, 1934.

96. George A. Hall to Chauncey J. Hamlin, March 22, 1934, Box 19, Group I, NYCLC Papers.

97. Courtenay Dinwiddie to Mrs. Francis H. Blake, December 7, 1933, "Minutes of the Child Labor Amendment Campaign Committee," January 19, 1934, NYCLC Press Release, February 5, 1934, Fred L. Porter to Mrs. Theodore C. Janeway, April 3, 1934, "Members of Child Labor Amendment Campaign Committee," January 8, 1935, ibid.; Robert W. Searle to HHL, March 2, 1937, "Child Labor, 1937," Reel 16, GP, HHLP; *New York Times*, April 18, 1934, January 24, 1935.

98. George A. Hall to Leo Eisen, March 15, 1934, Hall to Jeanne Marion Doane, March 15, 1934, Hall, "Why the Child Labor Amendment Failed in New York," May, 1934, Hall to Members of the Campaign Committee, February 26, 1935, NYCLC Papers, Group I, Box 19; Charles Burlingham to FDR, January 24, 1935, OF 58-A, FDRL.

99. Hall to Mrs. V. G. Simkhovitch, March 24, 1934, Box 19, Group I, NYCLC Papers.

100. Hall to Mrs. Horace A. Eaton, February 25, 1935, ibid.

101. Hilda S. Boyle to George A. Hall, February 1, 8, April 15, 1935, ibid.; HHL Message to the Legislature, February 26, 1935, *Public Papers, 1935*, pp. 121-22; New York *Herald Tribune*, April 14, 1935; *New York Times*, February 23, April 14, 1935.

102. The religious division on the vote is also reflected in the action of Jewish lawmakers. Among New York City Democrats, thirteen Jews voted for the amendment and one against. The religious affiliations of some lawmakers are indicated in the *New York Red Book, 1935* (Albany, 1935), and others can be obtained from obituaries.

103. George A. Hall to Roy F. Woodbury, September 9, 1935, Hall to Eugene Warner, October 3, 1935, Box 4-2, Group II, NYCLC Papers; "Minutes of Meeting of the Board of

Directors of the NYCLC," October 9, 1935, Box 10, Group I, NYCLC Papers; FDR to HHL, January 4, 1937, "Child Labor, 1937," Reel 16, GP, HHLP.

104. Albany *Knickerbocker Press*, February 3, 1937; New York *Herald Tribune*, February 3, 1937; *New York Times*, February 3, 7, March 16, 1937.

105. According to a statewide Gallup poll commissioned by a Rochester newspaper and released the day before the bishop spoke, 83 percent of the New Yorkers questioned favored the child labor amendment. Rochester *Democrat and Chronicle*, February 21, 1937.

106. Transcript of Public Hearing, February 22, 1937, p. 15, "Child Labor Amendment Hearing," Reel 18, GP, HHLP.

107. Only three identifiable Catholics voted for the amendment, and Jews split fourteen to one in favor of the measure. New York, *Assembly Journal, 1937*, pp. 868-69.

108. *Buffalo Evening News*, March 10, 1937.

109. Jeremy P. Felt, "The Child Labor Provisions of the Fair Labor Standards Act," *Labor History*, XI (Fall 1970): 467-81.

110. Felt, *Hostages of Fortune*, p. 120.

111. Manfred W. Ehrich to HHL, December 19, 1932, "Annual Message, 1933," Gen. Corr., 1933-40, HHLP.

112. HHL to Lillian Wald, December 24, 1910, Special File, HHLP; Courtenay Dinwiddie to HHL, August 22, 1940, "NCLC," Gen. Corr., 1933-40, HHLP; Fred S. Hall, *Forty Years, 1902-1942: The Work of the New York Child Labor Committee* (Brattleboro, Vt., 1942), pp. 28-29; Felt, *Hostages of Fortune*, pp. 120-22.

113. George A. Hall to HHL, April 18, 1934, "Federal Child Labor Amendment," Reel 31, GP, HHLP; Hall to HHL, September 21, 1934, "NYCLC," Reel 68, *ibid.*; "Minutes of Meeting of the Board of Directors of the NYCLC," October 11, 1933, Box 10, Group I, NYCLC Papers; Hall to Roy F. Woodbury, March 22, 1935, Box 4-2, Group II, NYCLC Papers; HHL Message to the Legislature, January 4, 1933, *Public Papers, 1933*, p. 29; HHL Address, October 25, 1934, *Public Papers, 1934*, pp. 799-800.

114. George Hall, "Review of Child Labor Legislation Before the New York Legislature of 1935," April 30, 1935, Box 19, Group I, NYCLC Papers; Albany *Knickerbocker Press*, March 6, 1935; New York, *Assembly Journal, 1935* (Albany, 1935), p. 2337; Felt, *Hostages of Fortune*, p. 126; Hall, *Forty Years*, pp. 30-31. In 1935, New York also reduced the workweek for youths sixteen to eighteen by cutting the maximum from fifty-four to forty-eight hours. *Laws of New York, 1935*, chap. 106, 107.

115. George A. Hall to HHL, April 24, 1935, Gen. Corr., 1933-40, HHLP.

116. Elmer F. Andrews to Robert F. Wagner, February 18, 1937, "1933-49 Miscellaneous Legislation," Wagner Papers; Felt, "The Child Labor Provisions," pp. 478-81.

117. New York State Department of Labor, *Some Social and Economic Aspects of Homework* (Special Bulletin No. 158, 1929), pp. 6-7 et passim; Roy Lubove, *The Progressives and the Slums* (Pittsburgh, 1962), pp. 209-13.

118. Ruth E. Shallcross, *Industrial Homework: An Analysis of Homework Regulation Here and Abroad* (New York, 1939), pp. 33-59; Felt, *Hostages of Fortune*, pp. 140-51.

119. *New York World-Telegram*, March 7, 1933, clipping, "New York Minimum Wage Clippings," CLNY Papers; Elmer F. Andrews to Rosilla M. Hornblower, March 1, 1934, New York State Department of Labor, Press Release, March 7, 1934, "New York Industrial Homework," CLNY Papers; New York State Department of Labor, *Report, 1933*, p. 39; "Worse than the Sweatshop," *Nation*, November 21, 1934, pp. 579-80.

120. New York State Department of Labor, Press Release, March 7, 1934; *New York Times*,

April 16, 1934; Rose C. Feld, "Sweatshops, Model 1935," *Forum,* LCLIII (March 1935): 168-71; New York, *Senate Journal, 1934,* p. 1091; New York, *Assembly Journal, 1934,* p. 2842; HHL Memorandum, May 22, 1934, *Public Papers, 1934,* pp. 359-60; *Laws of New York, 1934,* chap. 825.

121. Albany *Knickerbocker Press,* January 18, 1935; *New York Times,* January 18, 1935; *Laws of New York, 1935,* chap. 182. According to two observers of the national scene, New York (along with Connecticut) had adopted "the most restrictive [homework] legislation yet enacted in the country." John R. Commons and John B. Andrews, *Principles of Labor Legislation* (4th rev. ed.; New York, 1936), p. 207.

122. Mary E. Dreier and Maud Swartz to HHL, March 19, 1935, Bill Jackets (1935), chap. 182. (Original telegram in upper-case letters.)

123. "Report on Homework in the Men's and Boys' Outer Clothing Industry," n.d., in "New York Industrial Homework," CLNY Papers; Shallcross, *Industrial Homework,* pp. 65-66, 217-23; Felt, *Hostages of Fortune,* pp. 151-52.

VI

LENDING LABOR A HAND

During the early years of the Depression, organized labor faced an uncertain future in America. Membership in trade unions had fallen off in the 1920s for a combination of reasons, including rising wages and the antiunion climate of the times. By 1930, almost fifty years after the formation of the American Federation of Labor (AFL), only 10 percent of the country's nonagricultural workers held union cards. Based largely on skilled workers engaged in construction, mining and transportation, the AFL had made little headway in organizing employees in the nation's factories. When the economy collapsed, many unions fought simply to survive. The Amalgamated Clothing Workers, centered in New York City, saw its rolls drop from 177,000 in 1920 to only 7000 dues-paying members at one point in 1932. Scarcely able to sustain itself, Amalgamated cut staff salaries by 50 percent and eliminated most publications.[1] In the midst of this period of crisis, one trade union official candidly summed up the plight of the AFL: "I can't help but conclude that we are steadily declining in influence, certainly in membership and income, and the future looks dark." [2]

Weakened by the Depression, organized labor relied increasingly on government aid. Although traditionally opposed to public intervention in labor/management relations, the AFL had over the years gradually endorsed limited legislative action protecting the right to organize and setting minimum standards in areas largely unaffected by collective bargaining. Trade unionists had long sought, for example, curbs on antilabor injunctions, and they backed the crusade for workmen's compensation during the Progressive Era. However, not until the 1930s did the AFL broaden its narrow legislative program to include unemployment insurance and minimum wages for men. Under the impact of the Depression, organized labor not only approved many public welfare schemes, but also welcomed government's entry into the field of labor relations as a guardian of the right to organize.[3]

During the 1930s, trade unions actively sought state as well as federal assistance. While the AFL lobbied in Washington for protective legislation, local affiliates campaigned for similar measures at state capitals. The New York State Federation of Labor, the largest group of its kind in the country, drew on years of experience in Albany

131

and its close alliance with the Democratic party to win enactment of virtually its entire legislative agenda in the years 1933-37. The list of accomplishments included the adoption of government-sponsored welfare programs, such as unemployment insurance. Even more important, trade unions assured their very survival through the establishment of legal restraints on union-busting techniques and the creation of a State Labor Relations Board, which successfully guaranteed workers the right to organize and bargain collectively with their employers. This legislation put new life into the labor movement by facilitating the rapid growth of union membership.

1

The New York State Federation of Labor combined both the strengths and the weaknesses of American trade unionism. Dating its origins from 1865, the federation represented almost eight hundred local affiliates by 1935, and it spoke for an estimated 850,000 New Yorkers, over one-fifth of all union members in the entire country. Yet at least 80 percent of the state's nonagricultural wage earners remained unorganized, since unions had generally failed to gain a foothold in manufacturing, with the notable exception of the New York City clothing business.[4] Trade unionism in the state was based on the crafts in the construction, transportation, and communication industries.[5] In the 1930s, the young George Meany symbolized the traditional leadership of the New York State Federation of Labor. Trained as a plumber in the Bronx, Meany had worked his way up through union ranks and became federation president in 1934.[6]

Although speaking for a minority of New York's wage earners, the State Federation of Labor had a powerful voice in politics. Drawing on dues levied on affiliates and their members, the federation kept a staff in Albany to lobby for its legislative program adopted at annual statewide conventions. Additional leverage came from labor's active participation in political campaigns where it tried to reward friends and punish enemies. Through this process of legislative and elective politics, the federation developed a close alliance with New York's Democratic party. Governors Smith and Roosevelt, backed by Democratic lawmakers, championed union causes; and organized labor, in turn, supported them at the polls. This combination, however, brought trade unionists few victories, since unsympathetic Republicans invariably controlled at least one house of the legislature while Smith and Roosevelt led the state. As a result, even the federation's rather limited goals of the 1920s went largely unfulfilled.[7]

Despite some cooperation between government and organized labor in the pre-New Deal years, the philosophy of laissez-faire dominated the official attitude toward unionization. Federal and state governments largely confined their role in labor/management relations to that of a policeman, protecting property rights and deterring violence. Although workers could legally join unions, employers also had the right to combat such efforts. Theoretically, this left wage earners and businessmen on an equal footing, but in practice it heavily weighted the balance on the side of management.[8] One observer pointed out that, while permitting workers to form unions, the law recognized the equal freedom of the employer to destroy labor organizations. . . . An employer could coerce or threaten his employees to keep them from organizing. He could discharge them if they joined a union, and he could refuse to hire anyone who was a member. He could decline to deal with any union of his employees or to recognize the organization or any of its officers or agents as representatives of the employees. He was free to organize a company union of his own and force his employees to join it. It was not illegal for him to employ detectives to spy on his employees in order to find out whether they talked unionism among themselves. . . . Under such circumstances, to speak of labor's right to organize was clearly a misuse of terms. All that the employees had was a right to try to organize if they could get away with it; and whether they could or not depended on the relative economic strength of the employers' and employees' organizations.[9]

After the turn of the century, the injunction became the most common legal weapon of owners fighting the unionization of workers. As a court order, the injunction usually directed particular parties to refrain from committing certain specified acts. Anyone accused of violating an injunction could be charged with contempt and punished with a fine or imprisonment. In labor disputes, employers frequently secured sweeping injunctions which effectively prevented strikes by forbidding or strictly limiting a host of activities from picketing to boycotts. Indeed, these court orders sometimes banned even the suggestion or discussion of anything that might interfere with business operations. Court procedure in such cases invited abuse, since it omitted the traditional safeguards connected with criminal law. A judge could grant a temporary injunction, which might last months, solely on the complaint of an employer without giving workers any opportunity to answer the charges. Signed affidavits, rather than witnesses, established proof, and judges alone made the final decisions without the use of juries. The same official who issued the order tried the case of anyone accused of violating it, and he determined the guilt and passed sentence at his own discretion. Punishment ranged from substantial fines to months in jail.[10] Since courts proved overwhelmingly sympathetic to businessmen in these proceedings, organized labor became "100 per cent opposed to the injunction."[11]

Injunctions often worked in tandem with so-called yellow-dog contracts. According to these written agreements, laborers promised as a condition of employment not to join a union. After the Supreme Court upheld the legality of this device in 1917, its use became widespread throughout the country.[12] Employees sometimes unwittingly entered into such agreements. One girl who went to work for a New York hotel in 1925 later described her experience:

I took a job as a chambermaid, and after the housekeeper [hired] me she sent me down to the office to fill out the necessary blanks. The clerk in the office handed me this long printed form, and made little X's at three different places, and said, "Put your name here." I wrote very slowly and glanced back over what I was signing. One of the clauses was a promise not to join the union of hotel employees. He waited while I signed and then took it back without telling me to read it and without giving me an opportunity to read it. Most of the chambermaids were old women who probably could not have either read it or understood it without a great deal of difficulty.[13]

Although employers never sued for breach of yellow-dog contracts, they used them in appeals for injunctions which restrained union leaders from attempting to organize signers of the agreement. This technique also proved effective against strikes. If workers walked off the job, an employer could enter into yellow-dog contracts with professional strikebreakers and then seek an injunction to block picketing and any other interference with the business and its new employees.[14]

During the 1920s, the New York State Federation of Labor spearheaded a drive against court injunctions. In the Empire State, strong resentment built up against the injunction, often backed by the yellow-dog contract, because they both became common weapons in the arsenal of businessmen.[15] Organized labor complained that "injunctions are almost entirely sought by those who desire to break up existing labor unions and prevent the formation of new ones." [16] Although Governors Smith and Roosevelt supported the federation's appeal for legal curbs on these noxious court orders, enabling legislation made little headway owing to the strong opposition of business associations. In 1930, lawmakers finally adopted a compromise measure which prohibited the issuance of any injunction without notice of a hearing, but the bill permitted judges themselves to determine the time and manner of notification.[17] The legislature continued to reject labor's demand, endorsed by Roosevelt, for jury trials of persons accused of violating these court orders.[18]

A national campaign against the labor injunction resulted in congressional passage of the Norris-La Guardia Act in 1932. This law forbade injunctions by federal courts to sustain yellow-dog contracts or to prevent peaceful strikes. In addition, it extended procedural guarantees, including hearings and jury trials for alleged violators of the decrees. This far-reaching measure gave new impetus to the drive for similar restrictions on state courts.[19]

In New York, trade unionists looked to the state's new governor, Herbert Lehman, to help win curbs on injunctions. Despite his years as a businessman, Lehman had earned the respect of organized labor. As an investment banker, he had little personal contact with struggles over unionization, but on one occasion he had resigned from the board of directors of a southern textile mill because it refused to deal with an affiliate of the AFL.[20] Lehman's first exposure to labor relations had come in 1924, when Governor Smith appointed him to a commission to mediate a dispute in the New York garment industry. While serving on the panel, Lehman not only became acquainted with the grievances of clothing workers, but he also made lasting friendships with some of their leaders, such as David Dubinsky of the International Ladies Garment Workers Union (ILGWU). Lehman showed his strong commitment to the principle of trade unionism in 1928, when he rescued the ILGWU with an interest-free personal loan of $25,000.[21] By 1930, President William Green of the AFL could say publicly that Lehman "places such a great value upon those intangible things called human rights that he would make a good member of some national or international union affiliated with the American Federation of Labor." [22]

During his first term as governor, Lehman spoke out strongly in favor of expanding the legal rights of organized labor.[23] He called for a measure permitting jury trials for anyone charged with violating an injunction. In 1933, Lehman took no public position on the union demand for a complete ban on yellow-dog contracts similar to that in the Norris-LaGuardia Act, but the following year he added this item to his list of labor proposals. The governor also supported a goal long sought in vain by organized labor—the exemption of unions from the state's antitrust law.[24]

In spite of strong backing from Democratic lawmakers, these measures went down to defeat due to the opposition of Republicans who controlled the Assembly. During both the 1933 and 1934 sessions, the three proposals sailed through the Senate only to die in Assembly committees. Motions to discharge them lost by virtually solid party votes.[25] Even the Depression and the example of the federal government could not overcome the powerful alliance of businessmen and Republicans, as long as the latter dominated one house of the New York legislature.

When Democrats took control of both the Senate and the Assembly in 1935, they finally breached the Republican dam. In his first message to the legislature that year, Lehman recommended an eighteen-point agenda of labor reforms, including unemployment insurance, improved workmen's compensation, additional curbs on child labor and women's hours, and protection of workers' right to organize.[26] Although most of it had been offered piecemeal in the recent past, the governor's complete package represented, according to a leading union journal, the "greatest and most definite program of labor and human welfare legislation ever submitted to a legislature by a chief executive of our state." [27]

While workers cheered, employers found themselves on the defensive. Mark Daly of Associated Industries begged Lehman to consult businessmen on labor proposals in spite of the fact that "we are completely at your mercy." Noting that the procedure for considering bills remained unchanged, the governor suggested that Daly address himself to the appropriate legislative committees.[28] Unfortunately, from the point of view of businessmen, Democrats now controlled all these committees, and after years of frustration they opened the floodgates to permit a deluge of pro-labor measures to pour through.

Both houses of the legislature moved quickly. For the first time in memory, committees met the day after the opening of the session and reported favorably a number of bills which the governor's staff had already drafted. Breaking records for speed, lawmakers set early dates for hearings and forwarded measures to the full houses for final votes.[29]

Leading items on the Democratic agenda included those designed to enhance the right to organize. Early in the session the legislature adopted a bill exempting unions from the state's antitrust law through a declaration that "the labor of human beings is not a commodity or article of commerce." [30] Business groups continued to oppose stronger anti-injunction measures, modeled after the Norris-LaGuardia Act, but Democrats pushed through three bills over the objections of most Republicans. These laws required a detailed bill of particulars before any hearing on a temporary injunction, prohibited the use of such decrees to enforce yellow-dog contracts, and provided jury trials for anyone accused of breaking those orders.[31]

Before adjourning in 1935, lawmakers adopted all but two of Lehman's eighteen labor recommendations.[32] In addition to injunction reforms, the list of major achievements included unemployment insurance, improvements in workmen's compensation, reduction of the maximum workweek for women and minors, an increase in the school-leaving age from fourteen to sixteen, and additional controls on industrial homework.[33] This unparalleled record of accomplishment brought Lehman well-deserved praise. George Meany declared: "Taken together, these enactments establish an achievement in social and industrial well-being for men, women and children that has no parallel in the legislative history of this or any other state on the American continent." [34] Agreeing with the president of the state federation, Lucy R. Mason of the National Consumers' League asserted that the "complete record of labor legislation this year will undoubtedly show that New York has done far more for the protection of labor than any other state in the Union." [35]

The Citizens Union justifiably awarded the "lion's share of the credit for the session's accomplishments . . . to Governor Lehman." [36] Although his predecessors had laid the groundwork for some reforms, Lehman fulfilled earlier plans and offered some of his own. The Depression created a widespread demand for change, but it was Lehman's popularity that largely accounted for the 1934 election victory that gave Democrats control of the legislature. After achieving this indispensable margin in both houses, the governor put together a comprehensive program with the support of organized labor, the Consumers' League, and other groups crusading for particular reforms. It was Lehman too who cleared away the last obstacles by lining up Democratic legislators behind the sixteen labor bills.

2

While New York gradually expanded state protection of the right to organize in the early 1930s, the federal government was radically altering the imbalance in labor/management relations. In the National Labor Relations Act of 1935, Washington created machinery which guaranteed workers the opportunity to vote on the issue of unionization without any interference from employers or their agents. If a majority of workers chose to join a union, their employer had to bargain collectively with representatives of the organization selected by wage earners. The Wagner Act specifically prohibited businessmen from committing "unfair labor practices," such as firing workers for union membership, but the law imposed no restraints on organized labor. To administer this far-reaching statute, Congress set up an independent agency, the National Labor Relations Board (NLRB).[37]

The Wagner Act covered only wage earners engaged in businesses affecting interstate commerce. Although the Supreme Court subsequently interpreted this restriction on federal power very broadly, fear of the Court's conservative bias forced the NLRB to apply the law narrowly at first.[38] In any case, the board necessarily had to turn aside the pleas of strictly intrastate laborers who sought federal protection of the right to organize.[39]

New York State initially contained about one million workers excluded from the Wagner Act. The NLRB took no responsibility for New Yorkers employed in hotels and restaurants, some building construction, and various service industries.[40] Since wage earners in these occupations had no other recourse, many walked off their jobs in order to force recognition of their unions. As a result, the number of strikes involving the attempt to organize rose abruptly. The State Department of Labor recorded four times as many labor disputes involving intrastate workers during the period 1935-36 as compared with the previous three years, and the proportion caused by conflicts over union recognition jumped from one-third to two-thirds.[41]

New York City provided glaring evidence of the obstacles in the way of collective bargaining for intrastate workers. Local building employees, such as elevator operators, doormen, janitors, and scrubwomen, could not take advantage of the NLRB because their occupations lay outside interstate commerce as then defined. Nevertheless, many exercised the right to associate by joining the local branch of the Building Service Employees International Union, an affiliate of the AFL. Although not formally recognized by management as the employees' bargaining agent, the union won a wage increase for workers in 1935 through the intervention of Mayor La Guardia, who got both sides to submit their differences to arbitration. This agreement covered about 50,000 workers in 6000 buildings. In anticipation of the contract's expiration on March 1, 1936, the union sent employers a new list of demands, including higher wages and the closed shop which would have required all workers to be union members.[42] Owners, represented by the Realty Advisory Board, replied curtly in January: "Needless to say, your demands are impossible. That being so, they cannot even be the basis for discussion."[43]

Management prepared for a test of strength with the obvious hope of destroying the workers' attachment to the union. While asserting publicly that the Building Service Employees Union had too few members to call a successful walkout, the Realty Advisory Board set up an employment bureau to fill the places of any strikers. On March 1, thousands of workers ignored the threat and walked off their jobs in Manhattan and Bronx apartments. Within a few days, police estimated that 20,000 men and women had struck over 2000 buildings. Declaring a health emergency, Mayor La Guardia brought both sides together. After three days of fruitless talks, union leaders offered to end the strike if owners agreed to submit all issues in the dispute to binding arbitration, but employers adamantly refused to put the question of the closed shop in the hands of any third party.[44]

Meanwhile, owners tried to break the strike. They legally hired thousands of replacements from employment agencies which sprang up around the city. The new workers included jobless New Yorkers and professional strikebreakers who poured into the city from as far away as Ohio. The "finks," as strikers branded them, earned $6.00 to $9.00 a day, double the pay of regular employees. Since clashes between finks and pickets often occurred, owners also engaged private guards, so-called nobles, to protect the new employees. Despite the good wages, the number of strikebreakers soon dwindled as the walkout moved into its second week and finks tired of the unfamiliar work and confrontations with pickets.[45]

The passage of time also softened the attitudes of labor and management. After two weeks, pressure from the mayor finally produced a compromise settlement. The union abandoned its demand for the closed shop, and employers dropped their plan to retain a portion of the strikebreakers. In turn, both sides agreed to a three-year contract which provided for arbitration of most outstanding issues. Although the union still did not receive formal recognition, signature of the agreement by both parties achieved this end in effect.[46] Yet nothing required owners to bargain collectively with the union three years hence. Strikes by workers over the right to organize and negotiate would undoubtedly still confront employers' union-busting tactics as long as labor relations in intrastate businesses depended largely on the free play of market forces.

Since New York State led the country in the number of wage earners unprotected by the NLRB, it became the focus of a drive to extend the right to organize to local workers. In April 1936, within a year after passage of the Wagner Act, the general counsel of the AFL offered a labor relations measure which he had modeled after the federal statute. The State Federation of Labor immediately presented the bill to the legislature sitting in Albany, but it arrived too late in the session to receive serious consideration. Nevertheless, Lehman went over the bill carefully with a representative of the federal Division of Labor Standards who suggested minor revisions.[47]

The federation reintroduced its proposal in 1937. As sponsored by two Democrats, Senator Emmett L. Doyle of Rochester and Assemblyman Irving D. Neustein of Manhattan, the measure copied the broad outline, and at some points the exact wording, of the Wagner Act.[48] In a declaration of findings and policy, the Doyle-Neustein bill asserted that businessmen, often well organized themselves, "have superior economic power in bargaining with employees." This imbalance, according to the proposed legislation, adversely affected the general welfare of the state by curtailing the purchasing power of wage earners, creating sweatshops, and "tending to produce and aggravate recurrent business depressions." The denial of the right of workers to organize and the refusal to accept collective bargaining led to "industrial strife and unrest, which are inimical to the public safety and welfare." Therefore, the bill concluded that it should be

> the public policy of the state to encourage the practice and procedure of collective bargaining and to protect the exercise by workers of full freedom of association, self-organization, and designation of representatives of their own choosing, for the purpose of negotiating the terms and conditions of their employment . . . , free from the interference, restraint or coercion of their employers.

The measure proposed to extend these guarantees to virtually every New Yorker not covered by the Wagner Act.

The state bill created a Labor Relations Board to implement its provisions. Composed of three full-time members appointed by the governor, the panel was empowered to protect the right of workers to bargain collectively through unionization on the basis of majority rule. To prevent interference from employers, the legislation specifically prohibited nine "unfair labor practices." Lawmakers later added a tenth which brought the total to exactly double the number cited by the Wagner Act. The forbidden practices included the formation of employer-dominated company unions, the failure to bargain collectively with employee representatives, and the use of labor spies, blacklists, and yellow-dog contracts.[49]

New Yorkers split along predictable lines over the merits of this sweeping plan. Speaking for trade unionists, George Meany hailed the bill as one which would bring stability to labor and industry in the state. Elinore M. Herrick, a regional director of the NLRB who had helped lead the fight for a minimum wage law, warned that unless New York applied the principles of the Wagner Act to purely intrastate businesses, "we are going to have recurring industrial troubles." Officials of large corporations remained noticeably quiet on this controversial legislation, since their workers were already covered by the National Labor Relations Act. However, organizations of local employers, notably the New York City Merchants' Association and the New York Board of Trade, condemned the onesidedness of the Doyle-Neustein bill, which placed restraints solely on businessmen.[50] The head of the New York State Economic Council characterized the measure as "an invitation to irresponsible labor agitators to get by the throat the multitude of small local business concerns in the State." [51] Attacking from a different angle, the Board of Trade questioned the advisability of creating a state model of the NLRB before the Supreme Court ruled on the validity of the federal law.[52]

On April 12, 1937, the country's highest tribunal removed any doubts about constitutionality. Announcing decisions in a series of related cases, the Supreme Court upheld the Wagner Act in its entirety.[53] These rulings not only undermined resistance to the national law but also prepared the way for enactment of a similar measure in New York. Senator Wagner wired Lehman soon after the Court approved his legislation: THE TIME IS RIPE TO AFFORD THE SAME ADVANTAGES TO LOCAL INDUSTRIES IN NEW YORK.[54]

Since the federal law had passed the ultimate test, Albany legislators amended their proposal so that it followed the Wagner Act even more closely. Representatives of organized labor and Lehman's staff cooperated in redrafting parts of the Doyle-Neustein bill. As adopted by the legislature, the changes encompassed both revisions in administrative procedure and the exclusion of farm labor and employees of government, charitable, educational, and religious organizations.[55] Democrats defeated the attempt of some Republicans to add a ban on sit-down strikes, which were sweeping the country. Senator Doyle argued that this question lay outside the scope of his proposal, which represented "labor's bill of rights." [56]

As the time approached for a final vote on the Doyle-Neustein measure in early May, Governor Lehman recommended the creation of a State Board of Mediation to supplement the State Labor Relations Board (SLRB). While Lehman saw the SLRB as a means of fostering industrial peace by establishing equality between workers and their employers, he conceived of the Board of Mediation as an additional way of assuring the same goal. Since union recognition and collective bargaining did not preclude labor disputes over other matters such as wages and hours, the proposed mediation panel of five members would take steps "to effect a voluntary, amicable and expeditious adjustment and settlement of the differences which have precipitated or threaten to precipitate a labor dispute." [57]

Within a week after Lehman appealed for quick action on both bills, they sailed through the legislature. Except for a brief but sharp debate over including a ban on sit-down strikes, the Doyle-Neustein measure encountered little opposition. It first passed the Democratic-controlled Senate with only two dissenting votes cast by upstate Republicans, and it then easily cleared the Assembly when over thirty members of the Republican majority joined all Democrats save one, an upstate farmer. Both houses unanimously adopted the bill creating a Board of Mediation.[58]

In spite of these lopsided votes, representatives of small businessmen mounted an unsuccessful campaign to win Lehman's veto of the "Little Wagner Act." Letters poured into the executive chamber, particularly from local employer organizations in New York City.[59] Real estate operators, retailers, and building contractors argued that the bill was pro-labor, would increase labor/management conflicts, and drive business out of the state.[60] One of the most reactionary lobbyists in Albany charged that the SLRB "WOULD LITERALLY SOVIETIZE THE STATE OF NEW YORK." [61] Rejecting these dire predictions, Lehman signed into law both the "Little Wagner Act" and its companion measure which established the State Board of Mediation.[62]

The 1937 legislative session rivaled that of 1935 in producing victories for workers. In addition to guaranteeing the right to organize and bargain collectively, New York completed adoption of its social security program, upgraded unemployment insurance benefits, reenacted a minimum wage law, and cut the maximum hours permitted for several categories of women workers.[63] Lehman expressed particular satisfaction with the State Labor Relations Act because, as he correctly observed, it "unfolded a new type of social institution." [64]

Although a number of other states established similar agencies, New York's SLRB and Board of Mediation proved the most effective in the country. Unlike some governors, Lehman not only implemented these statutes but also helped assure their success by selecting experienced and dedicated administrators. The Reverend John P. Boland, a Catholic priest and a regional director of the NLRB, took the post of chairman of the State Labor Relations Board, and William H. Davis, a former deputy administrator of the NRA, became the first head of the Board of Mediation.[65] Close cooperation between the two agencies accounted in part for their remarkable records. Sharing offices in New York City, they referred cases to one another in a practical division of labors.[66]

The State Labor Relations Board also reached an agreement with the NLRB to avoid jurisdictional disputes. In 1937, the National Board recognized the state's exclusive responsibility for a specific list of predominantly local businesses including retail stores, service trades, and small industries which did not ship any large proportion of their goods outside New York. In addition, the SLRB asserted authority over employees in some New York companies affecting interstate commerce if the NLRB refused for any reason to accept the cases. Both Washington officials and the state courts approved this procedure, which prevented the growth of a "no-man's land" between the overburdened National Board and New York's powerful state panel.[67]

After beginning its work in July 1937, the State Labor Relations Board soon found itself flooded with cases. During the last five years of Lehman's administration, the board handled 10,000 disputes regarding both charges of unfair labor practices and petitions for representation elections. These cases involved 435,000 employees, most of whom participated in elections to decide whether the majority of workers in each of the potential bargaining units wanted union representation (see Table 4). Although the SLRB did not report the number of New Yorkers unionized as a result of votes it supervised, the large proportion of elections won by unions indicates that state intervention facilitated the spread of the labor movement (see Table 5). Moreover, the SLRB, in partnership with the NLRB, contributed to the growing acceptance of unions as a legitimate force in the state's economy.[68]

Table 4
Number of Employees Involved in Cases Processed by
the New York State Labor Relations Board, 1937–42

	1937–39[a]	1940	1941	1942	1937–42
Employees involved in unfair labor practice cases	91,892	11,492	12,019	7,619	122,410
Employees involved in representation cases	179,612	35,251	74,039	23,612	312,514
Total	270,892	46,743	86,058	31,231	434,924

[a] The SLRB reported no annual figures for the first three years.

Source: *Report of the New York State Labor Relations Board* (Albany, 1940-43).

The 1930s marked an abrupt shift in the American attitude toward the right to organize. Under the impact of the Depression, the federal and state government shed the laissez faire idea that labor/management relations should be a function of market conditions. New York initially enhanced the right of workers to associate freely by restricting the use of antilabor weapons such as the injunction and the yellow-dog contract. This limited state action was soon overshadowed by the Wagner Act, which committed the federal government to positive and permanent intervention through the NLRB. Following the example of Washington, New York adopted the so-called Little Wagner Act, which extended to intrastate workers the same guarantees of representation and collective bargaining. The creation of the State Board of Mediation

Table 5
Results of Representation Elections Held by the
New York State Labor Relations Board, 1937–42

Election Winner	1937–42	Percent of Total
AFL	630	44
CIO	284	20
Independent union[a]	59	4
Single employer union[b]	52	4
No union	395	28
Total	1420	100

[a]A labor organization unaffiliated with either the AFL or CIO but with membership in more than one company.

[b]An independent organization whose membership was limited to the employees of a single company.

Source: *Report of the New York State Labor Relations Board* (Albany, 1940-43).

also aided the settlement of labor disputes through public means, but the greatest boon to wage earners came from implementation of the Wagner Act and its state model. Supplementing efforts by the federal government, New York provided workers with a bill of rights, thereby ensuring a new equality in labor/management relations.

The union movement itself accounted for much of the change in the period. As the strongest organization of its kind in the country, the New York State Federation of Labor, under the leadership of George Meany, proposed most of the legislation which altered the imbalance in dealings between employees and their employers. Through its active support of Lehman's Little New Deal, organized labor won enactment of the major items in its legislative program and helped prevent New York from adopting any of the restrictive labor laws which other states began to approve in the late 1930s.[69] Affiliates of both the AFL and the Congress of Industrial Organizations (CIO) took advantage of not only the New Deal in Washington but also the Little New Deal in Albany to increase their strength in New York.

NOTES

1. Lyle W. Cooper, "The American Labor Movement in Prosperity and Depression," *American Economic Review*, XXII (1932): 641-59; Leo Wolman, *Ebb and Flow in Trade Unionism* (New York, 1936), pp. 33-42, 84-86, 116; Irving Bernstein, *The Lean Years: A History of the American Worker, 1920-1933* (Boston, 1960), pp. 84-90, 335-36 et passim.

2. Anonymous labor leader quoted in Louis Adamic, "The Collapse of Organized Labor," *Harpers,* January 1932, p. 168.

3. Irving Bernstein, *Turbulent Years: A History of the American Worker, 1933-1941* (Boston, 1970), passim.

4. U.S., Department of Commerce, Bureau of the Census, *Fifteenth Census of the United States, 1930: Population,* vol. III, pt. 2, p. 305; Belle Zeller, *Pressure Politics in New York* (New York, 1937), pp. 8-9.

5. Of fifteen state federation officers in 1930, all but one represented craft unions. Six were affiliated with the building trades and four with transportation and communications. New York State Federation of Labor (hereinafter referred to as NYSFL), Annual Convention, 1930, *Official Proceedings.*

6. See *supra,* chap. IV, p. 77. The subsequent split in labor's ranks between the AFL and the CIO had little immediate impact in New York in spite of the fact that unions from the state's garment industry were among the ten CIO unions suspended by the AFL in November 1936. For several years the dispute remained largely a national one. The New York State Federation of Labor did not formally break ties with local affiliates of the CIO until June 1938, a month after the AFL finally expelled the dissident groups. New York members of the CIO waited until 1938 to open a legislative office in Albany to lobby for their own program. The CIO's organizational drives initially focused on businesses such as steel, automobiles, and textiles centered in other states. The major breakthrough in New York came at General Electric where management gave in without a fight. *New York Times,* January 26, 1938; NYSFL Annual Convention, 1938, *Official Proceedings,* pp. 53-55; Bernstein, *Turbulent Years,* pp. 423-29, 612-13 et passim.

7. Zeller, *Pressure Politics in New York,* pp. 10-26; Paula Eldot, "Alfred E. Smith, Reforming Governor" (unpublished Ph.D. dissertation, Yale University, 1961), pp. 315-62; Bernard Bellush, *Franklin D. Roosevelt as Governor of New York* (New York, 1955), pp. 191-207.

8. John R. Commons and John B. Andrews, *Principles of Labor Legislation* (4th rev. ed.; New York, 1936), pp. 374-75; Irving Bernstein, *The New Deal Collective Bargaining Policy* (Berkeley, Calif., 1950), p. 8.

9. William M. Leiserson, *Right and Wrong in Labor Relations* (Berkeley, Calif., 1938), pp. 26-27. See also Edwin E. Witte, *The Government in Labor Disputes* (New York, 1932), pp. 230-31.

10. Commons and Andrews, *Principles of Labor Legislation,* pp. 413-15; Felix Frankfurter and Nathan Greene, *The Labor Injunction* (New York, 1930), pp. 53-60, 82-105.

11. Witte, *Government in Labor Disputes,* p. 7. One study found that of 118 recorded applications for injunctions in federal courts from 1901 to 1930, 100 were granted. These figures do not include requests that went unchallenged and, therefore, unreported. Frankfurter and Greene, *The Labor Injunction,* p. 49.

12. *Hitchman Coal and Coke Co. v. Mitchell,* 245 U.S. 229.

13. Quoted in Joel I. Seidman, *The Yellow Dog Contract* (Baltimore, 1932), p. 52.

14. Ibid., pp. 37, 41, 79-81; Witte, *Government in Labor Disputes,* pp. 220-24.

15. One study of the New York garment industry found that the use of injunctions increased markedly in the 1920s. P. F. Brissenden and C. O. Swayzee, "The Use of Labor Injunctions in the New York Needle Trades," *Political Science Quarterly,* XLIV (December, 1929): 548-68.

16. *NYSFL Bulletin,* January 10, 1930.

17. NYSFL Annual Convention, 1929, *Official Proceedings*, p. 77; Frankfurter and Greene, *The Labor Injunction*, pp. 77, 187-89; Witte, *Government in Labor Disputes*, pp. 89, 282.

18. Bellush, *Franklin D. Roosevelt as Governor of New York*, p. 315.

19. Bernstein, *The Lean Years*, pp. 391-415.

20. HHL to A. Mothwurf, April 18, 1929, William Green to HHL, May 14, 1929, "Glanzstoff Strike," Special Subject File, HHLP; NYSFL Annual Convention, 1929, *Official Proceedings*, pp. 9-10; HHL Memoir, COHC, pp. 71-72.

21. Morris Sigman to HHL, June 12, 1928, Special File, HHLP; Benjamin Schlesinger to HHL, January 19, 1932, "ILGWU," Reel 23, LGP, HHLP; Allan Nevins, *Herbert H. Lehman and His Era* (New York, 1963), pp. 85-91.

22. NYSFL Annual Convention, 1930, *Official Proceedings*, p. 19.

23. For the NYSFL's legislative program for 1933 and 1934, see *NYSFL Bulletin*, December 19, 1932, December 9, 1933.

24. HHL Messages to the Legislature, January 4, 1933, *Public Papers, 1933*, p. 28, January 3, 1934, *Public Papers, 1934*, p. 50.

25. For a good summary of the progress of labor legislation in Albany, see *NYSFL Bulletin*, May 12, June 10, 1933, May 4, 1934.

26. HHL Message to the Legislature, January 2, 1935, *Public Papers, 1935*, pp. 26-27. Lehman's program closely resembled that suggested by organized labor. *NYSFL Bulletin*, December 12, 1934.

27. *NYSFL Bulletin*, January 10, 1935.

28. Daly to HHL, January 5, 1935, HHL to Daly, January 7, 1935, "Daly, Mark," Reel 24, GP, HHLP.

29. Albany *Knickerbocker Press*, January 4, 5, 9, 16, 17, 1935.

30. *Laws of New York*, 1935, chap. 12.

31. Ibid., chaps. 298, 299, 477; Albany *Knickerbocker Press*, January 23, 1935; *New York Times*, January 21, 30, February 20, March 21, April 3, 13, 27, 1935; Osmond K. Fraenkel, "Recent Statutes Affecting Labor Injunctions and Yellow-Dog Contracts," *Illinois Law Review*, XXX (March 1936): 854-83.

32. The two proposals that failed to pass were ratification of the federal child labor amendment (see *supra*, chap. V) and statewide regulation of fee-charging employment agencies. With strong backing from organized labor and reform groups, Lehman tried at almost every session of the legislature to establish state controls over private employment agencies, some of which were little more than rackets which collected fees for nonexistent jobs. However, enabling bills annually went down to defeat due to the concerted opposition of employment agencies and the powerful newspapers in which they advertised. In addition, New York City officials resisted state supervision because the city had its own system of local regulation, staffed by political appointees. *New York Times*, February 29, 1934, March 11, 1936; Henry L. O'Brien to John B. Andrews, May 3, 1934, Harold C. Ostertag to Andrews, April 1, 1936, Andrews to Michael J. Murphy, April 28, 1939, Andrews Papers, New York State School for Industrial and Labor Relations, Cornell University.

33. For discussions of reforms not covered in this chapter, see *supra*, chaps. IV and V.

34. Meany Statement, April 15, 1935, *Public Papers, 1935*, p. 502. See also Meany Memoir, COHC, pp. 3-4.

35. Mason to HHL, May 2, 1935, "Lehman, Herbert H.," NCL Papers.

36. *New York Times*, November 3, 1935.

37. Bernstein, *The New Deal Collective Bargaining Policy*, pp. 84-153.

38. C. Herman Pritchett, *The Roosevelt Court: A Study in Judicial Politics and Values* (New York, 1948), pp. 199-200.

39. Elinore Herrick to Benedict Wolf, October 26, 1935, Legal folder, Correspondence with Regional Office II, Office of the Secretary, NLRB Records, Record Group 25, National Archives.

40. Albany *Knickerbocker Press,* April 21, 1937.

41. New York State Department of Labor, "Labor Relations: A Concern of the State," Section III, pp. 4-5, enclosed in Elmer F. Andrews to HHL, April 22, 1938, "Labor Department—Constitutional Amendments," Reel 54, GP, HHLP. The number of strikes by interstate workers also increased after passage of the National Labor Relations Act, because many employers throughout the country refused to give in to unionization without a fight. But employees covered by the Wagner Act at least had the law on their side in battles with employers. R. W. Fleming, "The Significance of the Wagner Act," in *Labor and the New Deal,* edited by Milton Derber and Edwin Young (Madison, Wis., 1957), pp. 130-33; Sidney Lens, *Left, Right and Center: Conflicting Forces in American Labor* (Hinsdale, Ill., 1949), pp. 273-86.

42. *New York Times,* January 1, 3, 1936.

43. Ibid., January 11, 1936.

44. Ibid., January 30, February 28, March 1-7, 1936.

45. *New York World-Telegram,* March 3-8, 1936.

46. *New York Times,* March 15, 1936.

47. Charlton Ogburn to Clara F. Beyer, April 23, 1936, Beyer to D. Y. Campbell, April 24, 1936, Campbell to Beyer, April 29, 1936, "Collective Bargaining Legislation, New York, 8-1 (34)," Classified General Files, Division of Labor Standards, Record Group 100, National Archives; NYSFL Annual Convention, 1936, *Official Proceedings,* p. 159.

48. *NYSFL Bulletin,* April 2, 1937.

49. For the complete text of the original Doyle-Neustein bill introduced on February 15, 1937, see Associated Industries *Monitor,* XXIII (March 1937): 229-32.

50. Albany *Knickerbocker Press, New York Times,* March 10, 1937.

51. *New York Times,* May 4, 1937.

52. Ibid., March 11, 1937.

53. *NLRB v. Jones & Laughlin Steel Corp.,* 301 U.S. 1; *NLRB v. Fruehauf Trailer Co.,* 301 U.S. 49; *NLRB v. Friedman-Harry Marks Clothing Co.,* 301 U.S. 58; *Associated Press v. NLRB,* 301 U.S. 103; *Washington, Virginia and Maryland Coach Co. v. NLRB.* 301 U.S. 142; Richard C. Cortner, *The Wagner Act Cases* (Knoxville, 1964), pp. 172-77 et passim.

54. Wagner to HHL, April 27, 1937, "L" (Labor Relations), Reel 52, GP, HHLP.

55. Albany *Knickerbocker Press,* April 16, 20, May 4, 1937; *New York Times,* April 15, 20, 1937. New York's statute ultimately conformed more than those of most other states to the pattern of the Wagner Act. Charles C. Killingsworth, *State Labor Relations Acts: A Study of Public Policy* (Chicago, 1948), p. 113.

56. Albany *Knockerbocker Press,* April 30, 1937.

57. HHL Message to the Legislature, May 3, 1937, *Public Papers, 1937,* pp. 250-51. New York already had a Bureau of Mediation and Arbitration which had been in operation since 1907, but it was largely ineffective in adjusting labor disputes. Howard S. Kaltenborn, *Governmental Adjustment of Labor Disputes* (Chicago, 1943), pp. 180-83.

58. Albany *Knickerbocker Press,* May 4, 1937; *New York Times,* May 5, 7, 8, 1937; New York, *Assembly Journal, 1937,* p. 3435.

59. The major reason for the absence of any opposition from large statewide business organizations was reflected in a statement by Mark Daly of Asociated Industries, who noted that the great majority of employers in his group were exempt from the state law since they were already covered by the Wagner Act. Daly concluded: "Industry did not fare badly at the hands of the 1937 Legislature." Associated Industries *Monitor,* XXIII (May 1937): 271, 282.

60. See correspondence in Bill Jackets, chap. 443 (1937).

61. Merwin K. Hart to HHL, May 14, 1937, ibid.

62. *Laws of New York, 1937,* chap. 443. No employer directly challenged the validity of the Doyle Act, but when one company questioned in court the right of insurance salesmen to take advantage of the law, it also argued the statute unconstitutionally violated "freedom of contract." New York's highest court summarily disposed of this point by citing the Supreme Court's rulings in the Wagner Act cases. *Metropolitan Life Insurance Co. v. NYS Labor Relations Board, et al.,* 280 N.Y. 194.

63. See *supra,* chaps. IV and V.

64. HHL Address, August 24, 1937, *Public Papers, 1937,* p. 716. Even after 1937, New York continued the drive to place additional curbs on union-busting techniques. In 1938, the legislature passed a law regulating private detective agencies to prevent them from acting simultaneously as so-called employment agencies which supplied strikebreakers. *New York Times,* January 21, 1938; *Laws of New York, 1938,* chap. 349.

65. Other members of the SLRB were John D. Moore, a former technical adviser to the NRA and the National Labor Board, and Paul M. Herzog, who became chairman of the NLRB under President Truman. The four other members of the mediation board were: Arthur S. Meyer, a member of the New York City Board of Industrial Relations; Mabel Leslie, a director of the Consumers' League and Women's Trade Union League; John C. Watson, a merchant; and Max Meyer, who had served on many mediation panels. HHL Statement, June 24, 1937, *Public Papers, 1937,* pp. 657-58; HHL to Jacob Billikopf, July 1, 1937, "Billikopf, Jacob," Gen. Corr., 1933-40, HHLP; William H. Davis Memoir, COHC, pp. 62-66.

66. Paul M. Herzog to Robert F. Wagner, February 19, 1940, "Assorted Important Subjects, 1933-38," Wagner Papers, Georgetown University Library; Herzog, "The New York Labor Relations Act in the Development of Administrative Law," *New York State Bar Association Bulletin,* XII (April 1940): 53-59; Herzog, "A State Labor Relations Act in Operation," *American Labor Legislation Review,* XXX (December 1940): 178; Walter P. Arenwald, "Mediation, Arbitration and Investigation of Industrial Disputes in New York State, 1937-1940," *Journal of Political Economy,* XLIX (February 1941): 76; Edwin E. Witte, "What the States Can Do to Improve Labor Relations," *State Government,* XVIII (December 1945): 224.

67. Kurt L. Hanslowe, *Procedures and Policies of the New York State Labor Relations Board* (Ithaca, N.Y., 1964), 128-43. The U.S. Supreme Court subsequently placed some limitations on the SLRB's authority over interstate businesses. *Bethlehem Steel Co. v S.L.R.B.,* 330 U.S. 767 (1947).

68. Union membership in New York jumped from 959,800 in 1939 to 2,051,800 in 1953. This change was brought about by a variety of factors including wartime advances and a period of prosperity, as well as the protection offered by both state and federal governments. While the total number of unionized workers more than doubled, the proportion of organized nonagricultural laborers rose from 23 to 34 percent. The latter figure showed not only how

far the union movement had come but also how far it still had to go in order to reach even a majority of the state's wage earners. Leo Troy, *Distribution of Union Membership among the States, 1939 and 1953* (New York, 1957), p. 4; Milton Derber, "Growth and Expansion," in *Labor and the New Deal*, ed. by Derber and Young, pp. 40-41.

69. For examples of the setbacks suffered by labor in some states, see James T. Patterson, *The New Deal and the States: Federalism in Transition* (Princeton, N.J., 1969), pp. 124-26.

VII

THE PROMISE OF PARITY

The Depression hit New York farmers hard. When the economy collapsed, agricultural prices fell faster than the general price level, and farm incomes dropped to a point where cash receipts often failed to cover the costs of production. In 1932, a New York milk producer complained:

> Our farms' fixed charges, such as interest, insurance, and taxes, are as high, if not higher, than they were two years ago. . . . These set charges we have to pay on a farm mean cash, and something has to be turned into cash. They won't take a cow for your taxes any more. Three years ago we could sell a cow that would pay all the taxes but today it would mean three cows at the market we have, provided someone would pay you cash.[1]

To stave off bankruptcy and the loss of their property, farmers stopped buying needed groceries and clothes, and they started keeping school-aged children at home as a source of cheap labor. One upstate farmer reported in 1932:

> Present returns are enough for not more than a mere existence. The boys and girls more and more are being used to take the place of a hired man.
> Farm families may apparently be well fed, but many are nearly destitute of suitable clothing, shoes and other present day necessities of life.

Some people living on farms lacked even proper nourishment. "One man came in last Saturday and said he hadn't had anything in his house for his wife and children to eat except fruit and vegetables and milk, and he wanted to know if I could not get a sack of flour for him," a rural legislator told his Albany colleagues.[2]

New Dealers in Albany and Washington instituted a number of programs to relieve rural distress. For farmers, the Welfare State sought "parity"—the restoration of agricultural purchasing power to the pre-World War I level. In New York this effort focused on the dairy industry, which constituted the largest and best-organized segment of local agriculture. From 1933 to 1937, the state tried government price-fixing as a means of improving the dairymen's lot. When this system proved of doubtful value, New York gave farmers themselves the power to bargain collectively with milk distributors, but dairymen soon despaired of winning broad acceptance of voluntary controls. At the request of farmers, lawmakers reinstated government-enforced minimum prices in 1938, and after years of negotiations, Albany also reached an agreement with Washington to regulate the price of milk which poured into New York from neighboring states. All these experiments ultimately failed to achieve the elusive goal of full parity, in part because dairymen refused to hold their output in check. Yet however flawed, the various attempts to boost farm prices reflected the desire of New Dealers to guarantee a minimum standard of living not only for industrial laborers but also for their country cousins.

1

Despite its reputation as an urban center, the Empire State long contained one of America's richest agricultural communities. In 1870, New York had more farms than any other state, and it led the country in the value of its agricultural property. After the turn of the century, the number of farms steadily declined until the 1930 census found only 700,000 people, 6 percent of the state's population, living on farms. Yet in that year New York ranked second nationally in the production of milk, vegetables, apples, and grapes. This high standing in perishable foods reflected the proximity of New York City—the country's largest single market for farm products.[3]

By the twentieth century, dairying dominated agriculture in the Empire State. America's industrial revolution in the post-Civil War era had brought a series of technological changes in transportation and refrigeration which permitted upstate farmers to send fresh milk to New York City where the demand for this nourishing food grew rapidly. When prices for fluid milk, as distinguished from by-products like cheese and butter, surpassed the returns for other agricultural commodities, the majority of New York farmers specialized in the dairy business. As a result, the state led all others in milk output until World War I, when Wisconsin captured first place. [4]

The growth of the milk industry created not only profits but also problems. Since dairymen far distant from the metropolitan area could not peddle their own milk to the consumer, they became dependent on middlemen for retail sales. By 1900, several large corporations controlled the New York City market, and they naturally tried to maximize profits by cutting the prices paid to isolated milk producers. To fight the dealers, dairymen combined into groups and even withheld their milk for brief periods during 1883 and 1902. Although these early associations soon collapsed, they prepared the way for the Dairymen's League which became New York's most powerful farm organization. In 1916 and 1919, the League directed successful milk strikes which forced distributors to increase returns to farmers. When these victories brought indictments against League officials for conspiracy to raise prices in New York City, dairymen won passage of legislation enabling farmers to join in cooperatives designed to improve prices for agricultural products.[5]

The Dairymen's League Cooperative Association, Inc., superseded the original League in the early 1920s. The group immediately signed up 50,000 dairymen, most of them New Yorkers, who agreed to let the League dispose of their entire production. As a nonstock, nonprofit interstate association of dairymen supplying the New York City area, the League not only bargained with dealers to get higher prices for members, but also went into the processing and distributing business. By 1932, after buying a number of plants and retail outlets, the organization had become New York City's third largest dealer, ranking behind Borden's Farm Products Company and Sheffield Farms Company. While peddling about half its milk directly to consumers, the League sold the rest of its pool to Borden's. Sheffield received all its milk from members of the Sheffield Producers' Cooperative Association, Inc., which supplied only its parent company.[6]

Despite the growth of the Dairymen's League and other cooperatives modeled after it, almost half the dairymen in New York State remained unorganized in the interwar years. Unaffiliated farmers tended to be less prosperous than those who joined various agricultural organizations. According to a study conducted in 1934-35, "The operators of farms of less than 55 acres in size are represented in only very small proportions in membership in the farm bureau, and in the Dairymen's League and other cooperatives." [7] Independent milk producers sold their output to the many small dealers in cities around the state.

The peculiar requirements of milk marketing handicapped farmers in their persistent struggle with distributors. Although the demand for milk and its supply varied sharply during different seasons and even from day to day, consumers expected at all times to find adequate quantities of this supposedly essential food. Since milk was perishable, farmers could fulfill a shifting demand only by producing more milk than needed in the liquid form. Under the most favorable conditions the dairy industry assumed that it must carry a daily surplus of about 20 percent to meet any unexpected fluctuations in the market. That portion of the output not consumed as fluid milk went into less profitable by-products such as butter and cheese. Since drinking milk brought the greatest returns, farmers naturally competed for this outlet and undercut each other when supplies far surpassed the demand.[8]

The Dairymen's League tried to assure its members equal shares of the fluid-milk market. Through a complicated system known as the classified price plan, the League labeled milk according to its ultimate use and paid dairymen a blended price based on the average rate received by the cooperative for the entire supply it sold each month. Thus, after producers turned their milk over to the League, they waited a month to find out its worth. If for that period 60 percent of the association's pool went into drinking milk and 40 percent into butter, each League member received a check which paid him for 60 percent of his production at the going rate for fluid milk and 40 percent at the lower price for butter. Some farmers bitterly opposed this scheme because they had no way of ensuring that the monthly checks accurately reflected the final uses of their milk.

According to critics, the League became such a large distributor that it lost interest in protecting farmers.[9]

After temporary disruptions caused by World War I, dairymen in the Empire State prospered until 1931. The consumption of milk remained high during the 1920s, and farmers kept the volume under control, which helped stimulate good prices for dairy products. Even the Depression initially had little effect on dairymen, since urban populations did not readily curb their intake of milk. However, in the winter of 1931-32, producers suddenly felt the full impact of the Depression. Within two months the price for 100 pounds of drinking milk dropped from $2.90 to $1.79 and it continued to decline through 1932.[10]

The collapse of the dairy industry struck with a fierce intensity. By 1933, milk prices had fallen 34 percent below the general price level.[11] A long-time observer of the agricultural scene concluded in 1932: "The present state of the dairy farmers in New York State is the most discouraging I have known in the [past] 60 years." [12] When milk returns failed to cover the costs of production, dairymen found themselves short of cash for fixed expenses and store-bought necessities. In desperation some families tried to exist entirely on foods which they raised themselves, such as fruits and vegetables. For these people rural magazines became survival manuals, packed with advice on how to stretch a dollar by, for example, feeding a family of four on 68 cents a day.[13]

Recognizing the plight of the dairymen, the state legislature created a temporary committee to investigate the milk industry in 1932. After a year of study, the committee found that milk prices covered little more than half the cost of production by January 1933. This decline in the dairy business, according to the state inquiry, was caused by a variety of factors including the curtailment of consumers' purchasing power, an expansion of milk output since 1927, and the prevalence of price-cutting and other destructive trade practices among dealers. The latter problem came about because during the period of glut small distributors, who contracted for little of the surplus and sold drinking milk exclusively, could undercut the Dairymen's League and Borden's, which had larger milk pools and had to dispose of the surplus by turning it into cheaper by-products.[14]

After citing overproduction as a primary cause of ruinous prices, the committee proposed to rescue farmers simply through manipulation of the market. To prevent bankruptcy and guarantee a continuous supply of milk, the inquiry recommended that New York create a temporary control board with the power to regulate the distribution of milk by licensing dealers, prohibiting unfair trade practices, and setting minimum retail prices. "The purpose of this emergency measure," the investigators emphasized, "is to bring partial relief to dairymen from the disastrously low prices for milk which have prevailed in recent months." [15] Committee members justified government assistance on the grounds that dairying represented the most important branch of agriculture in New York and milk constituted an essential item in the human diet.[16] Moreover, the legislative report concluded, "the state must come to the aid of these [farm] families as it has to the aid of the unemployed." [17] While suggesting a remedy for marketing problems, the investigators avoided the question of surplus, which they hoped farmers could cope with themselves through cooperatives such as the Dairymen's League.

Begun under the aegis of Governor Roosevelt, the Joint Legislative Committee to Investigate the Milk Industry issued its findings in April 1933, after Herbert Lehman had assumed leadership of the Empire State. As a product of Manhattan, the new governor knew little about agriculture, and he relied on advice from several quarters. The State Department of Agriculture and Markets proved of limited aid to Democratic chief executives, because the legislature had retained control over this agency when Alfred E. Smith had reorganized the state government during the 1920s. Constitutional amendments approved at that time had given the governor power to choose other department heads, but selection of the commissioner of agriculture remained in the hands of the legislative branch. This Republican-controlled body had naturally ensured the appointment of Republicans who operated independently of Democratic chief executives.[18] As his own tie to the farm community, Governor Roosevelt had created the Agricultural Advisory Commission, an unofficial panel dominated by leaders of farm associations, which convened periodically and recommended legislation to aid farmers.[19] Upon taking office, Lehman reappointed Roosevelt's Advisory Commission with a few changes in personnel, and soon thereafter the new governor selected Dr. Carl E. Ladd to head that body.[20]

Since the advisory board met infrequently, Lehman depended largely on Ladd for expert opinion. A graduate of the New York State College of Agriculture at Cornell, Ladd had subsequently taught there and had become dean of the college in 1932. Dedicated to the interests of New York farmers, the energetic Ladd emerged as a leader not only in education but also in politics. He cultivated friendships with Roosevelt and Lehman which permitted him to exercise unusual influence, particularly in the case of Lehman who had little familiarity with farming. While working behind the scenes for Lehman as an unpaid consultant and speech writer, the Cornell dean remained politically independent with close ties to leaders of state farm groups, most of whom were Republicans. Ladd considered himself a spokesman for New York farmers generally, but like his Cornell colleagues who ardently supported cooperation among farmers, Ladd most often reflected the views of organized agriculture, led by the Dairymen's League, the Grange, and the Farm Bureau.[21]

An air of tension surrounded the formulation of a state farm policy in 1933. After the legislature convened, one observer warned: "The farmers of New York State are in a desperate and ugly mood." [22] During February, two months before the committee investigating dairy problems finished its lengthy report, Senator Perley A. Pitcher, chairman of the group and a Republican from the dairy country of northern New York, introduced a measure creating a state milk control board with extensive authority, including the power to fix a minimum price to dairymen and a maximum price to consumers. A public hearing on the Pitcher bill showed that farmers overwhelmingly favored government regulation of milk marketing. After traveling long distances to Albany, over two thousand hard-hit dairymen literally shouted their approval of the Pitcher measure, which they seemed to embrace as their only hope of salvation.[23] One distressed farmer pleaded: "Give us something to pull us out of the hole. We want action." [24]

The Dairymen's League and its supporters firmly opposed the original Pitcher bill. Officials of the state's largest cooperative feared that the milk control proposal would undermine their organization, since the legislation made no provision for the League's classified price plan. Moreover, as a defender of the League's position pointed out to Lehman, the Pitcher measure did not

> preserve the principle of cooperative marketing, on which principle most of the farm leaders of the State believe any permanent solution of the problem must rest. League officers and directors are firmly convinced that the passage of this bill would wreck the Dairymen's League.[25]

Recognizing the force of producer demands for government action, the League hoped to win increased regulation of distribution without any state price-fixing. Dean Ladd and other farm spokesmen backed the cooperative in its resistance to price controls. The *American Agriculturist,* a prominent farm journal published in New York, objected to Pitcher's legislation because it would allegedly weaken or destroy the League. Edward R. Eastman, the magazine's dynamic editor who had formerly held the same position on the *Dairymen's League News,* usually echoed the views of organized farm interests with which he worked closely both as a newspaperman and as secretary of Lehman's Agricultural Advisory Commission.[26]

While the Dairymen's League opposed price controls, large distributors favored the idea. Big companies like Borden's which faced cutthroat competition from smaller dealers saw *minimum* prices to consumers as a means of restoring some stability to the milk business. The Pitcher bill, however, stipulated *maximum* retail prices and minimum returns to farmers, which the distributors claimed would ruin them.

In a bit of horse-trading, dealers and the Dairymen's League joined forces in Albany and effectively rewrote the milk control bill through a series of amendments. The resulting legislation set up a state board which was to fix *minimum* wholesale and retail prices for each of the milk classifications already used by the League. Dealers promised to pass along to farmers a fair share of any increased profits, but the revised measure no longer required the state to fix minimum returns to dairymen.[27] John J. Dillon, a long-time opponent of Borden's and the League, accurately observed in his magazine, *The Rual New-Yorker:* "It started out to be a farmers' bill. The change made it a dealers' bill." [28]

Unhappy about the measure's new slant, a group of western New York dairymen revolted. At the end of March, some one thousand independent producers withheld their milk from the Rochester market and dumped the milk of fellow dairymen who tried to cross picket lines on country roads. In a petition to Albany lawmakers, the strikers demanded prompt action on a bill providing for minimum milk prices for farmers. After days of battling police sent to the scene by the governor, dissident dairymen called a truce to await the response of state officials.[29]

The governor and the legislature moved quickly. After Lehman issued an emergency message to expedite adoption of a milk control law, the Senate immediately passed the amended measure with a provision permitting the state to set prices for farmers. Only five senators, four of them New York City Democrats, voted against the plan, because it would undoubtedly hurt the consumer.[30] In the Assembly the chairman of that body's Agriculture Committee tried unsuccessfully to add an amendment supported by the Dairymen's League which would have barred the state from fixing prices for producers.[31] When minor changes by the Assembly forced the Senate to reconsider the measure, violence erupted again in the Rochester area. After a day of skirmishes between police and dairymen, the legislature completed action on the Pitcher bill, and the strike came to a halt while the governor reviewed the measure. Lehman's position remained in doubt, since he had emphasized that his willingness to speed consideration of the legislation was not intended as an endorsement.[32] However, after the governor's Agricultural Advisory Commission approved the bill, Lehman signed the proposal into law.[33]

New York's establishment of milk control marked a new departure in government intervention in the economy. Although the state had long regulated monopolies, it now stepped in for an emergency period of one year for the expressed purpose of increasing profits in a highly competitive business disrupted by expanding supplies and a diminishing consumer demand. Intended originally to help milk producers through minimum *farm* prices, the Pitcher bill was rewritten under pressure from dealers and the Dairymen's League to set minimum *retail* milk prices and to protect the League's classified marketing system. The legislation also directed the state milk board to license distributors and end unfair trade practices. As finally enacted, the law made the fixing of minimum prices to dairymen entirely optional rather than mandatory, but even without implementation of this provision, farmers expected to share any increased profits resulting from higher retail prices. Although dealers and producers would reap their improved returns at the expense of powerless consumers, they maintained that the public also benefited because state controls assured an uninterrupted supply of quality milk. Many urban lawmakers accepted this argument, especially after some farmers temporarily withheld their milk from the market. The clamoring of dairymen brought passage of what the *American Agriculturist* accurately called

the most far-reaching, radical legislation that has ever been proposed for agriculture. It takes entire control of the business, not only out of the hands of the dealers but out of the hands of the farmers, and puts it into a State body.[34]

The New York law soon became a model for a number of other states that adopted similar measures.[35]

2

The Empire State's initial attempts to regulate milk prices met with a mixed reception. Two days after the Pitcher proposal went into effect in April 1933, the new control board set minimum retail prices for different grades of milk. The panel, composed of a director and the state commissioners of agriculture and health, had hoped to fix prices at prevailing rates, but it found such a wide range that it decided to peg them at the relatively high level already established by Borden's and Sheffield Farms, which represented a victory for New York City's two largest dealers. Farmers, unwilling to count on the generosity of distributors, insisted that the milk board also exercise its discretionary power to fix minimum returns to dairymen. When the state delayed taking this step, producers who had successfully used a strike to stampede lawmakers in April threatened similar action if officials did not immediately order a minimum price for farmers. The control board gave in to this demand in May, setting a price slightly over that called for by dairymen. As a result of the state's action, a brief period of calm settled over New York's dairy country.[36]

During the summer of 1933, dissident farmers again revolted. Hard hit by a drought which forced them to buy feed for their herds, some dairymen complained that the state's use of the League's classified price plan for determining returns to producers allowed dealers to pay farmers a blended rate for their milk which allegedly cheated them of a fair share of the consumer's dollar.[37] At the end of July, a group of independent producers led by Albert Woodhead, the farmer who had organized the spring milk strike, insisted that the state stop applying the League's complex price system and instead guarantee every dairyman a flat 45 percent of the total retail price for all milk. Woodhead warned of another strike on August 1 if Albany rejected this demand. While admitting that the classified plan was too complicated, the milk board responded that this system had increased returns to farmers and, furthermore, that the state could not institute an untested alternative simply upon the request of a minority of New York dairymen. Despite personal appeals from Woodhead, Lehman refused to intercede in matters legally under the jurisdiction of the milk board.[38] In the event of a strike, the governor promised that "the state will protect all law-abiding citizens in the legitimate conduct of their lawful affairs of business." [39]

On August 1, milk and blood mingled on upstate roads. Striking farmers, confined largely to four counties in the middle of the state, withheld their milk from market and tried to stop uncooperative neighbors by placing trees and spiked planks across highways and dumping the milk of trucks forced to halt. Violence erupted outside Boonville, a small town north of Utica, where a group of helmeted state troopers swinging nightsticks waded into a crowd of farmers who stood by a roadblock. In the resulting melee eight dairymen were injured and one was hospitalized. Although police claimed a farmer precipitated the assault by throwing a rock, the troopers' response seemed excessively brutal, and the Boonville incident enraged dairymen throughout the state, most of whom had not initially participated in the strike. Within two days "the milk holiday," as some called it, spread rapidly from central New York to western and southern counties, and over 10,000 of the state's 80,000 dairymen joined the withholding action out of sympathy for the Boonville farmers. Opposing groups of dairymen fought each other on several occasions and even exchanged gunshots, but strikers and police avoided any more pitched battles despite numerous confrontations and arrests.[40]

From his office in Albany, Lehman focused on quelling the violence. While accepting the right of dairymen to keep their milk at home, the governor sought to prevent strikers from interfering with producers, many of them members of the Dairymen's League, who wanted to deliver their milk to market. The League accused its opponents of using "tactics strikingly similar to those of Communistic agitators," and it demanded that the state crack down on the "other than 100 per cent American farmers [who] had a hand in the movement." [41] Despite insistent pleas from a variety of quarters, especially in organized agriculture, the governor refused to declare martial law and call out the National Guard. He relied instead on the state police to supplement the efforts of county officials whom Lehman prodded to beef up their forces.[42]

In addition to stemming the tide of lawlessness, the governor sought a thorough review of milk board activities. On the fourth day of the strike, he asked the legislature, which was already meeting in a special session on other business, to create a committee that could determine the attitudes of producers, distributors, and consumers toward the state regulation of milk. Lehman saw no reason to continue price-fixing if dairymen, who had insisted on its adoption, had really turned against it.[43] Republican assemblymen, however, blocked the proposed inquiry because, they argued, "No investigation can be effective while property is being destroyed and lives threatened." Lehman agreed that the strike was "both unwise and indefensible," but he contended that the state should give dairymen an opportunity to speak their minds.[44] Therefore, when lawmakers refused to provide a forum, the governor delivered a statewide radio appeal on August 12, and he promised that farmers would receive a full hearing before the milk board as soon as "violence and intimidation and other unlawful methods have ceased and are a thing of the past." Strikers offered a one-week truce while they aired their grievances in Albany, but Lehman immediately countered that no state official would meet with any farmer until the strike was definitely called off.[45]

The governor's use of the carrot and the stick brought peace to the dairy country. Within days after Lehman assured farmers of a hearing, Albert Woodhead asked his followers to abandon their strike because the governor was "willing to hear the farmers' side of the story." [46] When dairymen complied, Lehman formally requested the milk control board to commence a thorough study of the milk industry.[47] The governor's handling of the strike won him praise throughout New York. Upstate newspapers applauded his refusal to use the National Guard or bargain with strikers until they halted illegal interference with other dairymen.[48] One journal commended the chief executive as "splendidly courageous, fair, and effective." [49] Even the leader of the holiday movement expressed appreciation for Lehman's efforts to avoid martial law and secure dairymen a hearing in Albany. Yet although the governor succeeded in ending the strike, many dairymen remained disgruntled, since two weeks of turmoil had failed to bring any material improvement in their condition.[50] Lehman himself concluded in a letter to his secretary: "The whole milk situation is so extremely complicated that it seems almost impossible to satisfy any substantial group of producers." [51]

3

While trying to prove itself to farmers during the first year of its life, New York's milk control board survived a legal challenge to its authority. The test of the state's power to fix milk prices originated in Rochester where Leo Nebbia, a local grocer, was fined $5.00 in city court for disregarding an order of the milk board. Nebbia's crime—a misdemeanor—consisted of selling two quarts of milk and a loaf of bread for 18 cents after the state had set the minimum price of milk at 9 cents per quart.[52] In explaining his action, the storekeeper subsequently declared:

> I sell a bottle of milk at what the law says. At that price I make a good profit—so good, that to my best customers . . . I give a loaf of bread free and still make money.[53]

Although this practice violated a state decree, Nebbia's lawyer contended that the milk board's order contravened the equal protection and due process clauses of the Fourteenth Amendment, and therefore, the Pitcher milk control law should be ruled unconstitutional. When lower courts rejected these claims, Nebbia appealed his conviction to New York's highest tribunal.[54]

The *Nebbia* case focused primarily on the question of due process. In a long line of decisions extending back into the nineteenth century, the United States Supreme Court had severely restricted the power of state governments to regulate wages, hours, and prices on the grounds that such action deprived citizens of their property without the due process of law required by the Fourteenth Amendment. Although the Court admitted the right of states to control businesses "affected with a public interest," it had narrowly interpreted this phrase so that, according to a 1932 decision, "the production or sale of food or clothing cannot be subjected to legislative regulation on the basis of a public use." [55] This statement seemed to preclude government control of Nebbia's retail milk prices, but lawyers for the state argued that the importance of milk in the human diet made the general welfare dependent on its production. Thus the fixing of prices to ensure a steady flow of milk constituted a valid exercise of the state's police power, especially when limited to an emergency period of one year. [56]

On July 11, 1933, the New York Court of Appeals upheld the conviction of Nebbia by a vote of five to one. Speaking for the majority, Chief Judge Cuthbert W. Pound noted that an earlier generation probably would have condemned the milk control law

> as a temerarious interference with the rights of property and contract . . . [and] with the natural law of supply and demand. But we must not fail to consider that the

police power is the least limitable of the powers of government and that it extends to all the great public needs; that constitutional law is a progressive science; that statutes aiming to establish a standard of social justice, to conform the law to the accepted standards of the community, to stimulate the production of a vital food product by fixing living standards of prices for the producer, are to be interpreted with that degree of liberality which is essential to the attainment of the end in view . . . and that mere novelty is no objection to legislation.

Despite recognized limitations on legislative authority to abridge property rights, Pound concluded, "we do not feel compelled to hold that the 'due process' clause of the Constitution has left milk producers unprotected from oppression." [57] The lone dissenter on the Court of Appeals cited recent Supreme Court interpretations of the due process clause which, he argued, made price-fixing in the dairy industry unconstitutional.[58]

The nation's highest tribunal chose to ignore these precedents when reviewing the *Nebbia* case. By the slimmest of margins, the Supreme Court broke with recent tradition and sustained New York's milk control act in March 1934.[59] The majority decision, written by Justice Owen J. Roberts, avoided consideration of the emergency situation and asserted:

there is no closed class or category of businesses affected with a public interest. The phrase "affected with a public interest" can, in the nature of things, mean no more than that an industry, for adequate reason, is subject to control for the public good.[60]

Relying partially on an 1877 ruling *(Munn v. Illinois)*, the Court declared that states held the power to regulate the prices set by private companies even if the businesses were neither monopolies nor government franchises. In the issue at hand, Roberts considered New York's setting of milk prices "not to be unreasonable or arbitrary, or without relation to the purpose to prevent ruthless competition from destroying the wholesale price structure on which the farmer depends for his livelihood, and the community for an assured supply of milk." [61] The four dissenting judges questioned the foundation for the majority's concept of public interest and due process. "The Legislature," Justice James C. McReynolds maintained, "cannot lawfully destroy guaranteed rights of one man with the prime purpose of enriching another, even if for the moment, this may seem advantageous to the public." [62]

4

The Supreme Court's acceptance of milk control enabled New York to consider extending the law, due to lapse on April 1, 1934. A week after the Court handed down its decision on March 5, Lehman endorsed a report of the milk board which recommended the continuance of price-fixing for another year and the reenactment of the agency's other functions on a permanent basis. The latter powers included the authority to license dealers and investigate all aspects of the milk industry. In order to strengthen state regulation, the board also suggested that its administrative apparatus be incorporated into the Department of Agriculture and Markets as the Division of Milk Control. Above all, board members warned that if New York terminated strict supervision of the dairy business, "milk prices will undoubtedly fall to a very low level, and the conditions in the dairy industry will become chaotic." [63]

Table 6
Average Price per Hundred Pounds Received by Farmers for
Average Test Milk at New York State Plants, 1932–41 *

Month	1932	1933	1934	1935	1936	1937	1938	1939	1940	1941
(1)	(2)	(3)	(4)	(5)	(6)	(7)	(8)	(9)	(10)	(11)
January	$1.61	$1.17	$1.75	$1.96	$2.08	$2.07	$2.23	$2.06	$2.32	$2.23
February	1.58	1.12	1.71	1.96	2.07	2.05	2.07	1.92	2.26	2.15
March	1.48	1.01	1.58	1.93	1.91	1.93	1.84	1.49	2.08	2.08
April	1.30	.99	1.50	1.86	1.76	1.75	1.57	1.23	1.92	1.97
May	1.16	1.18	1.49	1.72	1.67	1.61	1.42	1.19	1.73	1.96
June	1.07	1.37	1.56	1.57	1.66	1.54	1.36	1.28	1.68	2.04
July	1.10	1.55	1.64	1.62	1.82	1.73	1.40	1.59	1.82	2.39
August	1.22	1.79	1.74	1.71	2.14	1.94	1.49	2.05	1.96	2.54
September	1.30	1.77	1.73	1.77	2.11	2.11	2.00	2.21	2.10	2.65
October	1.34	1.70	1.80	1.92	2.09	2.22	2.08	2.43	2.10	2.86
November	1.40	1.83	1.95	2.13	2.25	2.55	2.29	2.42	2.33	2.95
December	1.29	1.79	2.01	2.13	2.15	2.49	2.18	2.34	2.34	2.90

* Owing to seasonal variations, price changes are best reflected by comparisons based on the same month.

Source: New York, *Annual Reports of the Department of Agriculture and Markets for the Years 1940, 1941.*

During the first year of milk control, New York had witnessed marked improvements in the dairy trade. The average prices paid to farmers nearly doubled, and some stability returned to the distribution of milk (see Table 6, columns 3 and 4). Tracing the reasons for these changes proved difficult. Although state price-fixing orders had enabled dealers to regain control of their markets, increased returns to dairymen were caused by more than government intervention, in spite of Lehman's claim that "better prices for fluid milk . . . resulted from the work of the Milk Control Board." [64] The state had helped but so too had the drought, which reduced milk production during the summer of 1933. Moreover, the general price level had risen while New York had regulated the milk business. [65]

The 1934 bill extending milk control encountered some opposition, but organized producers and dealers pushed it through the legislature. Prominent farm groups supported the measure because they contended that the milk board had stabilized the industry and placed "several million dollars in the pockets of farmers." [66] However, independent dairymen who had struck against the board the previous summer still claimed that state supervision had helped dealers and the Dairymen's League at the expense of unaffiliated producers. Although leading distributors favored continuation of the milk board, they protested new provisions which made some regulations permanent. At a public hearing on the bill, a lone spokesman for consumers pointed out that they had borne the burden of improved returns to farmers through increased retail prices, but this appeal on behalf of unorganized milk drinkers won little sympathy in Albany. Working against a deadline of April 1, the legislature approved the extension of milk control with only four dissenting votes cast by urban lawmakers. [67]

In 1935, New York prolonged state price-fixing for another year. Leading farm associations backed the continuation of emergency controls until April 1, 1936, and the Democratic-dominated legislature quickly passed an enabling act with little fanfare. As long as farmers' returns steadily improved during this period, few questioned the value of government price-fixing (see Table 6). [68]

During the 1930s, the plight of dairymen elicited much sympathy from the majority of New Yorkers who lived in cities. Urban legislators overwhelmingly accepted regulations on milk designed to raise prices, and spokesmen for consumer groups asserted that an identity of interests bound farmers and workers, since both were exploited by milk dealers. [69] Writing late in the decade in a radical farm journal, an official of the Milk Consumers Protective Committee of the Consumers Union declared:

> One of the most gratifying accomplishments of the past year to my mind, has been the increased sympathy and understanding between city dwellers and farmers. . . . We have come to realize that our interests and welfare are inter-dependent and we are determined to work more and more closely for our common good. [70]

Such statements reflected the hope of some liberal New Yorkers that exploited city workers could politically join forces with hard-pressed dairymen. In 1938, New York's American Labor Party announced that "its chief purpose, aim and goal [was] an independent labor and farmer political party." [71] The dream of a farmer-labor coalition, coupled with compassion for suffering dairymen, led many urban lawmakers to support higher farm prices during the 1930s.

5

New York's milk program excluded controls on production, which became one of the most widely used means of raising farm prices during the 1930s. In the dairy business the supply of milk had traditionally stayed close to the demand of consumers, taking into consideration the fact that the industry normally carried a 20 percent surplus to meet any sudden increase in milk purchases. The number of dairy cows in New York had not risen significantly during the 1920s, which explained in part why dairymen had fared so well at a time when producers of staples like wheat and cotton had seen their prices drop sharply. After 1930, a leading cause of low milk prices was a shrinking demand rather than an unusual expansion of supplies. Following more than three decades of steady increase, New York's per capita consumption of milk had fallen about 10 percent during 1931-32, as a result of reduced purchasing power. In 1933, the legislative committee investigating the dairy industry had warned that "unless some form of arbitrary regulation is applied, the production of milk will not be satisfactorily adjusted to the demand for a period of several years." [72] However, the committee avoided recommending any specific plan for restricting output, in part because no one could decide how to control a perishable commodity produced largely by numerous small farmers.

New York dairymen also overwhelmingly opposed any government regulation of their production. Leaders of the farm community argued that "surplusses [sic] have been exaggerated and that impending shortages of useful things may result." [73] Emphasizing reduced rates of consumption, Edward R. Eastman of the *American Agriculturist* asserted: "Of course there can never be any real overproduction of these best foods in the world." [74] Yet statements like these failed to take into account the impact of government price-fixing which would almost certainly stimulate increased output if it achieved the desired goal of improved returns for farmers. Late in 1933, Charles H. Baldwin, New York's commissioner of agriculture and a member of the milk board, warned Farm Bureau members: "Any one acquainted with dairy conditions today will admit that we can no longer secure satisfactory prices with government control unless we have some means of regulating production." [75] The following year, the state milk board asked for and received discretionary power to institute production quotas, but the agency found "no need at present to reduce the amount of milk produced in New York State." [76] Apparently unwilling to face certain opposition from farmers, the milk board never attempted to regulate milk supplies at their source. State leaders even ceased reminding dairymen that they should keep an eye on their output.[77]

While overlooking their own responsibility for market conditions, New York dairymen tried to use advertising to encourage more milk drinking. During 1933 and 1934, Edward R. Eastman spearheaded a drive to win state backing for a publicity campaign designed to revive the sagging demand for dairy products.[78] In support of his plan, the editor of the *American Agriculturist* argued that state-sponsored advertising of milk would "do more to increase consumption, take care of surplus and improve prices for farmers than anything else that is being done." [79] After this proposal attracted the support of organized farm groups in 1934, the legislature passed a milk publicity bill which levied a small tax on producers and dealers to raise $500,000 for a year-long state campaign to promote the drinking of milk. Lehman initially had reservations about the propriety of government involvement in this enterprise, but he signed the measure after the Agricultural Advisory Commission came out in favor of it.[80]

Soon after New York started publicizing milk, the *American Agriculturist* originated a drive to win the ultimate endorsement for milk. During the summer of 1934, the magazine called on New Yorkers to celebrate "Milk Sunday" as a day devoted to the greater glory of the state's leading agricultural product. With surprising enthusiasm, worshipers dedicated whole church services to milk. Drawing on Ezekiel 20:6 ("A land flowing with milk and honey, which is the glory of all lands"), one upstate minister warmed to his subject:

> Jesus taught that human life is holy. Milk is essential to human life. Therefore, I say to you that milk is holy because human life is at stake in that pail of milk. There is nothing in this chancel more holy than milk.[81]

Another preacher blessed milk as a "food fit for God and His angels." [82]

The state-backed publicity campaign often resembled that carried on by ministers. Health officials complained that the advertising agencies hired by New York circulated statements, "some of which are quite inaccurate from a scientific point of view and many of which smack of quackery." [83] Emphasizing the usual Madison Avenue appeals to vanity, ads declared that "Milk is Not Fattening," and they called on women to "Clear up your Complexion with Milk." [84] Despite such extravagant claims, publicity proved of doubtful value in stimulating greater use of milk because, as a spokesman for consumers pointed out, people knew the importance of milk but curtailed their intake after the Depression cut incomes. The success of the milk control board in raising retail prices also discouraged increased consumption. When advertising failed to have any marked effect on milk sales, some farmers and dealers demanded an end to the program which they had to finance.[85] However, the original backers of this experiment, including publishers whose newspapers benefited from the windfall, persuaded the legislature and the governor to extend the "emergency" program year by year through 1942.[86]

The Depression-oriented concern with surpluses also stimulated a drive to rid dairy herds of diseased cows.[87] Fifteen years before Lehman became governor, New York had inaugurated a campaign to remove tubercular cattle by giving indemnities to dairymen as partial payment for animals that had to be destroyed. This idea proved more popular among farmers in the 1930s, when they faced a shrinking demand for milk; and in 1937, the state announced that it had finally eliminated TB from its dairy herds at a cost of $60 million spent over a period of two decades.[88] The *American Agriculturist* championed disease eradication as a means of controlling milk output, but, expressing the sentiments of New York farmers, the journal declared that "it is wrong to say to a dairyman that he should reduce the amount of feed given his best cows in order to reduce production, or that he should reduce the number of his good cows." [89]

Practical considerations also prevented New York from adopting restrictions on milk output. In addition to the lack of a proven scheme for regulating milk supplies and the difficulty of enforcing any program opposed by farmers themselves, the inability of New York to control the production of dairymen in neighboring states blocked action in Albany. The head of the Dairymen's League declared in 1933: "We can imagine the success we would have of obtaining the consent of the dairy farmers in New York State to reduce their production if it were possible for the producers of adjoining states to increase their production and sell it in the market that the New York State dairy farmers would lose." [90] Yet in the absence of any check on output, New York farmers predictably enlarged their dairy herds as a result of more favorable milk returns during the period 1933-36.[91] By 1937, the increased volume of milk contributed to a drop in prices, but dairymen continued to overlook their own responsibility for the turn of events. Even at the end of the decade, New York farm leaders were still telling their followers that "the apparent surplus has been caused by under-consumption." [92]

6

The reasons for the instability of New York's dairy business lay partly outside the state. The milkshed which supplied New York City with drinking milk extended for a radius of five hundred miles from the center of the metropolis. Although New York farmers furnished over two-thirds of the city's fluid milk, the remainder came from an area stretching from Maryland to Canada. The metropolitan market also encompassed parts of New Jersey and Connecticut. Therefore, effective regulation of New York's dairy industry necessitated cooperation among several states and the federal government, but these parties failed for years to reach a mutually satisfactory agreement.[93]

The first attempt to stabilize marketing and production throughout the New York milkshed came in the wake of the 1933 milk strike. New York, New Jersey, Connecticut, and Vermont—the four states in the area with milk control boards—created a Committee of Eighteen composed of representatives of the four boards, the federal Department of Agriculture, and leading milk distributors and producers. This group hoped to take advantage of the New Deal's Agricultural Adjustment Act, which sought to restore farmers' purchasing power through production controls, marketing agreements, and the removal of surpluses. The Agricultural Adjustment Administration (AAA) initially relied on regional agreements to improve the returns for drinking milk in each marketing area. According to this procedure, local dealers and producer associations drew up tentative contracts governing prices, output, and trade practices. If approved by the Secretary of Agriculture, the agreements could be enforced by the AAA, which had the power to license distributors handling dairy products. Any firm that violated the accepted price and trade regulations could have its federal license removed, thereby preventing it from doing further business. In effect, this system implemented at the interstate level the same activities carried on by New York's milk board. By the time interested groups in the New York City market requested federal help in stabilizing their fluid milk business, Washington had already certified agreements for several other cities.[94]

After working for over a month, the Committee of Eighteen submitted its proposal to the AAA in early October 1933. The tentative agreement applied the League's classified price system to all milk sold in the metropolitan area and established production quotas based on a percentage of milk supplied by each farmer for the respective month of the preceding year.[95] This plan represented a victory for the Dairymen's League, since, according to the counsel for New York's milk board, it would provide "for all producers not members of the large cooperatives all the activities which the Dairymen's League has in the past carried on for its producers."[96] All farmers would bear the cost of administration by paying the same fee the League charged for its services. Unaffiliated dairymen, none of whom participated in formulating the agreement, complained that they could not even obtain a copy of the proposal. The Community Councils of New York, Inc., also disapproved of the failure to include any representatives of consumers who would foot the cost of parity for farmers through higher retail prices.[97]

The Committee of Eighteen proposal ultimately died in Washington. Since the AAA had over 150 other milk agreements to review, its overburdened staff took more time than expected to examine the draft for New York. Furthermore, the AAA considered more carefully the tentative agreement for the country's largest single market, which handled fully 10 percent of the nation's drinking milk. When Washington finally insisted on extensive revisions, it encountered opposition from the Committee of Eighteen, which resented many of the alterations. Cooperatives and the state milk boards feared that the federal government would usurp their powers and prerogatives. With so many conflicting interests involved, Lehman could not get President Roosevelt to intervene and break the deadlock.[98]

After months of fruitless negotiations over the Committee of Eighteen proposal, the New York and New Jersey milk boards prepared an alternative plan in January 1934. At the same time a shakeup in the Agricultural Adjustment Administration forced out officials who had backed marketing agreements which proved of questionable value in the absence of strict production controls and effective enforcement. After announcement of a new federal policy which emphasized the restriction of surpluses, the New York/New Jersey plan was redrawn so that it relied more heavily on administration by the AAA.[99]

This proposal also failed to satisfy all interested groups. At a series of hearings in February 1934, the Dairymen's League endorsed the New York/New Jersey plan, but independent producers objected to the inclusion of the League's classified price system. Opponents of the cooperative still wanted a single price for all their milk determined in advance of its delivery to market. Conservative New York officials looking at the plan worried about the usurpation of state prerogatives. Although Commissioner of Agriculture Charles H. Baldwin, a Republican, had long called for federal regulation of interstate milk prices, he feared that strict controls by the AAA would undermine the authority of the state milk board.[100] New York's attorney general supported these suspicions by publicly airing his belief that the AAA proposal "will mean the end of state sovereign government as such. It will initiate a form of centralized national authority never within the contemplation of the Federal or State Constitutions." [101] With farmers split and Albany officials skeptical, attempts to regulate the entire milkshed again collapsed. Some New Yorkers, particularly Republicans, complained that Secretary of Agriculture Henry A. Wallace showed greater interest in western and southern producers of wheat, cotton, and hogs, but this charge overlooked the unwillingness of many New Yorkers to accept federal controls on milk recommended by the AAA.[102]

In the absence of federal regulations, New York tried unsuccessfully to stop cheaper out-of-state milk from washing out its minimum price structure. Following a provision of the Pitcher law, the New York milk board ruled that dealers who purchased milk outside the state could not sell it in New York unless they had paid at least the minimum price that farmers in the Empire State received. A New York City distributor, G. A. F. Seelig, Inc., which bought its milk in Vermont, challenged this prohibition as an unconstitutional impairment of interstate commerce.[103] Although New York admitted in federal court to an indirect burden on the flow of goods between states, it argued that this was permissible under local police powers in order to protect the general welfare of citizens. The United States Supreme Court unanimously disagreed in an opinion handed down in March, 1935.

Neither the power to tax nor the police power may be used by the state of destination with the aim of establishing an economic barrier against competition with the products of another state or the labor of its residents. Restrictions so contrived are an unreasonable clog upon the mobility of commerce.[104]

This decision revived interest in federal regulation of interstate milk. Governor Lehman immediately called for a conference of the seven states in the New York milkshed, and the participating governors demanded assistance from Washington to prevent price-cutting in the milk business.[105] Working in cooperation with the United States Department of Agriculture, a committee representing the seven states formulated a plan under provisions of the Agricultural Adjustment Act to license distributors as a means of enforcing minimum prices to dairymen. This proposal encountered opposition from dealers who would have had to pay the costs of administration and also would have lost their sources of cheap milk. Independent farmers objected to the plan because it included the League's classified price system and contained specific exemptions for cooperatives. Even the Dairymen's League, which strongly supported federal intervention, wanted certain amendments before adding its endorsement.

Since two-thirds of the producers had to ratify the proposal before it could go into effect, months were spent rewriting it in a futile attempt to win the approval of competing interest groups. A revised draft appeared in October 1935, but it met continued resistance from dealers and unaffiliated dairymen. Subsequent negotiations failed to produce a satisfactory compromise and, early in 1936, New York abandoned its effort to win acceptance of federal control of interstate milk prices.[106]

7

New York's inability to regulate out-of-state milk supplies created doubts about the value of local price-fixing. In late 1935, small independent dairymen called for repeal of the milk control law so that New York farmers could sell milk as cheaply as their counterparts in neighboring states. Lehman and the large cooperatives opposed any immediate relaxation of the enforcement of intrastate milk prices, but by the time the 1936 legislature convened, the Dairymen's League had prepared a substitute for government price-fixing.[107] Working in concert with other farm groups, the League proposed that the state transfer to associations of producers and distributors the power to negotiate milk prices, subject to approval of the commissioner of agriculture who would have the authority to enforce decisions of the dairy industry. This procedure required suspension of the state antitrust law, but New York's biggest farm organizations argued that private marketing agreements would restore stability to the milk business. In addition, as the Farm Bureau pointed out to its members, the League proposal would prevent consumers from using the existing state control apparatus to set maximum retail prices.[108]

As introduced in the legislature by Assemblyman Ernest J. Lonis, a Republican farm leader from Oswego County, the League plan won little support in 1936. Big distributors favored the idea of bargaining with dairymen to determine milk prices, but retail merchants preferred leaving such power in the hands of the state.[109] Speaking for unaffiliated farmers, an Albany lawmaker charged that industry-directed price-fixing would enslave dairymen:

> The essence of the Lonis bill is to enable the dealers and the cooperatives to fix the prices to be paid to the dairy farmers for no other purpose than to bring this price down and keep it down for all time.[110]

Peter G. Ten Eyck, the commissioner of agriculture and a dairy farmer himself, also distrusted the intentions of distributors, and he appealed for extension of state controls for another year.[111] At a legislative hearing in March, over two thousand farmers poured into Albany and cheered witnesses who backed the continuation of government supervision. Summing up the attitude of dairymen, one speaker declared: "Fix the price to the farmer and let the dealer go out and take care of himself!" Confronted by this display of sentiment, the Dairymen's League decided not to push the Lonis measure. The president of the League concluded that "the least difficulty and disturbance will result from re-enactment of the present law." [112]

The legislature took the path of least resistance. Since dairymen in favor of continued state controls predicted milk riots and bloodshed if New York abandoned the three-year-old system of price-fixing, lawmakers prolonged government regulation until

April 1937, in spite of objections from a few New York City Democrats who complained about high retail prices of milk.[113] The extension of milk control met with the approval of Lehman, who thought, as usual, that the state should "act in accordance with the very clearly demonstrated sentiment of the farmers." [114]

Support for government price-fixing finally evaporated during a drought in 1936. When a dry spell forced dairymen to feed expensive grain to herds in July and August, their agricultural associations called on the state to raise the minimum returns to milk producers. A group of dissidents from central New York also insisted on an end to the classified price plan, and they threatened to strike if the state rejected their demands. Responding to these pressures, the milk board boosted prices and reduced the number of milk classifications from nine to six, but this failed to satisfy many disgruntled farmers who considered it too little and too late. The state's action also precipitated a revolt among consumers when large dealers jacked up retail prices to cover higher returns to dairymen. Led by Mayor La Guardia's administration, which publicized the cheaper milk of small independent stores, New York City residents forced Borden's and Sheffield Farms to roll back price increases. By the winter of 1936, several months of turmoil in the dairy business had left producers, distributors, and consumers disgusted with the milk control board, which became a convenient scapegoat.[115]

With the opposition to state regulation mounting, Lehman called for a reevaluation of government price-fixing in 1937. As in the past, the governor promised to respect the wishes of farmers:

I feel that the future of milk control should be decided by dairymen themselves. The Governor and the Legislature have a right to expect producers of milk to come to some unanimity of agreement as to how the best interest of dairymen may be served. If such an agreement can be reached, then the State should throw its resources behind it.[116]

Lehman regretted that attempts to gauge the sentiment of farmers often brought forth "a veritable Babel of conflicting opinions counseling different courses," and he warned that "if agriculture is to prosper, if farmers are going to continue to hold their equality with others, they must organize." Only through cooperatives, according to the governor, could dairymen expect to solve their problems and speak with one voice to all levels of government.[117]

Early in 1937, the legislature followed Lehman's suggestion and created a temporary committee to study public sentiment on milk control. The inquiry held a dozen hearings around the state and took testimony from 372 witnesses, most of whom came out against the existing system of government intervention in the milk business. Spokesmen for the consuming public, represented principally by the Milk Consumers Protective Committee—a recently organized coalition of forty welfare, civic, and labor groups, objected to price-fixing at their expense, and they demanded a role in any state determination of prices.[118] Pointing to the rising number of violations of the milk law, large distributors and grocers called for repeal of unenforceable regulations which small wholesalers and peddlers could easily evade, thereby undercutting both the corner shopkeeper and companies like Borden's. The influx of interstate milk not subject to any supervision troubled New York dairymen, who had recently seen their share of the metropolitan market drop from 70 to 60 percent. Still smarting from their bitter experience the previous summer, many producers also complained that the milk board could not adjust prices quickly enough to meet changing market conditions. A minority of dairymen from northern sections of New York defended state price-fixing because, as suppliers of local cities such as Rochester and Syracuse, these farmers did not encounter the competition from interstate milk that wrought havoc with the price structure in New York City. After listening to the vast majority of consumers, distributors, retailers, and producers attack state price-fixing, the joint legislative committee recommended that New York allow the emergency statute to lapse on April 1, 1937.[119]

Athough generally opposed to the existing regulatory system, dairymen in New York refused to let the laws of supply and demand dictate their milk prices. They disagreed, however, on the best alternative to government controls. With the end of the state milk board in sight, the Dairymen's League revived its proposal to grant organizations of producers and dealers the power to negotiate milk prices through collective bargaining. If voluntary agreements failed to stabilize a marketing area of the state, the League's plan gave farmers and dealers the option of petitioning the commissioner of agriculture to issue minimum price orders which would have the force of law if approved by 75 percent of the dairymen as well as distributors of at least 50 percent of the milk in a particular market.[120] Introduced by Senator George F. Rogers, a Rochester Democrat, and Assemblyman Howard N. Allen, a Dutchess County Republican, the League's bill won the support of prominent farm associations and was presented as "the plan of organized agriculture." [121]

A competing proposal came from a group led by John J. Dillon. *The Rural New-Yorker's* irascible publisher, who with his well-trimmed white beard looked more like a continental diplomat than a rural firebrand, defended unaffiliated milk producers who often found themselves squeezed between the powerful Dairymen's League and the big distributors such as Borden's. The outspoken newspaperman had long opposed the so-called Borden-League alliance which, he charged, had created "the most sinister and ruthless monopoly that ever fastened its talons in the flesh and blood of a farm industry." [122] Although eighty years old in 1937, the still spry Dillon attacked the Rogers-Allen measure because he feared that distributors would dominate the collective bargaining procedure:

> I have no hesitation about discussing the dairy problem with dealers but after the experience of sixty-five years with them I cannot avoid the conclusion that there is no profit in such a discussion from the basic standpoint of producers. Oil and water just do not mix. Oil always comes to the top. In this case the oil represents the dealers.[123]

Dillon offered an alternative to the League plan. He suggested that New York establish a new statewide board representing dairymen which would negotiate a single price for milk before it left the farm. State officials could review agreements reached by delegates of producers, but they could not reduce prices unless dairy profits proved higher than those of other businesses. In defense of his idea, Dillon argued that it would place ultimate control of prices where it belonged—in the hands of dairymen—rather than in the grip of dealer-oriented cooperatives:

> The one thing that I am asking for is the fundamental principle of farmers' rights [sic] to determine the price and terms for the sale of their own milk. They have this right in economic law, civil law, and Divine law, and I want to give them the power and authority to exercise this right. That makes farmers their own control board and of course eliminates anything that would interfere with their authority to do this much.[124]

Dillon gathered independents who supported his proposal into the New York State Milk Committee, which coordinated a drive to push for enactment of the measure sponsored by Senator Francis L. McElroy, a Syracuse Democrat, and Assemblyman Fred A. Young, a Lewis County Republican.[125]

After months of maneuvering, organized agriculture won the battle in Albany. With farmers sharply divided, lawmakers avoided offending anyone by ratifying both the Rogers-Allen and the McElroy-Young bills. This strategy left the final decision in the hands of Governor Lehman, who could hardly sign into law conflicting proposals.[126] Before the League's plan cleared both houses, Lehman had insisted on an amendment which prohibited the fixing of retail prices. Both measures passed by large majorities, with the primary opposition coming from a small group of New York City Democrats, one of whom argued that the bills would place a "noose around the necks of the consumers."[127] Having promised to follow the dictates of farmers, Lehman finally accepted the proposal of the Dairymen's League, because it had the endorsement of leading farm groups which acted as spokesmen for New York agriculture. Upon signing the Rogers-Allen measure, the governor declared:

> This bill does not permit the fixing of prices to consumers. It does not give distributors control of the industry. Control under this bill is kept with the producers.
>
> The bill is strongly urged by the New York State Conference Board of Farm Organizations. It is approved, I believe, by a majority of the producers of the State.
>
> While this bill is not a cure-all, and in fact may not prove as effective as its proponents believe it will, I do think it is a sound measure containing machinery for substantial assistance to the producer.[128]

Lehman's action generated predictable responses from farmers. Speaking through the Conference Board of Farm Organizations, the agricultural establishment applauded adoption of the League's plan. Airing his disappointment, John J. Dillon bitterly asserted:

"The Governor has, unwittingly, we hope, given the sanction of law to one of the most sinister rackets on record." [129] The cantankerous newspaperman based this charge on his firmly held belief that cooperatives, such as the Dairymen's League, did not represent the interests of milk producers. The governor, however, had to make the opposite assumption or despair of ever determining the will of farmers. At a time when, in the words of an official of the Farm Bureau, "Government by pressure groups has become the order of the day," Lehman naturally looked for guidance in farm policy to organized agriculture, which usually spoke with one voice in New York.[130] In a rare moment of candor, a dissident farm leader once defended Lehman's readiness to cooperate with the Dairymen's League and similar groups:

> The Governor is not a farmer. His contacts are with those big, well financed farm "organizations" such as the League and Sheffield associations. How can the Governor know what farmers think of these organizations? He must take the position that these organizations represent the farmers. If these organizations do not represent farmers then why do farmers stand for them? Is the Governor's duty to clean up farm organizations? Why hate a governor for not doing something farmers should do for themselves? [131]

8

New York dairymen failed to solve their problems through the Rogers-Allen law. When milk prices tumbled after state controls lapsed on April 1, 1937, producers and distributors in the New York City market formed their respective bargaining agencies, which reached a partial agreement on minimum returns to dairymen. After this plan went into effect on July 1, prices paid to farmers supplying the metropolitan area improved considerably for several months, but expanding milk supplies soon disrupted the dairy business. Anxious to unload a burgeoning output, farmers readily sold to dealers who offered less than the established minimum price. According to Charles Baldwin, the former commissioner of agriculture who was now executive secretary of the dairymen's bargaining agency, the operation of the Rogers-Allen law "proved to everyone that voluntary agreements on prices between producer groups and distributors was [sic] quite impossible." [132] In February 1938, ten months after the expiration of government price-fixing, dairymen petitioned for a resumption of state controls backed by federal regulation of interstate milk shipments.[133]

Officials in Albany and Washington immediately went into action.[134] Under provisions of the Rogers-Allen law and the federal Agricultural Marketing Act, the state and federal departments of agriculture held a series of joint hearings and drew up a schedule of minimum producer prices which the vast majority of dairymen approved in a referendum. After seven months of negotiations, the combined state/federal orders, one governing returns to out-of-state farmers delivering milk to the metropolitan market and the other covering New York producers, went into effect on September 1, 1938.[135] These decrees initially brought dairymen increased prices, but unfavorable court decisions forced the temporary suspension of government controls early in 1939 (see p. 159, Table 6, columns 8 and 9). After higher tribunals upheld the constitutionality of the marketing orders, Washington and Albany restored price regulations.[136]

Despite periodic improvements in returns to dairymen, government intervention failed to bring stability to the milk business. Confronted by abrupt seasonal shifts in marketing conditions, state and federal administrators could not respond quickly enough to the demands of farmers. When droughts sharply increased the costs of production, impatient dairymen, unwilling to rely completely on cumbersome government procedures for raising prices, resorted to brief strikes. During the 1939 dry spell, a withholding action brought the dumping of milk and the death of a picket who was run down by a milk truck. In 1941, frustrated farmers staged another strike to show their displeasure with inadequate returns for milk.[137] Although strikes forced some upswing in prices, their recurrence emphasized the inflexibility of state and federal regulatory machinery.[138]

Overproduction also eroded government attempts to aid dairymen, since milk supplies ran too far ahead of the consumers' demand. After farmers had expanded their output as a result of improved returns in the late 1930s, New York's milk production had reached the highest level since the turn of the century by 1940.[139] Disturbed by such reports, Lehman finally began lecturing dairymen about basic economics:

> We must recognize, I think, that any price control plan promising a definite return and a stabilized market tempts producers to increase individual production to get a larger share of the market and a bigger gross return. Such a desire is only human.
>
> But we must remember that the market can absorb only so much milk . . . in the profitable fluid form.[140]

During the early 1940s, the governor called on farmers to cooperate in the voluntary regulation of milk output. But his pleas fell on deaf ears, and imbalances in supply and demand continued.[141]

New York ultimately failed to restore farmer's purchasing power to pre-World War I levels but not for lack of effort. The legislature spent much of its time listening to dairymen and putting into law their various panaceas.[142] In 1937, Lehman concluded that "in the five years I have been Governor I have devoted more time, thought, and energy to the milk problem in the hope of being helpful to our producers, than to any other ten subjects." [143] Despite his urban background, Lehman's obvious sympathy for farmers won their approval. Leaders of agricultural associations, most of whom were Republicans, frequently praised the Democratic governor's willingness to extend state aid to farmers.[144] In an editorial, the *American Agriculturist* expressed the gratitude of its readers:

> [F]armers and other citizens of New York State have a sympathetic governor. No other governor of our time or generation has given more personal time to

agriculture and particularly to milk marketing problems than has Governor Lehman. No other governor has been more constructive in what he is trying to do to help.[145]

All the energy and good will of New Dealers produced mixed results during the 1930s. With a deep sense of frustration, Edward R. Eastman declared in 1936: "Damn milk anyway! There never has been any real solution to it, and I am beginning to doubt if there is any." [146] Certainly New Deal experiments did not "solve" farm problems in the Empire State. At the insistence of farmers themselves, New York created the milk board to improve returns to dairymen, but government price-fixing in the absence of production controls stimulated increased output, which in turn depressed prices. Throughout this period, organized farmers largely dictated the shape of state agricultural programs, often to the detriment of the public at large, which had to pay the cost of higher returns to producers. The *New York Times* lamented in 1941: "As in many other examples of Government 'economic planning,' more attention has been paid in the milk control program to the interests of special groups . . . than to the general public welfare as represented by the interests of consumers as a whole." [147]

Despite significant shortcomings, the farm policies of the Little New Deal expanded the role of government in the Empire State. As a result of the Depression, New Yorkers accepted a series of measures designed to guarantee farmers a minimum standard of living. Although state and federal intervention failed to achieve the goal of parity with pre-World War I purchasing power, it helped bring some improvement in prices and showed, above all, the willingness of New Dealers to put government at the service of economically distressed groups.

NOTES

1. New York State, *Report of the Joint Legislative Committee to Investigate the Milk Industry,* Leg. Doc. No. 144 (1933), p. 61. (Hereinafter referred to as *Report on the Milk Industry.)*
2. Ibid., pp. 64, 67.
3. David M. Ellis et al., *A History of New York State* (Ithaca, N.Y., 1967), p. 485; Paul W. Gates, "Agricultural Change in New York State, 1850-1890," *New York History,* L (April 1969): 115-41; U.S., Department of Commerce, Bureau of the Census, *Fifteenth Census of the United States, 1930: Agriculture,* vol. II, pt. I, pp. 71, 95, 101, 106, vol. IV, pp. 40-41, 52.
4. Eric Brunger, "A Chapter in the Growth of the New York State Dairy Industry, 1850-1900," *New York History,* XXXVI (April 1955): 136-45; Ellis, *A History of New York State,* pp. 273-75.
5. John J. Dillon, *Seven Decades of Milk: A History of New York's Dairy Industry* (New York, 1941), pp. 5-18; Ellis, *A History of New York State,* pp. 500-2.
6. Dewey J. Carter, ed., *The Fifty Year Battle for a Living Price for Milk: A History of the Dairymen's League* (New York, 1939), pp. 3-14; *Report on the Milk Industry,* pp. 102-62. During the 1930s, a few of Lehman's opponents, including the Republican nominee for governor in 1936, charged that the state's chief executive, as well as Lehman Brothers, had a financial interest in Borden's and the National Dairy Corporation, a holding company which

owned Sheffield Farms and numerous upstate dairies. During the 1936 campaign, Lehman denied that he or Lehman Brothers possessed a single share of stock in any milk company. Saul Levitt and Allan Chase, "Herbert Lehman: 'Silent Dynamite,'" *American Mercury*, XXXIII (September 1934): 16-17; Joseph J. Doyle to James A. Farley, September 16, 1936, Box 83, OF 300, FDRL; HHL Address, October 21, 1936, *Public Papers, 1936*, pp. 974-75; John M. Hancock to HHL, December 28, 1936, Special File, HHLP.

7. Of the farmers surveyed, 27 percent owned less than fifty-five acres, but this group accounted for only 8 percent of the League's membership. W. A. Anderson, *The Membership of Farmers in New York Organizations* (Ithaca, N.Y., 1938), p. 20.

8. *American Agriculturist*, November 6, 1937, p. 699; *New York Times*, September 13, 1936.

9. *Report on the Milk Industry*, pp. 109-21, 156-69; Carter, *The Fifty Year Battle*, pp. 15-16. The most extreme opponents of the Dairymen's League charged that it was a tool of Borden's, because that company purchased almost its entire milk supply from the League. In 1937, a federal investigation concluded that "relations between Dairymen's League and the Borden Co. were that of vendor and vendee and no evidence was adduced showing the exercise of any control by The Borden Co. over the League." Dillon, *Seven Decades of Milk*, pp. 178-80; U.S., Congress, House, *Report of the Federal Trade Commission on the Sale and Distribution of Milk and Milk Products: New York Milk Sales Area*, House Doc. 95, 75th Cong., 1st sess., 1937, p. 56. For a defense of the League's point of view throughout this period (based largely on interviews with former League officials and their supporters), see Gould P. Colman, "Theoretical Models and Oral History Interviews," *Agricultural History*, XLI (July 1967): 255-66.

10. Carter, *The Fifty Year Battle*, pp. 21-22.

11. *Report on the Milk Industry*, p. 41.

12. Ibid., p. 70.

13. Ibid., p. 64; *Orange County Farm Bureau News*, October 1932.

14. *Report on the Milk Industry*, pp. 15-21.

15. Ibid., p. 19.

16. Throughout this period a variety of experts made extravagant claims about the benefits of milk. One historian declared: "A casual look at the races of people seems to show that those using much milk are the strongest physically and mentally, and the most enduring of the peoples of the world. Of all races, the Aryans seem to have been the heaviest drinkers of milk and the greatest users of butter and cheese, a fact that may in part account for the quick and high development of this division of human beings." Ulysses Prentiss Hedrick, *A History of Agriculture in the State of New York* (Albany, 1933), pp. 362-63.

17. *Report on the Milk Industry*, p. 14.

18. In 1935, Lehman took advantage of a Democratic-controlled legislature to win passage of a bill giving the governor power to appoint the commissioner of agriculture and markets. Farm spokesmen generally approved this step, since Lehman indicated in advance that he would select Peter G. Ten Eyck—an experienced farmer—to fill the post. HHL Message to the Legislature, January 2, 1935, *Public Papers, 1935*, p. 24; Albany *Knickerbocker Press*, January 25, 1935; *New York Times*, January 31, 1935; *Laws of New York, 1935*, chap. 16; Howard E. Babcock to J. D. Barnum, May 7, 1938, Box D-1, Howard E. Babcock Papers, Collection of Regional History, Cornell University.

19. Bellush, *Franklin D. Roosevelt as Governor of New York*, pp. 78-89.

20. In addition to members of the state government, Lehman's original appointments to the commission included the following private citizens: C. E. Ladd, Flora Rose, L. R. Simons,

Charles F. Warren (all of Cornell); H. E. Babcock (Grange League Federation cooperative and Cornell trustee); Maurice C. Burritt (original organizer of Farm Bureau and Cornell trustee); Walter Clark (State Horticultural Society); E. R. Eastman (*American Agriculturist);* Mrs. Edward Eddy (State Home Bureau); Fred Freestone (Grange); Clark W. Halliday (Sheffield Producers'); Berne A. Pyrke (former commissioner of agriculture and markets); Fred Sexauer (Dairymen's League); Jared Van Wagenen, Jr. (Farmers' Institutes); A. G. Waldo (State Vegetables Growers Association); C. R. White (Farm Bureau); Isaiah D. Carr, John F. Fallon, James R. Stevenson, H. R. Talmage ("Master Farmers"—an honor bestowed on particularly successful farmers). *Public Papers, 1933,* p. 369; Press Release, January 16, 1933, HHL to Carl E. Ladd, March 2, 1933, "Agricultural Advisory Commission," Reel 2, GP, HHLP.

21. Gould P. Colman, *Education & Agriculture: A History of the New York State College of Agriculture at Cornell University* (Ithaca, N.Y., 1963), pp. 414-17; Belle Zeller, *Pressure Politics in New York* (New York , 1937), p. 132. For evidence of Lehman's reliance on Ladd, see Ladd to HHL, February 10, 1933, August 18, 1938, HHL to Ladd, November 20, 1934, Gen. Corr., 1933-40, HHLP; Walter T. Brown to Ladd, January 8, 1940, "Farm and Home Week," ibid.; Ladd to Brown, February 9, 1940, "Master Farmer Dinner," ibid.

22. *New York Times,* February 8, 1933.

23. *American Agriculturist,* April 1, 1933, p. 155; New York *Herald Tribune,* March 15, 1933; *New York Times,* February 16, 1933; *The Rural New-Yorker,* March 25, 1933, p. 219.

24. *New York Times,* March 15, 1933.

25. Edward R. Eastman to HHL, March 3, 1933, "Milk Legislation—Pitcher-Bartholomew Bill," Reel 62, GP, HHLP.

26. Seward A. Miller to John D. Miller, January 26, February 17, 1933, Box 9, Dairymen's League Papers (#2900), Collection of Regional History, Cornell University; Maurice C. Burritt Diary, March 18, 1933, Maurice C. Burritt Papers, Collection of Regional History, Cornell University; *American Agriculturist,* April 1, 1933, p. 155; Colman, *Education & Agriculture,* p. 279.

27. *The Rural New-Yorker,* March 25, 1933, p. 219; *New York Times,* March 17, April 6, 1933. The Dairymen's League had convenient access to the legislature through League members who sat on the agriculture committees in both houses. Jewel Bellush, "Milk Price Control: History of Its Adoption, 1933," *New York History,* XLIII (January 1962): 86-87.

28. *The Rural New-Yorker,* April 8, 1933, p. 251.

29. *Rochester Times-Union,* March 29-31, 1933.

30. *New York Times,* March 30, April 1, 1933; *The Rural New-Yorker,* April 1, 1933, p. 235; Albert Woodhead to HHL, March 30, 1933, "Milk Strike—1933," Reel 62, GP, HHLP. The lone G.O.P. senator to vote against the bill did so because he doubted the wisdom of price-fixing. Thomas C. Desmond to HHL, August 9, 1933, "Desmond, Thomas C.," Reel 25, GP, HHLP.

31. *Buffalo Evening News,* April 4, 5, 1933; *Rochester Times-Union,* April 4, 5, 1933.

32. Before officially taking over as governor, Lehman had privately questioned the idea of state price-fixing. "[I]f the price of milk were to be fixed by State authority we should no doubt have to deal with demands that prices on many other commodities be similarly fixed. I doubt that general support could be found for such a policy." HHL to Jerry F. Sheehan, December 17, 1932, Gen. Corr., 1932, HHLP.

33. *Rochester Times-Union,* April 8, 10, 1933; *New York Times,* April 5, 7, 9, 11, 1933; "First

Report of Governor's Agricultural Advisory Commission," April 5, 1933, *Public Papers, 1933,* pp. 474-75; Maurice C. Burritt Diary, April 5, 1933, Burritt Papers; Dairymen's League Membership Service to Directors et al., April 11, 1933, League Papers (#2900), Box 9; *Laws of New York, 1933,* chap. 158.

34. *American Agriculturist,* April 1, 1933, p. 155.

35. John D. Black, *The Dairy Industry and the AAA* (Washington, 1935), pp. 311-312, 323.

36. *New York Times,* April 14, May 14, 1933; Edward R. Eastman to HHL, May 4, 1933, "Eastman, E. R.," Reel 27, GP, HHLP.

37. For an explanation of the classified price plan, see *supra,* p. 150.

38. Stanley A. Piseck to HHL, July 11, 1933, "PIO," Reel 75, GP, HHLP; *New York Times,* July 25, 26, 1933; New York *Herald Tribune,* July 28, August 8, 1933; *Rochester Times-Union,* July 27, 1933; *The Nation,* September 6, 1933, pp. 267-69.

39. *New York Times,* July 31, 1933.

40. *Rochester Times-Union,* August 4-8, 1933; Albany *Knickerbocker Press,* August 4, 1933, Syracuse *Post-Standard,* August 2-9, 1933, clippings, Metropolitan Co-operative Milk Producers Bargaining Agency Papers, Collection of Regional History, Cornell University. (Hereinafter referred to as Metropolitan Bargaining Agency Papers.)

41. *Dairymen's League News,* August 22, 1933. The governor's Agricultural Advisory Commission called on the attorney general to investigate evidence that outside "agitators . . . in league wtih Communists" participated in the milk strike, but a member of the commission who lived in the strike area questioned the commission's charges and accused it of "dragging . . . red herrings across the trail." Report on the Agricultural Advisory Commission, August 4, 1933, *Public Papers, 1933,* pp. 645-46; Maurice C. Burritt to Carl E. Ladd, August 7, 1933, Box 1, Burritt Papers.

42. *New York Times,* August 8, 1933; HHL Statements, August 5, 8, 1933, *Public Papers, 1933;* E. S. Foster to HHL, August 9, 1933, HHL to Foster, August 14, 1933, "New York State Conference Board of Farm Organizations," Reel 71, GP, HHLP. For Lehman's exchanges with county officials, see *Public Papers, 1933,* pp. 649-54.

43. HHL Message to the Legislature, August 4, 1933, *Public Papers, 1933,* pp. 146-49.

44. Albany *Knickerbocker Press,* August 9, 1933, CB, 19: 643, HHLP; HHL Statement, August 9, 1933, *Public Papers, 1933,* pp. 655-56.

45. HHL Address and Statement, August 12, 1933, *Public Papers, 1933,* pp. 774, 656.

46. *Rochester Times-Union,* August 14, 1933.

47. Charles H. Baldwin et al., to HHL, August 14, 1933, HHL to Baldwin et al., August 15, 1933, *Public Papers, 1933,* pp. 657-60; *New York Times,* August 15, 1933; Howard E. Babcock to Frank E. Gannett, August 14, 1933, Box C-2, #1, Babcock Papers.

48. Batavia *Times,* August 10, 1933, Poughkeepsie *Eagle News,* August 14, 1933, *Rochester Times-Union,* August 14, 1933, Troy *Morning Record,* August 14, 1933, Canadaigua *Messenger,* August 16, 1933, CB, 19: 95-97, HHLP.

49. Syracuse *Journal,* August 15, 1933, ibid., p. 97.

50. Albert Woodhead to HHL, August 19, 1933, "Milk Strike—1933," Reel 62, GP, HHLP; Lorena A. Hickok Report, September 12-19, 1933, "Hickok Reports," Harry Hopkins Papers, FDRL.

51. HHL to Carolin A. Flexner, August 17, 1933, "Flexner, C. A.," Flexner File, HHLP.

52. Under the law Nebbia was subject to a maximum penalty of $100 and/or a year's imprisonment, but the Rochester city court judge, aware that this might become a test

case, levied a nominal fine so that the matter could be ultimately decided solely on the merits of the case. *Nebbia v. New York*, 291 U.S. 502, "Transcript of Record," in *U.S. Briefs, 1933* (429).

53. *New York Times*, November 3, 1933.

54. Rochester *Democrat and Chronicle*, May 28, June 14, 1933; *Rochester Times-Union*, May 31, June 13, 1933.

55. *New State Ice Co. v. Liebmann*, 285 U.S. 262, quoted in Morris Duane, "*Nebbia v. People:* A Milestone," *University of Pennsylvania Law Review*, LXXXII (April 1934): 622.

56. *People v. Nebbia*, 262 N.Y. 259-61.

57. Ibid., 271.

58. Ibid., 272-77.

59. *Nebbia v. New York*, 291 U.S. 502; Nathan Levy, "Comment: Constitutional Law—Price-Fixing—Changing Attitudes," *Michigan Law Review*, XXXII (April 1934): 832-39; "The Supreme Court in Reverse," *New Republic*, November 21, 1934, pp. 35-36; Alfred H. Kelly and Winfred A. Harbison, *The American Constitution: Its Origins and Development* (4th ed.; New York, 1970), pp. 737-38.

60. *Nebbia v. New York*, 291 U.S. 536.

61. Ibid., 530.

62. Ibid., 538.

63. *Report of the Milk Control Board, March 1934*, Leg. Doc. No. 74 (1934), p. 27; HHL Message to the Legislature, March 12, 1934, *Public Papers, 1934*, pp. 87-88.

64. HHL Address, February 16, 1934, *Public Papers, 1934*, p. 705.

65. *Report of the Milk Control Board, March, 1934*, p. 3; Arthur M. Schlesinger, Jr., *The Coming of the New Deal* (Boston, 1958), pp. 236-46.

66. Statement by New York Conference Board of Farm Organizations, March 23, 1934, Box 4, New York State Farm Bureau Papers, Collection of Regional History, Cornell University.

67. Albany *Knickerbocker Press*, March 30, 1934, CB, 21: 1160; New York *Herald Tribune*, March 24, 29, 1934; *New York Times*, March 24, 28, 1934; John J. Dillon to Frank N. Decker, March 27, 1934, Milk File (1), Frank N. Decker Papers, Collection of Regional History, Cornell University; *Law of New York, 1934*, chap. 126.

68. *New York Times*, January 10, 15, 24, 26, 1935; E. S. Foster to HHL, February 4, 1935, "New York State Conference Board of Farm Organizations," Reel 71, GP, HHLP; *Laws of New York, 1935*, chap. 10.

69. New York *Herald Tribune*, May 21, 1938; *New York Times*, January 22, 1937; Emil Greenberg to HHL, October 2, 1939, "Milk Strike, 1939," Reel 62, GP, HHLP.

70. *The Dairy Farmer*, October 25, 1938, in Farmers' Union of the New York Milkshed Papers, Collection of Regional History, Cornell University. (Hereinafter referred to as Farmers' Union Papers.)

71. Quoted in Robert F. Carter, "Pressure from the Left: The American Labor Party, 1936-1954" (unpublished Ph.D. dissertation, Syracuse University, 1965), p. 104.

72. *Report on the Milk Industry*, pp. 79-91. Quotation on p. 15.

73. Howard E. Babcock quoted in "Minutes of the Annual Meeting," November 9-10, 1933, Box 30, New York State Farm Bureau Papers.

74. *American Agriculturist*, December 9, 1933, p. 505.

75. "Excerpts from Talk by Commissioner Charles H. Baldwin at Meeting of Farm Bureau Federation," November 9, 1933, Box 30, New York State Farm Bureau Papers.

76. *Report of the Milk Control Board, March, 1934,* p. 29; New York *Herald Tribune,* March 16, 1934, CB, 21: 1117, HHLP.

77. "Minutes of Annual Meeting," November 22-23, 1934, New York State Farm Bureau Papers, Box 30. For a rare warning issued by a state commissioner of agriculture, see Peter G. Ten Eyck to Fred Sexauer, October 21, 1935, Box S3-2, Dairymen's League Papers (#2614).

78. The idea of state publicity apparently originated in 1932 with Commissioner of Agriculture Charles H. Baldwin who established a Consumer Information Service to stimulate the sale of dairy products. In 1933, the legislative inquiry into the milk industry also recommended a program of state milk advertising. Rochester *Democrat and Chronicle,* September 29, 1932, clipping, Metropolitan Bargaining Agency Papers; *Report on the Milk Industry,* p. 263; *American Agriculturist,* September 30, 1933, p. 393.

79. *American Agriculturist,* April 14, 1934, p. 201.

80. "Resolutions, Annual Meeting," November 10, 1933, Box 30, New York State Farm Bureau Papers; E. R. Eastman to HHL, April 27, 1934, "Agricultural Advisory Commission," Reel 2, GP, HHLP; Charles H. Baldwin to HHL, May 9, 1934, Frank E. Gannett to "The Publishers Addressed," June 1, 1934, E. R. Eastman to HHL, June 4, 1934, "Agricultural and Markets—Milk Publicity," Reel 2, GP, HHLP; HHL to Carl E. Ladd, May 1, 1934, "Ladd, Carl E.," Reel 59, GP, HHLP; Eastman to Howard E. Babcock, May 1, 26, 1934, Boxes D-2, D-3, Babcock Papers; *Laws of New York, 1934,* chap. 882.

81. *American Agriculturist,* July 21, 1934, pp. 405-7.

82. Ibid., August 18, 1934, p. 460.

83. Thomas Parran to HHL, November 13, 1935, "Agriculture and Markets—Milk Publicity," Reel 2, GP,HHLP.

84. "Report of the Subcommittee on Milk Publicity," January 22, 1937, "New York Academy of Medicine," Reel 68, GP, HHLP.

85. Paul J. Kern to HHL, May 21, 1937, Bill Jackets, chap. 329 (1937); L. A. Van Bomel to HHL, March 1, 1935, Edward F. Brown to HHL, March 4, 1935, Bill Jackets, chap. 405 (1935); J. G. Horner to HHL, January 29, 1935, "Agriculture and Markets—Milk Publicity," Reel 2, GP, HHLP; *The Rural New-Yorker,* April 20, 1935, p. 335; New York State, *Report of the Joint Legislative Committee to Investigate the Milk Control Law,* March 22, 1937, Leg. Doc. No. 81 (1937), p. 12. (Hereinafter referred to as *Report on the Milk Law.)*

86. Fred H. Sexauer to HHL, June 5, 1934, Gen. Corr., 1933-40, HHLP; E. R. Eastman to HHL, January 11, 1935, "Agriculture and Markets—Milk Publicity," Reel 2, GP, HHLP; Frank E. Gannett to HHL, February 22, 1935, Bill Jackets, chap. 405 (1935); Gannett to Howard E. Babcock, April 5, 1935, Box C-2, Babcock Papers; "Report of the Legislative Committee, 1936," in "New York State Farm Bureau," Reel 71, GP, HHLP; *Rochester Times-Union,* February 3, 1935, March 27, 1936; Jared Van Wagenen, Jr., *Days of My Years: The Autobiography of a York State Farmer* (Cooperstown, N.Y., 1962), pp. 164-69.

87. See HHL's Annual Messages to the Legislature, 1933-36, in *Public Papers.*

88. *American Agriculturist,* November 20, 1937, p. 726; HHL Message to the Legislature, January 5, 1938, *Public Papers, 1938,* p. 41.

89. *American Agriculturist,* September 30, 1933, p. 393.

90. *Buffalo Evening News,* August 22, 1933.

91. *American Agriculturist,* June 19, 1937, p. 429. On July 1, 1937, the volume of milk produced

in New York State was the greatest for any July 1 since 1930. Ibid., August 14, 1937, p. 524.

92. Address by Herbert P. King, November 28, 1940, Box 30, New York State Farm Bureau Papers.

93. *Report on the Milk Industry,* pp. 32-34.

94. F. F. Lininger, *Dairy Products Under the Agricultural Adjustment Act* (Washington, 1934), pp. 1-3, 19-34; Clyde L. King to Kenneth F. Fee, August 15, 1933, General Correspondence, New York State Department of Agriculture, Agricultural Stabilization and Conservation Service (AAA) Records, Record Group 145, National Archives. (Hereinafter referred to as GC, NY, AAA Records).

95. Henry S. Manley to Clyde L. King, October 7, 1933, Subject Correspondence (hereinafter SC), Milk—New York, AAA Records; *American Agriculturist,* September 16, 1933, p. 385, October 28, 1933, p. 445.

96. Transcript of Informal Conference on Marketing Agreement for New York Milkshed, October 19, 1933, p. 10, Marketing Agreements (Abandoned)—New York-New Jersey, Agricultural Marketing Service Records, Record Group 136, National Archives. (Hereinafter referred to as Marketing Agreements—NY-NJ, AMS Records.)

97. Emil Greenberg to Charles H. Baldwin, November 11, 1933, ibid.; Fred J. Sisson to Clyde L. King, October 23, 1933, SC, Milk-NY, AAA Records; Thomas Parran to HHL, October 6, 1933, "Milk Control Board, 1933," Reel 2, GP, HHLP; *The Rural New-Yorker,* October 28, 1933, p. 549, November 11, 1933, p. 567.

98. Charles H. Baldwin to Frank Decker, November 16, 1933, Milk File (1), Decker Papers; B. B. Derrick to Mary S. Burton, November 13, 1933, Clyde L. King to George Peek, November 29, 1933, Derrick to Mrs. Edward L. Scofield, December 14, 1933, Henry A. Wallace to FDR, January 30, 1934, SC, Milk—NY, AAA Records; Transcript of Informal Conference on New York Marketing Agreement, December 12, 1933, Marketing Agreements—NY-NJ, AMS Records; HHL to FDR, January 5, 1934, FDR to HHL, January 13, 1934, "Agricultural Advisory Commission," Reel 2, GP, HHLP.

99. Murray R. Benedict, *Farm Policies of the United States, 1790-1950* (New York, 1953), pp. 304-5; Van L. Perkins, *Crisis in Agriculture: The AAA and the New Deal, 1933* (Berkeley, 1969), pp. 163-65; William B. Duryee to Henry A. Wallace, January 6, 1934, J. H. Mason to O. E. Southwick, January 22, 1934, SC, Milk—NY, AAA Records.

100. New York City Hearing Record, February 5-7, 1934, Docket No. 146, Office of Solicitor, Department of Agriculture Records, Record Group 16, National Archives; Elmer D. Hays to Jerome N. Frank, February 16, 1934, A. H. Lauterbach to Chester C. Davis, March 8, 1935, Marketing Agreements—NY-NJ, AMS Records; Frank to Victor Christgau, March 16, 1934, GC, NY, AAA Records; C. H. Baldwin to George J. Savage, September 17, 1934, SC, Milk—NY, AAA Records; *The Rural New-Yorker,* February 10, 1934, p. 109.

101. *Report of the Milk Control Board,* March 1934, p. 10.

102. M. V. Atwood Memorandum, August 10, 1933, Box C-2, #1, Babcock Papers; Francis D. Culkin to Frank Decker, February 24, 28, 1934, Charles H. Baldwin to Decker, February 23, March 2, 1934, Milk File (1), Decker Papers; *American Agriculturist,* March 3, 1934, p. 113.

103. *New York Times,* November 3, 1933.

104. *Baldwin v. G. A. F. Seelig,* 294 U.S. 527.

105. HHL to Governors of Connecticut, Maryland, Massachusetts, New Jersey, Pennsylvania, and Vermont, March 8, 19, 1935, HHL to Henry A. Wallace, March 25, 1935,

Representatives of Seven States to Wallace, March 26, 1935, HHLP, GP, Reel 62, "Milk Shed Conference, March 24, 1935"; HHL Statement, March 24, 1935, *Public Papers, 1935*, p. 499.

106. *American Agriculturist,* May 25, 1935, p. 330, June 22, 1935, p. 394, October 26, 1935, p. 641; *New York Times,* June 14, September 24, 1935; *The Rural New-Yorker,* June 22, 1935, p. 491, November 23, 1935, p. 747; Remarks of Peter G. Ten Eyck, February 19, 1936, Ten Eyck to HHL, February 20, 27, 1936, "Metropolitan Milk Shed," Reel 61, GP, HHLP; Ten Eyck to E. W. Gaumnitz, March 12, 1936, GC, NY, AAA Records.

107. HHL to R. J. Clemens, September 6, 1935, A. C. Pilger to HHL, September 11, 1935, HHL to H. V. Noyes, September 19, 1935, "Agriculture and Markets—Division of Milk Control, 1935-38," Reel 2, GP, HHLP; *New York Times,* September 11, 19, 1935.

108. E. S. Foster to HHL, December 27, 1935, "New York State Farm Bureau Federation," Reel 71, GP, HHLP; Foster to HHL, January 2, 1936, "New York State Conference Board of Farm Organizations," ibid.; Foster to Federation Advisory Committee et al., March 3, 10, 1936, Box 2, New York State Farm Bureau Papers (#2714 ADD.); *American Agriculturist,* February 1, 1936, p. 65; Carter, *The Fifty Year Battle,* p. 25.

109. *New York Times,* January 4, 1936: "Resolution Adopted by the 15th Annual Convention of the United Independent Retail Grocers and Food Dealers Association, Inc.," March 1, 1936, "Agriculture and Markets—Division of Milk Control, 1935-38," Reel 2, GP, HHLP.

110. *New York Times,* February 20, 1936.

111. Ten Eyck to HHL, February 8, 1936, "Agriculture and Markets—Division of Milk Control, 1935-38," Reel 2, GP, HHLP; Remarks of Ten Eyck, February 19, 1936, "Metropolitan Milk Shed," Reel 61, GP, HHLP.

112. *New York Times,* March 11, 1936.

113. New York *Herald Tribune,* March 27, 1936; *New York Times,* March 24, 27, 1936. The milk control law was extended by an overwhelming vote of 140 to 6 in the Assembly and 30 to 13 in the Senate. HHL to John J. Dillon, September 3, 1936, "Special Session, October 20, 1936," Reel 89, GP, HHLP.

114. HHL to Harold B. Johnson, March 16, 1936, Gen. Corr., 1933-40, HHLP; *Laws of New York, 1936,* chap. 215.

115. *American Agriculturist,* September 26, 1936; *New York Times,* July 7, 10, 12, August 11, 12, 14, 31, September 13, 19, 21, 23, 1936; John J. Dillon to HHL, September 1, 1936, Stanley A. Piseck to HHL, October 17, 1936, "Special Session, October 20, 1936," Reel 89, GP, HHLP; Piseck to HHL, September 16, 1936, "Milk Hearing, September 12, 1936," Reel 62, GP, HHLP.

116. HHL Message to the Legislature, January 6, 1937, *Public Papers, 1937,* p. 26.

117. HHL Address, February 19, 1937, ibid., p. 692.

118. Under the leadership of the Consumers Union, the Milk Consumers Protective Committee had been organized in September 1936 in response to increased retail prices. Although this group frequently identified with oppressed dairymen, its formation frightened distributors, and a former state commissioner of agriculture who worked for Sheffield Farms declared privately: "Price consciousness and consumer consciousness are building up very fast in this market and maybe the time is not very far distant when the consumers will be telling the producers what they will get for their milk rather than the producers telling the consumers what the consumers will pay for their milk." Susan Jenkins to Members of the Milk Consumers Protective Committee et al., n.d., "Milk Prices," Reel 62, GP, HHLP; Caroline Whitney to HHL, December 28, 1936, "Agriculture and Markets—Division of

Milk Control, 1935-38," Reel 2, GP, HHLP; Berne A. Pyrke to Frank N. Decker, February 26, 1937, Milk File (3), Decker Papers.

119. *Report on the Milk Law,* March 22, 1937, pp. 7, 12-20.

120. Fred H. Sexauer to George F. Rogers, March 10, 1937, "Agricultural and Markets—Division of Milk Control, 1935-38," Reel 2, GP, HHLP.

121. E. S. Foster to Chairman of County Farm Bureaus et al., April 14, 1937, Box 2, New York State Farm Bureau Papers (#2714 ADD.). The Rogers-Allen bill was commonly called "The Ithaca Plan," but Dean Carl Ladd denied that the College of Agriculture had participated in preparation of the measure. Ladd to Frank N. Decker, April 27, 1937, Milk File (3), Decker Papers.

122. *The Rural New-Yorker,* February 29, 1934, p. 601. (See *supra,* p. 173n9.)

123. Dillon to Frank N. Decker, April 30, 1937, Milk File (3), Decker Papers.

124. John J. Dillon to Frank N. Decker, January 13, 1937, ibid.

125. *The Rural New-Yorker,* January 30, 1937, p. 83, April 10, 1937, p. 329.

126. Frank N. Decker to John J. Dillon, April 20, 1937, Dillon to Decker, April 23, 1937, Milk File (3), Decker Papers.

127. New York *Herald Tribune,* May 4, 6, 7, 1937; *New York Times,* May 4, 6, 7, 1937; New York State *Assembly Journal, 1937,* pp. 2970-80, 3260-64; New York State *Senate Journal, 1937,* p. 1730. Quotation in *Herald Tribune,* May 4, 1937.

128. HHL Memorandum, May 19, 1937, *Public Papers, 1937,* p. 396.

129. *The Rural New-Yorker,* June 5, 1937, p. 467.

130. Report of the General Secretary to the Annual Meeting, November 10, 1937, New York State Farm Bureau Papers, Box 30; Howard E. Babcock to J. D. Barnum, May 12, 1938, Box D-1, Babcock Papers.

131. *The Dairy Farmer,* November 25, 1938, Farmers' Union Papers.

132. Baldwin Memoir, "Data Relative to the First Four Years of the Agency," p. 8, Metropolitan Bargaining Agency Papers, Box 1.

133. Holton V. Noyes to HHL, October 25, 1937, "Milk Prices," Reel 62, GP, HHLP; Noyes Memorandum to HHL, n.d. [1938], "Agriculture and Markets, 1933-38," Reel 2, GP, HHLP; E. W. Gaumnitz to Noyes, February 9, 1938, GC, NY, AAA Records; New York State, *Annual Report of the Department of Agriculture and Markets for the Year 1938,* Leg. Doc. No. 37 (1939), pp. 114-15. (Hereinafter referred to as *Department of Agriculture Report, 1938.)* Carter, *The Fifty Year Battle,* pp. 25-26.

134. Lehman had hoped voluntary agreements under the Rogers-Allen law would end the need for state regulation of milk prices, but he finally reached the conclusion that "in order to preserve reasonable order in any metropolitan milk market some form of government control is necessary." HHL to Frank N. Decker, January 5, 1938, "Decker, Frank N.," Reel 25, GP, HHLP; HHL to Alfred L. Rose, July 10, 1939, "Milk Prices," Reel 62, GP, HHLP.

135. *Department of Agriculture Report, 1938,* pp. 116-22. In addition to the marketing order for New York City, New York State issued two others—one for Buffalo and the other for Rochester. New York, *Annual Report of the Department of Agriculture and Markets for the Year 1939,* Leg. Doc. No. 37 (1940), p. 122.

136. *Noyes v. Erie & Wyoming Farmers Co-operative Corp.,* 10 N.Y.S. 2d 114 (1939), 281 N.Y. 187 (1939); *United States v. Rock Royal Cooperative, Inc., et al.,* 26 F. Supp. 534 (1939), 307 U.S. 533 (1939). While awaiting the outcome of appeals, New York amended the

Rogers-Allen law to rectify minor faults found by a lower court judge. *Laws of New York, 1939,* chap. 760.

137. Daniel M. Frisbie to HHL, August 14, 1939, "Milk Strike, 1939," Reel 62, GP, HHLP; *New York Times,* August 17, 1939, June 21, July 8, 1941; *The Union Farmer,* September 25, 1939, June and July, 1941, Farmers' Union Papers; Lowell K. Dyson, "The Milk Strike of 1939 and the Destruction of the Dairy Farmers Union," *New York History,* LI (October 1970): 523-43.

138. One historian concluded that by 1940, "The State and Federal governments . . . had stabilized the New York State milk industry." However, this judgment overlooks continued ferment in the milkshed. Paul Abrahams, "Agricultural Adjustment during the New Deal: The New York Milk Industry; A Case Study," *Agricultural History,* XXXIX (April, 1965): 101.

139. Address by Daniel M. Frisbie, March 16, 1939, "Frisbie, Daniel," Reel 34, GP, HHLP; Leland Spencer, "Public Regulation of the Milk Industry," *State Government,* XII (October 1939): 189-90; *Department of Agriculture Report, 1939,* p. 130; *New York Times,* January 15, 1940.

140. HHL Address, August 31, 1939, *Public Papers, 1939,* p. 626.

141. HHL Address, January 17, 1940, *Public Papers, 1940,* pp. 612-14; HHL Address, January 22, 1941, *Public Papers, 1941,* pp. 661-63.

142. Other segments of the state's farming community, in addition to dairymen, made demands on Albany during the 1930s, but they asked for traditional government aid, generally in the form of improved marketing facilities which included roads and regional markets. Lehman backed many of these proposals, but they received little attention, since they came from less numerous and less well-organized groups than dairymen. For the annual legislative programs of the New York Farm Bureau and the State Conference Board of Farm Organizations, showing their emphasis on dairy problems, see Box 4, New York State Farm Bureau Papers; "New York State Conference Board of Farm Organizations," Reel 71, GP, HHLP.

143. HHL to Edward R. Eastman, May 26, 1937, Gen. Corr., 1933-40, HHLP.

144. Edward R. Eastman to HHL, May 22, 1937, ibid.; Fred H. Sexauer to HHL, June 30, 1936, June 10, 1942, Box 2, Dairymen's League Papers (#3026); Howard E. Babcock to Thomas E. Dewey, October 19, 1938, Box D-2, Babcock Papers.

145. *American Agriculturist,* September 25, 1937, p. 602. See also *Ithaca Journal,* February 18, 1937, CB, 46: 879.

146. Eastman to Howard E. Babcock, December 16, 1936, Box D-3, Babcock Papers.

147. *New York Times,* February 4, 1941.

VIII

THE ADVENT OF PUBLIC HOUSING

During the 1930s, New Yorkers shed the illusion that either Progressivism or prosperity had brought much improvement in slum housing. Lawrence Veiller, a leader of the progressive crusade against tenements, declared in 1932 that American cities "have the worst slums in the civilized world; this is notably so [in] New York." [1] Descriptions of the poorest homes in the world's richest metropolis read like pages out of Charles Dickens. In 1934, almost half of the apartment buildings in New York City dated from before the turn of the century when primitive housing codes allowed virtually any kind of structure. Two million people, almost one-third of the city's population, lived in these decaying multifamily dwellings some of which still contained rooms without windows to let in light or fresh air. Over 387,000 families had no central heat, 244,000 went without hot running water, and 189,000 lacked private toilets. Diseases like tuberculosis and rickets thrived in apartments with inadequate light, ventilation, and sanitation.[2] Congestion intensified the misery, and a 1932 study found "unbelievable crowding" in one Manhattan block.

> In many [buildings], there were five and six persons in two rooms. In one case there were eight persons living in two rooms. . . . As the average family consisted of six members, there was over-crowding, lack of privacy, no space for recreation or study, and no possibility [for children] of decent hours of retiring.[3]

In 1938, a housing expert noted with dismay that "Jacob Riis described these conditions 40 years ago and, except for a few changes forced upon owners since that time, they remain much the same." [4]

Slums had also spread across upstate New York, which had virtually no local housing regulations. A 1928 survey of an unnamed community considered typical revealed that obsolete dwellings clogged the central district. Here the city's poor crowded into converted single-family houses and three- or four-story tenements, most of which had no gas, heat, or hot water. Many furnished electricity, but some still relied on oil lamps for light. Seventeen percent of the buildings had windowless rooms, and 12 percent provided outdoor privies as the only toilet facilities. Of all the dwellings in the area, one had a fire escape. Despite such reports, most New Yorkers conceived of poor housing as primarily a problem of New York City, owing to the magnitude of its slums which overshadowed any in the country.[5] Furthermore, local reformers with national reputations had focused attention on New York City so that even the word "slum" had become synonymous with the Lower East Side of Manhattan.[6]

The Depression stimulated a search for new ways of assuring adequate housing. With conditions actually growing worse, many Americans finally admitted the inability of restrictive legislation and private enterprise to produce decent homes for low-income families. As government vastly expanded its involvement in many areas of society during the 1930s, this country adopted for the first time programs of slum clearance and low-rent housing financed by the public treasury. The federal government initiated the movement for public housing, but the Empire State soon joined the campaign which ultimately required the financial resources of every level of government. Unable to improve standards through the enforcement of housing codes, New York established a system of state aid to supplement federal and local funds for low-rent housing. Although the New Deal certainly did not eliminate slums, it inaugurated a positive attack by shifting the emphasis of housing reform from the purely negative means of restrictive laws to the constructive approach of publicly financed housing.

1

The regulation of apartment buildings originated in New York City during the post-Civil War era. As immigrants poured into the city and squeezed into five- and six-story dwellings, disease and decay reached shocking proportions. In the wake of a cholera epidemic, local reformers persuaded the state to set minimum standards for slum housing. The Tenement House Law of 1867 defined a tenement as any building where four or more families lived independently of each other and did their cooking on the premises. The measure did not apply to hotels or clubs and covered in effect only slum quarters, since New York's middle and upper classes still resided in single-family houses. Emphasizing physical conditions, the 1867 law required that tenements have facilities such as sufficient water closets or privies, suitable garbage receptacles, and adequate safeguards against fire. But the vagueness of many standards, coupled with lax enforcement, undermined the statute's effectiveness. Although amendments adopted over the next thirty years generally failed to strengthen the Tenement House Law, its coverage was expanded to include dwellings with three families.[7]

At the turn of the century, progressives thoroughly overhauled New York's housing code. Under the guiding hand of Lawrence Veiller, the state established a commission which studied tenement conditions in New York City and then drafted a new statute to replace the one of 1867. As adopted by the legislature, the Tenement House Law of 1901 improved the regulations governing health and safety in existing buildings. In addition, all buildings subsequently constructed to house three or more families had to meet more stringent standards regarding light, ventilation, space, plumbing, and fire protection. The sharp distinction between present and future housing led to common use of the terms "old-law" tenements to describe those built before 1901 and "new-law" for all erected after the measure went into effect. To ensure better enforcement of the code, the 1901 law created a local Tenement House Department with sole responsibility for administration of the statute. Although the separate agency produced greater compliance, its effectiveness still depended on adequate staff and conscientious officials, both of which often proved lacking.[8]

The next major revision of New York City's tenement code came in 1929. This occurred as a result of advances in fireproofing techniques and the spread of so-called apartment hotels, which evaded application of the 1901 statute because they did not provide kitchens. The Multiple Dwelling Law of 1929 covered not only tenements but also all other buildings, such as rooming houses, hotels, apartment hotels, and clubs, which housed three or more families. Furthermore, the new measure upgraded minimum standards set by the 1901 code. Since the Multiple Dwelling Law applied exclusively to cities of over 800,000 people, it took effect only in New York City where it replaced the Tenement House Law of 1901.[9]

Advocates of restrictive housing legislation employed the same arguments to justify the measures enacted from 1867 through 1929. Pointing to the effect of slums on the poor, reformers stressed that disease and filth reaped a particularly heavy toll among children growing up in tenements. Although evidence of this won over professional altruists such as social workers, it had little impact on the community at large, for which the slums were out of sight and out of mind. Therefore, the campaign for better housing emphasized the social costs of slums. Disease and fire could spread from bad to good neighborhoods; crime, vice, and illness were a financial burden on taxpayers who had to foot the bills for police, prisons, and hospitals. Underlying these appeals was a crude environmentalism which assumed that poor housing produced the evils associated with it. Eradicate the slum, and crime, vice, and disease would also vanish.[10] Progressives never had the opportunity to test this theory, because their restrictive laws were directed not at abolishing slums but, rather, at trying to make tenements safer, cleaner, and more comfortable. As a result, environmentalist ideas survived the Progressive Era.[11]

During the 1920s, the Tenement House Law suffered the fate of many similar reforms. Lax enforcement, as a result of insufficient funds and indifferent officials, effectively nullified the housing code in New York City. While the number of dwellings grew, the staff of the Tenement Housing Department dropped by one-third in the twenty years after 1910. In 1930, the State Board of Housing concluded: "The Tenement House Law is not enforced today, nor has there been adequate enforcement . . . at any time within the past ten years." [12]

Mayor Fiorello La Guardia put new life into the moribund Tenement House Department. After taking office in January 1934, he appointed Langdon W. Post as head of the city's housing agency. Although only thirty-four, Post already had years of experience in the field of housing. He later recalled that his interest dated from the Progressive Era:

> I distinctly remember when Jacob Riis came . . . to my preparatory school and aroused for the first time in the minds of the 150 boys who listened to him a realization of the horrors that stalked in those areas of New York City which had been forbidden to us during the holidays and which we looked upon as a sort of compound into which no decent people should venture.[13]

As a New York State assemblyman, Post had introduced the bill that became the Multiple Dwelling Law of 1929. With a flair for attracting public attention, the politically ambitious Post "put slums and housing on the front pages of the newspapers" after he took over as tenement house commissioner.[14]

Early in 1934, a rash of fires dramatized the danger of slum housing. During February and March, twenty-four people died when flames consumed several old-law tenements. With wooden interiors and airshafts that became flues, these buildings burned like matchboxes once they caught fire. After discovering that several of the tenements which had gone up in flames had previously been cited for violations of the housing code, Commissioner Post immediately forced the closing of over a score of the city's worst firetraps by declaring them "unfit for human habitation." [15]

With New Yorkers shocked by the number of death-dealing fires, social workers formed the Emergency Committee for Tenement Safety to push for broad remedial legislation. Cooperating with Langdon Post, the group suggested amending the Multiple Dwelling Law to require the fire-retarding of public halls and stairways by 1936, a private toilet for every family by the same date and a window in every room used for living purposes by 1939. Reformers also wanted authority given to the city to order the demolition of abandoned buildings shown to be a nuisance. This four-point program won the endorsement of practically all civic, health, welfare, and labor organizations in New York City.[16] Relying on familiar arguments, the Emergency Committee for Tenement Safety declared that its proposals would "improve conditions for tenants in slum areas" and "reduce the social cost and economic losses of slum areas." In the midst of the Depression, the group also pointed out that upgrading minimum housing standards would "give employment to many thousands of men who would be engaged to make the necessary repairs." [17]

The committee found little sympathy among Albany lawmakers. On April 4, 1934, hundreds of social workers and slum residents marched to the Capitol with signs pleading: DON'T FIDDLE WHILE HOMES BURN! [18] At a public hearing, these outraged citizens confronted a large delegation of landlords who claimed they could not afford any increased expenses. The director of the Emergency Committee dismissed this objection:

> Some of these tenements are owned by the wealthiest estates in the country,

including the Astor, Wendel, Goelet and Stuyvesant estates. The greater proportion of these old-law tenements are actually in the hands of the first mortgagees, many of which are banks and other lending institutions. . . . The plea of poverty cannot be used by the wealthy estates, the absentee owners, the banks, insurance companies, and other first mortgagees.[19]

Recognizing the strong opposition of landlords, lawmakers killed three of the proposed changes in the Multiple Dwelling Law, but publicity given to fire hazards forced passage of the amendment requiring fireproofing of halls and stairways by 1936.[20]

In 1935, housing reformers renewed the campaign for better sanitary facilities in old-law tenements. Pointing to almost 200,000 New York City families who shared toilets with neighbors, local officials and social workers demanded for the sake of cleanliness and privacy that the state require a water closet for each apartment by 1936. Organized labor backed this proposal which would create much needed work for the construction trades. Small owners of old-law tenements naturally objected, but many leading real estate men who had no financial interest in such property privately expressed approval of the measure. After little opposition surfaced in Albany, the Democratic-controlled legislature adopted the enabling bill, and Lehman signed it into law.[21]

The 1935 revision of the Multiple Dwelling Law marked the end of the drive to raise legal standards for old-law tenements. Declaring himself satisfied with recent improvements in the housing code, Commissioner Post announced that the La Guardia administration would not sponsor any additional bills mandating physical changes.[22] Post had already revealed that he intended through such legislation to move "more definitely toward the elimination of the old-law tenement rather than toward the rehabilitation of these completely obsolete structures." [23] As a result of amendments approved during 1934 and 1935, he thought the Multiple Dwelling Law effectively prohibited old-law buildings, "because fewer owners will find it profitable to comply with the provision of fire-retarding the halls." [24]

Post's campaign exposed the weakness of restrictive legislation. Although within four years his strict enforcement policy reduced the number of old-law tenements from 67,000 to 59,000, it also brought rent increases due to improvements and contributed to a housing shortage which hit poor families hardest.[25] Protective laws could upgrade or even eliminate existing tenements, but they could not create new homes for slum residents. "If we keep on this course," one of La Guardia's advisers warned in 1937, "we shall have the highest housing standards in the world, while a third of the population sleeps on park benches." [26]

2

The problem of assuring sufficient low-rent housing had troubled reformers for years. Most progressives had simply assumed that private enterprise would meet the demand for better apartment buildings. While favoring government intervention, they strictly limited the public role to prohibiting dangerous and unhealthy conditions. Aware of the European trend toward state-financed low-cost housing, progressives rejected the idea as "both socialistic and the product of special class legislation." [27] Around the turn of the century, model tenements became the American alternative to public housing. Built entirely by private capital, these projects sought to furnish new apartments at low rents through voluntary limitations on profits. Perhaps predictably, this so-called investment philanthropy attracted few businessmen.[28]

During the 1920s, New York State initiated a scheme to stimulate the private construction of low-rent housing. In 1926, Governor Smith pushed through a law creating a permanent State Board of Housing of five unsalaried members to oversee the future development of shelter for New Yorkers. This agency could authorize the incorporation of limited-dividend companies to build housing at low rents. Approved firms were exempt from state taxes and fees if they restricted themselves to a 6 percent return, provided apartments at rentals under specified maxima, and met certain other requirements. Under the law, municipalities also had the power to waive local taxation on the projects. Many reformers hoped that this system of incentives would pump private money into low-rent housing, thereby avoiding any need for publicly financed construction.[29] Al Smith praised the 1926 law as "rational, economically sound and thoroughly American," because it "does not put government into the real estate or any other business." [30]

Limited-dividend housing never fulfilled its promise. During its first ten years, the State Board of Housing supervised the completion of fourteen projects in New York City under the terms of the 1926 measure. Although the new buildings supplied nearly 6000 apartments for about 20,000 people, they had little effect on slum dwellers, most of whom could not afford even the cheapest rents in limited-dividend projects. Since rentals in the latter averaged $40.00 a month, tenants came largely from the middle-income bracket. Tax exemption alone did not produce homes within reach of lower-class families.[31]

As government took the first positive, but faltering, steps to assure adequate shelter for the poor, Louis Pink emerged as a spokesman for "the new day in housing." An original member of the State Board of Housing, Pink approached this assignment with the insights of both a lawyer and a social worker. While growing up in Brooklyn just before the turn of the century, the middle-class youth had visited the Lower East Side of Manhattan where he discovered the vigor and horror of life in an urban slum. After graduating from a small upstate college in 1904, Pink returned to the city to study law. He and a friend rented an apartment on Avenue C in the heart of New York's worst slum, "thinking that in that way we might learn something about social problems and be useful." He later recalled his discovery, after a year of such living, that "there wasn't much we could do that was any help to anyone just by living in this tenement." [32] In the search for a more effective means of assisting his neighbors, Pink moved to the nearby University Settlement where he lived and worked for two years in the company of other middle-class reformers such as Belle Moskowitz.

After becoming a member of the bar, Pink devoted himself to the law, but he continued his involvement in social welfare activities. From 1910 to 1913, he interrupted his practice to serve as head worker of the United Neighborhood Guild, a combination of three Brooklyn settlement houses. Pink entered public life in 1926 when Belle Moskowitz, now Al Smith's leading adviser, recommended her fellow worker from University Settlement for appointment to the newly created State Board of Housing. After Lehman became governor, Pink briefly headed the housing agency while simultaneously holding the post of state superintendent of insurance. The active public official also accepted a position on the board of the New York City Housing Authority in 1934.[33] Remaining throughout this period a member of various private social welfare groups, Pink earned the admiration particularly of toughminded housing reformers like Helen Alfred, who declared that she could "think of no one so wise, realistic and dependably discriminating." [34]

Louis Pink sparked the movement for public housing in New York. Although he had originally endorsed limited-dividend corporations as a possible solution, he had done so with reservations. In his 1928 book on housing, Pink questioned whether tax exemptions would provide a sufficient inducement for large-scale private investment. He thought municipal or state loans might prove necessary in order to raise the funds so desperately needed for rehousing New York's vast slum population. By 1931, Pink recognized the failure of the limited-dividend experiment and called for more positive action by government. Using the New York Port Authority as a model, he proposed the creation of a municipal housing authority, a public corporation with the power to construct and operate low-rent housing through the sale of bonds. Although clearly a plan for public housing, this represented a cautious approach in that it stressed local control and did not include the use of government funds through either loans or direct grants.[35]

Support for Pink's idea came from the Public Housing Conference of New York. Organized in 1931 and headed by the social worker Mary K. Simkhovitch, this group flourished through the energy of its secretary, Helen Alfred, who helped transform it into the National Public Housing Conference (NPHC) by 1933. Born into an old American family in 1889, Helen Alfred had graduated from the New York School of Social Work and subsequently directed Madison House, a settlement on the Lower East Side. This outspoken woman had shown her radical nature by becoming a socialist and running for the New Jersey State Legislature as a Socialist party candidate in 1930. During the years that followed, she dedicated her considerable talents to speaking and writing in the cause of public housing, and her single-mindedness won many converts.[36] Working out of NPHC headquarters in New York City, Helen Alfred fought at every level of government for the group's stated goal: "To promote low-cost housing for workers through public construction and with the aid of government funds." [37]

The campaign began in the summer of 1932. After learning of Pink's plan for municipal housing authorities, Helen Alfred helped him draft enabling legislation with the advice of several legal experts. Introduced by Senator Samuel Mandelbaum of New York City during the regular session of the 1933 legislature, the measure passed the Democratic Senate without a dissenting vote, but it died in the Assembly.[38]

Soon thereafter, the federal government spurred the movement for public housing.

Following the suggestion of NPHC leaders, the National Industrial Recovery Act authorized the new Public Works Administration (PWA) to finance, among other things, slum clearance and low-rent housing. Under this provision designed to create jobs for the unemployed, local public bodies empowered to erect housing could receive federal grants covering up to 30 percent of the cost of project and loans for as much as 70 percent of the remaining expense. When this measure became law in June 1933, no properly constituted housing agency existed in the entire country.[39] Reformers in New York immediately called for a special session of the state legislature to enact a law permitting cities to apply for federal monies and undertake low-rent housing programs.[40] Pleading for Lehman's aid, Helen Alfred emphasized that New York finally had the opportunity to launch "a broad simultaneous attack upon slum occupation and unemployment." [41]

When the legislature reconvened in late July to consider a variety of issues, advocates of public housing split over whether New York should create state or local housing authorities. The original Mandelbaum bill, drafted by the NPHC, had permitted cities to establish independent municipal corporations subject only to limited regulation by the State Board of Housing. Supporters of this plan argued that each community could best meet local needs through decentralized public housing. Opponents questioned whether New York City would take advantage of permissive legislation, since the Democrats in power had shown no interest in low-rent housing despite pressure from numerous groups. Furthermore, if the city did initiate a housing program, its financial and political weakness might well doom any experiment in municipal construction and operation. For these reasons Robert D. Kohn, head of the Housing Division of the PWA, favored a state-run program.[42]

After attempts to resolve this difference failed, several bills went into the legislative hopper. In a message to the special session, Lehman endorsed the principle of municipal authorities because it placed "the initiative and fundamental control in the cities themselves." [43] With no administration bill, competing measures proposed varying degrees of state supervision over local authorities. The revised Mandelbaum bill did not even mention state control, but all others provided for some regulation by the Board of Housing.[44] The variety of plans confused lawmakers. While many undoubtedly distrusted New York City's Tammany leaders, others saw little reason to place their confidence in the state. After six years of "bungling," the State Board of Housing was "about as popular as poison ivy," according to Helen Alfred.[45] In any event, the split in reform ranks sealed the fate of enabling legislation, although the Mandelbaum bill again passed the Senate in August.[46]

In preparation for the 1934 session, proponents of public housing finally formed a united front. At the suggestion of Kohn of the PWA, New Yorkers organized the Slum Clearance Committee in October 1933. This unofficial group brought together housing experts and representatives of the Board of Housing and real estate interests. With the aid of Charles Poletti, the Slum Clearance Committee drafted legislation which satisfied all parties concerned by creating a municipal housing authority in New York City subject to limited controls by the State Board of Housing. While mandatory for New

York City, the measure gave other cities the option of establishing similar agencies.[47] Louis Pink summarized the rationale behind the compromise bill:

> It is essential that [the state board] have supervision of the projects in order to maintain housing standards and financial integrity, but it is unthinkable that any State body is wise enough or efficient enough or has time enough to go into each city, know what it needs and build and operate the projects. The emergency justifies many things, but there is no reasonable justification for depriving the cities not only of their rights but of their obligations to their own inhabitants.[48]

La Guardia's election as mayor in 1933 also renewed the confidence of those who wanted decentralized public housing but distrusted Tammany. After endorsing municipal housing in his campaign, La Guardia fulfilled his pledge by supporting the bill presented by the Slum Clearance Committee.[49]

Reformers used a variety of arguments to win popular backing for the municipal housing authority measure. Like progressives a generation earlier, they stressed the social costs of slums which required heavy expenditures for police, fire, health, and sanitation services.[50] While marshaling statistics to show the effects of poor housing on the community as a whole, Langdon Post noted that "it is unfortunately essential that we prove the necessity of slum clearance in terms of dollars and cents rather than in terms of human suffering." [51] Advocates of public housing also pointed out that low-rent projects would not compete with private enterprise, since businessmen had notably failed to build new apartments which the lowest one-third of the working class could afford.[52] Government-financed construction aimed at this forgotten group would create not only much-needed housing but also employment opportunities for jobless tradesmen. The PWA furnished the ultimate incentive for enabling legislation by announcing that it had earmarked $25 million for housing in New York City, which the community would lose if it did not establish a housing authority.[53]

When Albany lawmakers gathered in January 1934, New York's participation in public housing seemed assured. Louis Pink notified the governor that "everyone is now lined up behind the Municipal Housing Authority Bill from the president down. It ought to go through with a bang." [54] Addressing the National Public Housing Conference on January 2, Lehman observed that a radical change had recently overtaken public opinion:

> Previous to the existing crisis, the majority of the people of our State . . . held the attitude that housing was a matter of individual responsibility. . . . It has been commonly assumed that any man of industry and sturdy morals could secure for himself and his family a good home. Rather suddenly, a whole new set of attitudes has swept even the more conservative sections of the community into a willingness to accept as a joint responsibility the obligation to provide good housing for the lower income groups.
>
> This shifting of attitude has been accelerated, of course, by the exigencies of the existing industrial depression. A number of the more cherished and seemingly

changeless patterns have been redrafted. And so one of the most important new areas of social responsibility has been outlined in the field of housing. No longer do cast-off, run-down old houses seem good enough. . . . *Modern standards of housing for all of the people have come to seem not only a possibility but a right.*[55]

Reflecting this new sentiment, lawmakers unanimously adopted the municipal housing authority bill after no opposition materialized even among real estate interests.[56] Helen Alfred, "amazed and delighted beyond words," praised Lehman for securing "passage with such neatness and dispatch." [57] In the presence of Alfred and other leaders of the NPHC, the governor signed the measure into law on January 31, 1934.[58]

This legislation put New York in the forefront of the public housing movement. Although several states had already established municipal housing authorities, New York's 1934 statute soon became the model for the rest of the country. By 1939, all but ten states had adopted similar measures.[59] Unlike PWA's emergency relief program, the New York City Housing Authority was created as a permanent agency to take charge of rebuilding the slums. This led Helen Alfred to declare: "The year 1934 marks a milestone in the history of American housing. . . . As late as 1932 *public housing* had little meaning among us." [60] Pointing to the principal reason for the sudden acceptance of housing owned and managed by government, Langdon Post noted that "the ill winds of the depression have silenced the opposition and those who have fed on the misery of the slums find the bone scraped and are now willing that the government should step in." [61]

3

New York State's housing authority law provided the machinery but not the money needed for slum clearance and low-rent housing. Although the PWA had promised New York City $25 million, the full sum never reached the city, as a result of bureaucratic delays and cutbacks in appropriations. This precipitated an intensive search for new sources of money. By the late 1930s, reformers opened up both federal and state coffers, but limited funds continued to plague the public housing movement.

After passage of the housing authority law in 1934, New York City possessed a new weapon with which to attack the slums.[62] La Guardia assured that the positive approach of public construction would work hand-in-hand with restrictive legislation by appointing Tenement House Commissioner Post as chairman of the New York City Housing Authority. In this venture, Post had the services of Louis Pink and Mary K. Simkhovitch of the NPHC, who became unsalaried members of the authority.[63] For legal counsel, the agency secured Charles Abrams, lawyer and housing expert, who received no pay for the first four months because of the lack of funds.[64]

The shortage of money hampered the housing authority for some time. After organizing the new agency, Post found the PWA's housing program "had stalled completely, its wheels clogged up with indecision, red tape, semicolons and a general fear of doing something." [65] Unable to obtain PWA funds immediately, Post devised an ingenious scheme to construct a demonstration project. With a pledge of $300,000 from

Federal Relief Administrator Harry Hopkins to cover building materials, New York's penniless housing authority got a half block of land in the heart of the Lower East Side from Vincent Astor, who accepted authority bonds as payment. In January 1935, jobless New Yorkers on work relief began demolition of the old-law tenements on the site and, less than a year later, former residents of the slum started moving into the site's 122 new apartments which rented for an average of $6.00 per room per month. Appropriately called "First Houses," this project was the first low-rent public housing development in the United States.[66]

Construction of First Houses precipitated a legal test of the city's power to initiate slum clearance. In the midst of the land sold by Vincent Astor stood two old-law tenements owned by Andrew Muller, who refused to sell and argued in state court that the city had no right to take his property by condemnation because low-rent housing was not a public use. When the case finally reached the Court of Appeals in 1936, the state's highest tribunal upheld the constitutionality of the 1934 housing authority law by a vote of six to one. Citing the "unquestioned" social costs of slums, the majority declared:

> The menace of the slums in New York City has been long recognized as serious enough to warrant public action. . . . The slums still stand. The menace still exists. . . .
>
> Legislation merely restrictive in its nature has failed. . . . The cure is to be wrought, not through the regulated ownership of the individual, but through the ownership and operation by or under the direct control of the public itself. . . .
>
> In a matter of far-reaching public concern, the public is seeking to take the defendant's property and to administer it as part of a project conceived and to be carried out in its own interest and for its own protection. That is a public benefit and, therefore, at least as far as this case is concerned, a public use.[67]

Langdon Post hailed this ruling as "the most important judicial decision in the history of housing legislation." [68]

After work on First Houses started, the PWA finally got its housing program underway. As a result of financial cutbacks, Washington allotted New York City only $17 million instead of the $25 million promised in 1934. These federal funds built two projects, one in Brooklyn for 6000 persons and another in Harlem exclusively for 1900 Negroes. Completed in 1937, the two developments provided new quarters for only about .5 percent of the city's slum population; yet in conjunction with First Houses, they represented the extent of low-rent public housing in New York City.[69]

By 1937, the country's largest city faced a housing crisis. Enforcement of the Multiple Dwelling Law had reduced the number of existing low-rent apartments, and neither private nor public construction had significantly expanded the supply of comparably priced homes. In addition, improvements in the economy had increased the demand for such housing because families who had shared living quarters at the depth of the Depression now sought separate accommodations. As vacancy rates dropped sharply, local officials warned of a severe housing shortage.[70] In December, 1936, a group of savings banks produced an emergency when they sent eviction notices to four thousand families in four hundred tenements which did not comply with the Multiple Dwelling Law. After investigating the situation, the housing authority rejected pleas from real estate interests for a moratorium on enforcement, but it called for a six-month suspension of all penalities against owners who agreed to comply with the law or vacate their buildings in that time period. The state immediately adopted this amendment to prevent wholesale evictions.[71] While approving this stopgap measure, the housing authority stressed that restrictive statutes could never solve the housing crisis.

> There can be only one way out of the morass. A carefully considered program of legislation, with adequate appropriations, to provide new housing for the slum dwellers, the under privileged, and the low-income groups, should be enacted without delay.[72]

A national campaign for expanded government aid brought passage of the United States Housing Act in August 1937. First suggested by the NPHC and sponsored by Senator Wagner, this law authorized federal funds and credit for low-rent housing exclusively for families with small incomes. Assistance went directly to local public bodies and included both loans to cover up to 90 percent of a project's cost and also annual contributions to keep rents down. Localities had to pay for 10 percent of the building expenses and furnish at least 20 percent of the rent subsidies either in cash or through tax exemptions. In the law, Congress authorized a maximum of $500 million in loans and $60 million in subsidies for the following three years.[73]

The financial commitment of the Wagner Housing Act disappointed many New Yorkers. City and state officials estimated that it would take from $1.5 to $2.5 billion to demolish all old-law tenements and rehouse their residents in new quarters, but the federal measure limited each state to 10 percent of the $500 million loan program. Thus, the Empire State could obtain a maximum of $50 million for construction of low-rent housing over the next three years, and New York City could expect to receive only $30 or $40 million which could replace 2 or 3 percent of the old-law tenements.[74] Langdon Post judged this "an extremely small amount when we consider not only the need but the emergency we are facing." [75] Reflecting the sentiments of most reformers, the State Board of Housing called for local and state aid to supplement the deficient Wagner Act.

> It is clear that a public housing program relying wholly upon the severely limited Federal appropriation for loans and subsidies will be wholly inadequate to meet the housing requirements of the lowest income families. The State and its municipalities must now assume responsibility for providing necessary financial assistance to public housing agencies.[76]

Many Republicans and Democrats in New York had already displayed a willingness to aid public housing. As part of their increasing attempt to win support among urban voters, Republicans had endorsed the principle of government subsidies in their 1936 state platform.

We recognize the need for slum clearances initiated and executed by State and local authorities. Within the limits of a sound State financial policy, we favor public aid to provide homes for families now living in slum areas and unable otherwise to afford decent, safe, sanitary housing.[77]

In line with this pledge, Assemblyman Abbot Low Moffat of Manhattan introduced a bill in 1937 to authorize $100 million in state bonds for loans to municipal housing agencies.[78] Although Lehman favored federal, state, and local financial cooperation in a "long-range municipal housing program of slum clearance and low-cost housing," he thought state participation required enabling amendments to the constitution.[79] An impasse developed in 1937 when Moffat and other Republicans disputed the need for constitutional revisions which would take at least two years.[80] The following year, Lehman called for state grants as well as loans, and lawmakers in both parties agreed on three amendments to the constitution, one of which proposed a $200 million revolving fund for loans. However, the convening of the 1938 Constitutional Convention shifted the debate over public housing to a new forum.[81]

When the convention opened in April 1938, it quickly received a number of housing proposals. Although coming from a variety of different sources, including Mayor La Guardia, Senator Wagner, the State Board of Housing, and the NPHC, most amendments agreed in principle on the forms government assistance should take. All envisioned a revolving fund for state loans to both local housing authorities and private limited-dividend corporations. In addition, each suggested a system of state grants-in-aid to subsidize rents in public projects. To permit local funding, other provisions authorized cities and towns to go into debt for this purpose by increasing the usual limitations on borrowing. Finally, these measures were designed to facilitate land acquisition for public housing through broader use of the powers of eminent domain and excess condemnation. The various plans differed only on specifics such as the size of the revolving funds and the degree of restrictions on local indebtedness.[82]

These proposals encountered little opposition in the convention's housing committee. This group was dominated by Republicans, but a majority of the members came from New York City, as did its chairman, Councilman Joseph Clark Baldwin, and a leading Democratic expert on housing, Senator Robert F. Wagner.[83] At a public hearing in June, committee members gave a friendly reception to speakers who favored government aid. Delegates listened carefully to Mayor La Guardia's description of appalling conditions in New York City slums. "You give [children] hospitals, parks and playgrounds, schools," he observed, "then you shoot them home at night into dismal, tuberculosis-breeding tenements." [84] Among the numerous witnesses, the only dissenting opinion came from real estate spokesmen who objected solely to any potential increase in municipal costs which would bring higher property taxes. Emphasizing that his group had already endorsed slum clearance and low-rent public housing, an officer of the Real Estate Board of New York "wished only to see these results achieved without placing additional tax burdens on real estate." [85] Visits to slum areas in New York and Buffalo convinced some upstate delegates of the pressing need for government assistance.

After one of these tours, Baldwin declared that his committee had learned enough "so that it will roll up its sleeves and draft a proposal to wipe out disgraceful slum conditions." [86]

In this spirit the committee unanimously approved a liberal housing measure. The so-called Baldwin amendment created a $300 million revolving fund, as large as any yet suggested, and proposed up to $2.5 million in annual rent subsidies to make public housing available to many who could not otherwise afford it. The plan also facilitated local housing aid by permitting tax exemptions for projects, expansion of debt limits by 2 percent, and excess condemnation which allowed cities to take more land through eminent domain than just that needed for housing. Although the result of some compromises, this package failed to include the demand of real estate owners for a ban on the use of property taxes for funding public housing.[87]

When the Baldwin amendment went before the full convention, it came under attack from delegates sympathetic to real estate interests. Al Smith and Robert Moses led the opposition on the convention floor. In a memorandum to the delegates, Moses derisively asserted that "almost all thinking citizens" would reject the housing committee's proposal, because it did not exempt real estate from paying any part of a housing program. "I do not yield either to threats or to insults," Joseph Baldwin parried.

[W] hen a group, a pressure group . . . , comes to see me in my office and threatens me, unless I exempt real estate, . . . it simply makes me very determined in my conviction that the amendment as we drafted it in the committee and as submitted by the committee is a just amendment, and I do not intend to yield . . . to any pressure group.[88]

Former Governor Smith, now president of the Empire State Building, defended property holders.[89] Much to the chagrin of reformers, the man who had laid the foundation for government housing subsidies offered an amendment to the Baldwin proposal excluding real estate from any additional taxation due to future slum clearance or low-rent housing. Baldwin countered that such a decision should be left up to state and local lawmakers and not incorporated into the constitution since no one could predict the health of real estate ten or twenty years hence. After Baldwin also warned that housing bonds would be virtually unmarketable without a city's entire tax resources to back them up, delegates narrowly rejected the Smith amendment by a vote of sixty-six to sixty-one.[90]

In the wake of this defeat, Smith revised his proposal. He recommended that the constitution specify that before floating housing loans cities had to enact special taxes, other than imposts on property, to finance the debt. If these levies proved insufficient, then communities could draw on funds from general property taxes. Although this modification theoretically permitted use of a city's complete financial resources, Joseph Baldwin complained that in practice it would force dependence on nuisance taxes and the regressive sales tax. Smith answered that without this change in the housing amendment over two million incensed property owners "will be laying for it on election day." On

August 18, the convention adopted Smith's restriction by a tally of seventy-four to sixty. Although no roll call was taken, reporters noted that about half the Democratic delegates sided with Smith, while liberal Republicans from New York City rejected his plan. After undergoing several other changes, the complete housing amendment passed the convention by a wide margin and went on the November ballot.[91]

Advocates of public housing greeted the final amendment with mixed reactions. Although they applauded the authorization of state and local funds for loans and rent subsidies, reformers decried the numerous restrictions placed on the future development of housing. In addition to the limitation on local taxing powers, the revised amendment declared that no project could receive state money unless it provided for actual slum clearance. The intention was to confine public housing to slum areas, but the ambiguous directive apparently held the possibility of building elsewhere if coupled with a plan for the destruction of substandard tenements. Upstate delegates also cut the maximum allowable rent subsidies to $1 million the first year with increases to $5 million after five years. Last-minute changes in the housing amendment banned the use of funds for any purpose except the construction of "low rent dwelling homes." This choice of words appeared to prevent the incorporation of stores or nurseries into housing projects because, even if rented to private persons, they did not qualify as dwelling units. Owing to its "serious handicaps," Helen Alfred called the housing amendment "something of an embarrassment," but she joined others in hoping that broad interpretation would nullify some of the worst defects.[92]

In spite of the misgivings of many housing experts, the amendment drew little opposition during the 1938 campaign. All state parties and their candidates, as well as virtually every civic and labor group, endorsed the housing proposal. Nevertheless, Senator Wagner spoke for many reformers when he declared that the amendment was a step in the right direction but inadequate to meet fully the housing crisis. Leading business organizations divided on the issue. While the State Chamber of Commerce and Merchants' Association of New York urged a yes vote, most real estate groups opposed the plan because it potentially allowed use of property taxes to finance local aid. In addition, some real estate spokesmen continued to denounce the principle of public housing.[93] On election day New Yorkers overwhelmingly approved the amendment by an almost two to one margin.[94]

4

By 1938, public housing received strong support for a variety of reasons. Since the plight of slum dwellers apparently generated little sympathy except insofar as it touched the lives of more affluent citizens, mounting evidence of the social costs of tenements undoubtedly helped to make government aid popular. While presenting statistics to show the higher rates of crime and disease in slum areas, public officials continued to justify new housing as a means of attacking these evils. A 1934 study by legal experts cited both genetic and numerous environmental causes of crime, but it concluded that "slum clearance means crime prevention." [95] Moreover, sections of New York City with substandard housing ate up much of the taxpayer's dollar that went for essential municipal services. Langdon Post found that bankers who remained indifferent to the suffering of slum residents sat up and took notice when they realized more taxes went to a block on Delancey Street than to one on Park Avenue.[96] In defense of the 1938 housing amendment, Joseph Baldwin asserted that government subsidies "would not only permit the State to solve the problem of health and housing but would, in the long run, help to relieve the heavy financial burden now borne by the taxpayers." [97]

During the 1930s, the economic dislocation of American society provided new arguments to buttress traditional justifications of housing reform. Advocates of government action raised the specter of revolution. "We can definitely trace some of our labor unrest to bad housing," warned the counsel of the Board of Housing, "and we can understand why such surroundings encourage the growth of radicalism and anarchy." [98] In a pamphlet published by the New York City Housing Authority, Langdon Post appealed to the same fears:

> All revolutions are germinated in the slums; every riot is a slum riot. Housing is one of the many ways in which to forestall the bitter lessons which history has in store for us if we continue to be blind and stiff-necked. As I see it, it is a question of housing—or else.[99]

The persistence of the Depression also made slum clearance attractive as a means of pump priming. After the 1937 downturn in the economy, Lehman declared in a message to the legislature: "I am convinced that government can best contribute toward the stimulation of business in this period of recession by promoting a far-flung program of public low-cost housing." In addition, the housing shortage of the late 1930s pointed to the failure of private enterprise to supply adequate shelter, particularly for families with small incomes.[100]

Since government greatly expanded its responsibility for the welfare of Americans during the Depression, public housing seemed a less radical departure than it had a generation earlier. Even many Republicans, especially those from New York City, approved this element of the Welfare State. In 1938, Abbot Low Moffat sounded like an ardent New Dealer when he asserted that a statewide program of subsidies would ensure "the decent and adequate housing which is *the right of every American family.*" [101]

Despite such rhetoric, reformers did not promise government aid for all those in need. Generally overlooking the plight of the poorest segments of society, they directed their attention to working-class families whose low incomes forced them to live in dilapidated tenements. In 1933, the Welfare Council of New York, a coalition of the city's private social service organizations, talked of low-income housing for those who earned more than $1000 a year. According to a contemporary study, this would have excluded at least 20 percent of America's families which had incomes under $1000 even in the prosperous year of 1929.[102] Harold Riegelman, an adviser to La Guardia who helped draft a number of housing bills,said government had to solve the problem of assuring satisfactory homes for relatively well-to-do workers "before we undertake the more difficult task for families having a smaller income than $1,000 per year, which includes many unemployables and charity cases." [103] Langdon Post dismissed the "submerged section of our society" as unredeemable, "a problem for psychiatrists and not for housing experts."

> What we have in mind when we speak of low-rental housing is the provision of adequate decent homes which will guarantee certain minimum standards in fresh air, sunshine and human amenities for the millions of American *workers who constitute the productive army of America.*[104]

Talk of public housing for a particularly "deserving" class of workers helped sell programs which might otherwise have been rejected as government handouts; but during the 1930s this policy forced people with little or no earnings to remain in slums since federal and state aid provided insufficient money for rent subsidies.[105]

5

Since the 1938 housing amendment was entirely permissive, its implementation required legislative action. This seemed a mere formality after the strong support given the amendment by politicians and voters. In his first message to lawmakers in 1939, Governor Lehman called for enabling legislation, but he left the details in the hands of Republicans who controlled both the Senate and the Assembly.[106] Having endorsed the principle of state aid since 1936, Republican leaders pledged to adopt a housing program during the 1939 session. Thomas C. Desmond of Newburgh, chairman of the Senate Committee on Cities, declared: "All recognize it as a responsibility of the Republican party to solve the housing problem." [107] While backing for this position came immediately from New York City Republicans and party leaders, many upstate members showed little enthusiasm.[108] Appealing for "a more sympathetic understanding of unfamiliar New York City issues," Senator Desmond asked for an end to cleavages between upstate and downstate Republicans.[109]

Public housing advocates gave their opponents the upper hand by failing to agree on a single bill in 1939. During January, at least five different proposals to put the housing amendment into effect went before the legislature. The first plan came out of a committee appointed by Mayor La Guardia and dominated by Robert Moses. After weeks of preparation, this group suggested that during the coming year New York City receive $100 million in state loans and $1 million in rent subsidies. Following the advice of Moses, the committee asked that up to 10 percent of housing funds finance collateral public facilities for services such as transportation, recreation, and police and fire protection. Furthermore, the city requested that the legislature permit local control of housing development by reconstituting the State Board of Housing as a banking agency to approve loans and subsidies but without the power to regulate their disbursement. Senator Desmond and Assemblyman Moffat sponsored bills which carried out the recommendations of the mayor's committee.[110] Desmond conceded that these measures primarily benefited New York City, but he promised "a square deal" for upstate communities which requested similar aid.[111]

The initial attack on the La Guardia plan came not from rural lawmakers but from metropolitan housing experts. Many complained that spending limited state funds on supplemental facilities would further restrict the amount of housing erected. Some reformers called for greater state loans for the first year and stronger state supervision.[112] In response to this criticism, La Guardia defended his committee's plan as a skeleton bill subject to revision, but the mayor privately dismissed such objections as "legalistic technicalities." [113] Since many supporters of public housing considered these basic questions of policy, they soon introduced competing proposals. Separate bills came from the New York City Housing Authority, the State Board of Housing, Assemblyman Robert F. Wagner, Jr., the New York County Republican Committee, and a coalition of civic groups. Although these measures differed on details such as the size of the revolving fund for loans, they all confined expenditures to housing and provided for a powerful state agency to oversee the future development of public projects.[114]

In 1939, a drawn-out dispute over the state budget delayed consideration of housing bills until May. By that time sentiment against public housing had increased, particularly among rural legislators who demanded a general belt-tightening combined with tax reductions. Some lawmakers cited disagreements among housing proponents as evidence of a need for further study before the state initiated a system of subsidies.[115] Endorsing a policy of delay, the Real Estate Board of New York argued that it did "not regard the housing amendment approved last fall as a mandate to the Legislature to rush into a gigantic program of government housing this year." [116] After the troublesome budget passed both houses in late April, Republican leaders drafted a housing plan which authorized $150 million in loans and $1 million in rent subsidies. The state could extend only one-third of the loans and one-fourth of the subsidies during the first year, and New York City could receive no more than two-thirds of each sum. On two other controversial items, Republicans decided against any allocation for facilities other than housing, and they chose to replace the Board of Housing with a single superintendent to oversee the development of housing throughout the state.[117]

An outcry of protest greeted announcement of this plan. With little hope of getting more money from the tightfisted Republicans, housing experts said nothing about the size of the appropriations, but they loudly criticized a number of last-minute administrative changes. These included a requirement that localities match state rent subsidies, severe limitations on land acquisition, an inadequate budget for state supervision, and the injection of politics by making project and tenant selection subject to approval by locally elected officials.[118] Mrs. Samuel I. Rosenman, who headed a recently organized lobby for housing legislation, summarized the basis of these objections to the Republican package:

The amended bills . . . make available sufficient loans and subsidy funds with which the state can initiate a program of public low-cost housing. To burden that effort with the administrative amendments referred to would . . . doom it to failure from the start.[119]

Even Senator Desmond who had agreed to sponsor the Republican proposals joined the swelling chorus and declared that "serious defects" necessitated further revisions in the legislation. Meanwhile, other Republicans warned that the donnybrook could well destroy the chances for passage of any housing law in 1939.[120]

At this point Governor Lehman suddenly stepped into the fray. After months of silence on the housing issue, he called a conference of legislative leaders where he won acceptance of several amendments demanded by housing experts. Republicans agreed to permit tax exemptions in place of cash for local matching subsidies, to liberalize powers of land acquisition, and to put tenant selection in the hands of local housing authorities. However, the Republicans refused to accede to any other changes sought by civic and housing groups.[121] Lehman admitted that the compromise legislation was "by no means perfect," but he thought his efforts had greatly improved the measure.[122] Reformers agreed because, above all, the governor had gained a commitment from legislative leaders to push for quick passage of the revised proposal, which soon cleared both houses with only four dissenting votes.[123] In applauding Lehman's crucial intervention, Helen Alfred spoke for others when she observed that "the bill, while still leaving much to be desired, lays a solid and broad base for a state-wide public housing program." [124]

In spite of its flaws, the 1939 legislation kept the Empire State in the vanguard of the public housing movement. As the first state to put its resources behind municipal housing, New York did "pioneering work," which the National Association of Housing Officials praised because it provided a basis of experience for the rest of the country.[125] New York's pledge of $150 million in loans compared favorably with the maximum of $50 million initially available under the 1937 federal housing act. Nevertheless, the combined $200 million obtainable from parallel state and federal programs paled in light of the estimate that it would take $2 billion to rehouse New Yorkers living in substandard housing. "It is obvious from the foregoing data," the State Board of Housing concluded in 1939, "that even if the State and all its municipalities should exercise to the utmost the powers given them under the new housing amendment, and even if the Federal government should continue its modest program, only a slight percentage of the actual needs would be met." [126]

Implementation of Albany's aid program met with unexpected delays. Before contracts could be signed, the State Division of Housing had to work out administrative procedures, and local communities had to raise the necessary matching rent subsidies. While waiting for state assistance, New York City received $45 million from Washington to build over 10,000 dwelling units under the terms of the 1937 act.[127] In 1941, New York's Division of Housing finally approved $20 million in loans for a complex of 3500 apartments in Brooklyn, the largest public housing project in the country. Soon thereafter, the state authorized an additional $27 million for three more developments in New York City and $1 million for a project in New Rochelle.

However, American entry into World War II forced postponement of all but the Brooklyn project which, because of its location opposite the Navy Yard, received priority as housing temporarily for war workers.[128] Charles Abrams concluded in 1946: "Despite delays and setbacks, New York . . . has gone further than any other state to aid low-rent housing and slum clearance." [129] The future development of public housing raised a host of disputes regarding location, cost, planning, and tenant selection, but New Yorkers emerged from the 1930s firmly committed to the idea of housing, financed, owned, and managed by government.[130]

The Depression provided the impetus for public housing. In New York City during the early 1930s, reformers first organized to sell this experiment to a people sinking deeper into poverty. Advocates of government enterprise won wide support for a variety of reasons, including fear, the inability of private developers to supply sufficient housing for low-income families, the failure of restrictive legislation, and the need to produce jobs for the unemployed. The initial commitment to public construction came from Washington, which fostered local participation through the temporary Public Works Administration.

Born as an emergency relief scheme, public housing quickly became a permanent function of government. After the Empire State approved the creation of municipal corporations to erect and operate housing, the search for building funds stimulated a national campaign for increased federal expenditures. In 1937, Congress established the United States Housing Authority to finance a decentralized public housing program. The growing housing crisis in New York City, coupled with limited federal appropriations, led the state to join the Herculean effort to clear the slums. With bipartisan backing, New York inaugurated a system of state loans and rent subsidies, modeled after the national program. Like Washington, Albany did not actually build or manage any projects, but instead it helped finance local development. Although all levels of government combined failed to supply enough money to eradicate slums during this period, they assumed for the first time direct responsibility for ensuring adequate shelter for low-income families.

NOTES

1. The Editors of *Fortune, Housing America* (New York, 1932), p. 7.
2. *New York Times,* March 11, 1934; "Blue Sky for All Is Slum-Clearance Goal," *Literary Digest,* (April 28, 1934), p. 19; James Ford, "New York Resurveys Her Vast Housing Needs," *New York Times Magazine,* January 24, 1937, p. 8.
3. Harry Manuel Shulman, *Slums of New York* (New York, 1938), p. 44.
4. Langdon W. Post, *The Challenge of Housing* (New York, 1938), p. 38.
5. New York State, *Report of the State Board of Housing,* Leg. Doc. No. 95 (1929), pp. 43-50.
6. For a variety of contemporary definitions of the slum, see James Ford, *Slums and Housing with Special Reference to New York City* (2 vols; Cambridge, Mass., 1936), I: 3-14.
7. *Laws of New York, 1867,* chap. 908; Lawrence M. Friedman, *Government and Slum*

Housing: A Century of Frustration (Chicago, 1968), pp. 25-29; Roy Lubove, *The Progressives and the Slums: Tenement House Reform in New York City, 1890-1917* (Pittsburgh, 1962), pp. 25-28, 88-100.

8. In order to reduce to a simple majority the number of votes needed for passage of the 1901 law, it applied to all first-class cities, which at the time meant New York City and Buffalo. *Laws of New York, 1901*, chap. 334; Lubove, *The Progressives and the Slums*, pp. 117-36, 151-66.

9. Provision was made for the voluntary adoption of the 1929 statute by other cities, but none elected to do so at the time. *Laws of New York, 1929*, chap. 713; Gertrude M. Ruskin, "Restrictive and Constructive Housing Legislation in the State of New York" (unpublished M. A. thesis, New York University, 1941), pp. 14-32; MacNeil Mitchell, "Historical Development of the Multiple Dwelling Law," *Consolidated Laws of New York Annotated*, 35-A (1946): xvii-xix.

10. Friedman, *Government and Slum Housing*, pp. 3-14; Lubove, *The Progressives and the Slums*, pp. 71-73.

11. Lubove, *The Progressives and the Slums*, p. 133.

12. New York State, *Report of the State Board of Housing*, Leg. Doc. No. 84 (1930), pp. 71-73.

13. Post, *The Challenge of Housing*, pp. 102-3.

14. Charles Abrams, *The Future of Housing* (New York, 1946), p. 215. See also Louis Pink Memoir, COHC, p. 44.

15. New York *Daily News*, March 12-17, 1934; *New York Post*, March 13, 1934; *New York World-Telegram*, March 14, 21, 1934; "New York's War on Fire-Trap Tenements," *Literary Digest*, March 24, 1934, p. 21.

16. *New York Times*, March 30, 1934; Ira S. Robbins to HHL, April 18, 1934, chap. 526 (1934), Bill Jackets.

17. Ira S. Robbins to Members of the Legislature, April 2, 1934, chap. 526 (1934), Bill Jackets.

18. *Albany Evening News*, April 5, 1934.

19. New York *Herald Tribune*, April 15, 1934. Little information exists on the nature of New York City's slum owners during this period. Trinity Church, one of the largest holders of real estate in Manhattan, had been identified with run-down tenement properties since the Progressive Era. A 1929 study of realty records showed that prominent estates controlled 10 percent of the property on the Lower East Side, but this figure did not include buildings where ownership was concealed. Unlike absentee owners, numerous smaller landlords lived in or nearby their few tenements, but the Depression forced many of them to mortgage their holdings, some of which thereby passed into the hands of banks and insurance companies. Although the exact percentage of slum dwellings held by each of these various groups is unknown, banks and similar institutions accounted for a growing proportion in the 1930s. Langdon Post thought they had become "the largest single owners of slum tenements, instead of the wealthy families who held most of them 35 years ago." In 1937, a bank president offered striking evidence of this when he stated privately that his institution alone owned 245 old-law tenements and held mortgages on over two thousand more. *Report of the State Board of Housing* (1930), p. 57; Post, *The Challenge of Housing*, pp. 61-62; "The High Cost of Slums," *Review of Reviews*, LXXXIX (June 1934): 46; Charles G. Edwards to HHL, May 18, 1937, chap. 353 (1937), Bill Jackets.

20. Ira S. Robbins to HHL, April 30, 1934, chap. 526 (1934), Bill Jackets; Robbins Memorandum, May 3, 1934, "Housing Section, Welfare Council," Edith Elmer Wood

Papers, Columbia University; *New York Times,* May 16, 1934; *Laws of New York, 1934,* chap. 526.

21. *New York Times,* February 27, 1935; Lillian D. Wald to HHL,. April 2, 1935, George H. Hallett, Jr., to HHL, March 30, 1935, John M. O'Hanlon to HHL, April 8, 1935, Fiorello La Guardia to HHL, May 6, 1935, Greater New York Taxpayers Association to HHL, April 5, 1935, Ira S. Robbins to Charles Poletti, April 23, 1935, chap. 904 (1935), Bill Jackets; *Laws of New York,* 1935, chap. 904.

22. New York City, *Tenement House Department Report for the Year 1935,* p. 15.

23. New York City, *Tenement House Department Report for the Years 1932-34,* p. 7.

24. Post to La Guardia, January 3, 1936, "Housing," Box 2672, La Guardia Papers, New York City Municipal Archive.

25. New York City, *Tenement House Department Report for the Year 1936,* p. 9; *Tenement House Department Report for the Year 1937,* pp. 19-20

26. Harold Riegelman to the Editor, *New York Times,* March 13, 1937.

27. Lubove, *The Progressives and the Slums,* p. 179.

28. Ibid., pp. 33-44, 104, 178-81.

29. Louis H. Pink, *The New Day in Housing* (New York, 1928), pp. 98-114; Dorothy Schaffter, *State Housing Agencies* (New York, 1942), pp. 238-56.

30. Pink, *The New Day in Housing,* p. viii.

31. *Public Housing Progress,* November 15, 1934; Carl Randau, "New York's Great Luxury—Its Slums," *New York World-Telegram,* April 29, 1936; Edith Elmer Wood, *Slums and Blighted Areas in the United States* (Washington, 1936), pp. 103-5; Post, *The Challenge of Housing,* pp. 123, 216-17. In 1930, Herbert Lehman showed a strong interest in low-rent housing by investing $300,000 in a limited-dividend project built by Amalgamated Clothing Workers. Aaron Rabinowitz Address, April 29, 1931, p. 11, Rabinowitz to HHL, September 5, 1931, "Amalgamated Housing Project," Special Subject File, HHLP; Allan Nevins, *Herbert H. Lehman and His Era* (New York, 1963), p. 121.

32. Pink Memoir, p. 5.

33. Ibid., pp. 3-32.

34. Alfred to Edith Elmer Wood, [November] 1937, "NPHC, II," Wood Papers.

35. Pink, *The New Day in Housing,* p. 108; *Brooklyn Daily Eagle,* September 13, 1931; Pink Memoir, pp. 36-37, 40-41.

36. Helen Alfred, ed., *Toward a Socialist America: A Symposium of Essays* (New York, 1958), p. 12; Timothy L. McDonnell, *The Wagner Housing Act: A Case Study of the Legislative Process* (Chicago, 1957), pp. 54-55, 64.

37. See letterheads of the NPHC in the Wood Papers, "NPHC, I."

38. *New York Times,* November 6, 1932, February 16, March 30, 1933; *Public Housing Progress,* December 15, 1934; Pink Memoir, pp. 41-42; Helen Alfred to HHL, February 16, 1933, "Emergency Public Works Commission," Reel 29, GP, HHLP.

39. Michael W. Straus and Talbot Wegg, *Housing Comes of Age* (New York, 1938), pp. 33-40; McDonnell, *The Wagner Housing Act,* pp. 29-30.

40. Ira S. Robbins to HHL, June 26, 1933, "Municipal Housing Bill," Reel 65, GP, HHLP; Aaron Rabinowitz to HHL, July 18, 1933, "Special Session (1933)—Municipal Housing," Reel 89, ibid.

41. Alfred to HHL, July 11, 1933, "National Public Housing Conference," Reel 67, GP, HHLP. (Hereinafter referred to as "NPHC.")

42. Helen Alfred to Charles Poletti, July 24, 1933, ibid.; Louis Pink to Poletti, August 9, 1933, Paul Windels to Poletti, July 21, 1933, Kohn to HHL, July 25, 1933, "Secretary of State—Housing Board, 1933," Reel 91, GP, HHLP; Carl S. Stern to Poletti, August 10, 1933, "Municipal Housing," Reel 65, ibid.; Pink Memoir, pp. 49-50.

43. HHL Message to the Legislature, August 3, 1933, *Public Papers, 1933,* p. 144. In June, Lehman had declared: "Social justice demands that the community, through its police powers, and through its public conscience, insure decent housing conditions so that the ills that spring from congested slums will be largely eliminated." HHL Address, June 15, 1933, ibid., p. 764.

44. Schaffter, *State Housing Agencies,* pp. 69-70.

45. Alfred to Edith Elmer Wood, August 21, 1933, "NPHC, I," Wood Papers.

46. Ira S. Robbins to HHL, July 18, 1933, Robbins to Charles Poletti, July 25, 1933, "Municipal Housing," Reel 65, GP, HHLP; Helen Alfred to HHL, August 12, 1933, "NPHC," Reel 67, ibid. At a one-day special session in October 1933, the Mandelbaum bill went down to defeat for the third time despite a renewed appeal for passage from Governor Lehman. The Senate unanimously adopted the measure, but the Republican Assembly buried it in committee because of anti-Tammany feeling and continued opposition from the State Board of Housing to any bill that did not provide for state supervision. HHL Message to the Legislature, October 10, 1933, *Public Papers,* 1933, p. 181; Albany *Knickerbocker Press,* October 19, 1933; *New York Times,* October 19, 1933; Alfred to Poletti, October 23, 1933, "NPHC," Reel 67, GP, HHLP.

47. Helen Alfred to Officers of the NPHC, December, 1933, "NPHC, I," Wood Papers; Alfred to Poletti, December 11, 1933, "NPHC," Reel 67, GP, HHLP; Richard S. Childs to Fiorello La Guardia, February 1, 1934, "New York City Housing Authority," Box 662, La Guardia Papers. (Hereinafter referred to as "NYCHA.")

48. *New York Times,* November 12, 1933.

49. Arthur Mann, *La Guardia Comes to Power, 1933* (Chicago, 1965), pp. 107-8; *New York Times,* November 26, 1933.

50. Helen Alfred, *Municipal Housing* (New York, 1932), pp. 8-10.

51. "The First [NPHC] Washington Conference on Public Housing," January 27, 1934, p. 9, "NPHC," Reel 67, GP, HHLP.

52. Between 1927 and 1931, only 1.7 percent of all apartments newly built in New York City (excluding Staten Island) rented for less than $12.50 per room per month or at rentals families in slums could even remotely afford. New York State, *Report of the State Board of Housing,* Leg. Doc. 84 (1932), p. 23.

53. NPHC, "New York Opinion Expects Municipal Housing Legislation," n.d., "NPHC, I," Wood Papers; *New York Times,* January 14, 23, 1934.

54. Pink to HHL, December 15, 1933, "Pink, Louis H.," Gen. Corr., 1933-40, HHLP.

55. HHL Address, January 2, 1934, *Public Papers, 1934,* p. 691. (Italics added.) See also HHL Address to the Legislature, January 3, 1934, ibid., p. 47.

56. New York, *Assembly Journal, 1934,* p. 132; New York *Herald Tribune,* January 31, 1934; *New York Times,* January 30, 31, February 1, 1934. The Real Estate Board of New York, which had cooperated with the Slum Clearance Committee and approved its bill, soon had second thoughts. After passage of the measure, the board tried unsuccessfully to have it amended to fix maximum rents, bar families earning over $1500 annually, and confine public housing to slum areas. *New York Times,* February 18, 25, 26, March 4, 22, 1934.

57. Alfred to HHL, February 8, 1934, "Alfred, Helen," Gen. Corr., 1933-40, HHLP. See also Langdon Post to HHL, February 1, 1934, "POS," ibid.

58. HHL Memorandum, January 31, 1934, *Public Papers, 1934*, p. 331; *Laws of New York, 1934*, chap. 4.

59. Helen Alfred to Abbot Low Moffat, May 11, 1939, chap. 808 (1939), Bill Jackets; Robert Moore Fisher, *20 Years of Public Housing* (New York, 1959), p. 89.

60. *Public Housing Progress*, December 15, 1934.

61. "The First [NPHC] Washington Conference," January 27, 1934, p. 7.

62. By 1939, ten upstate cities had also created municipal housing authorities under the 1934 law, but only six of these actually developed any projects. Throughout this period, New York City led the housing movement by initiating thirteen projects as compared to four in Buffalo and one each in Lackawanna, Schenectady, Syracuse, Utica, and Yonkers. New York State, *Report of the State Superintendent of Housing*, Leg. Doc. No. 70 (1940), p. 15.

63. Other appointees were Rev. E. Roberts Moore of Catholic Charities and B. Charney Vladeck, general manager of the *Jewish Daily Forward*. La Guardia to Post, February 13, 1934, "NYCHA," Box 2565, La Guardia Papers; La Guardia to John Ihlder, January 10, 1936, "Housing," Box 2672, ibid.

64. Post to La Guardia, June 4, 1934, "NYCHA," Box 662, ibid.

65. Post, *The Challenge of Housing*, p. 180. For a discussion of setbacks in PWA's Housing Division, see Straus and Wegg, *Housing Comes of Age*, pp. 121-33.

66. Post, *The Challenge of Housing*, pp. 182-90; NYCHA, *Twenty-five Years of Public Housing, 1935-1960* (New York, 1960), p. 1. During World War I, the federal government had built and operated housing for workers in defense plants. However, these public dwellings were not designed specifically for poor families, and they were sold at the end of the war. Edith Elmer Wood, *Recent Trends in American Housing* (New York, 1931) pp. 66–82. Friedman, *Government and Slum Housing*, pp. 95–96.

67. *New York City Housing Authority v. Muller*, 270 N.Y. 333, 341-43.

68. *New York Times*, March 18, 1936. This decision had national significance because federal courts had blocked PWA's attempts to clear slums by eminent domain. Thus, Washington had to rely on local powers of condemnation, first affirmed in the *Muller* case. E. H. Foley, Jr., "Legal Aspects of Low-rent Housing in New York," *Fordham Law Review*, VI (January 1937): 16-17; William Karlin, "New York Slum Clearance and the Law," *Political Science Quarterly*, LII (June 1937): 241-58; William Ebenstein, *The Law of Public Housing* (Madison, Wis., 1940), pp. 57-66.

69. *New York World-Telegram*, October 9-10, 1935; *New York Times*, January 3, 1937; Post, *The Challenge of Housing*, pp. 190-95. PWA projects were federally constructed, owned, and operated, but in the single case of New York City, Washington leased the completed developments to the local housing authority because of its demonstrated expertise. In upstate New York the PWA built three projects for 1148 families in Buffalo, Lackawanna, and Schenectady. Arnold H. Diamond, "The New York City Housing Authority; A Study in Public Coporations" (unpublished Ph.D. dissertation, Columbia University, 1954), pp. 8-9; Straus and Wegg, *Housing Comes of Age*, pp. 151, 194, 207-8, 221.

70. *Tenement House Report*, 1936, pp. 8-10.

71. Langdon Post to Fiorello La Guardia, December 31, 1936, *Public Papers, 1937*, pp. 38-39; *New York Times*, January 23, 1937; *Laws of New York, 1937*, chap. 1.

72. NYCHA Report, [January 25, 1937], *Public Papers, 1937*, p. 215.

73. McDonnell, *The Wagner Housing Act,* passim. For Lehman's endorsement of the Wagner bill, see HHL to Robert F. Wagner, May 18, 1937, "City Affairs Committee of New York," Reel 17, GP, HHLP.

74. *New York World-Telegram,* May 2, 1936; New York State, *Report of the State Board of Housing,* Leg. Doc. No. 66 (1938), p. 11.

75. *New York Times,* October 19, 1937. Soon after making this statement, Post abruptly resigned as chairman of the NYCHA because La Guardia ordered city officials not to confer with Nathan Straus, U.S. housing administrator. Frustrated by delays in implementing the new federal program, the mayor said that he would cooperate with Washington only when and if it was ready to start building. Post thought La Guardia's interference would "have disastrous results for public housing" and quit in protest. Charles Abrams, housing authority counsel, followed suit. Reformers feared that La Guardia's highhandedness would bring politics into the housing authority and thereby destroy its independence. This proved to be the case as La Guardia became more involved in the work of the authority. His actions were on behalf of public housing, but reformers worried that the same tactics would be used by less committed mayors to subvert the housing movement. *New York Times,* November 23, December 2-3, 1937; La Guardia to Post, December 1, 1937, Post to La Guardia, December 2, 1937, "NYCHA," Box 662, La Guardia Papers; La Guardia to Straus, December 17, 1937, "NYCHA," Box 2565, ibid.; Arthur Garfield Hays to HHL, December 5, 1937, "NYCHA," Reel 69, GP, HHLP; Edith Elmer Wood to Evans Clark, December 22, 1937, "NPHC, I," Wood Papers; Abrams, *The Future of Housing,* pp. 287-88.

76. *Report of the State Board of Housing* (1938), p. 17. For other criticisms of the federal program, see Ira S. Robbins Memorandum, November 15, 1937, "New York State," Wood Papers; Helen Alfred to Fiorello La Guardia, November 15, 1937, La Guardia to the Board of Estimate, January 25, 1938, "NYCHA," Box 2565, La Guardia Papers.

77. *New York Times,* September 30, 1936.

78. Ibid., January 11, February 1, 1937.

79. HHL Message to the Legislature, January 6, 1937, *Public Papers, 1937,* pp. 33-34.

80. *New York Times,* March 24, 1937; Schaffter, *State Housing Agencies,* pp. 280-84.

81. HHL Message to the Legislature, January 5, 1938, *Public Papers, 1938,* pp. 34-36; *New York Times,* January 6, February 24, March 4, 16, 18, 1938.

82. NPHC Resolution, January 21, 1938, Helen Alfred to Edith Elmer Wood, May 18, 1938, "NPHC, II," Wood Papers; New York State Board of Housing, Press Release, June 9, 1938, "Housing—Department of, 1938," Reel 46, GP, HHLP; *New York Times,* April 18, 19, May 1, 1938.

83. Schaffter, *State Housing Agencies,* p. 295.

84. *New York Post,* June 9, 1938.

85. *New York Times,* June 10, 1938.

86. Ibid., June 12, 1938. Baldwin also noted: "Housing is proving itself to be a common denominator not only between Republicans and Democrats in the convention, but between so-called upstate and downstate representatives." New York *Herald Tribune,* June 12, 1938.

87. The committee's plan won the endorsement of the State Board of Housing. New York *Herald Tribune,* July 14, 1938; *New York Times,* July 14, 26, 1938. For Baldwin's explanation of the proposal, see *Record of the Constitutional Convention of the State of New York* (Albany, 1938), pp. 1560-69. (Hereinafter referred to as *Record of the Convention.)*

88. *Record of the Convention,* pp. 1541, 1605-6.

89. Smith initially claimed to "represent no realty interest of any kind," but when debate heated up several weeks later, he bragged that "I am working for a concern that pays more taxes for one building than is paid any place in the world." Ibid., pp. 1624, 3084.

90. Ibid., pp. 1627, 1636-37, 1760. Although no roll call was taken, observers noted that the balloting split party lines as conservative Democrats and Republicans backed Smith's measure and liberals from both parties opposed it. *New York Times,* July 28, 1938.

91. *Record of Convention,* pp. 3081-96 (quotation on p. 3084); New York *Herald Tribune* and *New York Times,* August 18, 1938.

92. Alfred to Edith Elmer Wood, September 1, 1938, Wood to Alfred, September 2, 1938, "NPHC, II," Wood Papers; Louis Pink to Alfred E. Smith, August 18, 1938, "Housing—Department of, 1938," Reel 46, GP, HHLP; New York State, *Report of the State Board of Housing,* Leg. Doc. No. 60 (1939), pp. 16-20; Robert F. Wagner to FDR, August 31, 1938, OF 88, FDRL.

93. *New York Times,* September 30, October 1, 4, 14, 26, 30, November 2, 6, 7, 1938; HHL to Helen Alfred, November 6, 1938, "HOU," Gen. Corr., 1933-40, HHLP; Mary K. Simkhovitch Address, November 7, 1938, Mary K. Simkhovitch Papers, Schlesinger Library, Radcliffe College.

94. New York City voters ratified the measure by a three to one margin, while upstaters accepted it by a bare majority, but Helen Alfred expressed particular satisfaction with the upstate returns. *New York Red Book, 1939* (Albany, 1939), p. 443; Alfred to Edith Elmer Wood, [November, 1938] "NPHC, II, Wood Papers; N.Y. Const., art. 18 (1938).

95. Irving W. Halpern et al., *The Slum and Crime: A Statistical Study of the Distribution of Adult and Juvenile Delinquents in the Boroughs of Manhattan and Brooklyn* (New York, 1934), p. 21. For a summary of contemporary findings regarding the social costs of poor housing, see Ford, *Slums and Housing,* I: 350-437.

96. Carl Randau, "New York's Greatest Luxury—Its Slums," *New York World-Telegram,* April 28, 1936.

97. *New York Times,* June 28, 1938. For a critique of the assumptions about the causal relation between slums and other problems, see John P. Dean, "The Myths of Housing Reform," *American Sociological Review,* XIV (April 1949): 281-88.

98. Ira S. Robbins, Memorandum, October 1, 1934, "Housing Legislation," Reel 46, GP, HHLP.

99. Post, *Housing . . . or Else* (New York, 1936), p. 22.

100. HHL Message to the Legislature, January 5, 1938, *Public Papers, 1938,* pp. 34-35.

101. *New York Times,* January 29, 1938. (Italics added.) See also Judith Stein, "The Birth of Liberal Republicanism in New York State, 1932-1938" (unpublished Ph.D. dissertation, Yale University, 1968), pp. 187-89.

102. "Minutes of Meeting of Housing Section," December 7, 1933, "Housing Section, Welfare Council," Wood Papers; Maurice Leven et al., *America's Capacity to Consume* (Washington, 1934), p. 55.

103. *New York World-Telegram,* April 28, 1936.

104. Post, *Housing . . . or Else,* p. 15. (Italics added.)

105. For a rare critique of the effective exclusion of many slum dwellers from public housing, see Albert Mayer, "New Homes for a New Deal, " *New Republic,* February, 14, 1934, p. 8.

106. HHL Message to the Legislature, January 4, 1939, *Public Papers, 1939,* pp. 27-28; HHL to Sidney Maslen, April 16, 1939, chap. 808 (1939), Bill Jackets.

107. *New York Times,* January 1, 1939.

108. New York *Herald Tribune,* January 11, 1939; *New York Times,* December 27, 1938, January 18, 1939.

109. *New York Times,* January 14, 1939.

110. Helen Alfred to Edith Elmer Wood, [November, 1938], "NPHC, II," Wood Papers; Paul Windels to Fiorello La Guardia, January 9, 1939, "Mayor's Committee on Housing," Box 685, La Guardia Papers; La Guardia to Newbold Morris, November 14, 1938, "NYCHA," Box 2565, ibid.; Minutes of Mayor's Committee on Housing Legislation, November 29, December 7, 13, 20, 1938, Dorothy Rosenman Papers, Columbia University; *New York Times,* January 10, 15, 1939.

111. Albany *Knickerbocker News,* January 11, 1939.

112. Helen Alfred to Edith Elmer Wood, January 13, 1939, "NPHC, II," Wood Papers; Alfred Rheinstein to Fiorello La Guardia, January 18, 1939, "NYCHA," Box 2565, La Guardia Papers; *New York Times,* January 11, 14, 1939.

113. La Guardia to Alfred Rheinstein, January 20, 1939, "NYCHA," Box 2565, La Guardia Papers.

114. Albany *Knickerbocker News,* February 18, 1939; New York *Herald Tribune,* January 18, 28, 1939; *New York Times,* January 18, 26, 28, February 8, 18, 1939; *Report of the State Board of Housing* (1939), pp. 21-23.

115. Albany *Knickerbocker News* and *New York Times,* March 8, 1939; Alex Rose to Affiliated Organizations of the American Labor Party, March 16, 1939, "ALP, 1939," Sidney Hillman Papers, Amalgamated Clothing Workers of America Library.

116. "Slum Clearance and Low Cost Housing," *Real Property,* XVIII (March 1939): 2.

117. *New York Times,* April 30, May 10, 1939.

118. Louis Pink to HHL, May 10, 1939, "Housing Board, 1939-40," Reel 45, GP, HHLP; Alfred Rheinstein to HHL, May 15, 1939, "Housing Legislation," Reel 46, ibid.; Robert P. Lane to HHL, May 10, 1939, Helen Alfred to Abbot Low Moffat, May 11, 1939, Harold S. Buttenheim to Thomas C. Desmond, May 11, 1939, Charles Abrams to HHL, Mary 15, 1939, Fiorello La Guardia to HHL, May 15, 1939, chap. 808 (1939), Bill Jackets; *New York Times,* May 12, 1939.

119. Dorothy Rosenman to Abbot Low Moffat, May 13, 1939, "Housing Legislation," Reel 46, GP, HHLP.

120. Albany *Knickerbocker News,* May 15, 1939.

121. HHL to Joseph R. Hanley et al., May 14, 1939, "Housing Legislation," Reel 46, GP, HHLP; *New York Times,* May 15, 16, 1939.

122. HHL to Alfred Rheinstein, May 17, 1939, "Housing Legislation," Reel 46, GP, HHLP.

123. *New York Times,* May 21, 22, 1939; Louis Pink to HHL, May 15, 1939, "Housing Legislation," Reel 46, GP, HHLP; Ira S. Robbins to HHL, May 24, 1939, George H. Hallett to HHL, May 29, 1939, Paul Kellogg to HHL, June 2, 1939, chap. 808 (1939), Bill Jackets; *Laws of New York, 1939,* chaps. 808, 946, and 953.

124. Alfred to HHL, May 16, 1939, "Housing Legislation," Reel 46, GP, HHLP. See also Alfred to Edith Elmer Wood, June 12, 1939, "NPHC, II," Wood Papers.

125. "New York State to Finance Low-Rent Housing," *NAHO News,* June 23, 1939, pp. 41-43.

126. *Report of the State Board of Housing* (1939), p. 13.

127. Diamond, "The New York City Housing Authority," pp. 12, 20-21.

128. New York State, *Report of the State Commissioner of Housing,* Leg. Doc. No. 29 (1942), pp.

23-26; *Report of the State Commissioner of Housing,* Leg. Doc. No. 25 (1943), pp. 11-13, NYCHA, *Twenty-five Years of Public Housing,* pp. 2-3.

129. Abrams, *The Future of Housing,* p. 209.
130. New York's continued leadership in public housing is reflected in the fact that by 1968 the New York City Housing Authority had about 500,000 tenants, almost one-quarter of the total number of people living in government projects in the United States. Lawrence M. Friedman, "Government and Slum Housing," in *Housing,* ed. by Robinson O. Everett and John D. Johnston (Dobbs Ferry, N.Y., 1968), pp. 175-76.

IX

BATTLING THE UTILITIES

Consumers rarely received much attention in Albany unless blatantly scandalous business practices forced government to act. Privately owned utilities had long invited close scrutiny because the powerful monopolies often took a public-be-damned attitude in spite of the fact that most citizens depended on them for vital services. In New York the battle for reasonable utility rates dated from the Progressive Era when Governor Charles Evans Hughes won passage of a law creating a Public Service Commission (PSC) to regulate all utilities.[1] Although considered a model in 1907, the PSC showed signs of weakness by the 1930s. Under the impact of the Depression, New York strengthened the agency in an attempt to reduce rates which did not decline with other prices. But the widely heralded legislative victory proved in many ways a hollow one. As in the case of housing, government regulation of utilities was a cumbersome and inefficient process. This increased the demand for electricity produced by the government, but opponents prevented state development of New York's water power resources during this period.

1

Government regulation of private business requires at least three essentials to have any hope of success. In addition to adequate power, a watchdog public commission needs an able and conscientious staff and sufficient funds to make enforcement possible.[2] By 1930, New York's Public Service Commission lacked all three preconditions for effective regulation.

Since its creation in 1907, the PSC had stood still while the utility industry underwent radical changes. Most important, control over electric and gas production had passed into the hands of a few men who headed giant holding companies that had bought up local power plants. Groups of holding companies had also merged into larger combinations. In New York this process of pyramiding resulted in creation of the Niagara-Hudson Power

210

Corporation in 1929. Financed by the investment bankers J. P. Morgan and Floyd L. Carlisle, Niagara-Hudson took over three smaller holding companies that owned most of the state's individual generating plants located outside New York City. Another holding company, the Consolidated Gas Company of New York City, owned nearly all the gas and electric utilities in the metropolitan area, and its output almost equaled that of its upstate relative. Although independent corporations, Consolidated Gas and Niagara-Hudson were both dominated by the Morgan-Carlisle interests. Carlisle sat as chairman of the board of directors for each firm, and the transmission lines of both systems connected at a point north of New York City.[3] This colossus lay largely outside the jurisdiction of the Public Service Commission. Despite the fact that the holding companies were incorporated under New York statutes, the PSC had the authority to supervise operating utilities but not their parent organizations. The latter did everything possible to prevent the state from closing this gap.[4]

In order to deter effective regulation anywhere in the country, the public utilities mounted a national campaign aimed at winning popular approval of their activities. Working primarily through newspapers and schools, the companies sustained a steady barrage of propaganda. The manipulation of the press encompassed everything from the purchase of newspapers to the distribution of pro-utility editorials. Power companies also advertised heavily because, as one midwestern executive emphasized, "when you talk advertising to most newspapermen they warm to you." [5] In an unusual assault on schools, privately owned utilities contributed to colleges, paid professors and teachers, formulated utility courses, published books, and induced corrections in "unfair" texts. Material circulated in classrooms presented the utility point of view as established fact. "Public utilities are properly and thoroughly regulated," asserted one pamphlet given to school children.[6] The purpose of all this, as the secretary of the National Educational Association understood it, was "to prepare the next generation of voters to appreciate and stand for private ownership of utilities." [7] Toward the same end, the companies sought opportunities for trained speakers to explain utilities at virtually any public meeting. In a five-month period during the 1920s, 613 addresses were given throughout New York State and resulted in 360 columns of free newspaper coverage. Although these widespread efforts entailed the expenditure of millions of dollars, utility magnates cared little, since the cost could be passed on to consumers through higher rates. "Don't be afraid of expense," a director of the National Electric Light Association (NELA) told fellow publicity agents, "the public pays the expense." [8] At the centers of political power, like Albany, the companies maintained flocks of lobbyists to promote their interests, but not until 1934 did the Federal Trade Commission (FTC) disclose that these tactics included actual payments to New York legislators. When asked if his organization had neglected any means of influencing public opinion, an official of NELA replied: "Only one and that is sky writing." [9] Assessing the extent of propaganda carried on by private utilities, the FTC concluded that "no campaign approaching it in magnitude has ever been conducted except possibly by governments in war time." [10]

As the only check on the activities of local power companies, New York's Public Service Commission proved "entirely too docile." [11] Under the leadership of a chairman sympathetic to the utilities, the five commissioners failed even to exercise the body's limited authority during the 1920s. Rarely initiating any investigations of rates or service, they conceived of their role as that of a judge to settle disputes between giant companies and individual customers. When complaints arose, the cards were stacked on the side of the utilities, since they had the money and staff to overwhelm the PSC with evidence supporting their position. Disregarding its potential as a defender of consumer interests, the passive commission chose not to use its engineers, accountants, and lawyers to compile data on the utilities and cross-examine witnesses in hearings.[12]

Governor Roosevelt helped reverse the policy of the PSC. After forcing the retirement of the group's chairman, he appointed in his place Milo R. Maltbie, one of the original commissioners during the Progressive Era, who had usually stood against the utilities. With a Ph.D. in economics from Columbia, the aging Maltbie had written several books on public utilities and won a reputation as an expert in the field. Most important, he declared upon taking office in 1930 that the PSC should take the initiative in protecting the general public. Under the prodding of Governor Roosevelt, Albany lawmakers authorized an investigation of the Public Service Commission, but the inquiry's majority, selected by the Republican legislature, suggested only minor changes in the powers of the PSC. Although the legislature adopted these, it turned down the far-reaching revisions proposed by the Roosevelt appointees to the study panel.[13] The G.O.P. reflected the sentiment of the president of New York Edison who declared in 1930: "State regulation of utilities has not broken down or failed. On the contrary, it has proved, in my judgment, to be one of the best examples in our government structure of how capably a public agency . . . can deal with important, complicated and frequently highly technical matters." [14]

The determination of rates presented the most difficult problem for public utility commissions around the country. All interested parties agreed that rates must allow for a fair return upon the value of property used in the public service. But this standard raised more questions than it answered. What property is actually "used"? What is the "value"? What constitutes a "fair return"? Competing theories of establishing value caused the most debate. The private companies preferred to equate the value of a utility with the hypothetical, present-day cost of replacing an existing plant. This so-called doctrine of reproduction cost, long accepted by the PSC and endorsed by the Supreme Court, took into account price fluctuations, but during a period of rising prices it often inflated the worth of a utility. Critics complained: "Like stock watering, it tends to conceal from the public the high rate of profits and enables the companies to charge as high rates as their business judgment dictates." [15] Furthermore, the state had to spend enormous amounts of time and money to determine constantly changing reproduction costs. Since ordinary citizens, in their dual role as consumers and taxpayers, ultimately paid the bill for property valuations, a Republican commissioner privately called this a "futile method." [16]

The prudent investment doctrine offered an alternative means of deciding rates. As set forth by Supreme Court Justice Louis D. Brandeis in a 1923 dissenting opinion, this standard proposed the cost of capital prudently invested as the fairest return due a utility.[17] Since this value stayed relatively stable and could be determined from company records, its use could have expedited the settlement of rate disputes without violating the rights on stockholders. However, the state still had to compute accrued depreciation, a figure open to question. Moreover, courts had not accepted the prudent investment rule as a valid rate base.[18]

Faced with complex questions of valuation, the PSC often resorted to private negotiations rather than formal proceedings. Under the leadership of Milo Maltbie, the PSC bargained with utility executives to win rate reductions during the early 1930s. Both sides found this system advantageous. While the PSC saved time and money, thereby permitting it to cover more ground, the companies avoided the possibility of even greater cuts if the state instituted a legal case. In defense of this policy, commissioners pointed out that negotiated rate adjustments brought immediate decreases in gas and electric charges amounting to $10 million in 1931.[19] Nevertheless, attempts at informal regulation proved the failure of the existing system, which required lengthy and costly studies of value.[20]

2

The Depression sparked widespread dissatisfaction with privately owned utilities. While government investigations exposed the evils of "the power trust," consumers found that gas and electric rates did not drop with other prices. New York's Public Service Commission received more complaints of excessive rates in 1932 than in any other year since its formation.[21]

Aware of the rising discontent, Herbert Lehman talked about utilities frequently during his 1932 campaign. Calling for both stricter regulation and public power, he promised that "people of this state shall have available to them . . . the lowest possible reasonable rates for electricity, gas, and telephone." Although he added that utility stockholders were entitled to a fair return, he thought this standard should apply only to the actual investment of "legitimate investors." Speculators with inflated securities could apparently expect little sympathy from the former Wall Street banker. According to Lehman, the principal obstacle in the way of cheaper electric rates was the utility monopoly which dominated the state and was "interested primarily in profits and not in lower rates." This trust "controlled the policy of the Republican party," thereby thwarting attempts by Democrats to strengthen the Public Service Commission. When the PSC tried to cut rates, "the companies with their great resources have been able to block such efforts by retaining lawyers, expending huge sums on elaborate valuations, and in other ways using the consumers' money to defeat the consumers' interest." Lehman demanded increased authority for the commission so that it could become "an effective agent of the people, taking the initiative in assuring consumers abundant service at the lowest possible rates." [22]

In his first message to Albany lawmakers, the new governor recommended several measures to improve the PSC. Suggested by Milo Maltbie, they were but a portion of what gradually became Lehman's public utility program. Most of the proposals did not reach the legislature in the form of bills until more than two months later. During this period, the commission submitted more ideas to the governor and drafted the necessary legislation in cooperation with Charles Poletti.[23]

As the PSC carefully explained, it confronted a variety of obstacles in trying to protect the public. Above all, the agency was frustrated in its attempts to supervise transactions between holding companies and local utilities. The Associated Gas and Electric Company, for example, "had used the holding company idea to siphon funds from the operating utilities." Despite persistent efforts, the PSC could not halt this practice because it lacked sufficient authority. Therefore, the commissioners called for a ban on "upstream" loans from any subsidiary to a parent company and a similar prohibition against "lateral" loans from one operating firm to another. The PSC also advocated several minor reforms. To stimulate rate reductions through competition, villages operating their own power plants should be permitted to extend their services to adjacent areas. Furthermore, the state should require gas and electric companies to return to customers the interest accrued from their deposits every two years, and the corporations should turn over to the state all unclaimed deposits. In addition, Maltbie asked the governor to reintroduce a 1932 bill placing gas transmission lines within the jurisdiction of the PSC.[24]

Effective regulation necessitated not only expanded powers but also adequate funds. The problem of securing money became especially acute during the Depression, because the PSC faced a mounting number of complaints at a time when the state had difficulty maintaining even previous budget levels. As an escape from this dilemma, the commission proposed assessing public utilities at least a portion of the costs connected with special investigations, particularly for property valuations. Since other New York regulatory bodies, notably those for banking and insurance, had already instituted a system of charging part of their expenses to the businesses affected, this plan did not represent a radical departure. Yet Maltbie suggested it with reluctance, because it might jeopardize the commission's independence. To guard against this possibility, he stressed that utilities should not pay state employees directly. Instead, Albany should establish a revolving fund which the companies could replenish and from which the agency could draw money to enlarge its operations. Although consumers would undoubtedly bear the burden of any assessments, Maltbie thought this fair, since they also benefited from more efficient regulation.[25]

By the beginning of March, the Public Service Commission had prepared a number of bills implementing its ideas, but few had actually gone into the legislative hopper. In part, this delay was caused by Lehman's preoccupation with more pressing problems of unemployment relief and the budget. Also, the failure to move faster against the public utilities reflected an underlying pessimism about the chances of pushing through legislation which curbed the monopolies. Both Lehman and Maltbie doubted whether their bills could pass, but they hoped to begin the educational process by introducing them. If the goal for the 1933 session was merely to offer a set of reforms, then the loss of time mattered little.[26]

After several months of work behind the scenes, the governor presented his utility program on March 21. In a special message to the legislature, he declared that "rates have been retained at levels distinctly too high for these days." Relief for the oppressed consumer lay in strengthening the PSC "in accordance with the expressed desire of the people and in their primary interest." Toward this end, Lehman recommended eliminating certain holding company abuses such as inflated service charges; prohibiting upstream loans and other drains on operating companies; permitting any city to appear in utility proceedings before the PSC or courts; authorizing the extension of municipal electric lines to adjacent territory; and requiring companies to return the collected interest on customers' deposits and to give unclaimed deposits to the state. The governor thus endorsed fully the reforms sought by the PSC.[27] A week later, Lehman appealed for legislation permitting cities to own and operate power plants. The threat of government competition, he argued, would discourage private utilities from charging exorbitant rates.[28]

By the time Lehman announced his utility program, the 1933 legislature had begun its drive toward adjournment. During the last few weeks of the session, lawmakers spent their time debating the repeal of Prohibition and reforms in local government.[29] Most of the utility bills never emerged from committee. Although the governor had anticipated resistance in the Republican Assembly, he suffered unexpected defeats in the Senate where Democrats held a single-vote majority. In the final hours of the session, Senate Democrats ignored Lehman's pleas for legislation allowing municipal ownership and the assessment of utilities. When brought to a vote, the two bills were rejected overwhelmingly because of the opposition of more than ten Democrats, most of them members of Tammany or its allies in Brooklyn. Only two minor measures passed both houses; one outlawed upstream loans and the other gave cities the right to appear as parties in utility proceedings.[30]

After his utility program bogged down in the legislature, Lehman sought relief for consumers through the PSC. In May, the governor called Maltbie's attention to the "widespread dissatisfaction among the people of the state concerning the existing gas and electric rates." Since utilities showed little inclination to cut charges voluntarily, Lehman wanted the PSC to take action. As a first step, he asked Maltbie to proceed "as rapidly as possible to investigate utility rates now in effect in New York City using the utmost legal power of the State." Recognizing that the commission suffered from limited funds, the governor promised to seek more money if the agency ran short.[31] When the PSC agreed to his plan, Lehman announced on May 24 that public hearings would begin immediately in New York and soon thereafter in the rest of the state.[32]

On the first day of the inquiry, Milo Maltbie revealed his sympathy for consumers. Taking note of the "belief that the utilities have not borne their fair burden of the depression," he proposed to set temporary rates for electricity "in this extreme emergency." Maltbie did not indicate on what basis the PSC would determine these rates, but he stressed the need for cooperation from utilities: "[I]f they offer a policy of resistance to such reasonable reductions as the Commission may direct and resort to litigation, the efforts of the Commission for temporary relief will be fruitless." [33] Floyd Carlisle responded with a pledge of "cooperation based upon reason." [34] However, the question remained whether the two men could agree on what constituted fair rates.

Local officials quickly endorsed the idea of temporary price changes. The president of the State Conference of Mayors urged "aggressive cooperation . . . in a State-wide movement for emergency reductions of utility rates." [35] At its annual convention in early June, the group adopted a resolution calling for immediate decreases, and it backed legislation permitting municipalities to produce and distribute their own electricity.[36] Soon thereafter, Albany's mayor warned the utilities that "the cities of the state are well organized, thoroughly united and determined to get redress." [37]

Unmoved by these appeals, the power companies resorted to familiar obstructionist tactics. Consolidated Gas, the object of the New York City investigation, used a variety of maneuvers to thwart PSC decrees after the commission spent three months collecting and sifting testimony. When the PSC ordered a one-year cut of $9 million in the electric rates of six utilities owned by Consolidated Gas, the holding company applied for a reconsideration on grounds that the NRA utility code would increase operating expenses. The commission held another two months of hearings on the effects of the planned code, and it narrowly decided by a three to two vote to sustain its decision under pressure from Maltbie and Lehman.[38] Consolidated Gas then began the lengthy process of appeal through the state courts which postponed indefinitely implementation of the rate decreases.[39] Thus the commission's six-month campaign to aid consumers ended with no prospect of savings in sight.

Although the Public Service Commission generally failed to achieve its goal of lower rates in 1933, its highly publicized hearings confirmed suspicions about the power trust. A vice president of New York Edison revealed that the salaries of company executives had increased in the previous year while the wages of all other Edison employees had declined. Between 1929 and 1933, dividends paid to Consolidated Gas stockholders had either remained constant or in some cases risen, and the wholesale rates for gas and electricity had gone up although other prices had dropped sharply. Testimony before the PSC also suggested how public utilities maintained their privileged position. Among the officials of New York Edison was an assistant to the chairman of the board who earned $15,000 annually but whose identity was mysteriously listed as "H.E." in company records. When questioned by the press, H. Edmund Machold, a former Republican state chairman and onetime speaker of the Assembly, admitted he worked for the firm. He said nothing about the nature of his job, but the attempt to hide his connection with New York Edison could scarcely allay the notion that such men wielded improper influence in Albany.[40]

While the PSC had pursued its investigation of public utilities, Lehman had reconvened the legislature in July. The special session was to deal with unemployment relief, but the governor also took the opportunity to request enactment of four utility measures. First, he asked again that the PSC be authorized to charge utilities for valuations. Second, he suggested the creation of a revolving fund of $300,000, which the utilities would replenish, to permit the commission to expand its activities at once. Third, in apparent anticipation of a legal challenge from companies, the governor called for extension of the PSC's power to set temporary rates. Finally, he renewed his bid for legislation forcing gas and electric corporations to pay immediately the accrued interest on deposits which amounted to an estimated $1 million.[41]

A small group of Democrats again blocked action on most of these bills. When the Senate Public Service Committee, dominated by Tammany Democrats, first voted on the legislation, a single Democrat backed the governor. Lehman fired off another special message defending his proposals as necessary to safeguard the interests of consumers. In response both houses passed the bill providing for the return of interest payments, but the Senate committee killed the other three measures, as did its counterpart in the Assembly.[42] A Republican member of the PSC had no doubts about the source of opposition in both parties. "Although it will be a very difficult thing to prove," Maurice Burritt declared confidentially, "I think most people who know anything about it believe that the legislation was defeated by the public utilities themselves." [43]

Support for this theory soon came from the G.O.P. state chairman. Elected head of the party in 1930, W. Kingsland Macy had seemed unlikely to challenge the status quo. A descendant of Nantucket whalers who had arrived from England in 1635, Macy had attended Groton and Harvard. He had held a seat on the New York Stock Exchange, but he preferred the life of a politically active country gentleman, working from his power base in Suffolk County, Long Island. Despite his social standing, Macy's independent and critical spirit turned him into a reformer.[44] In the wake of La Guardia's 1933 election victory, Macy attempted to rejuvenate the moribund Republican party on the state level. He focused on the G.O.P. Assembly which, he argued, was a tool of public utility interests. In a remarkable speech to Republican county chairmen during December 1933, Macy described the way utilities exercised their power:

> Let us tear the mask aside. This is a fight between the public utilities and an uncontrolled Republican party.
> The Republican party cannot afford to be dominated by H. Edmund Machold. . . . The trouble is not that Mr. Machold believes in the private ownership of public utilities, but that he apparently believes in the private ownership of the State government.

Macy asserted that Machold headed an "invisible government" in Albany which operated through the office of the Assembly clerk, Fred Hammond, who had held that post for twenty-one years. The state chairman also tied Democrats to "the power ring":

> [T]he secret control in the Assembly . . . has worked, and still is working, with Tammany Hall. . . . Tammany has always been ready to order its legislators to give its votes to protect the power interests, if in return the power interests will swing their influence to protect Tammany from investigation.

Backing up Macy, another G.O.P. leader called for "a party of sane and effective liberalism; a party which will appeal to the younger as well as the older elements in the population; a party which will not permit itself to be jockeyed into the position of being regarded as the supporter of any special interest." [45]

While the Macy forces sought change, the Republican Old Guard tried to stand pat. In response to Macy's accusations, the party's legislative caucus appointed a committee of lawmakers to examine the charges. However, Macy refused to cooperate with any inquiry unless it had the power of subpoena and an independent counsel. Proceeding without the state chairman, the panel held a day of public hearings at which Machold and Hammond denied any wrongdoing. When the 1934 legislature convened the following week, the committee reported to the full party caucus that "none of the charges against the Assembly and its officers has been sustained." [46]

Nevertheless, progressive Republicans continued their fight to oust Hammond as Assembly clerk. Defeated in the party caucus, some twenty G.O.P. legislators prevented the Assembly from organizing, because no candidate for clerk could secure the necessary majority. Speaker Joseph A. McGinnies, a Hammond supporter, ruled that until the lower house elected a clerk, it could not conduct any other business, but Hammond was opposed by all except one of the Republican assemblymen from New York City, four of five from Buffalo and two from Suffolk Country, plus four others. Finally, after twenty-two ballots and a ten-day delay, the stalemate was broken through a face-saving device which permitted Speaker McGinnies to designate a clerk. His reappointment of Hammond solved the immediate problem of organizing the Assembly, but the Republican party would never be the same after the challenge of urban progressives.[47]

The G.O.P. power struggle set the stage for Lehman's reintroduction of his public utility proposals. On January 22, 1934, the governor forwarded a package of eleven utility bills to the legislature. With a single exception, the suggestions were similar to the ones rejected in 1933. The three most important measures permitted municipal ownership of gas and electric services, empowered the PSC to establish temporary rates, and authorized the commission to assess utilities.[48] Kingsland Macy immediately endorsed Lehman's program in telegrams sent to every Republican member of the legislature. "Strongly urge prompt consideration and passage of legislation carrying into effect Governor's utility program," he wrote.[49] Although the majority of his party had refused to follow his lead in the Hammond fight, Macy was potentially a strong ally, since his bloc of progressive assemblymen held the balance of power between Democrats and Old Guard Republicans.

In the face of mounting public pressure for curbs on utilities, conservative Republicans fixed on a new strategy. Rather than simply oppose the governor's recommendations, the Old Guard countered with several bills of its own designed to weaken two of Lehman's proposals. Disturbed by the possibility of competition between public and private utilities, Republicans offered a municipal ownership plan under which a community would have to buy existing private companies before it could build and operate a power plant that would furnish the same service. The G.O.P. also proposed to charge all utilities of the same type, not just the ones investigated, for the cost of rate valuations.[50]

Utility executives chose the municipal ownership bill as the focus of their attacks on Lehman's entire program. Led by Floyd Carlisle, utility men voiced their objections in public hearings at Albany. Government competition, according to Carlisle, would bring the "complete and utter eventual ruin" of private companies, because public enterprises would possess the unfair advantage of freedom from taxation. Therefore, any statute permitting municipal plants should require the purchase of competing private utilities. The president of the New York State Bankers' Association agreed: "Public and tax exempt competition would seriously impair and ultimately destroy the earning power and hence the value of the properties and the securities of privately owned companies." [51]

Using these arguments, company officials enlisted an army of small investors in the battle to defeat the governor's utility bills.[52] Through a massive letter-writing campaign, corporate executives warned of the danger to investments in utilities. The president of Consolidated Gas told stockholders that under municipal ownership they "should have the right to be reimbursed for what would be destroyed." Furthermore, he predicted that enactment of the temporary rate bill "would require the reduction and possible passing of the dividend on the common stock of this Company." He suggested that interested people write their representatives or appear personally at Albany hearings.[53] "Ask that the Municipal Bill be amended and that the Temporary 5% Return Bill be defeated so your investment will not be endangered," the president of a Niagara-Hudson subsidiary wrote stockholders.[54] Frightened by such pronouncements, investors throughout the state flooded the governor with letters and joined newly formed pressure groups such as the New York State Federation of Public Utility Investors.[55]

Reformers tried to defuse the explosive issue of municipal ownership. At the legislative hearing, Milo Maltbie ridiculed the assertion that any of the governor's bills would jeopardize the investments of "widows and orphans." [56] More to the point, Dr. James C. Bonbright, professor of finance at Columbia's School of Business, argued that the municipal ownership measure represented a threat only "to the securities of badly mismanaged companies or of companies that are so overcapitalized that they are compelled to charge exorbitant rates in order to support this bloated capitalization. . . . A progressive company that treats its customers fairly has nothing to fear from municipal ownership. A company that refuses to make reasonable rates *ought* to have something to fear." Looking at Lehman's entire utility program, Bonbright emphasized "how extremely conservative are these proposed measures when compared with the only alternative that presents itself if our general system of regulation cannot be made to work—outright government ownership on a wholesale basis." [57] Lehman himself doubted that many communities would take advantage of municipal ownership. "But where a utility corporation fails to give even reasonably fair rates and decent service, cities and other municipalities should have this weapon of defense." [58]

After lawmakers sat on his utility program for over two months, Lehman appealed over their heads to the people of New York. Speaking over the radio on March 26, he reviewed the rise of holding companies and explained that the PSC needed greater powers to protect consumers. In an attack on propaganda circulated by utilities, the governor deplored the use of absolutely unjustified statements "to frighten the small and frequently uninformed investor." He pointed to his years of experience in the financial world and assured stockholders that his recommendations would not harm "any investment prudently made." After carefully explaining each bill, Lehman called for "an expression of popular demand from the consumers of this State, . . . so powerful as to overwhelm any opposition that may be mustered by public utility companies." [59] The governor's reasoned but frank address had the desired effect. Phone calls, telegrams, and letters of support, including an unprecedented number from housewives, poured into Albany, and the Democratic chairman of the Senate Public Service Committee announced that the legislation would receive a favorable report the following week.[60]

Several days later a lucky break insured passage of the utility bills. On March 29, the Federal Trade Commission released correspondence between the Associated Gas and Electric Company and New York State Senator Warren T. Thayer, a Republican member of the Public Service Committee. Dating from 1927-28, when Thayer chaired the committee, the letters included one in which the senator reported on his activities in Albany.

> In keeping with your instructions of March 22, regarding my expense account . . . I herewith hand you bill as suggested.
>
> The legislature adjourned last Friday. . . . If at any time I can be of further service to you, please do not hesitate to call upon me. I hope my work during the last session was satisfactory to your company; not so much for the new legislation enacted, but from the fact that many detrimental bills which were introduced we were able to kill in my committee.[61]

This disclosure supplied proof for Macy's accusations about the influence of utilities in Albany. A Republican newspaper in Buffalo concluded that Thayer was only the tip of the iceberg, since that city also had "legislators whose direction of service has been toward the utilities and away from the public interest." [62]

When news of the Thayer letters reached Albany, the legislature had recessed for the weekend, but Lehman went on the offensive. "I cannot conceive," the governor exclaimed, "how the Legislature would, in view of . . . developments in the last two days, refuse to report my bills out and vote on them." [63] He demanded "a complete and impartial and thoroughgoing legislative investigation of the relations, past and present, between public utilities and any one in the service of the State Government." He added, however, that such an inquiry should not further postpone enactment of his utility program.[64]

The following Monday, an overflow crowd gathered in the Senate gallery to hear Thayer respond to the FTC revelations. When he took the floor, the senator emotionally denied "anything improper or unethical in connection with . . . the alleged letters," and he asked that the Judiciary Committee examine the entire matter.[65] The Senate quickly approved Thayer's request, and both houses also adopted concurrent resolutions providing for a broad investigation of the state's utilities. The two inquiries commenced after the annual session of the legislature adjourned.[66]

In the wake of the Thayer scandal, Senate Democrats took quick action on the governor's utility bills. Even before the upper house had met to hear Thayer's defense, members of the Public Service Committee hurriedly discharged the legislation they had ignored for over two months. During the next week, Senate Democrats, voting as a bloc, turned back G.O.P. attempts to amend the municipal ownership and temporary rate plans. Then senators of both parties overwhelmingly approved seven of the measures that utility executives had not openly condemned. Of the three remaining proposals, only the one authorizing temporary rate decreases cleared the upper house, because it had solid support from Democrats. By breaking ranks, a handful of Democrats from both New York and upstate cities caused the defeat of the municipal ownership and assessment bills.[67]

Unwilling to accept anything short of a complete victory, Lehman declared that "the fight has only just commenced." [68] Two days after the partial setback in the Senate, he threw down the gauntlet at a Jefferson Day dinner in New York City which brought together Democrats from the state and nation. In an unusual plea for party regularity, Lehman charged that although Senate Republicans had voted against the municipal ownership and assessment bills, this "does not excuse destructive action on the part of Democrats contrary to our party pledges." After citing Democratic platforms going as far back as 1918, he lectured his listeners about party responsibility. "I have the right to demand that the legislators of my own party support me in carrying out a pledge made by our party, and one to which all of them subscribed by their very candidacy on the Democratic ticket." [69] The national Democratic chairman, James Farley, put his weight behind Lehman. While in New York for the Jefferson Day dinner, Farley told local leaders that enactment of the governor's utility program intact was essential for Democratic victory in the upcoming election. Yielding to the pressure, seven insurgents reversed themselves when the upper house next met. However, two Democrats refused to give in, and the votes of three Republicans provided the margin of victory for the municipal ownership and assessment bills.[70]

Upon completion of the Senate fight, attention turned to the Republican Assembly where the aid of Kingsland Macy proved invaluable. In his first trip to Albany since the abortive attempt to reorganize the lower house, the Republican state chairman received assurances from his long-time foe, Speaker McGinnies, that the utility bills would not die in committee. When the Public Service Committee then took the rare step of reporting most of the measures but without the favorable recommendation that usually accompanied legislation, Macy worked fast to prevent a stalemate over obstructionist amendments. He met with G.O.P. assemblymen from the metropolitan area and persuaded them to accept all the proposals in their original form. Defying their majority leader in the Assembly, this bloc of almost twenty progressive Republicans united with a solid phalanx of Democrats to defeat numerous amendments to the municipal ownership and assessment bills. With the Old Guard routed, the lower house overwhelmingly approved all the governor's utility measures with the exception of a minor one that was delayed in the Senate and later died in the Assembly.[71] "To the surprise of everyone," Milo Maltbie exclaimed, we "have obtained the Governor's utility program without any material change." [72]

3

The sense of triumph faded quickly. After the legislature had acted, the utilities successfully delayed application of the most important new statutes. When the Public Service Commission ordered three companies to lower their rates in 1934, the firms won a stay in court pending a test of the temporary rate law's constitutionality. Fourteen of sixteen utilities also fought attempts by the PSC to assess the cost of investigations. Furthermore, litigation blocked commission efforts to make companies keep up-to-date property inventories so the state could readily determine whether profits were excessive. Since the PSC expected state courts to sustain all these orders, it concluded that utilities sought only to postpone the day of reckoning.[73] "At present," the regulatory body admitted, "there is every inducement for the companies to delay and procrastinate. . . . The companies stand to lose nothing by delay and may gain considerable sums." [74]

As anticipated, New York's highest tribunal ultimately ruled against the utilities. In separate decisions, the Court of Appeals upheld the powers to set temporary rates, assess companies, and require property records.[75] Going to the heart of the issue, Chief Judge Frederick E. Crane declared in one case:

> The fixing of a reasonable rate by these public service corporations . . . to be of any value should be a matter of speedy regulation. The courts should not encourage such *finesse* in figuring as to make these hearings upon rate questions an obstruction instead of a relief.[76]

However, this judicial endorsement of quick action came in July 1936, more than two years after the legislature gave the PSC authority to intiate savings for consumers. Although the litigants had to refund the difference between their rates and those previously ordered by the state, their appeals to the courts had discouraged the PSC from instituting many other cases until the question of constitutionality was settled. In the wake of these 1936 rulings, the PSC finally found the utilities more inclined to accede to commission directives without first going to court.[77]

Despite setbacks during the 1930s, the Public Service Commission cut rates more than in any period since its formation. Although some decline would have been expected anyway at a time when other prices were falling, utilities showed repeatedly that little change would have occurred in their electric and gas rates without heavy pressure from the state.[78] After reaching a record high of $14 million in 1935, the total amount of annual rate reductions dropped off toward the end of the decade as a result of utilities' increased costs (see Table 7). New taxation, principally for unemployment relief, accounted for much of the rise in expenses of power companies.[79] A 1944 study pointed

Table 7
Reductions in Utility Rates in New York State, 1939–42[a]
(amounts in dollars)

Year	Negotiated without Formal Case	Negotiated during Formal Case	Ordered as a Result of Formal Case	Voluntary	Total
1931	382,000	9,516,000	39,000	118,000	10,055,000
1932	1,371,000	346,000	37,000	461,000	2,215,000
1933	1,571,000	1,917,000	1,829,000	610,000	5,918,000
1934	849,000	860,000	2,443,000	614,000	4,766,000
1935	26,000	10,723,000	703,000	4,414,000	14,460,000
1936	165,000	173,000	5,707,000	1,023,000	7,068,000
1937	601,000	7,308,000	1,310,000	1,647,000	10,866,000
1938	368,000	1,178,000	937,000	850,000	3,333,000
1939	458,000	2,103,000	1,262,000	873,000	4,696,000
1940	1,524,000	761,000	262,000	732,000	3,297,000
1941	206,000	1,796,000	5,000	171,000	2,178,000
1942	20,000	224,000	89,000	122,000	211,000

[a]Includes rates for gas, electricity, telephone, water and steam.

Source: *Annual Report of the PSC, 1942,* p. 37.

galley 134 part

On the balance, the 1930s proved the limitations of regulation as a means of assuring the lowest possible utility rates. With good cause, Commissioner Burritt declared in 1939 that "New York State never had more efficient utility regulation." [81] But such statements, although certainly true, overlooked the obstacles still in the way of protecting customers. Even a conscientious Public Service Commission had to undertake lengthy investigations of each company before it could order permanent rate reductions. Meanwhile, utilities called for increases that the state often could not deny, since it was bound by laws and legal precedents which affirmed the right of these privately owned businesses to make a profit. Throughout PSC inquiries into company finances, the powerful monopolies held the upper hand because they could ultimately pass on to consumers the cost of retaining an army of accountants and lawyers to defend their position. As a New Dealer pointed out in 1934: "[T]he electric industry with its far-flung battle line and illimitable resources watches us and as we move they take the necessary steps to neutralize whatever we do." [82]

4

Owing to the ineffectiveness of regulation, public power offered the best hope of cheaper electricity. "No matter what we may think of the policy of public ownership of utilities . . . , it may be the only weapon which the people have left to use against exploiting companies whose operations are subversive of the public welfare," declared Frank Walsh, head of New York's Power Authority, in 1934.[83] Although virtually no one advocated a state takeover of existing utilities, New York had an untapped source of energy in the St. Lawrence River, which ran along the state's northern boundary with Canada. Since it drained the entire Great Lakes area, the river had an enormous but steady flow that made it ideal for producing hydroelectric power. Estimates of its potential energy went into millions of horsepower.[84]

Both private businesses and Albany officials had long eyed this natural resource. During the Progressive Era, the Aluminum Company of America had sought state permission for the exclusive right to develop the water power of the St. Lawrence. At about the same time, Governor Hughes asserted that this "should not be surrendered to private interests but should be preserved and held for the benefit of the people." [85] Hughes, and subsequently Al Smith, blocked private exploitation of the St. Lawrence, but both failed to implement their plans for public power because of opposition from the utilities and G.O.P. lawmakers. The stalemate continued throughout the 1930s and 1940s despite steady growth of the movement for state production of electricity.[86]

In 1931, Governor Roosevelt won passage of a law creating the Power Authority of the State of New York. This agency, led by five trustees appointed by the governor, was charged with responsibility for developing and marketing the hydroelectric power of the St. Lawrence. However, the Authority had to await ratification of an American agreement with Canada before it could actually begin construction of power stations that would divert the international waterway. Unwilling to stand by idly, the agency's trustees, headed by the energetic and outspoken labor lawyer Frank Walsh, became the leading pressure group in the campaign to gain approval of a Canadian-American accord. The Authority also engaged experts to study production costs, and it opened negotiations with Niagara-Hudson on rates for the private transmission of public power.[87]

Development of the latent energy of the St. Lawrence was inextricably tied to its improvement as a waterway, since the river formed an essential link in the 2350-mile chain stretching from Duluth, Minnesota, to the Atlantic Ocean. By the 1930s, most of the Great Lakes-St. Lawrence seaway could accommodate oceangoing ships to a depth of twenty-seven feet except for a section of the St. Lawrence which was only fourteen feet deep. Therefore, when the United States and Canada successfully negotiated a treaty providing for power plants along the river, they also agreed to make the St. Lawrence navigable for vessels drawing up to twenty-seven feet. The power project was expected to create over two million horsepower in electrical energy which the countries would divide equally. America's share amounted to half the entire output of New York's private utilities in 1932.[88]

After it was signed on July 18, 1932, the St. Lawrence Treaty ran into trouble in the U.S. Senate. The agreement had only emerged from committee by the time of FDR's inauguration in March 1933, and the new president hesitated to force a vote because he doubted that he could muster the necessary two-thirds majority. Despite continued pressure from New York's Power Authority and midwestern proponents of the seaway, the treaty did not finally come up for a vote until 1934, after Roosevelt formally asked senators to ratify it. On March 14, 1934, the president suffered his first major defeat in Congress when the Senate rejected the St. Lawrence Treaty by a tally of forty-two to forty-six, twenty-one votes short of a two-thirds majority. Both parties split sharply on the issue, with Democrats divided thirty-one to twenty-two and Republicans fourteen to twenty, for and against the agreement.[89]

Sectional economic interests largely determined the outcome. Since farmers looking for cheaper transportation were leading proponents of the St. Lawrence seaway, senators from all the states near the Great Lakes, except Illinois, supported the plan. Chicago authorities worried about diversion of water from Lake Michigan. But the most significant resistance came from thirteen Atlantic seaboard states, backed by three from the Mississippi Valley, which feared that their ports would lose traffic if grain and other products could travel directly to and from the midwest without being transshipped through eastern and southern seaports. For this reason both New York's senators cast ballots against the treaty, even though Robert Wagner favored public development of St. Lawrence water power. During the 1933-34 debate over the accord, opponents focused on the seaway portion, rarely mentioning the hydroelectric project. Nevertheless, as advocates of the entire plan pointed out, the same financial interests, notably J. P. Morgan and Company, which stood behind the threatened eastern railroads also controlled the utilities menaced by public power. Yet bankers, undoubtedly wary of the sympathy they could generate for utility companies, apparently decided that the navigation feature excited the most widespread opposition, and they used this issue to prevent New Yorkers from gaining access to cheaper electricity.[90]

After the 1934 setback, Roosevelt tried unsuccessfully to revive the St. Lawrence plan. At first he attempted to renegotiate the treaty to make it more palatable, but intermittent talks with the Canadian officials dragged on and ultimately broke off in the late 1930s. Since it remained unlikely that two-thirds of the Senate would back a treaty in any case, American proponents pushed for an executive agreement, which required only a simple majority for congressional approval. Such an accord, resembling the original 1932 treaty draft, was signed in March 1941, but the outbreak of war delayed further action, owing to the shortage of manpower and material. Not until 1954 did New York finally get Washington's authorization to build power plants along the St. Lawrence.[91]

New Yorkers won few victories against privately owned utilities during the 1930s. A combination of Lehman's vigorous leadership and Senator Thayer's indiscretion brought a legislative breakthrough in 1934, but the power companies prevented application of the laws for several years. Even after the Court of Appeals upheld the Public Service Commission's new authority, the PSC still faced a number of obstacles in trying to lower electricity rates. Not the least of these barriers was a state fiscal policy that increased taxes on utilities which, in turn, could pass along to consumers any rise in costs.

Above all, advocates of cheaper electricity could not match the political power of private utility corporations. Lehman himself took an advanced position on every question involved in the regulation of utilities, but he could not even line up all members of his own party behind measures requested by the PSC. Furthermore, there was no well-organized pressure group outside the legislature to back up Lehman on this issue. Letters of protest from consumers scarcely compared with the influence exerted by utility monopolies, which maintained full-time lobbyists in Albany. State officials, notably Lehman and members of the PSC and the Power Authority, carried the burden of the fight for improved regulation and public power, and they were outgunned by utility interests in Albany and Washington. Although reformers won a few battles during the decade, the state's privately owned utilities triumphed in the war against effective regulation and public power.

NOTES

1. New York originally established two commissions—one for New York City and another for the rest of the state—but in 1921, the two were combined into one unit headed by five commissioners.
2. Martin G. Glaeser, *Public Utilities in American Capitalism* (New York, 1957), p. 249.
3. A third holding company, the Associated Gas and Electric Company, accounted for less than 10 percent of the state's electrical energy.
4. *Summary Report of the Federal Trade Commission to the Senate of the United States, Pursuant to Senate Resolution No. 83, 70th Congress, 1st Session, on Economic, Financial, and Corporate Phases of Holding and Operating Companies of Electric and Gas Utilities* (Washington, 1935), pp., 84, 96-114, 734-38; James C. Bonbright and Gardiner C. Means, *The Holding Company: Its Public Significance and Its Regulation* (New York, 1932), pp. 90-148.
5. Quoted in Stephen Raushenbush, *The Power Fight* (New York, 1932), p. 16.
6. Quoted in Jack Levin, *Power Ethics* (New York, 1931), p. 73.
7. Quoted in Raushenbush, *The Power Fight*, p. 38.
8. Levin, *Power Ethics*, pp. 129, 167. Quotation on p. 167.
9. Ibid., p. 153.
10. *Summary Report of the Federal Trade Commission to the Senate of the United States, Pursuant to Senate Resolution No. 83, 70th Congress, 1st Session, on Efforts by Associations and Agencies of Electric and Gas Utilities to Influence Public Opinion* (Washington, 1934), p. 18.
11. William E. Mosher to Morris L. Cooke, June 12, 1930, Box 94, Morris L. Cooke Papers, FDRL.
12. Morris L. Cooke to William E. Mosher, February 6, 14, 1930, Mosher to Cooke, February 11, 1930, Cooke Papers; New York State, *Annual Report of the Public Service Commission for the Year 1939* (Albany, 1940), pp. 217-19. (Hereinafter referred to as *Annual Report of the PSC*.)
13. Bernard Bellush, *Franklin D. Roosevelt as Governor of New York* (New York, 1955), pp. 243-68.
14. Quoted in Raushenbush, *The Power Fight*, pp. 118-19.

15. Minority Report of the New York Commission on Revision of the Public Service Commissions Law, quoted in ibid., p. 69.

16. Maurice C. Burritt to Edward R. Eastman, August 30, 1933, Box 1, Maurice C. Burritt Papers, Collection of Regional History, Cornell University.

17. *State of Missouri ex. rel. Southwestern Bell Tel. Co. v. Public Service Commission of Missouri,* 262 U.S. 276.

18. For discussions of the theories of valuation, see William E. Mosher and Finla G. Crawford, *Public Utility Regulation* (New York, 1933), pp. 180-224; James C. Bonbright, *Principles of Public Utility Rates* (New York, 1961), passim; Charles F. Phillips, Jr., *The Economics of Regulation: Theory and Practice in the Transportation and Public Utility Industries* (Homewood, Ill., 1965), pp. 214-400.

19. Maurice C. Burritt to C. G. Marshall, [April 1933], Box 4, Burritt Papers; Milo R. Maltbie to HHL, June 12, 1933, "Maltbie Milo," Reel 62, GP. HHLP.

20. The Twentieth Century Fund Power Committee, *The Power Industry and the Public Interest* (New York, 1944), p. 235.

21. Milo R. Maltbie to HHL, February 17, 1933, "Public Service Commission," Reel 79, GP, HHLP. (Hereinafter referred to as "PSC.")

22. HHL Addresses, October 22, 25, November 1, 4, 1932, Speech File, pp. 831, 853-56, 979, 1014, HHLP.

23. Maltbie to HHL, December 17, 1932, "Annual Message, 1933," Gen. Corr., 1933-40, HHLP; HHL Message to the Legislature, January 4, 1933, *Public Papers, 1933,* pp. 29-30.

24. *Annual Report of the PSC, 1932,* I: 11-15, 24-26; Maltbie to HHL, January 27, February 4, 1933, HHL to Maltbie, February 7, 1933, "PSC," Reel 79, GP, HHLP.

25. *Annual Report of the PSC, 1932,* I: 23-24; Maltbie to HHL, February 17, 1933, "PSC," Reel 79, GP, HHLP.

26. HHL to Frank P. Walsh, January 20, 1933, "Power Authority," Reel 77, GP, HHLP; HHL to Maltbie, February 16, 1933, Maltbie to HHL, February 22, 1933, Charles Poletti to Maltbie, March 8, 1933, "PSC," Reel 79, GP, HHLP.

27. HHL Message to the Legislature, March 21, 1933, *Public Papers, 1933,* pp. 100-1. In his budget message, Lehman had already recommended the assessment plan for utilities. HHL Message to Legislature, January 30, 1933, ibid., p. 54.

28. HHL Message to the Legislature, March 28, 1933, ibid., pp. 104-5.

29. President Roosevelt refused to put the federal government behind the municipal ownership bill (through a proposed congressional resolution recognizing the right of New York to generate power on the St. Lawrence) because he thought such matters would receive scant attention in Albany where the question of beer control was paramount. Basil Manly to Frank P. Walsh, April 4, 1933, Frank P. Walsh Papers, New York Public Library.

30. HHL Messages to the Legislature, April 10, 1933, *Public Papers, 1933,* pp. 121-22; New York *Senate Journal, 1933* (Albany, 1933), p. 1538; *Laws of New York, 1933,* chaps. 255-56.

31. HHL to Maltbie, May 4, 1933, "PSC," Reel 79, GP, HHLP.

32. HHL Statement, May 24, 1933, "Maltbie, Milo," Reel 62, GP, HHLP.

33. Maltbie Statement enclosed in Maltbie to HHL, May 25, 1933, ibid.

34. *New York Times,* May 27, 1933.

35. Ibid., June 1, 1933.

36. William P. Capes to HHL, June 20, 1933, "Conference of Mayors, 1932-33," Reel 20, GP, HHLP.

37. *New York Times,* July 1, 1933.

38. Maurice C. Burritt to Edward R. Eastman, July 21, August 21, 1933, Box 1, Burritt Papers; Burritt Diary, November 21-23, 1933, Burritt Papers; Maltbie to Charles Poletti, August 31, 1933, "PSC," Reel 79, GP, HHLP; Maltbie to HHL, November 23, 1933, HHL to Maltbie, December 4, 1933, Gen. Corr., 1933-40, HHLP; *New York Times*, August 21, 22, November 25, 1933.

39. Consolidated Gas argued that any rate decreases, even temporary ones, required a complete property valuation. The Appellate Division of the State Supreme Court upheld this contention and ruled the cuts illegal in June 1935. *New York Edison v. Maltbie*, 279 N.Y.S. 949.

40. *New York Times*, June 21, 23, 27, 1933.

41. HHL Message to the Legislature, August 3, 1933, *Public Papers, 1933*, pp. 144-46.

42. HHL Message to the Legislature, August 22, 1933, ibid., pp. 171-72; *New York Times*, August 18, 23, 1933; *Laws of New York, 1933*, chap. 808.

43. Burritt to Edward R. Eastman, August 21, 1933, Box 1, Burritt Papers.

44. Alva Johnston, "Profiles: The King," *The New Yorker*, September 12, 1931, pp. 25-28.

45. *New York Times*, December 9, 1933.

46. Ibid., December 27, 28, 1933, January 3, 1934.

47. Albany *Knickerbocker Press*, January 3-13, 1934; *New York Times*, January 4, 13, 1934; Judith Stein, "The Birth of Liberal Republicanism in New York State, 1932-1938" (unpublished Ph.D. dissertation, Yale University, 1968), pp. 45-67.

48. HHL Message to the Legislature, January 22, 1934, *Public Papers, 1934*, pp. 72-75.

49. *New York Times*, January 24, 1934.

50. George Gercke to Joseph J. Canavan, January 17, 1934, "Power Authority," Reel 77, GP, HHLP; *New York Times*, February 21, 1934.

51. *New York Times*, February 21, 1934. See also Chamber of Commerce of the State of New York, *Monthly Bulletin*, XXV (March 1934): 447-55.

52. HHL to James C. Bonbright, February 26, 1934, "Public Utility Legislation," Reel 79, GP, HHLP.

53. George B. Cortelyou to Venetia S. Gale, February 13, 1934, chap. 281 (1934), Bill Jackets.

54. W. Kelly to All Stockholders, February 14, 1934, enclosed in George A. Hobe to HHL, February 20, 1934, Gen. Corr., 1933-40, HHLP. For similar letters, see *New York Times*, February 19, March 8, 1934.

55. New York *Herald Tribune*, February 18, March 20, 1934.

56. *New York Times*, March 1, 1934.

57. Power Authority of the State of New York, Press Release, February 20, 1934, "Power Authority," Reel 77, GP, HHLP.

58. *New York Times*, February 24, 1934. Studies by the PSC showed that rates of the towns which already had public power were consistently lower than private companies in the same area. Milo Maltbie to HHL, March 13, 1934, "PSC," Reel 79, GP, HHLP.

59. HHL Address, March 26, 1934, *Public Papers, 1934*, pp. 706-14.

60. *Buffalo Evening News*, March 27, 1934; *New York Times*, March 28, 1934. The decision to discharge the bills may have been reached before the governor's address, but the speech itself brought public confirmation of the decision. *New York Times*, April 2, 3, 1934.

61. *New York Times*, March 30, 1934.

62. *Buffalo Evening News*, April 4, 1934.

63. Ibid., March 30, 1934.

64. *New York Times*, March 30, 31 1934.

65. New York *Herald Tribune*, April 3, 1934.

66. The Senate Judiciary Committee ultimately recommended censure of Thayer, but he announced his resignation before the hearings ended. The joint investigation into public utilities took almost two years and finally suggested eleven revisions in the law to strengthen the Public Service Commission. Five relatively minor changes were enacted. *Proceedings of the Judiciary Committee of the Senate in the Matter of the Investigation Requested by Senator Thayer*, Leg. Doc. No. 102 (1934); *Joint Legislative Committee to Investigate Public Utilities, Final Report*, Leg. Doc. No. 78 (1936); *Laws of New York, 1936*, chaps. 295, 655, 696, 780, 816; *Annual Report of the PSC, 1939*, pp. 38-39.

67. New York *Herald Tribune*, April 3, 5, 1934; New York, *Senate Journal, 1934* (Albany, 1934), pp. 820-28.

68. New York *Herald Tribune*, April 6, 1934. Lehman refused to accept amendments particularly in the municipal ownership bill which his advisers had warned would be emasculated by any further changes. James C. Bonbright to HHL, March 8, 1934, GP, HHLP.

69. HHL Address, April 7, 1934, *Public Papers, 1934*, pp. 717-20.

70. New York *Herald Tribune*, April 9, 1934; *New York Times*, April 8-10, 1934; *Senate Journal, 1934*, pp. 848-50.

71. New York *Herald Tribune*, April 10, 16, 1934; *New York Times*, April 11, 13, 15, 1934; New York, *Assembly Journal, 1934* (Albany, 1934), pp. 2154-62, 2400-3, 2907; *Laws of New York*, 1934, chaps. 212, 279-87.

72. Maltbie to Morris L. Cooke, April 25, 1934, Box 60, Cooke Papers.

73. *Annual Report of the PSC, 1934*, pp. 5, 12-17.

74. *Annual Report of the PSC, 1935*, p. 11.

75. *Yonkers Electric Light and Power Companies v. Maltbie, et al.*, 271 N.Y. 364; *Bronx Gas and Electric Company v. Maltbie, et al.*, 268 N.Y. 278.

76. 271 N.Y. 364.

77. *Annual Report of the PSC, 1936*, p. 24; *Annual Report of the PSC, 1938*, p. 12.

78. Maurice C. Burritt to Edward R. Eastman, August 30, 1935, Box 1, Burritt Papers.

79. *Annual Report of the PSC, 1937*, pp. 24-25; *Annual Report of the PSC, 1940*, pp. 17-19. See *supra*, chap. III.

80. Twentieth Century Fund, *The Power Industry*, p. 10.

81. Maurice C. Burritt to HHL, January 30, 1939, Box 1, Burritt Papers.

82. Morris L. Cooke to James C. Bonbright, June 29, 1934, Box 132, Cooke Papers.

83. Walsh to Morris L. Cooke, June 24, 1934, Box 137, ibid.

84. Roscoe C. Martin, *Water for New York: A Study in State Administration of Water Resources* (Syracuse, N.Y., 1960), pp. 196-97.

85. Quoted in ibid., p. 40.

86. Paula Eldot, "Alfred Emanuel Smith, Reforming Governor" (unpublished PhD. dissertation, Yale University, 1961), pp. 379-427.

87. Bellush, *Roosevelt*, pp. 208-42. For details of Power Authority activities, see *Annual Report of the Power Authority of the State of New York*, issued each year and entered as Leg. Doc.

88. For the background of this agreement and a copy of it, see *Annual Report of the Power Authority, 1931*, pp. 32-42; *Annual Report of the Power Authority, 1932*, pp. 54-62.

89. Delos M. Cosgrove to Morris L. Cooke, May 23, 1933, Box 246, Cooke Papers; Arthur H. Vendenberg et al., to FDR, May 18, 1933, Frank P. Walsh to FDR, June 2, 1933, Memorandum to FDR with vote estimate, [June 1933] OF 156, FDRL; FDR Message to

the Senate, January 10, 1934, *Public Papers and Addresses of Franklin D. Roosevelt* (New York, 1938), III: 29-31; *The New York Times,* March 15, 1934. For Lehman's support of the treaty, see HHL to Thomas J. Walsh, December 5, 1932, Special File, HHLP.

90. Delos M. Cosgrove to Morris L. Cooke, April 17, 1933, Box 246, Cooke Papers; Robert La Follette, Jr., to Thomas W. Lamont, February 10, 1934, "Power Authority," Reel 77, GP, HHLP; R. G. Sucher to Frank P. Walsh, August 23, 1933, Walsh memorandum, January 23, 1936, Judson King, "The Great Lakes-St. Lawrence Seaway and Power Project: A Brief Narrative, Prepared for President Franklin D. Roosevelt," March 10, 1937, pp. 84-86, OF 156, FDRL; Howard B. Wilson, "Economic Objections to the St. Lawrence Waterway Project," Part I, *Public Utilities Fortnightly,* February 15, 1934, pp. 199-206, Pt. II, ibid., March 1, 1934, pp. 267-74; Raushenbush, *The Power Fight,* p. 10; *Buffalo Evening News,* March 15, 1934; *Buffalo Courier-Express,* February 1, 1940.

91. Martin, *Water for New York,* pp. 198-201. Developments after 1934 can be followed in the *Annual Report of the Power Authority.* See also "Confidential Notebooks," Boxes 4-B and 5, Leland Olds Papers, FDRL.

X

THE END OF AN ERA

During Herbert Lehman's last term as governor, an era of reform came to an end in New York. Lehman emerged from the 1938 election with the first four-year lease on the state's executive mansion, but his margin of victory was small.[1] Republicans also controlled both the Assemby and the Senate for the first time since 1932. The social worker Homer Folks reflected in the wake of the election: "Not every year can be one of notable forward steps, and I am inclined to feel that 1939 may well be one primarily of holding the ground already gained, refining methods, getting ready for well demonstrated advances in the following year or two."[2] Folks's suspicion about the 1939 session proved correct, but the projected breakthrough in succeeding years never materialized. As the G.O.P. tightened its grip on the legislature, well-organized business and property interests mounted a campaign against rising taxes to finance swelling state budgets. Republican lawmakers joined the attack and forced Lehman to reduce expenditures, which precluded any further expansion of social services.

The reform impulse was also weakened by its very success. Many local groups that had long fought for welfare and labor legislation had accomplished their objectives by 1939. During the late 1930s, leaders of the New York Child Labor Committee turned their attention "to matters of administration of the child labor laws as we feel that the New York statutes are now in a fairly satisfactory condition—particularly after the unusually successful legislative efforts of the Committee in 1935."[3] Toward the end of 1939, George Meany told State Federation of Labor officials that "for the time being the major part of our Legislative Program has been achieved." Citing the reactionary trend around the country, Meany advised organized labor to focus on guarding against any revision of New York's existing social welfare laws.[4] Soon thereafter, Abraham Epstein's New York Permanent Conference on Social Security stopped holding regularly scheduled meetings because its "major program . . . has been achieved beyond its original expectations."[5]

Reflecting this growing sense of satisfaction among reformers, Lehman talked

231

increasingly about the need for preserving recent advances rather than taking on additional responsibilities. "The splendid program of social and labor legislation on our statute books must be safeguarded," he asserted defensively during the 1938 campaign.[6] The following year the governor set the tone for his fourth term.

> At the present we must devote our attention principally to the perfection and consolidation of the social gains we have already achieved.
>
> The new laws of the past six years have placed upon the administrative branch of the State intricate and difficult tasks. There is no question that the efficiency of some of these laws can be improved. . . . This is a good time to re-examine the legislative acts in order to strengthen the process of their administration. We should smooth out any rough edges; we should correct any mistakes disclosed by experience.[7]

This conservative goal encountered no resistance in the legislature. The question of taxes to support rising budgets produced the only controversy during 1939 and 1940; and the following year, lawmakers witnessed the dullest session in memory because of the absence of major issues and the decline of public interest in state affairs to the lowest point in two decades.[8] The specter of war also preoccupied Lehman as he allotted more and more of his time first to civil defense and then to mobilization. Yet in spite of the distraction of foreign affairs and restrictions on public spending, the Welfare State created by New York during the 1930s survived the period intact.

1

At the start of Lehman's fourth term, "economy" became the watchword in Albany. In 1939, Republican attempts to cut the budget ended with the governor contesting the G.O.P. plan in court. Although the Republican-controlled legislature lost the so-called battle of the budget because of a seemingly minor point of procedure, it successfully reversed Lehman's spending policy, which vocal business and taxpayer groups also opposed.

The dispute erupted when Lehman recommended a record budget of $415 million for the fiscal year 1939-40.[9] This represented a net increase of $20 million over the previous year, but the governor declared that he had arrived at the figure only after months of careful analysis and drastic pruning of the requests originally submitted by state agencies. With an anticipated deficit due to expanding costs and declining revenues, Lehman also called for new taxes amounting to $64 million in order to balance the budget as required by the state constitution. When compared with previous budgets, this one contained few surprises, since it represented but another step in a series of annual increases in state expenses (see Table 8). Indeed, as Lehman pointed out, a large part of the 1940 financial program "was in effect dictated by the legislation of other years creating the various departments, prescribing the services they should render, and agreeing to contribute large sums of State aid to the counties, cities, towns, villages and school districts." [10]

Table 9
New York State Expenditures, 1933-42
(money amounts in millions of dollars)

Fiscal Year	Total Expenditures	Selected Departments[a]							
		Education		Mental Hygiene		Public Works		Social Welfare	
		Amount	Per-cent	Amount	Per-cent	Amount	Per-cent	Amount	Per-cent
1933	271.4	115.5	43	27.2	10	28.9	11	8.8	3
1934	225.7	90.2	40	25.6	11	24.7	11	7.5	3
1935	281.6	123.1	44	29.3	10	26.9	10	8.0	3
1936	288.5	129.2	45	29.0	10	22.4	8	9.2	3
1937	314.5	131.8	42	34.2	11	26.7	8	9.3	3
1938	371.6	133.8	36	36.0	10	35.9	10	50.6[b]	14
1939	395.7	136.3	34	36.2	9	33.6	8	79.1	20
1940	394.5	127.7	29	34.2	9	36.3	9	78.1	20
1941	391.0	132.1	34	36.1	9	31.3	8	75.2	19
1942	374.2	131.8	35	38.7	10	26.7	7	63.8	17

[a]Of the departments not listed, each accounted annually for less than 3 percent of the state's total expenditures.
[b]Sudden increase a result of the takeover of the Temporary Emergency Relief Administration.

SOURCE: New York State, Department of Audit and Control, *Annual Report* (Albany, 1933–43).

Although Lehman had become governor as a former banker pledged to economy in government, the exigencies of the Depression and the cost of his Little New Deal had reversed this stance. After ordering sharp retrenchment during his first year in office, Lehman had backed a series of budgets that took state expenditures from $225 million in 1933-34 to $395 million in 1938-39. The bulk of these additional funds went not for functions or services actually carried on by the state but for aid to localities for public education and new social welfare programs, notably unemployment relief and old age assistance (see Fig. 4). Throughout the 1930s, contributions to local communities accounted for more than half the entire state budget.[11]

Under Lehman's leadership, New York used relatively progressive taxation to finance increased spending. While twenty-three states resorted to the sales tax during the 1930s, Lehman abandoned this expedient after employing it briefly in 1933-34 to help reduce the deficit he had inherited from Governor Roosevelt. Lehman disliked the sales tax because "it imposes an undue burden on the little fellow, as compared to the men of wealth or ample means." [12] As revenues from existing levies dropped owing to the sagging economy, the governor turned to higher taxes on businesses and personal income. The latter accounted for 11 percent of New York's total revenues in fiscal 1933

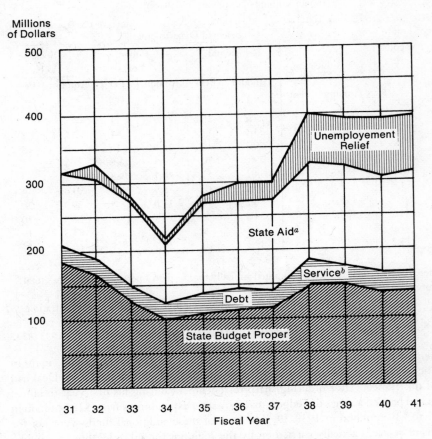

Millions
of Dollars

4. New York State's four-fold budget, 1931-1941.

a Excluding unemployment relief.
b Excluding relief bonds.

Source: HHL Message to the Legislature, January 22, 1940, *Public Papers, 1940*, p. 31.

Table 9
New York State Revenues, 1933–42
(money amounts in millons of dollars)

Fiscal Year	Total Revenues	Leading Tax Sources					
		Corporations		Personal Income		Inheritance and Estates	
		Amount	Per-cent	Amount	Per-cent	Amount	Per-cent
(1)	(2)	(3)	(4)	(5)	(6)	(7)	(8)
1933	221.8	45.7	21	24.9	11	34.0	15
1934	258.9	37.6	15	37.4	14	33.0	13
1935	251.2	38.4	16	48.0	19	29.7	12
1936	330.5	67.9	21	74.3	22	26.4	8
1937	360.9	58.3	16	104.9	27	33.6	9
1938	389.0	78.0	20	107.2	27	34.0	9
1939	359.8	74.1	21	89.2	25	35.5	10
1940	393.5	72.0	19	92.7	24	28.0	7
1941	428.1	66.5	17	101.2	24	27.7	6
1942	421.3	83.5	20	82.3	19	21.0	5

Fiscal Year	Leading Tax Sources							
	Stock Transfer		Motor Vehicles		Motor Fuel		Alcoholic Beverages	
	Amount	Per-cent	Amount	Per-cent	Amount	Per-cent	Amount	Per Cent
(9)	(10)	(11)	(12)	(13)	(14)	(15)	(16)	(17)
1933	31.6	14	29.9	13	37.0	17	. . . .	.
1934	33.3	13	29.8	11	36.1	14	10.8	4
1935	15.9	6	32.2	13	43.4	17	19.0	8
1936	34.4	10	33.4	10	52.6	16	18.5	6
1937	33.8	9	35.5	10	43.6	12	21.4	6
1938	20.7	5	37.3	9	59.3	15	21.6	5
1939	19.3	5	35.1	10	58.8	16	22.3	6
1940	19.2	5	38.1	10	62.1	16	32.2	8
1941	12.0	3	41.8	10	66.0	15	33.1	8
1942	12.0	3	37.1	9	61.7	15	35.4	8

Source: New York State, Department of Audit and Control, *Annual Report* (A bany, 1933-43).

Table 10
New York State Budgetary Surplus, 1933–42

Fiscal Year	Annual Surplus[a]	Accumulated Surplus	Fiscal Year	Annual Surplus	Accumulated Surplus
1933	−51.6	−94.4	1938	16.7	6.5
1934	29.7	−64.7	1939	−35.3	−28.9
1935	−32.3	−97.0	1940	−1.2	−30.0
1936	41.2	−55.9	1941	37.1	7.1
1937	45.7	−10.2	1942	47.1	54.1

[a] Minus sign (−) denotes a deficit.
Source: New York State, Department of Audit and Control, *Annual Report* (Albany, 1933–43).

and 25 percent by 1937 (see Table 9, column 6). When compared with other states, New York had one of the most progressive tax systems because it relied on imposts other than the regressive sales tax. This was especially remarkable since, throughout this period, the Empire State also had one of the highest per capita tax levels in the country.[13]

As a result of his banking experience, Lehman devoted much of his time to formulating the state's financial policy. He took particular pride in the annual executive budget, which he carefully prepared over a period of months in consultation with advisers and department heads.[14] To help assure favorable newspaper coverage, the governor invited editors and reporters to Albany for a briefing prior to public release of his budget.[15] Despite reverses in the general economy, Lehman managed both to expand the state's services and to reduce the accumulated deficit (see Table 10). This pay-as-you-go policy helped win widespread acceptance of spiraling budget requests during Lehman's first three terms as governor. In 1939, the *Herald Tribune,* which often opposed spending programs of the New Deal, concluded that "throughout his service, [Lehman] has been consistently sound and conservative in his administration of the state's finances." [16]

Protests against rising taxes and expenditures remained isolated and muted in New York until 1939, when a small group of powerful taxpayers staged a revolt.[17] The opposition crystallized around Lehman's request for a new impost on businesses and a revival of the direct tax on real estate which the state had abandoned in 1928. Since property owners had long objected to the burden of local real estate taxes, the *Herald Tribune* thought the governor's 1939 budget message might "finally startle the public from the dangerous lethargy with which it has too long received these documents." [18] This surmise proved correct as mail poured into Albany from organizations of merchants and property owners, as well as individual businessmen, who opposed any new taxation, expecially on real estate. Instead, they called for drastic retrenchment in spending to

eliminate the need for additional revenues.[19] Reflecting the overwhelming sentiment of
these New Yorkers, the Bronx Chamber of Commerce issued a "vigorous protest against
the adoption of a State Budget which will require not only retention of existing onerous
taxes, but in addition will require further imposts on real estate and business. *As a
substitute for taxes let there be a reduction of expenditures.*"[20]

Lehman's budget became the most controversial item in the 1939 legislative session,
which lasted longer than any since 1911.[21] In late February, a public hearing revealed
both the interest aroused in state finances and the sharp division of opinion among New
York's leading power blocs. A record crowd of six thousand people jammed the Capitol,
and the proceedings were broadcast over radio for the first time in legislative history.[22]
While officials of numerous business and real estate groups demanded specific cutbacks
in spending amounting to as much as $60 million, a woman from Westchester County
spoke generally for organized taxpayers:

> This is the last straw budget, breaking the camel's back—in this case the taxpayer's.
> The taxpayer who has been buffeted from pillar to post has finally reached the
> breaking point. His ire is up. From one end of the state to the other, there has been
> a roar of disapproval over this soaring, cloud-high budget. From Lockport to
> Greepoint, groups of citizens have voiced their indignation against any new taxes.
> They are opposed to all new taxes. They want economy.

Support for the governor's budget came from representatives of teachers, civil service
employees, and organized labor, who defended outlays for education and social welfare
programs.[23] The general director of the Charity Organization Society warned that
arbitrary cuts would cause "very genuine suffering and distress."[24]

Although G.O.P. lawmakers had initially offered no objections to Lehman's budget,
they quickly echoed the cries for economy which came from traditionally Republican
voters in the business community. However, legislators had trouble coming up with an
alternative fiscal plan, particularly since they needed virtual unanimity in the Senate
which they controlled by a slim two-vote margin. Party leaders originally hoped to
couple some cuts in spending with a shift from the proposed levies on business and realty
to a sales tax, but resistance to the latter from a group of Republican Senators forced the
G.O.P. to concentrate on reduced expenditures as the only means of avoiding unpopular
tax increases. While Republicans sought ways to trim state costs, advocates of
retrenchment kept the pressure on lawmakers. New protest groups sprang up in large
cities around the state, and mail demanding tax cuts continued to pile up in the Capitol.[25]
In the desperate search for savings, one assemblyman suggested that legislators should
"bale these communications asking for government economy and sell them to paper
reclaimers."[26]

After ten weeks of studying Lehman's budget, Republicans finally presented a revised
plan on April 17. They pruned over $30 million from the governor's $415 million
program by cutting state aid for education almost 10 percent and slashing road-building
funds more than 50 percent. The rest of the savings came from reduced appropriations

for most state departments. Although Republicans accepted Lehman's proposal for a hike in liquor taxes, they substituted a cigarette tax for his suggested levies on property and businesses. The estimated $33 million in new revenues would balance the budget when combined with the recommended cuts in spending. The Republican package was largely the work of Abbot Law Moffat, the thirty-eight-year-old chairman of the Assembly Ways and Means Committee, who had established himself as the G.O.P. fiscal expert since coming to Albany from Manhattan's silk stocking district in 1929. With the aid of eight assistants and after breaking three adding machines, Moffat had turned inside out practically every one of the 35,000 items in Lehman's 1939-40 budget in order to trim both taxes and expenses. At a party conference, Republican legislators unanimously endorsed Moffat's handiwork.[27]

Opposition to the plan focused on the question of its constitutionality. Under the amendment which established the executive budget system in the 1920s, the governor possessed primary responsibility for formulating a yearly financial program. This was designed to bring order to state fiscal policy by ending legislative logrolling in the budget-making process. Accordingly, the revised constitution decreed that the legislature could not alter the governor's plan except to reduce or eliminate specific items in the budget which, unlike other legislation, became law when passed by both houses without further action by the chief executive. The legislature could also increase individual appropriations, but these changes were subject to the governor's veto.[28] In 1939, however, Republicans in effect rewrote Lehman's budget by dropping itemized appropriations for most departments and substituting a lump sum from 5 to 10 percent less than that requested for each agency. Since this shifted to the executive branch the burden of deciding exactly where to cut costs, Republicans defended lump-sum allotments as the best way of trimming state expenditures.[29]

Attacks on the G.O.P. plan came not only from the Lehman administration but also from several anti-New Dealers. To everyone's surprise, former governor Alfred E. Smith first raised doubts about the constitutionality of the legislature's action. While agreeing with the need for economy, Smith recalled his successful fight for the 1927 amendment which authorized the executive budget, and he declared that "the system proposed by Moffat would force every governor to logroll with legislative leaders in preparing the budget, would leave the public and department heads in a complete fog as to appropriations and would require every department head to lick the boots of obscure legislative leaders."[30] Lehman initially refused to comment on the developing controversy, but he released an opinion by Attorney General John J. Bennett, Jr., advising that "the Legislature is without authority under the Constitution to amend . . . the appropriation bill in the manner now proposed."[31] Support for this position came from Robert Moses, who noted that the issue "goes far beyond partisanship" and who branded the Republican proposal "a slick, tricky way of [effecting economies], and . . . wholly unconstitutional."[32]

After consulting with his cabinet, Lehman also objected strenuously to the disputed plan, but he could not prevent Republicans from adopting it. While admitting the power of lawmakers to reduce or even scrap particular items in his budget, the governor dismissed as unconstitutional the replacement of his executive budget with unitemized lump-sum appropriations.[33] On April 28, Lehman warned that those "who have decided to railroad and jam the Republican budget through the Legislature must bear the full responsibility" for "deliberately violating the Constitution" and impairing essential public services.[34] Disregarding these pleas, Republicans enacted their proposal by a virtually straight party vote. Rather than veto the legislation, Lehman allowed it to become law without his signature because G.O.P. leaders pledged to cooperate in a court test of the measure's constitutionality.[35]

The case pitting Lehman against the Republican-dominated legislature moved quickly through the state courts. In arguments before the Appellate Division, attorneys for both sides agreed that "the fundamental question [is] whether the power of the Legislature to deal with the Governor's appropriation bills is full and complete or is in some way limited and constrained under the Constitution by the Governor." [36] On June 15, the Appellate Division ruled in favor of Lehman by a vote of three to two. The majority opinion declared:

The bill passed by the Legislature . . . goes much further than striking out items or reducing items or adding items of appropriation. In effect it destroys the Executive budget completely and substitutes therefor a legislative bill. In other words, the Legislature completely emasculated the Governor's Appropriation Bill. . . . This is contrary to the spirit and purpose of the Constitution.[37]

New York's highest tribunal unanimously upheld this decision a week later. While recognizing the need for some lump sums in an executive budget, the Court of Appeals ruled that where "a whole appropriation has been stricken out, including the items of which it is made, and compensation for clerks and services as well as maintenance is lumped together, the words of the Constitution have not been followed and such appropriation is illegal." [38]

Lehman won the constitutional battle of the budget, but he lost the campaign to win passage of his record spending program. After hailing the opinion of the Court of Appeals as "a real victory for sound government," Lehman reconvened the legislature to adopt a budget for the coming fiscal year.[39] The Republican majority predictably ignored pleas for the restoration of proposed cuts, and both houses simply reenacted the Republican financial plan with the appropriations fully itemized. Nevertheless, Lehman took great satisfaction in his successful defense of the executive budget system, which he considered more important than the temporary issue of economy in government.[40]

The 1939 session proved only the first round in a continuing fight over taxes and spending. The following year G.O.P. leaders accepted Lehman's invitation to cooperate in preparing the state's upcoming budget. As presented to the legislature in January 1940, the executive budget called for a modest increase in state spending of only $5 million, and it included a request for a rise in the income tax to offset an expected decline in revenues.[41]

Although lawmakers initially responded favorably to the governor's budget, the temporary political truce collapsed when New Yorkers again split openly over the issue. In renewing their protests against additional taxes, business and real estate interests continued to represent themselves as spokesmen for ordinary citizens.[42] The president of the State Chamber of Commerce charged that the "economy results obtained by the State-wide crusade of taxpayers last year have been undermined." [43] However, at a legislative hearing which drew over six thousand interested New Yorkers to Albany in mid-February, advocates of economy were outnumbered by teachers, parents, and civil service employees who defended the budget.[44]

Yet appeals for cutbacks did not fall on deaf ears. Sensitive to complaints from businessmen, Republicans withdrew their support for Lehman's financial program. But the search for savings proved difficult, since party leaders who had cooperated in planning the executive budget knew only too well that it had already been scraped to the bone. Any additional reductions would force the liquidation of some state services. Republicans, therefore, trimmed only $2 million, but they eliminated the need for an immediate tax increase through several sleights of hand such as inflating estimates of forthcoming revenues.[45] With unusual bluntness Lehman condemned the G.O.P. plan as "dishonest," "deceptive," and "just plain hocus-pocus," because it would undoubtedly leave the budget unbalanced.[46]

Lehman felt double-crossed by Republican leaders who had effectively promised to support the executive budget they had helped to draft.[47] "I have never known a more distressing situation," he reflected privately. "The only thing that encourages me is that [Republican lawmakers] are so stupid in their feeling of power that in the end they are bound to be '[hoist] by their own petard.' " [48] Ignoring repeated pleas from the governor for a truly balanced budget, which required $10 million in additional taxes or spending cuts, the Republican majority pushed its proposal through the legislature.[49]

After his experience of 1939 and 1940, Lehman stole the thunder from budget-cutters by joining their ranks. His fiscal plan for 1941-42 called for a nine-million-dollar decrease in appropriations and a twenty-one-million-dollar reduction in income taxes. Although some proponents of economy in government demanded greater savings, Lehman's proposal won the support of Republicans.[50] In 1942, the governor again surprised New Yorkers by recommending the smallest budget in six years coupled with a 25 percent cut in personal income taxes. This step, according to Lehman, was designed to save money to "further the task of pushing our war effort to the highest possible limit." [51] Thus, as a result of both tax protests and American entry into World War II, New York's appropriations remained below the 1938-39 peak during Lehman's last four years in Albany (see p. 233, Table 8).[52]

2

State finances dominated legislative sessions during Lehman's last term, but the threat of war also drew the governor's attention. Although Lehman had always shown an interest in foreign affairs, the plight of European Jews sharpened his sensitivity to international developments after 1933. Within months following Hitler's assumption of power,

Lehman spoke at a mass rally in New York City to protest the persecution of German Jews.[53] During succeeding years, he repeatedly condemned the German "campaign to exterminate the dwindling minority of Jews," and he appealed for money to aid those in distress.[54] Herbert Lehman personally contributed thousands of dollars to the cause and joined other members of his family in creating a fund to finance the emigration of close relatives threatened by Nazism.[55]

Lehman soon feared for the security of America. He became convinced, he later recalled, "that we were bound to go to war with Germany, not particularly [to protect] minority groups there in Germany . . . , but because I felt there was a real desire to dominate the world." [56] In 1938, even before the Munich conference, the governor warned New Yorkers about "the threat which dictatorship constitutes to democracy." [57] At his inauguration in 1939, Lehman surprised his audience by devoting his entire address to a plea for national unity in the face of tyranny abroad.[58] Shortly before the outbreak of World War II in Europe, he asserted that in view of the international situation the United States should have an army

at least the equal of any army in the world in equipment, training and morale. . . .

With the progress of science, the development of new methods of transport and warfare, we in this country can no longer count ourselves safe merely because of geographical isolation. No one can study the record of the past few years and fail to recognize the need of adequate preparedness.[59]

After France's quick defeat in the spring of 1940, Lehman repeatedly urged "immediate and all out aid to England; the prompt introduction of compulsory selective service and the establishment of an army, navy, and air force, the equal of any in the world." [60]

Lehman devoted his last two and one-half years in Albany to preparing New York for war.[61] "The execution of a plan of national defense," the governor told state officials in June 1940, "has become the primary job of the people of America." [62] Through an executive order Lehman created the New York State Council of Defense, composed of business, labor, and farm leaders, "to promote State and national security by formulating and assisting in the execution of plans for the mobilization . . . of the resources and facilities of the State." [63] In 1941, Lehman outlined a state defense program in his annual address to the legislature, and only in subsequent messages did he recommend any measures not related to the war.[64] Although Republicans generally supported the preparedness campaign, they refused to authorize Lehman's budget request for over $1 million to finance activities such as guarding state armories, because, Republicans charged, the proposal reflected "an intense emotional alarm . . . rather than sane business judgment." [65] However, after the attack on Pearl Harbor, the war dominated state affairs; during 1942, there was considerably greater bipartisan cooperation in Albany.[66] Recalling his last years as governor, Lehman subsequently admitted that his administration had overreacted to international developments.

We did an enormous amount of work [preparing the state for war,] most of which, of course, we never availed ourselves of. It wasn't necessary. We were prepared—probably we took more measures than were necessary, but . . . I've never regretted it.[67]

3

Financial belt-tightening and mobilization for war generally prevented expansion of the Little New Deal in the years 1939-42. Indeed, these concerns hampered administration of some existing programs, particularly in the field of labor legislation. Yet no reforms were actually repealed, and in a few cases lawmakers adopted amendments which improved the coverage of welfare measures.

The state's minimum wage statute suffered most as a result of the drive for economy in government. In 1938, the Advisory Committee on Minimum Wage Laws declared that New York contained 400,000 women and minors, in addition to those already covered, who awaited application of wage orders in their industries. This step, however, required an estimated $500,000 to pay the cost of enforcement. Despite annual appeals from groups including the Consumers' League and the Women's Trade Union League, the money was not forthcoming.[68] The chairman of the advisory committee pointed out: "The lack of an adequate appropriation for minimum wage enforcement means that we have a law on our statute books which . . . cannot be made to work because of grossly inadequate enforcement machinery." [69] Since Republicans spurned requests for additional funds, Lehman argued that reformers who wanted expansion of minimum wage protection should undertake the necessary educational campaign to win public backing.[70]

American entry into World War II also weakened enforcement of New York's labor code. Within days after the attack on Pearl Harbor, Lehman authorized the state's industrial commissioner to grant immediate dispensations from maximum hour and night work laws in cases where their enforcement would impair war production. The legislature soon accepted suspensions of up to six months on an individual basis subject to approval by the industrial commissioner. This step, which largely affected women workers, won the endorsement of the State Federation of Labor and the CIO, but the Women's Trade Union League opposed any relaxation of labor laws.[71]

Although the war eased restrictions on women's work, it stimulated numerous improvements in unemployment insurance. At the time of its enactment in 1935, New York's unemployment compensation law was highly praised because its provisions far surpassed those of the only other statute in existence.[72] By 1942, however, New York had one of the country's most regressive job insurance systems as a result of the failure to update the measure. All but three states, for example, had waiting periods shorter than that in New York. The Empire State also extended fewer weeks of benefits than any of the sixteen states, which set a single maximum for all claimants. Only three states, including New York, paid no compensation to partially unemployed workers. On the basis of these findings, New York's Department of Labor described the law it administered as "illiberal." [73]

In 1942, economic dislocation caused by the war provided the impetus for a thorough overhaul of job insurance. Although state officials had previously acknowledged weaknesses in New York's social security system, the war brought to the foreground some of the deficiencies of the unemployment insurance law. Specifically, the Department of Labor anticipated a rapid rise in temporary layoffs as the country retooled for war.[74] Early in 1942, Lehman warned that

the war effort would require renewed attention to the unemployment problem. . . . In the conversion of our national energies to war production, [many] workers will encounter periods of idleness before their skills can be diverted to new fields.[75]

Under the pressure of war time, state officials suggested a variety of changes in job insurance. The nine members of the Unemployment Insurance Advisory Council offered the most comprehensive amendments. The six representatives of the public and employers recommended radical changes in the benefit structure, including allowances for dependents, compensation for partial unemployment, coverage for wage earners in small businesses, increases in minimum payments, a reduced waiting period, and additional weeks of benefits. To finance these reforms, the council's majority called for the imposition of a tax on employees to match that already paid by employers.[76] Labor members of the council, driven by their long-standing opposition to any assessment on workers, issued a minority report in which they rejected five of the majority's seven recommendations, those which required additional funds. The Department of Labor also urged more limited changes owing to its concern with problems of cost and administration.[77] A joint legislative committee dominated by Republicans backed four revisions in the law. After a year of study, the group suggested an increase in the duration of compensation from thirteen to sixteen weeks, a reduction in the waiting period from three to two weeks, a rise in maximum benefits from $15.00 to $18.00 weekly, and extension of coverage to the partially unemployed. Following the lead of the legislature's G.O.P. majority, Lehman recommended the same four changes except that he urged twenty weeks of benefits. In support of organized labor, the governor opposed any tax on workers.[78]

With the governor and Republican leaders in substantial agreement, the package of four amendments won quick acceptance. Republicans first altered their bill to provide for a full twenty weeks of coverage, and then lawmakers passed the four improvements with little opposition.[79] "This measure . . . represents one of the greatest advances which New York has made in the field of social legislation," the state's industrial commissioner declared.[80] As Lehman pointed out when signing the bill in May 1942, the state finally accepted these reforms because American participation in World War II raised the threat of widespread temporary unemployment during the conversion to war production.[81]

Despite some setbacks during the years 1939-42, New York's Little New Deal survived the period intact. While the legislature's economy-minded Republican majority generally foreclosed the possibility of additional reforms, Lehman's hold on the executive branch precluded any attempt to dismantle the Welfare State. This political standoff gave the Little New Deal time to win greater acceptance as a part of the state's new status quo.

For Lehman the prospect of war overshadowed domestic events after 1939. His own subsequent evaluation of the period confirms this:

> I've always thought that my fourth term, while it did not result in much progressive legislation, was nonetheless a very important period, largely . . . because it became evident to many of us that war was inevitable in Europe, and that in all probability we would be drawn into the conflict, so that it was very necessary to make preparations for that situation, educate people, arouse public opinion, and to take steps to fortify the state, in civil defense, and also to a very considerable extent in military defense.[82]

In part because of the war, Lehman announced in May 1942 that he would not run for governor again. Eager to do something connected with the war, he resigned from office on December 2, 1942, leaving Albany a month early in order to take over immediately as director of Foreign Relief and Rehabilitation Operations.[83] After ten years of helping New Yorkers recover from the Depression, Herbert Lehman went to the aid of people ravaged by the scourge of war.

NOTES

1. See *supra,* chap. 1. pp. 14, 17.
2. Folks to HHL, December 19, 1938, "Folks, Homer," Gen. Corr., 1933-40, HHLP.
3. George A. Hall to Mrs. Leonard Jones, November 22, 1937, Box 11, Group II, New York Child Labor Committee Papers, New York State Library; see *supra,* chap. V, p. 120.
4. *NYSFL Bulletin,* December 28, 1939.
5. "Minutes of the Executive Committee Meeting of the New York Permanent Conference on Social Security," April 22, 1941, Box 41, Epstein Papers (Columbia).
6. HHL Address, October 27, 1938, *Public Papers, 1938,* p. 577.
7. HHL Message to the Legislature, January 4, 1939, *Public Papers, 1939,* p. 22. See also HHL Address, February 11, 1941, *Public Papers, 1941,* pp. 619-21.
8. New York *Herald Tribune,* February 23, 1941, Albany *Knickerbocker News,* April 4, 1941, *New York Times,* April 5, 1941 (CB, 90: 10897; 91: 11119, 11126, HHLP).
9. This sum included the original proposal for $411.7 million in appropriations plus $3.3 million subsequently recommended in the supplemental budget. HHL Message to the Legislature, March 1, 1939, *Public Papers, 1939,* pp. 101-3.
10. HHL Message to the Legislature, January 30, 1939, *Public Papers, 1939,* p. 55.
11. *New York Times,* February 13, 1940 (CB, 83: 8326).
12. HHL Memoir, COHC, p. 370. In New York State, retailers naturally opposed the sales tax while real estate interests favored it as a means of relieving the burden of property taxes. In 1934, Republicans fought unsuccessfully to continue the sales tax and increase it from 1 to 2 percent. Percy C. Magnus to HHL, February 16, 1933, "Magnus, Percy C.," Reel 58, GP,

HHLP; Press Release by George R. Fearon, February 12, 1934, "Sales Tax," Reel 85, ibid.; Chamber of Commerce of the State of New York, *Monthly Bulletin,* XXIV (January 1933): 373-75; *New York Times,* February 12, 14, 20, March 5, 9, 1933, March 14, 15, 1934.

13. New York State, *Report of the Joint Legislative Committee on State Fiscal Policies,* Leg. Doc. No. 41 (1938), pp. 160-67; Clara Penniman, "The Politics of Taxation," in *Politics in the American States,* ed. by Herbert Jacob and Kenneth N. Vines (Boston, 1965), p. 311; U.S. Department of Commerce, Bureau of the Census, *Historical Review of State and Local Government Finances,* State and Local Government Special Studies, No. 25 (Washington, 1948), p. 32.

14. In pursuit of expert opinion outside the state bureaucracy, Lehman often sought advice on financial matters from Robert M. Haig, professor of economics at Columbia University. See "Haig, Robert M.," Gen. Corr., 1933-40, HHLP.

15. *New York Times,* January 19, 1940 (CB, 83: 8157); HHL Memoir, pp. 507, 705; Carolin A. Flexner Memoir, COHC, p. 56; Jewel Bellush, "Selected Case Studies of the Legislative Leadership of Governor Herbert H. Lehman" (unpublished Ph.D. dissertation, Columbia University, 1959), pp. 314-15.

16. New York *Herald Tribune,* January 5, 1939 (CB, 75:6866).

17. Prior to 1938, Lehman's office staff did not even keep a separate file for constituent mail on taxation, but in that year the first letters of protest began to appear. See Reels 94 and 95, GP, HHLP.

18. New York *Herald Tribune,* January 31, 1939 (CB, 76: 7042).

19. Albany *Knickerbocker News,* February 2, 9, 1939, New York *Herald Tribune,* February 1, 2, 7, 8, 16, 1939 (CB, 76: 7040, 7058, 7060, 7062, 7070, 7072, 7078, 7092).

20. George F. Mand to HHL, February 3, 1939, "Taxes, A-L, 1939," Reel 94, GP, HHLP. (Italics added.) See also the Merchants' Association of New York et al., "How to Balance the State Budget without Additional Taxes," February 1939, "Budget—General, 1939," Reel 13, GP, HHLP.

21. New York *Herald Tribune,* May 22, 1939 (CB, 78: 7439).

22. Ibid., February 22-23 (CB, 76: 7140, 7144).

23. *New York Times,* February 23, 1939 (CB, 76: 7142-43).

24. Stanley P. Davies to HHL, March 1, 1939, "Taxes, A-L, 1939," Reel 94, GP, HHLP.

25. *New York Times,* March 20, April 13, 1939, New York *Herald Tribune,* April 9, 1939, Albany *Knickerbocker News,* April 10, 1939 (CB 77: 7202, 7246, 7250, 7256).

26. Albany *Knickerbocker News,* March 31, 1939 (CB, 77: 7225).

27. *New York Times,* April 18, 1939, Albany *Knickerbocker News,* April 8, 22, June 17, 1939 (CB, 77: 7244, 7287-88, 7311, 7562).

28. N.Y. Const., art. IV-A (1927) and art. VII (1938); New York State Constitutional Convention, *Problems Relating to Taxation and Finance* (Albany, 1938), pp. 17-22; Frederick C. Mosher, "The Executive Budget, Empire State Style," *Public Administration Review,* XII (Spring 1952): 73-84.

29. "Report Submitted to the Republican Conference by Republican Members of the Senate and Assembly Committees on Finance and Taxation on Governor Lehman's Budget, 1939-40," April 17, 1939, "Budget—Appropriation Act, 1939," Reel 13, GP, HHLP.

30. Statement by Alfred E. Smith, April 20, 1939, "Budget—General, 1939," Reel 13, GP, HHLP.

31. Bennett to HHL, April 26, 1939, *Public Papers, 1939,* p. 490. See also New York *Herald Tribune,* April 19, 26, 1939 (CB, 77: 7299, 7321).

32. Moses quoted in HHL Statement, April 24, 1939, *Public Papers, 1939*, p. 487.
33. HHL Message to the Legislature, April 27, 1939, ibid., p. 146.
34. HHL Message to the Legislature, April 28, 1939, ibid., p. 156.
35. *New York Times*, April 29, May 5, 13, 1939 (CB, 77: 7336, 7373, 7403); HHL Message to the Legislature, May 12, 1939, *Public Papers, 1939*, pp. 156-57; *Laws of New York, 1939*, chap. 460; HHL Memoir, pp. 708-9.
36. *New York Times*, June 14, 1939 (CB, 78: 7542).
37. *People v. Tremaine*, 13 N.Y.S. 2d 125 at 128.
38. *People v. Tremaine*, 281 N.Y. 1 at 8.
39. HHL Statement, June 22, 1939, *Public Papers, 1939*, p. 493.
40. HHL to Franklin D. Roosevelt, June 23, 1939, "Budget—Appropriation Act, 1939," Reel 13, GP, HHLP; HHL to Allan Nevins, January 4, 1962, "Nevins, Allan," Special File, HHLP.
41. *New York Times*, January 16, 1940, New York *Herald Tribune*, January 21, 1940 (CB, 83: 8139, 8159); HHL Message to the Legislature, January 22, 1940, *Public Papers, 1940*, pp. 30-74.
42. *New York Times*, January 23, 1940, New York *Herald Tribune*, January 24, 1940, Albany *Knickerbocker News*, January 24, 1940 (CB, 83: 8217, 8252); *Buffalo Courier-Express*, February 11, 1940.
43. *New York Times*, January 24, 1940 (CB, 83: 8247).
44. Albany *Knickerbocker News*, February 13, 1940, New York *Herald Tribune*, February 13, 1940 (CB, 83: 8327-30). See also the letters to HHL, in "Budget, 1940," Reel 13, and "Taxes, 1940," Reel 94, GP, HHLP.
45. *New York Times*, February 4, 18, 29, 1940 (CB, 83: 8287, 8360, 8388).
46. HHL Statement, February 29, 1940, *Public Papers, 1940*, p. 498.
47. Albany *Knickerbocker News*, March 5, 1940 (CB, 84: 8410).
48. HHL to Carolin A. Flexner, March 21, 1940, "Flexner, C. A.," Gen. Corr., 1933-40, HHLP. See also Thomas V. Brunkard to Flexner, March 18, 1940, "BRUN," ibid.
49. HHL Messages to the Legislature, March 4, 6, 11, 1940, *Public Papers, 1940*, pp. 168-77; *New York Times*, March 8, 31, 1940 (CB, 84: 8421, 8548).
50. HHL Message to the Legislature, January 27, 1941, *Public Papers, 1941*, pp. 50-91; Albany *Knickerbocker News*, January 28, February 13, 1941, *New York Times*, January 28, 29, March 8, 13, 1941 (CB, 90: 10752, 10760, 10823; 91: 10977, 10993).
51. HHL Message to the Legislature, January 26, 1942, *Public Papers, 1942*, p. 98. See also *New York Times*, January 27, 1942 (CB, 97: 12210).
52. Albany *Knickerbocker News*, March 12, 1942, New York *Herald Tribune*, March 25, 1942 (CB, 98: 12409, 12461).
53. HHL Address, March 27, 1933, *Public Papers, 1933*, pp. 737-38; HHL Memoir, p. 538.
54. HHL Address, December 13, 1936, *Public Papers, 1936*, p. 940. See also HHL Addresses: June 21, 1934, *Public Papers, 1934*, pp. 729-33; August 31, 1935, *Public Papers, 1935*, pp. 890-92; September 20, 1937, *Public Papers, 1937*, pp. 725-27.
55. HHL to Carolin A. Flexner, April 29, 1937, "Flexner, C. A.," Gen. Corr., 1933-40, HHLP; HHL to S. M. Lehman, November 17, 1938, "LEHMAN," ibid.; Allan Nevins, *Herbert H. Lehman and His Era* (New York, 1963), pp. 199-200.
56. HHL Memoir, pp. 541-42.
57. HHL Address, June 6, 1938, *Public Papers, 1938*, p. 509.
58. HHL Address, January 2, 1939, *Public Papers, 1939*, pp. 11-17.

59. HHL Address, August 22, 1939, *Public Papers, 1939*, pp. 623-24.

60. HHL, "Forward," *Public Papers, 1940*, p. 7. See also HHL to Nathan R. Sobel, May 16, 1940, "Sobel, Nathan R.," Gen. Corr., 1933-40, HHLP.

61. HHL to Irving Lehman, August 16, 1940, Special File, HHLP; Nevins, *Herbert H. Lehman*, pp. 209-16.

62. HHL Executive Order, June 12, 1940, *Public Papers, 1940*, p. 556.

63. *Report of the New York State Council of Defense for the Period of August 1, 1940 to December 1, 1941*, in *Public Papers, 1942*, p. 25. For a list of the council's original members, see *Public Papers, 1940*, p. 585. In 1941, lawmakers approved establishment of the council and added legislative leaders to the panel. *Laws of New York, 1941*, chap. 22.

64. HHL to Charles Poletti, November 23, 1940, "Annual Message, 1940," Gen. Corr., 1933-40, HHLP; HHL Message to the Legislature, January 8, 1941, *Public Papers, 1941*, pp. 9-23; *New York Times*, January 8, 1941 (CB, 89: 10530).

65. *New York Times*, March 6, 1941 (CB, 90: 10947).

66. New York *Herald Tribune*, January 4, 8, 1942; *New York Times*, January 5, 16, 1942, Albany *Knickerbocker News*, January 13, February 28, 1942 (CB, 97: 12005-6, 12057, 12117, 12125; 98: 12363).

67. HHL Memoir, p. 557.

68. Benjamin H. Namm to Frieda S. Miller, December 27, 1938, "Miller, Frieda," Gen. Corr., 1933-40, HHLP; Helene P. Gans to HHL, December 4, 1940, "GAM," ibid.; New York State Department of Labor, "Maintaining Labor Standards in 1939," pp. 6-7, Miller to HHL, January 17, 1940, "Labor Department—State Insurance Fund, 1939-40," Reel 54, GP, HHLP; Gans to HHL, March 29, December 13, 1939, "Consumers' League of New York," Reel 21, GP, HHLP; Clara Cook to HHL, January 3, 1940, "Minimum Wage—Laws and Hearings," Reel 63, GP, HHLP; HHL to Mrs. Leopold K. Simon, September 22, 1939, Juliet N. Bartlett to HHL, December 16, 1941, "WOLFE," Reel 105, GP, HHLP.

69. Benjamin H. Namm to HHL, February 3, 1939, "Minimum Wage—Laws and Hearings," Reel 63, GP, HHLP.

70. Benjamin H. Namm to HHL, January 26, 1939, "Miller, Frieda," Gen. Corr., 1933-40, HHLP; HHL Address, February 11, 1941, *Public Papers, 1941*, pp. 619-21.

71. HHL Statement, December 12, 1941, *Public Papers, 1941*, p. 591; *Laws of New York, 1942*, chaps. 4, 544, 618; "Labor Conference," January 1942, Reel 52, GP, HHLP; New York *Herald Tribune*, January 30, 1942 (CB, 97: 12245); HHL Statement, March 14, 1942, *Public Papers, 1942*, pp. 521-23.

72. See *supra*, chap. IV.

73. New York State Department of Labor, "Comparison of New York Unemployment Insurance Law with Laws of Other States," March 27, 1942, "Labor Department—Unemployment Insurance State Advisory Council, 1941-42," Reel 55, GP, HHLP. (Hereinafter referred to as "Labor Dept.—UISAC.")

74. Frieda S. Miller Memorandum, April 24, 1942, chap. 640 (1942), Bill Jackets.

75. HHL Message to the Legislature, March 16, 1942, *Public Papers, 1942*, p. 143.

76. Abraham Epstein hailed these recommendations as "the most enlightening development in this subject since the program was established in New York State over six years ago." Epstein to the Editor, *New York Times*, March 25, 1942.

77. "Report of the New York State Unemployment Insurance Advisory Council for the Year 1941," March 5, 1942, pp. 3-4, 22-23, "Labor Dept.—UISAC, 1941-42," Reel 55, GP,

HHLP; "Report of the Industrial Commissioner on the Unemployment Insurance Legislative Program, 1942," March 5, 1942, "Labor Department—Division of Placement and Unemployment Insurance, 1941-42," Reel 54, GP, HHLP.

78. *New York Times,* March 16, 20, 1942; HHL Message to the Legislature, March 16, 1942, *Public Papers, 1942,* pp. 143-45.

79. *New York Times,* April 17, 1942; *Laws of New York, 1942,* chap. 640.

80. Frieda S. Miller Memorandum, April 24, 1942, chap. 640 (1942), Bill Jackets.

81. HHL Memorandum, May 5, 1942, *Public Papers, 1942,* pp. 344-45.

82. HHL Memoir, pp. 716-17.

83. HHL Statement, May 7, 1942, *Public Papers, 1942,* p. 545; HHL to the Legislature, December 2, 1942, ibid., p. 640; HHL to Franklin D. Roosevelt, May 15, 1942, Cordell Hull to HHL, December 4, 1942, Special File, HHLP; Charles Poletti Memoir, COHC, pp. 26-27.

THE LITTLE NEW DEAL
IN RETROSPECT

During the 1930s, government touched the lives of New Yorkers as it never had before, and all levels of government participated in the expansion of public services. Drawing on federal and state aid, local communities improved their welfare systems and constructed an array of new facilities from airports to sewage-treatment plants. Municipal housing authorities around the state built and managed low-rent apartments for working-class families. In addition to supporting a variety of local projects, Washington made its presence felt directly through a host of exclusively federal programs which created jobs, saved homes from foreclosure, guaranteed workers' right to organize, and helped to raise farm incomes. The state government went to the aid not only of the jobless but also of numerous other groups including slum dwellers, factory workers, farmers and the elderly.

The programs that originated in Albany combined elements of both continuity and change. Some of the less spectacular victories of New York's Little New Deal extended gains of the Progressive Era. During the 1930s, the state relied on a traditional means of curbing child labor—raising the minimum school-leaving age. Albany lawmakers also effectively banned industrial homework, an evil first attacked by progressives at the turn of the century. In addition, the Little New Deal brought improvements in the twenty-year-old system of workmen's compensation. Finally, utility legislation sponsored by Lehman strengthened the Public Service Commission created in 1907.

Yet, in spite of these few direct links to Progressivism, the Little New Deal marked a sharp break with the past. During the Depression, New Yorkers approved a significant expansion of government services. Lehman noted in 1936: "There have been important changes in the public view of the standards of care due to dependent groups. . . . The purpose of government is not only to protect the lives and property of its people . . . but also to bring increased happiness, contentment and security into the homes of its people." [1] The search for security led New York to adopt a number of programs based

249

on the principle of the Welfare State—a government-guaranteed minimum standard of living as a matter of right.[2]

During the previous decades, reform governors had stressed other goals, notably equal opportunity and political democracy. Sounding the themes of Progressivism, Governor Charles Evans Huges once declared:

> It is not our part to plan an ambitious scheme for the reconstruction of society. . . .
> Our immediate duty is more practical than that. It is to obtain from our existing institutions that full measure of freedom of political action and of equal opportunity which they were intended and able to confer.[3]

As progressive chief executives, Hughes and Alfred E. Smith focused on devices to make government more efficient and responsible. Governor Franklin D. Roosevelt had tried, but largely failed, to put the state at the service of underprivileged groups like the aged. Although New York had abandoned the tradition of laissez-faire long before 1933, it had generally stopped short of extending positive government benefits in the form of social insurance or other welfare programs which guaranteed a minimum standard of living.

Like FDR, Lehman was no ideologue but his rhetoric reflected the new attitude of the 1930s. "The changes of the last three years have been essential to the preservation and to the greater development of what we proudly cherish as 'the American system,'" he argued defensively in 1937.[4] Yet within the limits of "the American System" which he obviously accepted, Lehman shifted his emphasis from that of previous generations.

> I believe in the profit motive, individual opportunity, reward for individual effort, but not through uncontrolled exploitation of the under-privileged.
> I believe in the rights of capital. But I believe with equal ardor in the rights of labor and of the consumer. . . .
> I believe, with abiding faith, in liberty and freedom. But I want the liberty to be the freedom to live fully and prosper greatly—not the freedom to be exploited by circumstances or starved by want.[5]

Expressions like "rights of labor" and "freedom from want," which were foreign to Progressivism, became the rallying cries of the New Deal in Washington and the Little New Deal in Albany.

Following the imperatives of the 1930s, New York adopted a variety of programs that laid the foundation for the Welfare State. The poor received aid from Albany for unemployment relief and social security against the burdens of old age, physical disabilities, and fatherless families. Labor legislation instituted a minimum wage system and raised other barriers against the exploitation of women and child laborers. Workers in intrastate businesses received the right to organize and bargain collectively with their employers. Abandoning complete reliance on private enterprise, New York initiated public housing to provide low-rent homes for working-class families. Upstate milk producers got government-fixed prices designed to boost the incomes of the majority of

New York farmers. On a number of fronts the state intervened to assure a minimum standard of living for many New Yorkers unable to earn it themselves. Despite New York's history of reform, more breakthroughs came under Lehman than any of his predecessors. "In his quiet and methodical way, this ex-banker has achieved far more than was accomplished by either Smith or Roosevelt," *The Nation* observed in 1940.[6]

The causes of Lehman's remarkable successes are more difficult to explain than his list of achievements. New York naturally benefited from the national forces, notably FDR's New Deal and the Depression, which stimulated change. But, in addition, unique local conditions helped to make the 1930s a turning point in New York State.

The New Deal in Washington created a favorable climate for reform, but the president and Congress played a limited role in the passage of Albany's Little New Deal. Except for parts of the Social Security Act, the federal government offered few direct incentives for state legislative action. Indirectly, national programs like the NRA codes encouraged New York to apply similar labor standards to intrastate workers. Albany also sometimes moved in advance of Congress, as with umemployment relief, job insurance, and minimum wages. Despite the large number of Washington officials, including the president, who had come from New York, there was surprisingly little contact between state and federal New Dealers, whose programs often dovetailed without any conscious effort. "I don't think it requires any plan or liaison for a liberal governor to follow some of the measures of the liberal Federal administration," FDR's speech writer and confidant, Samuel Rosenman, later reflected.[7]

For the most part, Albany and Washington went their separate ways during the 1930s. Although some scholars point to the decade as a period marked by cooperative federalism in which state and federal governments shared overlapping responsibilities, this was generally not the case in New York.[8] With the exception of social security, Albany developed its own Welfare State independent of the national one. To supplement federal aid for public housing and unemployment relief, New York instituted a long-range system of loans and grants-in-aid for local communities. In the field of labor legislation, Albany lawmakers established minimum wages, controls on child labor, the Board of Mediation, and the State Labor Relations Board to cover intrastate workers excluded from U.S. statutes. State and federal measures often paralleled each other, but they delineated separate, not overlapping, spheres of responsibility in attacking common problems.

Yet Washington often provided a model for Albany. Enabling legislation for several state programs, such as the Labor Relations Board and public housing subsidies, was copied almost verbatim from federal laws. Even more important, the host of reforms adopted in Washington lent an air of legitimacy to change at every level of government. Indeed, the description "Little New Deal" implied a sanction that Lehman would have lacked without Roosevelt.

The Depression also gave reform much of its impetus in New York. The collapse of the economy decimated the middle class, revealed the impersonal causes of poverty, and stimulated a rising demand for government action. Advocates of state intervention used the economic crisis to prove the need for unemployment insurance, permanent public assistance for dependent groups, minimum wages, and public housing. Driven by a sense of urgency, lobbyists, politicians, and judges repeatedly testified to the effect of the Depression on their thinking. Opponents of change, especially businessmen, also cited poor economic conditions as a reason for postponing adoption of welfare legislation which would increase costs or in any way hamper recovery, but this plea usually failed to block passage of reforms. After the crisis had hit so many people and hung on for years, a willingness to permit previously unthinkable innovations swept the state. This new spirit led Lehman to declare: "We are living in an exciting era—an era in which things are moving so rapidly and with an unprecedented will to progress." [9]

A number of factors made New York an especially fertile ground for reform ideas. Although Progressivism did not supply a rationale for the Welfare State, New York's progressive heritage and tradition of strong executives prepared New Yorkers to accept further change. Even the Court of Appeals, one of the most important tribunals in the country, went along with all of the Little New Deal, except for the 1933 minimum wage law, at a time when the United States Supreme Court was overturning much federal legislation. As a result of favorable state rulings, contested programs like unemployment insurance and farm price supports had the blessing of the Court of Appeals when they reached the Supreme Court.

The Empire State's urban character also gave reform much of its momentum. Time and again, social workers appealing for some kind of state aid pointed to conditions in New York City as evidence of the pressing need. Whether it was unemployment, housing, or sweatshops, the nation's largest city invited action because of the severity of its crises. New York City not only generated problems but also produced leaders who called for some of the most radical solutions. In addition to a variety of social welfare agencies, the metropolis contained several important groups, notably the Socialist and American Labor parties, which stood to the left of the Democrats. While prodding liberal politicians, these minority parties offered policies which made programs like the Little New Deal appear less radical by contrast. Writing to Norman Thomas about legislative strategy in Albany, Abraham Epstein of the Conference for Old Age Security held that "our Association should be as pregmatic [sic] as possible and it is up to you and the socialist party to contend that the bills are insufficient." [10]

The wealth of the Empire State helped make the Little New Deal possible. Although the Depression sometimes prevented the prompt implementation of costly measures like job insurance, New Yorkers generally believed that local employers could afford improved benefits at least as well as their counterparts around the country. Moreover, even during the economic crisis, New York raised money for programs such as unemployment relief more easily than sister states, because, as contemporary studies pointed out, New York had access to much greater tax resources.[11]

New York's progressive tradition, urban character, and wealth were significant preconditions for the success of reform in the 1930s, but the energy for change came from a small number of New Yorkers. Advocates of the Welfare State, particularly social workers who had long backed increased government services, swung into action during Lehman's administration. Many, including members of the National Consumers' League, the American Association for Labor Legislation, and the American Association for Social Security, led national movements, but working out of headquarters in New York City, they focused much of their attention on nearby Albany which, after all, was the capital of the country's most populous state. Well-organized groups stood behind virtually every program that became a part of the Little New Deal. The NCL spearheaded the drive for minimum wages; the New York Child Labor Committee took care of its speciality; the AALL and the AASS backed unemployment insurance; the State Federation of Labor fought for collective bargaining rights; the Dairymen's League supported government aid for agriculture. On the other hand, enabling legislation for social security went down to defeat in 1936 because reformers failed to organize a campaign behind it. Although many groups had championed their particular causes for years, they suddenly found widespread popular approval among voters and lawmakers after the Depression hit. In this more favorable atmosphere, social workers often expanded their demands, as in the case of job insurance, or developed new programs, such as public housing.

The impact of interest groups also explains some of the shortcomings of the Little New Deal. When organized labor opposed minimum wages for men, the proposal never reached the floor of the legislature. Private utility corporations blocked public development of the state's power resources. Physicians and pharmacists stood in the way of health insurance. With these few exceptions, however, the Little New Deal achieved most of its objectives. Yet its very goals were largely determined by established reform groups so that people in need, but without a voice in Albany, received fewer government benefits. Early in the 1940s, when blacks and aliens constituted the bulk of New York City's welfare cases, many were temporarily forced to go on municipal work relief, which was used in effect to test the worthiness of people who had previously received home relief as a right. The poorest slum dwellers were not permitted in public housing because they could not afford the rents. Unorganized agricultural workers did not get the protection of labor laws. "Whether we like it or not," the general secretary of the State Farm Bureau observed in 1939, "we must face the fact that this is the day and age of pressure government. At Albany many organized forces are at work in behalf of special interests. Agriculture is no exception nor can it afford to be an exception." [12]

Governor Lehman often reflected on the role of various interest groups in state affairs. He denied the claim that "in the enactment of economic and social reforms advantage is given to certain classes or groups, while discrimination is practiced against others. That I am confident is not true . . . in this State." [13] Nevertheless, Lehman pictured government as an arbiter among economic blocs.

Government must instill in all groups faith and confidence in the future. In turn each of these groups must trust in and co-operate with government and with each other. . . .

Within [New York's] borders are many farmers, large and small business enterprises, millions of wage earners and salaried employees and thirteen million consumers.

The interests of all these groups are in the last analysis common. Their interdependence has time and again been demonstrated in the economic history of the Nation. If one group is not adequately compensated and protected, the others soon[er] or later will suffer. Business cannot prosper at the cost of labor. Labor cannot prosper by destroying business. The consumer cannot flourish at the sacrifice of the farmer. The same principle controls the relations between business and the farmer, the consumer and the wage earner.

During the past five years *we have done much, by governmental policies, to balance these different interests.*[14]

Since the Little New Deal strengthened the power of farmers and laborers, businessmen felt left out and threatened. They were not even relied on for advice, as Lehman later pointed out. "I usually got much more out of my consultations with the labor leaders than I did with the state Chamber of Commerce, or the state equivalent of the National Association of Manufacturers," he recalled. "I knew perfectly well the answer I was going to get from those fellows, almost invariably." [15] Employers did not draft a single piece of reform legislation, and they rarely supported measures sponsored by competing interests. Although members of the laundry industry backed minimum wages as a means of regulating destructive competition, such outright endorsements of reform legislation by businessmen were unusual in the period. Recalling those days, Lehman later declared that corporate interests "fought everything, and . . . at that time, there were very, very few liberal-minded employers." [16]

In spite of the hostility of business groups, most of the Little New Deal passed with the aid of Republican lawmakers. Except for the year 1935, the G.O.P. controlled at least one house of the legislature, as it had during the terms of Governors Smith and Roosevelt when Old Guard Republicans tried, often successfully, to block welfare measures. Under the impact of the Depression and the New Deal's proven popularity, a new generation of G.O.P. legislators from urban areas accepted an expanded role for government in society. As early as 1933, a small number of Republicans supplied the votes to ensure adoption of minimum wage legislation, but most of their colleagues stood against the Little New Deal for several more years. In the wake of the 1936 election, most G.O.P. lawmakers approved passage of social security, the State Labor Relations Board, and Public Housing, even though they continued to protest rising budgets and taxes. By 1938, with the rout of the Old Guard largely completed, the Republican-dominated constitutional convention accepted a sweeping amendment which set down the principle of the Welfare State. The platform on which Thomas E. Dewey ran for governor later that year generally endorsed the advances of the Little New Deal and promised simply better administration under Republicans.[17]

In addition to the numerous other factors which helped bring about the Little New Deal in New York, one man—Governor Herbert H. Lehman—also contributed to the extraordinary success of reform in the 1930s. None of the Little New Deal proposals originated with Lehman, but he embraced virtually everything suggested by the forces of change. "Lehman," one federal official accurately recalled, "was really the fountainhead of all activity in the state of New York." [18] Genuinely interested in the plight of those

Americans who had not fared as well as he, Lehman, unlike most New Yorkers of his class, saw "no inconsistency between being a business man, and a liberal." [19] He listened to social workers and union leaders who presented government-sponsored remedies for economic exploitation and dependency, and then in his unspectacular manner the governor fought doggedly for legislative approval. Organized labor and social welfare groups frequently carried the burden of the struggle, but Lehman lent an air of legitimacy to radical proposals, some of which the state had rejected in the past. His accomplishments evoked praise from the political left and right. One man wrote the governor in 1936: "Being a socialist, I could hardly be expected to approve the acts of your administration. . . . Yet candor compels the admission that you have given the citizens of New York an honest, efficient, humane and enlightened administration." [20] "The State has made progress toward a businesslike humanitarianism," the *New York Times* reflected editorially in 1938. "For much of that progress our modest, hard-working and undramatic Governor can take credit. He has guided us in a labor and social program transcending any ever executed in America." [21]

NOTES

1. HHL Address, April 25, 1936, *Public Papers, 1936,* p. 876. A recent history of New York State agreed with Lehman. "The welfare program adopted during Lehman's administration as governor reflected a basic change in the public's attitude toward the government's responsibility to the people of New York. Poverty, which had once been a mark of opprobrium, was now considered a misfortune for which the individual was not responsible. Public relief, which many people had earlier referred to as a 'dole,' was now generally accepted as a more equitable and efficacious method than private charity for relieving human misery. What had once been considered 'socialistic' and 'un-American' [was] now accepted as commonplace." David M. Ellis et al., *A History of New York State* (Ithaca, N.Y., 1967), p. 426.
2. For a discussion of the concept of the Welfare State, see Leonard Krieger, "The Idea of the Welfare State in Europe and the United States," *Journal of the History of Ideas,* XXIV (October-December 1963): 553-68.
3. Quoted in Merlo J. Pusey, *Charles Evans Hughes,* (2 vols.; New York, 1951), I: 216.
4. HHL Address, January 1, 1937, *Public Papers, 1937,* p. 13.
5. HHL Address, October 24, 1936, *Public Papers, 1936,* p. 984.
6. *The Nation,* January 13, 1940, p. 30.
7. Samuel I. Rosenman Memoir, COHC, p. 21. See also Henry Morgenthau, Jr., Memoir, COHC, p. 2.
8. For studies of federalism which emphasize its cooperative elements, see Jane Perry Clark, *The Rise of a New Federalism: Federal-State Cooperation in the United States* (New York, 1938); Daniel J. Elazar, *American Federalism: A View from the States* (New York, 1966); Morton Grodzins, *The American System: A View of Government in the United States,* ed. by Daniel J. Elazar (Chicago, 1966).
9. HHL Address, February 13, 1934, *Public Papers, 1934,* p. 699.

10. Epstein to Thomas, February 23, 1929, Box 38, Epstein Papers (Columbia).
11. See, for example, Mabel Newcomer, *An Index of the Taxpaying Ability of State and Local Governments* (New York, 1935), passim.
12. "Report of the General Secretary to the Annual Meeting," November 19, 1939, Box 30, New York State Farm Bureau Federation Papers, Collection of Regional History, Cornell University.
13. HHL Address, January 1, 1937, *Public Papers, 1937,* p. 12.
14. HHL Message to the Legislature, January 5, 1938, *Public Papers, 1938,* p. 32. (Italics added.)
15. HHL Memoir, COHC, p. 454.
16. Ibid., p. 362.
17. Judith Stein, "The Birth of Liberal Republicanism in New York State, 1932-1938" (unpublished Ph.D. dissertation, Yale University, 1968), pp. 205-37 et passim.
18. Anna Rosenberg Memoir, COHC, p. 4.
19. HHL Address, October 24, 1935, *Public Papers, 1936,* p. 984.
20. Manuel C. to HHL, May 21, 1936, CB, 40.
21. *New York Times,* January 6, 1938.

BIBLIOGRAPHY

1. MANUSCRIPT COLLECTIONS

Agricultural Marketing Service Records. Record Group 136, National Archives.

Agricultural Stabilization and Conservation Service (AAA) Records. Record Group 145, National Archives.

American Association for Labor Legislation (John B. Andrews) Papers. New York School of Industrial and Labor Relations, Documentation Center, Cornell University.

American Association for Social Security (Abraham Epstein) Papers. New York School of Industrial and Labor Relations, Documentation Center, Cornell University.

Howard E. Babcock Papers. Collection of Regional History, Cornell University.

Maurice C. Burritt Papers. Collection of Regional History, Cornell University.

Citizens Union Papers. Special Collections, Columbia University.

Civil Works Administration Records. Record Group 69, National Archives.

Civilian Conservation Corps Records. Record Group 35, National Archives.

Consumers' League of New York Papers. New York School of Industrial and Labor Relations, Documentation Center, Cornell University.

Morris L. Cooke Papers. Franklin D. Roosevelt Library.

Royal S. Copeland Papers. Michigan Historical Collections, University of Michigan.

Edward F. Corsi Papers. Syracuse University Library.

Dairymen's League Papers. Collection of Regional History, Cornell University.

Frank N. Decker Papers. Collection of Regional History, Cornell University.

Department of Agriculture Records. Record Group 16, National Archives.

Mary W. Dewson Papers. Franklin D. Roosevelt Library.

Mary W. Dewson Papers. Schlesinger Library, Radcliffe College.

Division of Labor Standards Records. Record Group 100, National Archives.

Abraham Epstein Papers. Special Collections, Columbia University.

Farmers' Union of New York Milkshed Papers. Collection of Regional History, Cornell University.

257

Federal Emergency Relief Administration Records. Record Group 69, National Archives.

Homer Folks Papers. Special Collections, Columbia University.

Walter Gellhorn Papers. Special Collections, Columbia University.

Sidney Hillman Papers. Amalgamated Clothing Workers of America Library, New York City.

Harry Hopkins Papers. Franklin D. Roosevelt Library.

Fiorello La Guardia Papers. New York City Municipal Archives.

Herbert H. Lehman Papers. School of International Affairs, Columbia University.

Metropolitan Co-operative Milk Producers Bargaining Agency Papers. Collection of Regional History, Cornell University.

Henry Morgenthau, Jr., Diaries. Franklin D. Roosevelt Library.

National Consumers' League Papers. Library of Congress.

National Labor Relations Board Records. Record Group 25, National Archives.

National Youth Administration Records. Record Group 199, National Archives.

New York Child Labor Committee Papers. New York State Library, Albany, N.Y.

New York State Bill Jacket Collection. New York Public Library.

New York State Farm Bureau Papers. Collection of Regional History, Cornell University.

Leland Olds Papers. Franklin D. Roosevelt Library.

Charles Poletti Papers. Herbert H. Lehman Papers, Columbia University.

Public Works Administration Records. Record Group 135, National Archives.

Lindsay Rogers Papers. Special Collections, Columbia University.

Franklin D. Roosevelt Papers. Franklin D. Roosevelt Library.

Dorothy Rosenman Papers. Special Collections, Columbia University.

Mary Kingsbury Simkhovitch Papers. Schlesinger Library, Radcliffe College.

Social Security Administration Records. Record Group 47, National Archives.

Nathan Straus Papers. Franklin D. Roosevelt Library.

Norman Thomas Papers. New York Public Library.

Robert F. Wagner Papers. Georgetown University Library.

Lillian Wald Papers. New York Public Library.

Lillian Wald Papers. Special Collections, Columbia University.

Frank P. Walsh Papers. New York Public Library.

Edith Elmer Wood Papers. Avery Library, Columbia University.

Works Progress Administration Records. Record Group 69, National Archives.

2. ORAL HISTORIES

Collection of Regional History, Cornell University:
    Charles H. Baldwin Memoir

Oral History Collection, Columbia University:

George W. Alger Memoir
Helen Altschul Memoir
William H. Davis Memoir
Paul Douglas Memoir
David Dressler Memoir
Julius C. C. Edelstein Memoir
James A. Farley Memoir
Carolin Flexner Memoir
Edward J. Flynn Memoir
Homer Folks Memoir
Eugene J. Keogh Memoir
Herbert H. Lehman Memoir
George Meany Memoir
Henry Morgenthau, Jr., Memoir
Warren Moscow Memoir
Louis H. Pink Memoir
Chalrles Poletti Memoir
Eleanor Roosevelt Memoir
Anna Rosenberg Memoir
Samuel I. Rosenman Memoir
Marc Tanenbaum Memoir
George S. Van Schaick Memoir

3. GOVERNMENT PUBLICATIONS

New York City. Housing Authority. *Twenty-five Years of Public Housing, 1935-1960.* New York, 1960.

New York City. *Report of Mayor La Guardia's Committee on Unemployment Relief.* New York, 1935.

———. *Tenement House Department Report.* New York, 1934-38.

New York Red Book. Albany, 1900-42.

New York State. *Annual Report of the Department of Agriculture and Markets for the Year 1938.* Leg. Doc. No. 37, 1939.

———. *Annual Report of the Department of Agriculture and Markets for the Year 1939.* Leg. Doc. No. 37, 1940.

———. *Annual Report of the Department of Social Welfare, July 1, 1941-June 30, 1942.* Leg. Doc. No. 11, 1943.

———. *Annual Report of the Power Authority of the State of New York.* New York, 1932-44.

———. *Annual Report of the Public Service Commission.* Albany, 1933-43.

———. *Assembly Journal,* Albany, 1933-42.

New York State. Board of Social Welfare. *Annual Report for the Year 1938.* Leg. Doc. No. 68, 1939.

————. *Annual Report for the Year 1939*. Leg. Doc. No. 67, 1940.

————. *Annual Report for the Year 1940*. Leg Doc. No. 68, 1941.

————. *Annual Report for the Year 1941*. Leg. Doc. No. 28, 1942.

————. *Annual Report for the Year 1942*. Leg. Doc. No. 38, 1943.

New York State. Constitutional Convention Committee. *New York City Government Functions and Problems*. Albany, 1938.

————. *Problems Relating to Bill of Rights and General Welfare*. Albany, 1938.

————. *Problems Relating to Taxation and Finance*. Albany, 1938.

New York State. Department of Audit and Control. *Annual Report*. Albany, 1933-43.

New York State. Department of Labor. *Annual Report of the Industrial Commissioner*. Leg. Doc No. 21, 1934-41.

————. *Annual Report of the Industrial Commissioner, 1941*. Leg. Doc. No. 90, 1942.

————. *Minimum Wage and the Laundry Industry*. Special Bulletin No. 201, 1938.

————. *Trend of Employment in New York State Factories from 1914 to 1939*. Albany, 1940.

————. *Some Social and Economic Aspects of Homework*. Special Bulletin No. 158, 1929.

New York State. Department of Social Welfare. *Democracy Cares: The Story Behind Public Assistance in New York State*. Albany, 1941.

New York State. Governor's Commission on Unemployment Relief. *The Administration of Home Relief in New York City*. Albany, 1935.

————. *The Public Employment Services in the State of New York*. Albany, 1935.

————. *Public Relief for Transient and Non-Settled Persons in the State of New York*. Albany, 1936.

————. *State and Local Welfare Organization in the State of New York*. Albany, 1936.

————. *Work Relief in the State of New York*. Albany, 1936.

————. *Work Relief Projects of the Public Works Type in the State of New York*. Albany, 1935.

New York State. *Joint Legislative Committee to Investigate Public Utilities, Final Report*. Leg. Doc. No. 78, 1936.

————. *Laws of the State of New York*. Albany, 1933-42.

————. *Manual for the Use of the Legislature of the State of New York*. Albany, 1933-42.

————. *Proceedings of the Judiciary Committee of the Senate in the Matter of the Investigation Requested by Senator Thayer*. Leg. Doc. No. 102, 1934.

————. *Public Papers of Herbert H. Lehman, Forty-ninth Governor of the State of New York*. 10 vols. Albany, 1934-47.

————. *Record of the Constitutional Convention of the State of New York*. Albany, 1938.

————. *Records and Briefs of the New York State of Appeals*. Albany, 1934-37.

————. *Report of the Joint Legislative Committee on State Fiscal Policies*. Leg. Doc. No. 41, 1938.

————. *Report of the Joint Legislative Committee on Unemployment*, February 20, 1933. Leg. Doc. No. 66, 1933.

————. *Report of the Joint Legislative Committee to Investigate the Milk Control Law*, March 22, 1937. Leg. Doc. No. 81, 1937.

———. *Report of the Joint Legislative Committee to Investigate the Milk Industry*. Leg. Doc. No. 114, 1933.

———. *Report of the Milk Control Board, March, 1934*. Leg. Doc. No. 74, 1934.

———. *Report of the New York Commission on Old Age Security*. Leg. Doc. No. 67, 1930.

———. *Report of the New York State Labor Relations Board*. Albany, 1940-43.

———. *Report of the State Board of Housing for the Year 1928*. Leg. Doc. No. 95, 1929.

———. *Report of the State Board of Housing for the Year 1929*. Leg. Doc. No. 84, 1930.

———. *Report of the State Board of Housing for the Year 1931*. Leg. Doc. No. 84, 1932.

———. *Report of the State Board of Housing for the Year 1937*. Leg. Doc. No. 66, 1938.

———. *Report of the State Board of Housing for the Year 1938*. Leg. Doc. No. 60, 1939.

———. *Report of the State Commissioner of Housing for the Year 1941*. Leg. Doc. No. 29, 1942.

———. *Report of the State Commissioner of Housing for the Year 1942*. Leg. Doc. No. 25, 1943.

———. *Report of the State Superintendent of Housing for the Year 1939*. Leg. Doc. No. 70, 1940.

———. *Senate Journal*. Albany, 1933-42.

New York State. Temporary Emergency Relief Administration. *Administration of Public Employment Relief in New York State: Its Scope, Accomplishments and Cost, April 1, 1934-March 31, 1935*. Albany, 1935.

———. *Five Million People, One Billion Dollars*. Albany, 1937.

U.S. Congress. House. Committee on Appropriations. *Hearings* before a Subcommittee of the Committee on Appropriations, U.S. House of Representatives, on the Emergency Relief Appropriation Act of 1938, 75th Cong., 3d sess., 1938.

U.S. Congress. House. *Report of the Federal Trade Commission on the Sale and Distribution of Milk and Milk Products: New York Milk Sales Area*. House Doc. 95, 75th Cong., 1st sess., 1937.

U.S. Congress. Senate. Committee on Manufacturers. *Hearings* before a Subcommittee of the Committee on Manufacturers, U.S. Senate, on S. 5125, 72d Cong., 2d sess., 1933.

U.S. Department of Commerce. Bureau of the Census. *Fifteenth Census of the United States, 1930: Agriculture*, Vol. II, pt. 1.

———. *Fifteenth Census of the United States, 1930: Population*, Vol. III, pt. 2.

———. *Historical Review of State and Local Government Finances*. State and Local Government Special Studies, No. 25. Washington, 1948.

———. *Sixteenth Census of the United States, 1940: Population*, Vol. I, pt. 1.

U.S. Department of Labor. Women's Bureau. *A Brief History of the New York Minimum Wage Case*. Washington, 1936.

4. COURT CASES

Associated Industries of New York State v. Department of Labor, et al. 286 N.Y.S. 465 (1936).

Baldwin v. G. A. F. Seelig. 294 U.S. 499 (1935).

Bronx Gas and Electric Company v. Maltbie, et al. 268 N.Y. 278 (1935).

Metropolitan Life Insurance Co. v. NYS Labor Relations Board, et al. 280 N.Y. 194 (1939).

Morehead v. New York ex rel. Tipaldo. 298 U.S. 587 (1936).

Nebbia v. New York. 291 U.S. 502 (1934).

New York City Housing Authority v. Muller. 270 N.Y. 333 (1936).

Noyes v. Erie & Wyoming Farmers Co-operative Corp. 10 N.Y.S. 2d 114 (1939).

People ex rel. Tipaldo v. Morehead. 282 N.Y.S. 576 (1935).

People ex rel. Tipaldo v. Morehead. 282 N.Y.S. 233 (1936)

People v. Nebbia. 262 N.Y. 259 (1933).

People v. Tremaine. 281 N.Y. 1 (1939).

United States v. Rock Royal Cooperative, Inc., et al. 307 U.S. 533 (1939).

West Coast Hotel Co. v. Parrish. 300 U.S. 387 (1937).

W. H. H. Chamberlin, Inc. and E. C. Stearns v. Elmer F. Andrews, et al. 286 N.Y.S. 242 (1936).

W. H. H. Chamberlin, Inc. v. Elmer F. Andrews, et al. 299 U.S. 515 (1936).

Yonkers Electric Light and Power Company v. Maltbie, et al. 271 N.Y. 364 (1936).

5. NEWSPAPERS

Albany *Knickerbocker News*
Albany *Knickerbocker Press*
Brooklyn Daily Eagle
Buffalo Courier-Express
Buffalo Evening News
New York American
New York *Daily News*
New York Evening Post
New York *Herald Tribune*
New York Sun
New York Times
New York World-Telegram
Rochester *Democrat and Chronicle*
Rochester Times-Union

6. CONTEMPORARY PERIODICALS

American Agriculturist
American Labor Legislation Review
Chamber of Commerce of the State of New York *Monthly Bulletin*
The Dairy Farmer
Dairymen's League News
Monitor (Associated Industries)
Monroe Country Farm and Home Bureau News
National Association of Housing Officials News
New York State Federation of Labor Bulletin
New York State Federation of Labor, *Official Proceedings of Annual Conventions*
Public Housing Progress
The Rural New-Yorker
S.C.A.A. News
Social Security (American Association for Social Security)

7. BOOKS

Abrams, Charles. *The Future of Housing*. New York, 1946.

Alfred, Helen. *Municipal Housing*. New York, 1932.

Alfred, Helen, ed. *Towards a Socialist America: A Symposium of Essays*. New York, 1958.

Alsop, Joseph, and Catledge, Turner. *The 168 Days*. Garden City, N.Y., 1938.

Altmeyer, Arthur J. *The Formative Years of Social Security*. Madison, Wis., 1966.

Anderson, W. A. *The Membership of Farmers in New York Organizations*. Ithaca, N.Y., 1938.

Bellush, Bernard. *Franklin D. Roosevelt as Governor of New York*. New York, 1955.

Benedict, Murray R. *Farm Policies of the United States, 1790-1950*. New York, 1953.

Bernstein, Irving. *The Lean Years: A History of the American Worker, 1920-1933*. Boston, 1960.

———. *The New Deal Collective Bargaining Policy*. Berkeley, Calif., 1950.

———. *Turbulent Years: A History of the American Worker, 1933-1941*. Boston, 1970.

Black, John D. *The Dairy Industry and the AAA*. Washington, 1935.

Bonbright, James C. *Principles of Public Utility Rates*. New York, 1961.

Bonbright, James C., and Means, Gardiner C. *The Holding Company: Its Public Significance and Its Regulation*. New York, 1932.

Brown, Josephine C. *Public Relief, 1929-30*. New York, 1940.

Burner, David. *The Politics of Provincialism: The Democratic Party in Transition, 1918-1932*. New York, 1968.

Burnham, Walter Dean. *Critical Elections and the Mainsprings of American Politics*. New York, 1970.

Caldwell, Lynton K. *The Government and Administration of New York.* New York, 1954.

Callcott, Mary Stevenson. *Child Labor Legislation in New York.* New York, 1931.

Carpenter, Jesse Thomas. *Competition and Collective Bargaining in the Needle Trades.* Ithaca, N.Y., 1972.

Carter, Dewey J., ed. *The Fifty Year Battle for a Living Price for Milk: A History of the Dairymen's League.* New York, 1939.

A Centennial: Lehman Brothers, 1850-1950. New York, 1950.

Chambers, Clarke A. *Seedtime of Reform: American Social Service and Social Action, 1918-1933.* Ann Arbor, Mich., 1963.

Charles, Searle F. *Minister of Relief: Harry Hopkins and the Depression.* Syracuse, N.Y., 1963.

Citizens' Housing Council. *Housing the Metropolis.* New York, 1938.

Clark, Jane Perry. *The Rise of New Federalism: Federal-State Cooperation in the United States.* New York, 1938.

Colman, Gould P. *Education & Agriculture: A History of the New York State College of Agriculture at Cornell University.* Ithaca, N.Y., 1963.

Commons, John R., and Andrews, John B. *Principles of Labor Legislation.* 4th rev. ed. New York, 1936.

Connable, Alfred, and Silberfarb, Edward. *Tigers of Tammany: Nine Men Who Ran New York.* New York, 1967.

Cortner, Richard C. *The Wagner Act Cases.* Knoxville, 1964.

Derber, Milton, and Young, Edwin, eds. *Labor and the New Deal.* Madison, Wis., 1957.

Dillon, John J. *Seven Decades of Milk: A History of New York's Dairy Industry.* New York, 1941.

Dubofsky, Melvyn. *When Workers Organize: New York City in the Progressive Era.* Amherst, Mass., 1958.

Ebenstein, William. *The Law of Public Housing.* Madison, Wis., 1940.

Elazar, Daniel J. *American Federalism: A View from the States.* New York, 1966.

Ellis, David M.; Frost, James A.; Syrett, Harold C.; and Carman, Harry J. *A History of New York State.* Ithaca, N.Y., 1967.

Epstein, Abraham. *The Challenge of the Aged.* New York, 1928.

———. *Insecurity: A Challenge to America.* New York, 1933.

Everett, Robinson O., and Johnston, John D., eds. *Housing.* Dobbs Ferry, N.Y., 1968.

Fabricant, Solomon. *The Trend of Governmental Activity in the United States Since 1900.* New York, 1952.

Farley, James A. *Behind the Ballots.* New York, 1938.

———. *Jim Farley's Story: The Roosevelt Years.* New York, 1948.

Felt, Jeremy P. *Hostages of Reform: Child Labor Reform in New York State.* Syracuse, N.Y., 1965.

The Finances and Financial Administration of New York City: Recommendations and Report of the Sub-committee on Budget, Finance, and Revenue, of the City Committee on Plan and Survey. Herbert H. Lehman, chairman. New York, 1928.

Fisher, Robert Moore. *20 Years of Public Housing.* New York, 1959.

Flick, Alexander C., ed. *History of the State of New York,* Vol. VII. New York, 1933-37.

Flynn, Edward J. *You're the Boss: The Practice of American Politics.* New York, 1947.

Ford, Corey. *Donovan of OSS.* Boston, 1970.

Ford, James. *Slums and Housing with Special Reference to New York City.* 2 vols. Cambridge, Mass., 1936.

Fortune, editors of. *Housing America.* New York, 1932.

Frankfurter, Felix, and Greene, Nathan. *The Labor Injunction.* New York, 1930.

Freedman, Max, ed. *Roosevelt and Frankfurter: Their Correspondence, 1928-1945.* Boston, 1967.

Freidel, Frank. *Franklin D. Roosevelt: The Triumph.* Boston, 1956.

Friedman, Lawrence M. *Government and Slum Housing: A Century of Frustration.* Chicago, 1968.

Fuchs, Lawrence M. *American Ethnic Politics.* New York, 1968.

———. *The Political Behavior of American Jews.* Glencoe, Ill., 1956.

Garrett, Charles. *The La Guardia Years, Machine and Reform Politics in New York City.* New Brunswick, N.J., 1961.

Glaeser, Martin G. *Public Utilities in American Capitalism.* New York, 1957.

Goldmark, Josephine. *Impatient Crusader: Florence Kelley's Life Story.* Urbana, Ill., 1953.

Goulden, Joseph C. *Meany.* New York, 1972.

Grodzins, Morton. *The American System: A View of Government in the United States.* Edited by Daniel J. Elazar. Chicago, 1966.

Haber, William, and Murray, Merrill G. *Unemployment Insurance in the American Economy.* Homewood, Ill., 1966.

Hall, Fred S. *Forty Years, 1902-1942: The Work of the New York Child Labor Committee.* Brattleboro, Vt., 1942.

Hall, Helen. *Unfinished Business in Neighborhood and Nation.* New York, 1971.

Halpern, Irving W.; Stanislaus, John N.; and Botein, Bernard. *The Slum and Crime: A Statistical Study of the Distribution of Adult and Juvenile Delinquents in the Boroughs of Manhattan and Brooklyn.* New York, 1934.

Handlin, Oscar. *Al Smith and His America.* Boston, 1958.

Hanslowe, Kurt L. *Procedures and Policies of the New York State Labor Relations Board.* Ithaca, N.Y., 1964.

Hedrick, Ulysses Prentiss. *A History of Agriculture in the State of New York.* Albany, 1933.

Horton, John T.; Williams, Edward T.; and Douglass, Harry S. *History of Northwestern New York: Erie, Niagara, Wyoming, Genesee and Orleans Counties.* 3 vols. New York, 1947.

Hughes, Rupert. *Attorney for the People: The Story of Thomas E. Dewey.* Boston, 1940.

Huthmacher, J. Joseph. *Senator Robert F. Wagner and the Rise of Urban Liberalism.* New York, 1968.

Jacob, Herbert, and Vines, Kenneth N., eds. *Politics in the American States: A Comparative Analysis.* Boston, 1965.

John B. Andrews Memorial Symposium on Labor Legislation and Social Security. Madison, Wis., 1949.

Josephson, Matthew and Hannah. *Al Smith: Hero of the Cities.* Boston, 1969.

Kaltenborn, Howard S. *Governmental Adjustment of Labor Disputes.* Chicago, 1943.

Killingsworth, Charles C. *State Labor Relations Acts: A Study of Public Policy.* Chicago, 1948.

Laidlaw, Walter, ed. *Population of the City of New York, 1890-1930.* New York, 1932.

Leiserson, William M. *Right and Wrong in Labor Relations.* Berkeley, Calif., 1938.

Lens, Sidney. *Left, Right and Center: Conflicting Forces in American Labor.* Hinsdale, Ill., 1949.

Leuchtenburg, William E. *Franklin D. Roosevelt and the New Deal, 1932-1940.* New York, 1963.

———. *The Perils of Prosperity, 1914-32.* Chicago, 1958.

Leven, Maurice; Moulton, Harold G.; and Warburton, Clark. *America's Capacity to Consume.* Washington, 1934.

Levin, Jack. *Power Ethics.* New York, 1931.

Lindley, Ernest K. *Franklin D. Roosevelt: A Career in Progressive Democracy.* Indianapolis, 1931.

Lininger, F. F. *Dairy Products under the Agricultural Adjustment Act.* Washington, 1934.

Lubell, Samuel. *The Future of American Politics.* 3rd ed., rev. New York, 1965.

Lubove, Roy. *The Progressives and the Slums: Tenement House Reform in New York City, 1890-1917.* Pittsburgh, 1962.

———. *The Struggle for Social Security, 1900-1935.* Cambridge, Mass., 1968.

McDonnell, Timothy L. *The Wagner Housing Act: A Cast Study of the Legislative Process.* Chicago, 1957.

McGee, Cushman. *The Finances of the City of New York.* New York, 1940.

McKelvey, Blake. *Rochester: An Emerging Metropolis, 1925-1961.* Rochester, N.Y., 1961.

McQuade, Vincent A. *The American Catholic Attitude on Child Labor Since 1891.* Washington, 1938.

Mann, Arthur. *La Guardia Comes to Power, 1933.* Chicago, 1965.

Martin, Roscoe C. *Water for New York: A Study of Water Resources.* Syracuse, N.Y., 1960.

Maxwell, James. *Financing State and Local Government.* Washington, 1965.

———. *The Fiscal Impact of Federalism.* Cambridge, Mass., 1946.

Mayer, George H. *The Republican Party, 1854-1966.* New York, 1967.

Missall, John Ellsworth. *The Moreland Act: Executive Inquiry in the State of New York.* New York, 1946.

Moscow, Warren. *The Last of the Big-Time Bosses: The Life and Times of Carmine De Sapio and the Rise and Fall of Tammany Hall.* New York, 1971.

———. *Politics in the Empire State.* New York, 1948.

Moses, Robert. *Public Works: A Dangerous Trade.* New York, 1970.

Mosher, Frederick C., and Poland, Orville F. *The Costs of American Government: Facts Trends, Myths*. New York, 1964.

Mosher, William E., and Crawford, Fina G. *Public Utility Regulation*. New York, 1933.

Munger, Frank J., and Straetz, Ralph A. *New York Politics*. New York, 1960.

Nelson, Daniel. *Unemployment Insurance: The American Experience, 1915-1935*. Madison, Wis., 1969.

Nevins, Allan. *Herbert H. Lehman and His Era*. New York, 1963.

Newcomer, Mabel. *An Index of the Taxpaying Ability of State and Local Government*. New York, 1935.

O'Rourke, Vernon A., and Campbell, Douglas W. *Constitution-Making in a Democracy: Theory and Practice in New York State*. Baltimore, 1943.

Patterson, James T. *The New Deal and the States: Federalism in Transition*. Princeton, N.J., 1969.

Peel, Roy V. *The Political Clubs of New York*. New York, 1935.

Perkins, Van L. *Crisis in Agriculture: The AAA and the New Deal, 1933*. Berkeley, Calif., 1969.

Phillips, Charles F., Jr. *The Economics of Regulation: Theory and Practice in the Transportation and Public Utility Industries*. Homewood, Ill., 1965.

Pink, Louis H. *The New Day in Housing*. New York, 1928.

Piven, Frances Fox, and Cloward, Richard A. *Regulating the Poor*. New York, 1971.

Post, Langdon W. *The Challenge of Housing*. New York, 1938.

———. *Housing . . . or Else*. New York, 1936.

Pritchett, C. Herman. *The Roosevelt Court: A Study in Judicial Politics and Values*. New York, 1948.

Pusey, Merlo J. *Charles Evans Hughes*. Vol. I. New York, 1951.

Radomski, Alexander Leopold. *Work Relief in New York State, 1931-1935*. New York, 1947.

Raushenbush, Stephen. *The Power Fight*. New York, 1932.

Rayback, Robert J., ed. *Richards Atlas of New York State*. Rev. ed. New York, 1965.

Robinson, Dwight E. *Collective Bargaining and Market Control in the New York Coat and Suit Industry*. New York, 1949.

Rodgers, Cleveland. *Robert Moses, Builder for Democracy*. New York, 1952.

Roosevelt, Eleanor. *This I Remember*. New York, 1949.

Roosevelt, Elliott, ed. *F.D.R.: His Personal Letters*. 4 vols. New York, 1947-50.

Rosenman, Samuel I. *Working with Roosevelt*. New York, 1952.

Salmond, John A. *The Civilian Conservation Corps, 1933-1942: A New Deal Case Study*. Durham, N.C., 1967.

Sayre, Wallace S., and Kaufman, Herbert. *Governing New York City*. New York, 1960.

Schaffter, Dorothy. *State Housing Agencies*. New York, 1942.

Schlesinger, Arthur M., Jr. *The Coming of the New Deal*. Boston, 1959.

———. *The Crisis of the Old Order, 1919-1933*. Boston, 1957.

———. *The Politics of Upheaval*. Boston, 1960.

Schneider, David M., and Deutsch, Albert. *The History of Public Welfare in New York State, 1867-1940.* Chicago, 1941.

Seidman, Joel I. *The Yellow Dog Contract.* Baltimore, 1932.

Shallcross, Ruth E. *Industrial Homework: An Analysis of Homework Regulation Here and Abroad.* New York, 1939.

Sharkansky, Ira. *Spending in the American States.* Chicago, 1968.

Shaw, Frederick. *The History of the New York City Legislature.* New York, 1954.

Shulman, Harry Manuel. *Slums of New York.* New York, 1938.

Smith, Alfred E. *Up to Now: An Autobiography.* New York, 1929.

Stein, Leon. *The Triangle Fire.* Philadelphia, 1962.

Steiner, Gilbert Y. *Social Insecurity: The Politics of Welfare.* Chicago, 1966.

Straus, Michael W., and Wegg, Talbot. *Housing Comes of Age.* New York, 1938.

Terkel, Studs. *Hard Times: An Oral History of the Great Depression.* New York, 1970.

Thompson, John H., ed. *Geography of New York State.* Syracuse, N.Y., 1966.

Trattner, Walter I. *Homer Folks: Pioneer in Social Welfare.* New York, 1968.

Troy, Leo. *Distribution of Union Membership among the States, 1939 and 1953.* New York, 1957.

Tugwell, Rexford G. *The Brains Trust.* New York, 1968.

———. *The Democratic Roosevelt.* Garden City, N.Y., 1957.

Twentieth Century Fund Power Committee. *The Power Industry and the Public Interest.* New York, 1944.

Van Wagenen, Jared, Jr. *Days of My Years: The Autobiography of a York State Farmer.* Cooperstown, N.Y., 1962.

Walker, Stanley. *Dewey: An American of this Century.* New York, 1944.

Weiss, Nancy J. *Charles Francis Murphy, 1858-1924: Respectability and Responsibility in Tammany Politics.* Northampton, Mass., 1968.

Wesser, Robert F. *Charles Evans Hughes: Politics and Reform in New York, 1905-1910.* Ithaca, N.Y., 1967.

Whyte, William. *Financing New York City.* American Academy of Political and Social Science, Pamphlet Series, No. 2. New York, 1935.

Witte, Edwin E. *The Government in Labor Disputes.* New York, 1932.

Wolman, Leo. *Ebb and Flow in Trade Unionism.* New York, 1936.

Wood, Edith Elmer. *Recent Trends in American Housing.* New York, 1931.

———. *Slums and Blighted Areas in the United States.* Washington, 1936.

Writers' Program of the Work Projects Administration. *New York: A Guide to the Empire State.* New York, 1940.

Yellowitz, Irwin. *Labor and the Progressive Movement in New York State, 1897-1916.* Ithaca, N.Y., 1965.

Zeller, Belle. *Pressure Politics in New York.* New York, 1937.

8. ARTICLES

Signed Articles

Abrahams, Paul. "Agricultural Adjustment during the New Deal; The New York Milk Industry: A Case Study." *Agricultural History*, XXXIX (April 1965): 92-101.

Adamic, Louis. "The Collapse of Organized Labor." *Harpers*, CLXIV (January 1932): 167-78.

Adie, David C. "The Organization of a National Welfare Program." *Social Service Review*, VIII (September 1934): 423-33.

———. "A State Handles Its Public Welfare Problems." *Social Service Review*, VII (September 1933): 407-23.

Amidon, Beulah. "Due Process." *Survey Graphic*, XXV (July 1936): 413-14.

Andrews, John B. "Unemployment Reserves." *The Management Review*, XXIII (December 1934): 356-57.

Arenwald, Walter P. "Mediation, Arbitration and Investigation of Industrial Disputes in New York State, 1937-1940." *Journal of Political Economy*, XLIX (February 1941): 58-89.

Bellush, Jewel. "Milk Price Control: History of Its Adoption, 1933." *New York History*, XLIII (January 1962): 79-104.

———. "Roosevelt's Good Right Arm: Lieutenant Governor Herbert H. Lehman." *New York History*, XLI (October 1960): 423-43.

Brissenden, P. F. and Swayzee, C. O. "The Use of Labor Injunctions in the New York Needle Trades." *Political Science Quarterly*, XLIV (December 1929): 548-68.

Bromley, Dorothy Dunbar. "The Newspapers and Child Labor." *Nation*, CXL (January 30, 1935): 131-32.

Brunger, Eric. "A Chapter in the Growth of the New York State Dairy Industry, 1850-1900." *New York History*, XXXVI (April 1955): 136-45.

Burgess, Ernest W. "Aging in Western Culture." *Aging in Western Societies*. Edited by Ernest W. Burgess. Chicago, 1960.

Chambers, John W. "The Big Switch: Justice Roberts and the Minimum-Wage Cases." *Labor History*, X (Winter 1969): 44-73.

Cheyney, Alice S. "The Course of Minimum Wage Legislation in the United States." *International Labour Review*, XXXVIII (July 1938): 26-43.

Colman, Gould P. "Theoretical Models and Oral History Interviews." *Agricultural History*, XLI (July 1967): 255-66.

Cooper, Lyle W. "The American Labor Movement in Prosperity and Depression." *American Economic Review*, XXII (1932): 641-59.

Dean, John P. "The Myths of Housing Reform." *American Sociological Review*, XIV (April 1949): 281-88.

Duane, Morris. "*Nebbia v. People:* A Milestone." *University of Pennsylvania Law Review*, LXXXII (April 1934): 619-23.

Dyson, Lowell K. "The Milk Strike of 1939 and the Destruction of the Dairy Farmers Union." *New York History,* LI (October 1970): 523-43.

Feld, Rose C. "Sweatshops, Model 1935." *Forum,* CLIII (March 1935): 168-71.

Felt, Jeremy P. "The Child Labor Provisions of the Fair Labor Standard Act." *Labor History,* XI (Fall 1970): 467-81.

Flynn, John T. "Starvation Wages: The Plight of the Employed." *The Forum,* LXXXIX (June 1933): 327-31.

Foley, E. H., Jr. "Legal Aspects of Low-rent Housing in New York." *Fordham Law Review,* VI (January 1937): 1-17.

Ford, James. "New York Resurveys Her Vast Housing Needs." *New York Times Magazine,* January 24, 1937.

Fraenkel, Osmond K. "Recent Statutes Affecting Labor Injunctions and Yellow Dog Contracts." *Illinois Law Review,* XXX (March 1936): 854-83.

Gates, Paul W. "Agricultural Change in New York State, 1850-1890." *New York History,* L (April 1969): 115-41.

Gill, Corrington. "Local Work for Relief." *Survey Midmonthly,* LXXVI (May 1940): 157-59.

Goldmark, Josephine. "The New Menace in Industry." *Scribner's Magazine,* LXLIII (March 1933): 141-43.

Habel, William. "Relief: A Permanent Program." *Survey Graphic,* XXVII (December 1938): 591-94.

Halle, Rita S. " 'Lucky' to Have a Job." *Scribner's Magazine,* LXLIII (April 1933: 235-38.

Hauser, Philip M., and Vargas, Raul. "Population Structure and Trends." *Aging in Western Societies.* Edited by Ernest W. Burgess. Chicago, 1960.

Herzog, Paul M. "The New York Labor Relations Act in the Development of Administrative Law." *New York State Bar Association Bulletin,* XII (April 1940): 53-59.

Huthmacher, J. Joseph. "Charles Evans Hughes and Charles Francis Murphy: The Metamorphosis of Progressivism." *New York History,* XLVI (January 1965): 25-40.

———. "Urban Liberalism and the Age of Reform." *Mississippi Valley Historical Review,* XLIX (September 1962): 231-41.

Johnston, Alva. "Profiles: The King." *The New Yorker,* September 12, 1931, pp. 25-28.

Karlin, William. "New York Slum Clearance and the Law." *Political Science Quarterly,* LII (June 1937): 241-58.

Kerr, Thomas J., IV. "The New York Factory Investigating Commission and the Minimum Wage Movement." *Labor History,* XI (Summer 1971): 373-86.

Kirkendall, Richard S. "The Great Depression: Another Watershed in American History?" *Change and Continuity in Twentieth-century America.* Edited by John Braeman, Robert H. Bremner and Everett Walters. Columbus, Ohio, 1964.

———. "The New Deal as Watershed: The Recent Literature." *Journal of American History,* LIV (March 1968): 839-52.

Krieger, Leonard. "The Idea of the Welfare State in Europe and the United States." *Journal of the History of Ideas,* XXIV (October-December 1963): 553-68.

La Gumina, Salvatore J. "The New Deal, the Immigrants and Congressman Vito Marcantonio." *The International Migration Review,* IV (Spring 1970): 57-75.

Lehman, Herbert H. "A Business Man Looks at Politics." *Atlantic Monthly,* CXLVIII (November 1931): 555-64.

Leuchtenburg, William E. "Franklin D. Roosevelt's Supreme Court 'Packing' Plan." *Essays on the New Deal.* Edited by Harold M. Hollingsworth and William F. Holmes. Austin, Texas, 1969.

Levitt, Saul, and Chase, Allan. "Herbert Lehman: 'Silent Dynamite.' " *American Mercury,* XXXIII (September 1934): 11-20.

Levy, Nathan. "Comment: Constitutional Law—Price-Fixing—Changing Attitudes." *Michigan Law Review,* XXXII (April 1934): 832-39.

Liebmann, William B. "A Friendship: Pro Bono Publico." *Columbia Library Columns,* XVIII (November 1968): 10-15.

Link, Arthur S. "What Happened to the Progressive Movement in the 1920's." *The American Historical Review,* LXIV (July 1959): 833-51.

Lubin, Isador, and Pearce, Charles A. "New York's Minimum Wage Law: The First Twenty Years." *Industrial and Labor Relations Review,* XI (January 1958): 203-19.

McKelvey, Blake. "Rochester's Political Trends: An Historical Review." *Rochester History,* XIV (April 1952): 1-24.

Malisoff, Harry. "The Emergency of Unemployment Compensation." *Political Science Quarterly,* LIV (June, September, December, 1939): 237-58, 391-420, 577-99.

Mayer, Albert. "New Homes for a New Deal." *New Republic,* February 14, 1934, pp. 7-9.

Mitchell, MacNeil. "Historical Development of the Multiple Dwelling Law." *Consolidated Laws of New York Annotated,* vol. 35-A (1946): ix-xxi.

Mosher, Frederick C. "The Executive Budget, Empire State Style." *Public Administration Review,* XII (Spring 1952): 73-84.

Owen, Russell. "The Man Behind the 'Little New Deal.' " *New York Times Magazine,* March 15, 1936.

Parry, Albert. "A Minimum Wage Comes to New York." *American Mercury,* XXXIV (February 1935): 235-39.

Patterson, James T. "Mary Dewson and the American Minimum Wage Movement." *Labor History,* V (Spring 1964): 134-52.

Perkins, Frances. "The Cost of a Five-Dollar Dress." *Survey Graphic,* XXII (February 1933): 75-78.

Powell, Hickman. "Profiles: The Governor." *The New Yorker,* May 2 and 9, 1936, pp. 21-26, 25-29.

Shientag, Bernard L. "Chief Judge Irving Lehman, Citizen and Jurist: An Appreciation." *The Menorah Journal,* XXXV (Spring 1947): 155-75.

Smith, Alfred E. "Child Labor." *New Outlook,* CLXIII (March, 1934): 12.

Spencer, Leland. "Public Regulation of the Milk Industry." *State Gvoernment*, XII (October 1939): 189-90.

Szajkowski, Zosa. "Budgeting American Jewish Overseas Relief, 1919-1939." *American Jewish Historical Quarterly*, LIX (September 1969): 83-113.

———. "Disunity in the Distribution of American Jewish Overseas Relief, 1919-1939." *American Jewish Historical Quarterly*, LVIII (March 1969): 376-407.

———. " 'Reconstruction' vs. 'Palliative Relief' in American Jewish Overseas Work, 1919-1939." *Jewish Social Studies*, XXXII (January 1970): 14-42.

Vose, Clement E. "The National Consumers' League and the Brandeis Brief." *Midwestern Journal of Political Science*, I (November 1957): 267-90.

Walker, Forrest A. "Compulsory Health Insurance: 'The Next Great Step in Social Legislation.' " *The Journal of American History*, LVI (September 1969): 290-304.

Weinbaum, Marvin G. "New York County Republican Politics, 1897-1922: The Quarter Century after Municipal Consolidation." *The New-York Historical Quarterly*, L (January 1966): 63-94.

Wiecek, William M. "The Place of Chief Judge Irving Lehman in American Constitutional Development." *American Jewish Historical Quarterly*, LX (March 1971): 280-303.

Wilson, Howard B. "Economic Objections to the St. Lawrence Waterway Project." *Public Utilities Fortnightly*, XIII (February 15, and March 1, 1934): 199-206, 267-74.

Witte, Edwin E. "What the States Can Do to Improve Labor Relations." *State Government*, XVIII (December 1945): 224-25, 238.

Woolf, S. J. "Lehman or Bleakley?" *New York Times Magazine*, October 11, 1936.

———. "Lehman Outlines His Social Philosophy." *New York Times Magazine*, August 9, 1936.

Unsigned Articles

"An American Plan for Unemployment Reserve Funds." *American Labor Legislation Review*, XX (December 1930): 349.

"Blue Sky for All Is Slum-Clearance Goal." *Literary Digest*, April 28, 1934, p. 2.

"The Civil Works Administration and Nursery Schools in New York." *School and Society*, January 20, 1934, pp. 79-80.

"The High Cost of Slums." *Review of Reviews*, LXXXIX (June 1934): 46.

"In Memoriam: David C. Adie, 1888-1943." *Social Service Review*, XVII (June 1943): 227-28.

"New York's War on Fire-Trap Tenements." *Literary Digest*, March 24, 1934, p. 21.

"Slum Clearance and Low Cost Housing." *Real Property*, XVIII (March 1939): 2.

"A State Labor Relations Act in Operation." *American Labor Legislation Review*, XXX (December 1940): 178.

"States and Cities: Concerns and Commencements." *Time*, December 31, 1934, pp. 7-10.

"The Supreme Court in Reverse." *New Republic*, November, 21, 1934, pp. 35-36.

"Worse than the Sweatshop." *Nation*, CXXXIX (November 21, 1934): 579-80.

9. UNPUBLISHED MATERIAL

Brandt, Lilian. "Relief of the Unemployed in New York City, 1929-1937." Preliminary draft, 1939.

Bellush, Jewel. "Selected Case Studies of the Legislative Leadership of Governor Herbert H. Lehman." Unpublished Ph.D. dissertation, Columbia University, 1959.

Carter, Robert F. "Pressure from the Left: The American Labor Party, 1936-1954." Unpublished Ph.D. dissertation, Syracuse University, 1965.

Colville, Lorraine. "A Comparison and Evaluation of the Organization and Techniques of the Major Political Parties in New York City and the Reaction of the Electorate to the Organizations, 1929-1949." Unpublished Ph.D. dissertation, New York University, 1954.

Crown, James T. "The Development of Democratic Government in the State of New York Through the Growth of the Power of the Executive Since 1920." Unpublished Ph.D. dissertation, New York University, 1954.

Duncker, Alfred Elfert. "Policies for the Aged in New York State." Unpublished Ph.D. dissertation, Columbia University, 1971.

Eldot, Paula. "Alfred Emanuel Smith, Reforming Governor." Unpublished Ph.D. dissertation, Yale University, 1961.

Feldman, Martin I. "An Abstract of the Political Thought of Alfred E. Smith." Unpublished Ph.D. dissertation, New York University, 1963.

Gillette, J. William. "Welfare State Trail Blazer: New York State Factory Investigating Commission, 1911-15." Unpublished M.A. essay, Columbia University, 1956.

Lappin, Phillip. "Herbert H. Lehman: His Background and Public Career." Unpublished M.A. essay, Columbia University, 1958.

Lehman, Orin. "Herbert H. Lehman: His First Year as Governor of the State of New York." Unpublished M.A. thesis, New York University, 1956.

Morsell, John Albert. "The Political Behavior of Negroes in New York City." Unpublished Ph.D. dissertation, Columbia University, 1950.

Rawick, George Philip. "The New Deal and Youth: The Civilian Conservation Corps, the National Youth Administration and the American Youth Congress." Unpublished Ph.D. dissertation, University of Wisconsin, 1957.

Rosenthal, Herbert Hillel. "The Progressive Movement in New York State, 1906-1914." Unpublished Ph.D. dissertation, Harvard University, 1955.

Ruskin, Gertrude M. "Restrictive and Constructive Housing Legislation in the State of New York." Unpublished M.A. thesis, New York University, 1941.

Spinrad, William. "New Yorkers Cast Their Ballots." Unpublished Ph.D. dissertation, Columbia University, 1955.

Stein, Judith. "The Birth of Liberal Republicanism in New York State, 1932-1938." Unpublished Ph.D. dissertation, Yale University, 1968.

Weinberger, Kate M. "The Life and Political Philosophy of Herbert H. Lehman." Unpublished M.A. essay, Columbia University, 1940.

INDEX

AAA. *See* Agricultural Adjustment Administration

AALL. *See* American Association for Labor Legislation

AASS. *See* American Association for Social Security

AFL. *See* American Federation of Labor

Abrams, Charles, 191, 201, 206n75

Acheson, Dean, 111

Adie, David, 52; background of, 49; and Welfare State, 49-50; on reorganization of Department of Social Welfare, 57

Agricultural Adjustment Administration (AAA), 163-65 *passim*

Agricultural Advisory Commission, 153; origins of, 152; approves milk control bill, 154; supports state publicity for milk, 162; condemns 1933 milk strike, 175n41

Agriculture, 148-49. *See also* Milk industry

Aldrich, Winthrop W., 66n20

Alfred, Helen: background of, 188; and municipal housing, 188-89, 191; praises Lehman, 191, 200; cites limits of 1938 housing amendment, 196

Allen, Howard N., 168

Aluminum Company of America, 224

Amalgamated Clothing Workers of America, 131, 203n31

American Agriculturist, 153, 162, 171

American Association for Labor Legislation (AALL), 72, 76, 93, 252. *See also* Andrews, John B.

American Association for Old Age Security, 76, 87

American Association for Social Security (AASS), 76, 89, 252, 253. *See also* Epstein, Abraham

American Federation of Labor (AFL), 77, 134, 135, 137, 142; and unemployment insurance, 73; and labor legislation, 131; impact of Depression on, 131; drafts state labor relations bill, 138; split with Congress of Industrial Organizations, 143n6. *See also* New York State Federation of Labor

American Labor Party, 28n61, 160, 252

American Legion, 118

Andrews, Elmer F.: background of, 77; and unemployment insurance, 77, 80, 81, 84-85; and minimum wage, 108-09, 112, 114

Andrews, John B.: author of "American plan" for unemployment insurance, 72; organizes campaign for unemployment insurance, 73-75; and Abraham Epstein, 76-77; seeks union support for American plan, 77-78; attacks Ohio plan, 79, 80; endorses modified Ohio